JOURNALISTS

100 Years of the NUJ

TIM GOPSILL AND **GREG NEALE**

P
PROFILE BOOKS

First published in Great Britain in 2007 by
Profile Books Ltd
3A Exmouth House
Pine Street
Exmouth Market
London EC1R OJH
www.profilebooks.co.uk

A CIP catalogue record for this book is available from the British Library.

ISBN 10: 1 86197 808 1
ISBN 13: 978 1 86197 808 0

Text design by Sue Lamble
Typeset in Bembo by MacGuru Ltd
info@macguru.org.uk

Printed and bound in Great Britain by Clays, Bungay, Suffolk

The paper this book is printed on is certified by the © 1996 Forest Stewardship
Council A.C. (FSC). It is ancient-forest friendly. The printer holds FSC chain of
custody SGS-COC-2061

FSC
Mixed Sources
Product group from well-managed
forests and other controlled sources

Cert no. SGS-COC-2061
www.fsc.org
© 1996 Forest Stewardship Council

Items should be returned on or before the last date shown below. Items not already requested by other borrowers may be renewed in person, in writing or by telephone. To renew, please quote the number on the barcode label. To renew online a PIN is required. This can be requested at your local library.
Renew online @ **www.dublincitypubliclibraries.ie**
Fines charged for overdue items will include postage incurred in recovery. Damage to or loss of items will be charged to the borrower.

Tim Gopsill has been editor of the *Journalist*, the magazine of the NUJ, since 1988. Before that he was a journalist in newspapers, magazines and radio. He was a member of the NUJ national executive from 1984 to 1987 and has held most voluntary posts in the union. He is also co-chair of the Campaign for Press and Broadcasting Freedom.

Greg Neale, who has written mostly on the NUJ's history before the 1960s in this book, as well as the sections on women and race, has worked for more than 25 years in newspapers, magazines and broadcasting. He has won two 'editor of the year' awards for his work with BBC *History* magazine, and is a Centenary Fellow of the Historical Association.

CONTENTS

PART TWO: OUR WORLD

PART THREE: OUR WORK

PREFACE

In 2004, the National Union of Journalists decided to produce a new history of the union to mark its centenary in March 2007. An advertisement in the union's monthly magazine, the *Journalist*, invited writers to submit proposals. From among the applicants the committee that interviewed the would-be writers decided to ask us to work together.

This book is the result. It is not an 'official' history in the sense of a formal catalogue of the words and deeds or the comings and goings of union worthies over the years. Instead we have tried to tell how men and women, working in newspapers, radio, television and the internet, in magazines and books and in public relations, in Britain and Ireland, have striven for decent working lives for themselves and a decent and responsible media for society.

There has been no pressure on the writers to conform to any particular 'line', or to reflect the views of any section of the union. The typescript was checked by a group of senior members of the National Executive Council and some amendments were made, but there was no coercion.

A lot of people in the NUJ have put themselves out to help us get this book together in a fairly short time. Thanks to John Bailey, Mike Bower, Harry Conroy, Peter Dodson, Barry Fitzpatrick, John Foster, Chris Frost, Roy Greenslade, Anita Halpin, Tony Harcup, Ron Knowles, Pete Lazenby, the late Ernie McIntyre, Chris Morley, Gary Morton, Tom Nash, Bob Norris, Pauline Norris, Dick Oliver, Alex Pascall, Chris Reekie, Mike Sherrington, Aidan White, Dave Wilson, Harry Woodhead and Peter Wrobel.

Special thanks are due to Jim Barrow, Jim Boumelha, Jeremy Dear, Tony Delano, John Devine, Seamus Dooley, Jim Eadie, John Fray, Trevor Goodchild, Barbara Gunnell, Gary Herman, Alan Knowles, Hilary Macaskill. Denis MacShane, Lionel Morrison, John O'Sullivan, Alan Pike, Alan Slingsby and Christine Woodland.

And very special thanks to David Ayrton, Francis Beckett, John Horgan, Paddy Smyth, picture researcher Emma Wood and researchers Isabella Di Vanna and Catherine Maddison.

We have drawn on any amount of NUJ documentation written over the years, so appreciation is due to those, particularly the minutes clerks, who wrote it all; and to the various editors of the *Journalist*. Among published sources, we have relied heavily on the two previous histories – *Gentlemen, the Press!* by F. J. Mansfield (1941) and *The National Union of Journalists, a Jubilee History*, by Clement Bundock (1957).

Tim Gopsill
Greg Neale
February 2007

TIMELINE

1906 General: Liberal Party wins landslide election victory, introduces legislation including legal protection for unions.

Journalism: Newspaper Proprietors Association formed by Fleet Street employers.

NUJ: Journalists meet around Britain to discuss forming a union. Meeting in Manchester on 17 November decides to call a founding conference in Birmingham the next March.

1907 NUJ: Union founded at conference in Birmingham, 30 March, officially registered 15 August. Joining fee is 5 shillings (25p), annual subscription £1 12s 6d (£1.62p). Wins first legal case, for journalist sacked by the *Salford Times*.

1908 Journalism: Local Authorities (Admission of the Press to Meetings) Act passed as result of NUJ campaigning – its first press freedom success.

NUJ: First Annual Delegate Meeting (ADM), in Leeds; first issue of the *Union Journal* in November.

1909 Journalism: *Daily Sketch* launched, subsumed into *Daily Mail* 1971. *Sheffield Evening Mail* and *Bristol Mercury* closures prompt first NUJ action to place dismissed members in new jobs.

NUJ: Union wins Appeal Court action over the Sheffield 'radius' case. London venue for second ADM. There are now 1,217 NUJ members, and 40 branches, including first in Scotland and Ireland.

1911 Journalism: *Daily Herald* launched. First Copyright Act.

NUJ: First strike, at the *York Herald*. Union becomes Approved Society under National Insurance Act, able to provide unemployment pay, hardship benefits and legal aid.

1912   NUJ: Union appoints its first paid clerk, J. Gladwin. Membership now 3,338. Lloyd George, Chancellor of the Exchequer, guest of honour at fifth anniversary dinner.

1913   Journalism: *New Statesman* founded.

        NUJ: First office opened at 1 Strutt Street, Manchester.

1914   General: First World War begins.

        NUJ: Newspapers lay off staff, levy of 2.5p per week to fund wartime unemployment pay.

1915   Journalism: *Sunday Pictorial* launched. Becomes the *Sunday Mirror* in 1963.

1916   Journalism: Max Aitken (later Lord Beaverbrook) buys *Daily Express*.

        NUJ: First Scottish ADM, Glasgow.

1917   NUJ: First pay agreement concluded with NPA, representing national papers. Death of founding General Secretary William Newman Watts; Henry Richardson, *Journalist* editor, takes over. Alice Chalmers-Lawford the first woman delegate to ADM.

1918   Journalism: *Sunday Express* launched.

        NUJ: National pay agreement with provincial newspaper owners.

1919   NUJ: Union affiliates to Printing and Kindred Trades Federation.

1920   Journalism: First experimental British radio stations.

        NUJ: Chalmers-Lawford the first woman elected to the NEC. Union affiliates to TUC for first time. *Daily Mail* attacks union's 'jam factory journalism'.

1921   NUJ: First unsuccessful attempt to merge with the Institute of Journalists.

1922   Journalism: Lord Northcliffe, first modern press baron and unlikely supporter of the NUJ, dies. British Broadcasting Company established, first news broadcast 14 November. Wireless licence (50 pence) introduced.

NUJ: Union pulls out of TUC over call to give money to the *Daily Herald*.

1923 General: First Labour government elected

Journalism: *Radio Times* launched. First BBC outside broadcast.

NUJ: Union appoints first full-time organiser, Clement Bundock.

1924 General: Labour defeated in election after *Daily Mail* publishes forged letter on supposed Soviet plot. Conservatives form government.

Journalism: First crossword, *Sunday Express*. King George V makes first royal broadcast.

NUJ: Trade and Periodical branch established, the first for non-newspaper journalists.

1925 Journalism: BBC transmitter at Daventry opened, enabling radio broadcasting to most of the country.

1926 Journalism: Newspapers stopped or reduced to emergency editions in General Strike. BBC expands news coverage, allows PM Stanley Baldwin to broadcast but not Labour leader Ramsay Macdonald. Crawford committee recommends broadcasting by independent public service corporation.

NUJ: Union split over General Strike. Union participates in formation of the International Federation of Journalists (IFJ) with unions from twelve other nations.

1927 Journalism: British Broadcasting Company becomes the Corporation under Royal Charter.

1929 Journalism: BBC transmits experimental TV picture.

1930 Journalism: *Daily Worker* launched as newspaper of the Communist Party. BBC broadcasts that 'there is no news', on Good Friday. *News Chronicle* published.

1931 Journalism: Audit Bureau of Circulations established.

NUJ: Launch of the *Irish Press*, first Irish paper to have majority NUJ membership. First overseas branch in East Africa.

1932 Journalism: BBC moves into Broadcasting House, new HQ in central London; begins Empire broadcasts. British Newspaper Library opens in Colindale, north London.

1933 Journalism: Sheila Barrett becomes BBC's first woman announcer.

1934 Journalism: Radio Luxembourg first commercial broadcast to Britain.

1935 Journalism: Selsdon committee recommends television broadcasting be established within the public sector.

1936 Journalism: Death of King George V announced on air by John Reith, BBC director-general. Edward VIII's abdication broadcast. BBC television broadcasts begin; Elizabeth Cowell first woman TV announcer.

NUJ: Death of Henry Richardson. Bundock becomes General Secretary.

1937 Journalism: Ten thousand people watch coronation procession of George VI on television.

NUJ: Strike by reporters at the Law Courts in London over unfair dismissal of a colleague, who is reinstated.

1938 Journalism: *Picture Post* launched. BBC launches foreign language services in Arabic, Spanish and Portuguese. First TV news bulletin, TV coverage of FA Cup Final.

1939 General: Second World War begins with German invasion of Poland. Britain enters war, 3 September.

Journalism: BBC TV closed on outbreak of war – midway through a cartoon – amid fears German aircraft could use its transmissions to help navigate, but expands its foreign-language broadcasts to include Czech, Polish, Hungarian, Rumanian, Greek and Turkish. BBC radio announcers first give their names on-air to authenticate the broadcast but no longer required to wear dinner jackets. Ministry of Information introduces press censorship.

NUJ: Headquarters moved for safety from London to Hertfordshire.

1940   Journalism: Newsprint rationing. Broadcasting House hit by
           German bombs. Lord Rothermere, brother of Lord Northcliffe, dies.

           NUJ: Union rejoins the TUC, wins first pay rises for 20 years to
           meet reduced wartime conditions.

1941   Journalism: BBC begins 'V for Victory' broadcasts to occupied
           Europe. Government closes communist *Daily Worker* and
           independent *The Week* over criticisms of the war.

           NUJ: First history of the union, *Gentlemen, the Press!* by F. J.
           Mansfield, published. As IFJ ceases to function in war, union
           organises International Federation of Journalists of Allied or Free
           Countries in London. Crisis over registration of union in Ireland
           leads to resignation of president D. M. Elliott.

1944   General: D–Day invasion of Normandy.

1945   General: war ends. Clement Attlee's Labour government elected.

1946   Journalism: Alistair Cooke begins his 'Letter from America'
           broadcasts on BBC radio (it continues until March 2004). BBC
           launches Third Programme.

           NUJ: Union joins newly formed International Organisation of
           Journalists (IOJ) to replace IFJ, but it soon splits along cold war lines.
           First chapel in BBC and London Radio branch founded.

1947   Journalism: First Royal Commission on the Press recommends
           establishment of Press Council, an NUJ proposal.

           NUJ: Agreement achieved covering all newspapers in Dublin.

1948   NUJ: Communist Allen Hutt elected editor of the *Journalist*, faces
           frequent 'cold war' calls for dismissal. Nora Wiles becomes only
           second woman on the NEC.

1949   NUJ: Union leaves IOJ in protest at conduct of unions from
           communist countries. First agreements covering provincial papers in
           Ireland.

1950   Journalism: George Orwell and George Bernard Shaw, both NUJ
           members, die. Beveridge committee recommends BBC continues as
           sole broadcaster, with union recognition.

1951   General: Conservative government elected under Winston
Churchill.

1952   NUJ: Clem Bundock retires, first General Secretary not to die in
office. Jim Bradley elected new GS. Union joins re-formed IFJ in
Brussels.

1953   Journalism: Twenty million people watch coronation of Elizabeth II
on television. General Council of the Press, forerunner of the Press
Council, established. National Council for the Training of Journalists
also set up. NUJ has representation on both.

1954   NUJ: Union formally recognised by BBC.

1955   Journalism: ITV begins broadcasting, with news from ITN.

1956   General: Prime Minister Anthony Eden accuses BBC of 'giving
comfort to the enemy' by broadcasting criticism of government in
Suez Crisis.

1957   Journalism: *Picture Post*, *Glasgow Evening News* close. BBC radio
launches 'Today' programme. Prime Minister Harold Macmillan lifts
the 14-day rule, introduced in wartime, by which BBC could not
broadcast discussion of any item due to be debated in parliament.

NUJ: Lord Rothermere, nephew of Lord Northcliffe, chief guest
at golden jubilee dinner. Others include Iain Macleod, Minister of
Labour, and Sir Ian Jacob, director-general of the BBC. Second book
on the union published for anniversary, written by Bundock.

1959   Journalism: *Manchester Guardian* changes to the *Guardian*, begins
transfer to London.

NUJ: National printing strike divides the union, much as the
General Strike had done.

1960   Journalism: Nan Winton becomes first woman television news
reader. Closure of *News Chronicle* a trauma for the industry.

1961   Journalism: *Sunday Telegraph* launched. *Sunday Times* launches first
newspaper colour magazine.

1963   NUJ: 'Silent reporters' Brendan Mulholland and Reg Foster jailed for protecting sources in Russian spy case – last journalists sentenced to prison in UK. Nine-week pay strike at RTE in Dublin.

1964   Journalism: General Council of the Press replaced by the Press Council. BBC2 launched.

1965   Journalism: BBC Radio launches 'The World at One'.

NUJ: Jim Eadie becomes first full-time official in Ireland.

1966   Journalism: Roy Thomson, owner of the *Sunday Times*, buys *The Times*, prints news instead of advertising on front page for the first time. Rupert Murdoch buys *News of the World*.

NUJ: HQ moves into Acorn House in London, first building owned and built by the union.

1967   NUJ: 'Chapel power' movement begins with strike at *Middlesbrough Gazette*.

1968   Journalism: Murdoch relaunches the *Sun*, bought from IPC, publishers of the *Mirror*.

NUJ: General Secretary Jim Bradley retires, replaced by Ken Morgan. National papers agree to house deals for first time. Longest-serving NEC member Charles Turner of Manchester stands down after 48 years.

1970   General: New UK Conservative government requires unions to register.

NUJ: Murdoch signs first NUJ house agreement on national papers at the *Sun*.

1971   Journalism: Irish government introduces 'Section 31' censorship of reporting republican organisations.

NUJ: ADM refusal to register under Industrial Relations Act overturned by membership ballot. Breakdown of fourth attempt to merge with IoJ.

1972   NUJ: 'Bonanza' as Fleet Street chapels win big pay rises. Hutt stands down as *Journalist* editor after 24 years. ADM sets up first Equality

Committee to help women members. London Television branch
launched at Hilton Hotel.

1973   Journalism: Launch of commercial radio with Capital in London,
followed by 24-hour news station LBC. BBC introduces Ceefax
service of on-screen news.

NUJ: Chapel power militant Ron Knowles elected editor of the
Journalist.

1974   General: Labour wins two UK elections, introduces first Prevention
of Terrorism Act after IRA bombing of Birmingham.

Journalism: Closure of *Scottish Daily Express* (SDE) in Glasgow.

NUJ: Bid by 'chapel power' militants to have Morgan sacked fails at
ADM.

1975   Journalism: Redundant SDE workers launch *Scottish Daily News*,
a workers' co-op. Entrepreneur Robert Maxwell takes controlling
interest and paper collapses after six months. Angela Rippon, former
NUJ rep, becomes first presenter of BBC TV's Nine O'Clock News.

NUJ: Magazine journalist Rosaline Kelly first woman to become
President in 68 years. Race Relations Working Party set up to boost
ethnic minority journalists. Membership refused to National Front
members.

1976   Journalism: *Nottingham Evening Post* introduces direct input of copy
by journalists, replacing typesetting by printers.

NUJ: First official strike in Fleet Street, at *Daily Telegraph*. Union
structure revamped from geographical to 'industrial' system.

1977   Journalism: Annan Committee Report proposes fourth TV channel.

NUJ: Ken Morgan quits NUJ to become director of Press Council.
Fellow Mancunian Ken Ashton becomes General Secretary. BBC
Radio Sheffield strike against greengrocer doing sports reporting.

1978   Journalism: the *Daily Star* launched in Manchester by Express
Newspapers. *The Times* and *Sunday Times* suspend publication for 11
months in dispute over new technology.

NUJ: Newspaper Society strike, the union's biggest, by 9,000
members on provincial newspapers, lasts seven weeks over freezing

winter, wins 14 per cent after 5 per cent offer. ABC official secrets
trial ends in discharges for union members.

1979 General: Labour loses power; Margaret Thatcher becomes Prime
Minister.

Journalism: *Financial Times* launches international edition in
Germany.

NUJ: Start of seven-year dispute at *Nottingham Post* as owners TBF
refuse to re-hire journalists sacked in *NS* strike. Journalists produce
their own weekly paper, supported by football manager Brian
Clough. Talks on merger with NGA begin.

1980 Journalism: *London Evening News* closed; 271 journalists lose jobs.

NUJ: Book members at Maxwell's British Publishing Corporation
occupy central London office for three months. Union leaves Press
Council.

1981 Journalism: Rupert Murdoch buys *The Times* and *Sunday Times* from
Thomson organisation.

NUJ: Membership hits peak of 32,667, unmatched for 20 years.

1982 Journalism: *Mail on Sunday* launched.

1983 Journalism: BBC launches breakfast television.

NUJ: Merger talks with the NGA break down.

1984 General: Miners' strike begins

Journalism: Robert Maxwell, owner of Pergamon Press, buys the
Mirror Group. *Birmingham Daily News*, first daily free newspaper,
launched.

NUJ: Dispute at Dimbleby Newspapers leads to threat of seizure of
union assets by the courts; funds transferred from London to Ireland.
Bitter disputes at Portsmouth and Wolverhampton over technology,
with NUJ and NGA at odds. Jim Campbell, Belfast editor of the
Sunday World, shot at his home by loyalists but survives.

1985 Journalism: Conrad Black, Canadian publisher, buys the Telegraph
group.

NUJ: Accord signed with NGA over introduction of new
technology ends disputes and leads to more than 100 joint
agreements around the UK. Strike throughout UK broadcasting
over *Real Lives* censorship at the BBC. General Secretary Ken
Ashton quits following row over pensions scheme. Harry Conroy
becomes first Scot to take top job. Ethics Council set up.

1986   Journalism: Rupert Murdoch transfers the *Sun*, *The Times*, the *News
of the World* and the *Sunday Times* to a secretly-prepared plant at
Wapping, east London. More than 5,000 print and clerical workers
are sacked, precipitating 13-month dispute. Launches of low-
cost national papers using new technology: *Today* by Eddy Shah,
publisher of the *Stockport Messenger*; the *Independent* by three *Daily
Telegraph* journalists; and *Sunday Sport*.

NUJ: Member John McCarthy kidnapped by Hizbollah in Lebanon.
'Gadafi Telegram' affair as ADM reacts to bombing of Libya. George
Viner Memorial Fund set up to help ethnic minority journalism
students. Establishment of Irish Council.

1987   Journalism: Maxwell launches the London *Daily News*, first 24-hour
newspaper, lasts five months. Murdoch buys *Today*. Wendy Henry
first national woman editor of modern times at the *News of the World*.
News on Sunday, left-wing tabloid, launched in Manchester with
support from unions, lasts four months.

NUJ: South African-born Lionel Morrison becomes first black
President. NUJ executive member Aidan White becomes General
Secretary of the IFJ.

1988   Journalism: *Scotland on Sunday* launched. UK Government bans
broadcasting voices of Sinn Fein and other 'organisations associated
with terrorism in Northern Ireland', similar to Irish Section 31
provisions.

NUJ: Start of employers' offensive of 'derecognition' by Thomson
Regional Newspapers. Barbara Gunnell and Scarlett MccGwire
elected as first job-share Presidents – only the second women to
hold the post. RSI outbreak at *Financial Times* hits more than 100.

1989   Journalism: Launches of *Sunday Correspondent* and *Wales on Sunday*.
BBC begins to broadcast Parliament.

NUJ: Members in four offices begin long strikes against union 'derecognition'.

1990   Journalism: *Independent on Sunday* launched, *Sunday Correspondent* closes. Maxwell launches the *European*. BBC and ITV lose exclusive rights to publish programme listings. Broadcasting Act begins process of deregulating ITV.

NUJ: Financial crisis with debt of £1.5 million; a third of staff are made redundant. Conroy beaten in re-election for General Secretary by Steve Turner of the *Daily Mirror*; six-month row ensues over terms of Turner's contract. Black Members Council set up. Press for Union Rights campaign launched to win legal right to recognition as *Daily Mail* FoC Dave Wilson launches legal case. Union rejoins Press Council.

1991   Journalism: Calcutt report into intrusions of privacy recommends statutory penalties. Press Council superseded by Press Complaints Commission. Maxwell dies mysteriously at sea as his companies collapse; huge frauds revealed. BBC launches World Service Television. First journalism degree courses launched at four universities.

NUJ: Turner sacked by NEC for defying policy on merging with print unions, wins case in court. John McCarthy freed after five years.

1992   Journalism: Introduction of first UK national press card with NUJ support. The *Dundee Courier* last British daily to put advertisements instead of news on front page.

NUJ: Attempt by Turner to be reinstated fails at ADM in London. John Foster, former print union activist, elected General Secretary. Strike at Pergamon Press, longest of derecognition disputes, ends after three and a half years.

1993   Journalism: Guardian Media Group buys the *Observer*. Mirror group sackings and victimisation of union activists in wake of Maxwell debacle.

NUJ: First big RSI test case lost in High Court. Let in the Light campaign in Ireland.

1994   Journalism: Telegraph group launches first national newspaper into
          on-line publishing. BBC launches Radio 5 Live. Irish and UK
          governments lift broadcasting bans.

          NUJ: Anita Halpin is third NUJ woman President.

1995   Journalism: Murdoch closes *Today*.

          NUJ: first union website launched by London freelance members.
          Dave Wilson sacked by *Daily Mail* after losing case at House of
          Lords. Free student membership introduced.

1996   NUJ: Member Bill Goodwin wins landmark victory for protection
          of sources at European Court.

1997   General: 'New' Labour wins power after eighteen years of
          Conservative rule.

          Journalism: BBC Newsnight presenter Jeremy Paxman asks Home
          Secretary Michael Howard the same question twelve times. BBC
          launches on-line news and BBC News 24 television service.

          NUJ: *Irish Sunday Independent* crime reporter Veronica Guerin shot
          dead in Dublin. Deputy General Secretary Jake Ecclestone sacked by
          the NEC after dispute with Foster.

1998   Journalism: The *European* ceases publication. Deaths of the third
          Lord Rothermere and *Daily Mail* editor Sir David English.

1999   General: National parliaments set up in Scotland, Wales and
          Northern Ireland.

          Journalism: *Glasgow Herald* launches *Sunday Herald*.

          NUJ: Scottish Council set up, partly in recognition of national status.

2000   Journalism: public concern about news as BBC and ITV move times
          of their main bulletins.

          NUJ: First recognition agreements regained under New Labour's
          Employment Relations Act.

2001   NUJ: *Sunday World* Belfast reporter Martin O'Hagan shot dead by
          loyalists outside his home in Lurgan.

2002   NUJ: John Foster retires. Jeremy Dear becomes youngest ever (and first graduate) leader at 35. Members at Bradford *Telegraph and Argus* stage first pay strike on newspapers for thirteen years. Official NUJ website launched. Dave Wilson wins European Court case on union rights.

2003   Journalism: UK Communications Act further deregulates broadcasting.

NUJ: More women than men join the union for the first time.

2004   Journalism: BBC slated by Hutton Report over reporting the background of government decision to invade Iraq. Director-general Greg Dyke, chairman Gavyn Davies and reporter Andrew Gilligan resign.

2005   Journalism: Increase in 'citizen journalism' – media taking stories and images from the general public.

2006   Journalism: Provincial evening papers begin to convert to morning publication in panic at sales lost to online media.

NUJ: Membership passes 40,000, including 7,000 student members. More than 40 per cent are women.

GLOSSARY

Every effort has been made to avoid the use of initials, acronyms, union jargon and so on, but there are some NUJ bodies that crop up so frequently that their mention is unavoidable.

Journalists' union branches in offices are called 'chapels', an archaic term the origins of which are explored on page 170. Chapels are led by Mothers and Fathers; their secretaries are called clerks.

The union's top decision-making bodies are the Annual Delegate Meeting (ADM) and, between conferences, the National Executive Council (NEC).

The General Secretary – the chief executive of the NUJ – and the Deputy General Secretary are sometimes referred to, for the sake of brevity, as the GS and DGS respectively.

There is a breakdown of the decision-making processes and organisational structure of the NUJ in Appendix 2 on page 341.

PART ONE

OUR UNION

JOURNALISTS: WHO WE ARE

'There are some people on the pitch … they think it's all over – *it is now!*'

'Big Brother is watching you.'

'A dollar a word in America. In this country, anything I can get.'

'Let's face the music and dance.'

These quotations have something in common: all were written or spoken by figures who at one stage or another in their careers were prominent members of Britain's largest trade union for journalists. Kenneth Wolstenholme, BBC television commentator on the afternoon in 1966 when England won the World Cup, was previously an NUJ branch chairman in Manchester. George Orwell, author of *1984* and of some of the most powerful English prose of the twentieth century, joined the NUJ as a freelance journalist – his membership card is among the union's prized possessions. In 1931, George Bernard Shaw complained about his low earnings in Britain when he completed his membership application form – which today hangs on a wall at the union's headquarters, alongside Orwell's. And the fourth quotation? Well she didn't coin the phrase herself – Irving Berlin did – but Angela Rippon, the BBC newsreader, said it when she broke off from reading a dummy news bulletin to dance with comedians Morecambe and Wise on their television Christmas Special in 1976. Earlier in her career, Rippon had been a union activist,

the 'Mother of the Chapel', in union jargon, at the *Sunday Independent*
in Plymouth.

All four have figured prominently in their profession – if journalism
really *is* one. Or is it a trade, a craft, a skill – a calling, even? It is all of
these. But though journalists like to consider themselves professionals,
journalism does not work in the manner of a profession as most people
understand the term when they think of, say, medicine, accountancy or the
law. These are closed shops, with high barriers to entry; they are regulated
by professional associations; and, most importantly, the practitioners often
control the fees they are paid. Many of them are self-employed (or in
partnerships) and can take advantage of the market strength to name their
price. It is true that there are self-employed journalists – eight thousand
of them in the NUJ – but most are employed. And the self-employed
ones certainly do not control the market. In economic terms journalists
are simply hired hands, or pens. This is why they need, and why a hundred
years ago they formed, a union.

Is journalism a competitive or a cooperative profession? It is both: journalists are encouraged to compete, not just between different publications
or media but between themselves. Yet their work has also to be cooperative:
the production of a daily newspaper – more recently, a radio or TV bulletin
– is one of the great organisational achievements. Hundreds of people are
involved, producing tens of thousands of words and hundreds of pages which
are then processed into a coherent whole and printed into tens of thousands
– sometimes millions – of copies, and all done in about twelve hours. From
the raw material of the first facts gathered by the reporter to the finished
pages or broadcast is a kind of production process, but few factory assembly
lines work under greater pressure or, hopefully, to higher standards.

Paul Foot, the crusading investigative journalist, has written about the
excesses of competition among journalists in Glasgow, where he was a
trainee in the early 1960s. The city's rival papers had a history of buying up
figures in prominent court cases, and reporters had been literally fighting
on the streets to preserve one such 'exclusive'. Foot recalled – in a 1995
article for the *Journalist's Handbook* – how the row had spread to an NUJ
branch meeting and officials had intervened to resolve it: 'Eventually a
resolution was passed which condemned the violence and blamed it on
the wild circulation war … Employers and news editors were told in
no uncertain terms that journalists were never again going to abuse and
assault one another just because they had been told to do so.'

When the NUJ was formed in 1907 nearly all its members' work was for newspapers. Journalism then was seen by some as a respectable profession, by others as an opportunity for the quick-witted social climber, and by others as the resort of the disreputable chancer. Most journalists were male, working-class, and had left school aged thirteen to fifteen. They shared much in common with the printers with whom they worked closely, but at the same time there was a sense of some qualitative difference between the two. The celluloid collar and tie that marked out the clerical worker was also a badge of respectability. By the turn of the twentieth century the printers' trade unions had enabled them to secure better pay and conditions than most journalists.

But things had started to change in journalism too: in 1896 the entrepreneur Alfred Harmsworth (later Lord Northcliffe, an early and – one might think – unlikely supporter of the NUJ) had launched the *Daily Mail*. Journalism now became livelier, acquiring a tendency to greater sensationalism and a keen commercial eye on what new readers were interested in: sport, crime, gossip, fashion and other social preoccupations. The *Mail* soon became the first paper to sell a million copies.

The Harmsworth revolution created a system in which the enterprising reporter, the star writer and the gifted sub-editor could rise a long way. Journalism was becoming increasingly commercial and competitive, and the reporter who could secure a scoop, or whose shorthand exceeded another's for speed and accuracy, might hope soon to move to larger and better-paying papers.

The two world wars led to an increase in the number of women working on newspapers and magazines. The spread of broadcasting – radio in the 1920s, television after the Second World War – brought recruits from the middle classes; men at first, then women, as public service broadcasting was seen as both respectable and innovative. Radio and television also had glamour, swelling the competition for entry. The BBC increasingly attracted university graduates, and would institute training courses specifically for them, in addition to those it recruited from traditional journalistic backgrounds. The media were no longer the stamping ground of the bright working-class boy.

The image of journalism in the Hollywood films of the 1930s and 40s, widely watched – and much resented at the time by union members – perpetuated the idea of the raffish reporter in hat and raincoat, a not entirely trustworthy figure. But the educated tones of the early radio announcers and reporters – and early BBC radio and television newsreaders were drawn from the ranks of actors rather than newspaper reporters – added a certain social cachet to the new media, and began to change the public perception of journalism in general. Then, the rapid expansion of further education in the 1960s created more graduates keen to explore journalism as a career. The foundation in 1953 of the National Council for the Training of Journalists, in part as a result of pressure from the NUJ, emphasised the growing professionalised nature of journalism. Between 1964 and 1974, the proportion of graduates entering regional journalism quadrupled, from 4 to 17 per cent of the total entry, while the number entering with A Levels more than doubled from 29 to 60 per cent. More women were going to university, and the number of female trainees likewise doubled.

As they became more securely middle-class, journalists gradually became less socially deferential. Before the crisis over the abdication of Edward VIII in 1936 British newspapers had kept quiet about the King's relationship with Wallis Simpson, for example. By the mid-1950s attitudes had changed so much that the *Daily Mirror* felt able to counsel the Queen's sister on her love life, a front-page editorial headlined 'Come On, Margaret'. Furthermore, the work of the journalist was becoming increasingly appreciated by the public. Crowds lined the streets of Manchester in 1958 to pay their respects to the six football writers who perished along with the Manchester United players, the 'Busby Babes', in the Munich air disaster. NUJ President Tom Bartholomew wrote in the *Journalist*, the union's newspaper:

> Seldom, if ever, can a city have demonstrated its affection more than
> Manchester did as each funeral cortege passed slowly through the
> streets … Traffic stopped, police stood to attention – some even at
> the salute – workmen doffed their caps and stood with heads bowed,
> women wept – even the children stopped playing in the yard of one
> school as the cortege passed.

But amid the mourning arose controversy that prefigured later public unease at journalists' conduct: there was criticism of the apparently intrusive behaviour of some reporters and photographers in the Munich hospital where the crash survivors were taken.

The reputation of journalists for exposing scandal in the 1960s suggested that they were broadly on the side of the angels. Those working under Harold Evans at the *Sunday Times* in the 1970s were not alone in their belief that the purpose of their brand of journalism was 'to comfort the afflicted, and afflict the comfortable'. And just as the 1960s satire boom in Britain helped accelerate the trend away from social deference, so the Watergate scandal in the United States, when President Nixon's wrong-doings were exposed by the investigative journalists of the *Washington Post*, gave journalism a new allure. The next decade saw increased numbers of the well educated middle class knocking on editors' doors for trainee-ships, or applying to the growing number of colleges offering postgraduate courses.

It would be wrong to see public perceptions of journalism moving inexorably from disdain to approbation. By the end of the century public trust in journalism and journalists was waning. The concentration by newspapers and TV programmes on 'celebrity', the tabloid trends towards reporting show-business scandal in place of serious news, and concerns that invasion of privacy had replaced worthy investigation led to revival of journalists' previous unsavoury reputation. There was a low point in 1997 with the death of Diana, Princess of Wales, in a car crash in Paris.

George Bernard Shaw

George Bernard Shaw (1856–1950) was a moderate socialist propa-gandist and playwright. Born in genteel poverty in Dublin, he went to London at the age of 20, established himself as a music, theatre and art critic for *The World* between 1886 and 1890, and joined the Fabian Society. By the turn of the century he was an established playwright, earning early success with *The Devil's Disciple*. His early plays were vehicles to convey the Fabian message, and themes running through them were the evils of capitalism, the unjust subjection of women, and the need to rebel against accepted wisdom. The years between the turn of the century and the First World War were among his most productive, when he wrote plays including *Caesar and Cleopatra, Man and Superman* and *Pygmalion*. He won the Nobel Prize for Literature in 1926, and joined the NUJ in 1931, at the age of 75, perhaps in recogni-tion of the fact that he was now called upon for comment pieces on all sorts of social and political subjects. He remained an NUJ member until his death on 2 November 1950.

Claims were made – but largely disproved – that her death resulted from harassment by freelance photographers. Widespread vilification of journalists ensued from her adoring public, and reporters covering the Princess's funeral at Westminster Abbey were asked by their newsdesks to be particularly discreet. Diana was the most photographed human being of all time; editors used to reckon that her picture on the front page could add 100,000 copies to daily sales. Her adoration had been the creation of the popular press that was now reviled.

'Celebrity journalism' can describe the work of well-known writers as much as the pursuit of otherwise inconsequential individuals. Just as Wells, Shaw and others were celebrated figures in their day for their journalism, so the increasing amount of column space and airtime available to some journalists raised the profile of the profession. Some columnists appear better informed and respected than many politicians; a trend that has arguably surely added to journalism's leverage, even if some sections of the press have declined – or remained at a low ebb – in the public's opinion.

These ambivalent attitudes were reflected in opinion polls. When in 2003 the *Daily Telegraph* commissioned a survey of public attitudes, asking the question 'How much do you trust the following to tell the truth?', TV journalists scored 80 per cent; broadsheet newspaper journalists 65; local newspapers 60; mid-market newspapers (such as the *Daily Mail* and *Daily Express*) 36, and the tabloids 14 per cent – lower than estate agents (16) and Conservative politicians (20 per cent). When the *Telegraph* conducted a similar poll in early 2006, public trust in journalists had declined further. BBC journalists enjoyed a comfortable lead, though their approval ratings had fallen to 71 per cent. Some 62 per cent of respondents trusted broadsheet newspaper journalists; and the 'red-top' tabloids now notched up a trust rating of just 12 per cent. Journalists were constantly taunted about being more despised than estate agents. But the public still bought the papers – if in smaller numbers.

1

THE NUJ

From the beginning

The year 1907 was an eventful one in British labour history. The election of 1906 had resulted in a landslide victory for the Liberals, who would enact significant social reforms including bringing in national insurance and old age pensions. One of the new government's first moves was to push through the 1906 Trade Disputes Act. This reversed an anti-trade union legal ruling, the 'Taff Vale judgement' of 1901, which had left unions liable to be sued for damages by employers if their members went on strike. The 1906 Act gave unions protection, as well as legalising peaceful picketing. It was an early instance of the Liberals' desire to work with, if not placate, the trade unions who were increasingly seen as having the ability to deliver working-class votes. For another result of the election had been the return to Parliament of twenty-nine MPs representing the union-backed Labour Representation Committee, which was soon to rename itself the Labour Party.

There were also at this time new moves towards organisation within journalism. Since the 1880s, a new, commercial journalism had come into existence, through the activities of such journalist-cum-entrepreneurs as Alfred Harmsworth, later the first Lord Northcliffe. They had used new technology, such as the recently introduced linotype machine and improved rotary printing, and improved communications to provide for a new mass market – not just a slew of magazines and periodicals, but new newspapers such as the *Daily Mail* (established in 1896), the *Daily Express* (1900) and the *Daily Mirror* (1903).

In turn, printers and other workers sought to respond to these developments, to improve their conditions and protect their interests. In 1900, a group of printing unions had come together to form the Printing and Kindred Trades Federation. In 1906, the owners of Fleet Street papers established the Newspaper Proprietors' Association – later the Newspaper Publishers' Association – as the employers' trade body. Around the country, meanwhile, working journalists were beginning to discuss forming their own trade union. In Manchester, in Leeds, in south-east London, the talk was of poor conditions, the inability or unwillingness of the existing Institute of Journalists to do much about them, and how journalists could combine to improve their lot.

● ● ● ● ● ● ● ● ● ● ● ● ● ● ● ● ● ● ●

'Monster of the Fleet Street Deep'

'I am a warm supporter of the principles on which the Union is founded, and of many of the policies it is pursuing … The main points of the Union's programme – better pay, shorter hours and longer holidays – have my unreserved approval.'

Supportive words from a surprising source: an interview published in the *Journalist* in 1919 with the mightiest press baron of the times, Viscount Northcliffe – progenitor of the most successful newspaper dynasty in British history. In its early days the NUJ basked in his patronage; unfortunately, unlike his newspapers, this was not passed on to succeeding generations.

In 1917 it was Northcliffe's intervention that broke the deadlock between the union and the Newspaper Proprietors' Association, leading to the NUJ's first national agreement on salaries.[1] He sent executives from the *Daily Mail* and *The Times* – the latter he had recently bought – to the NPA to tell them to come to terms with the union.

Northcliffe was a maverick, and his motivation for encouraging the union was complex. One factor was a running feud with his fellow proprietors. In 1922 he published a belligerent and rambling pamphlet, *Newspapers and Their Millionaires*, which mounted a quite savage attack on what he called the 'monsters of the Fleet Street deep' – the 'amateur millionaires who are seeking titles and social advancement' through the ownership of national papers. Big capitalists were being drawn to the rapidly expanding and profitable popular press.

> Behind every single London daily paper, with the possible exception of some sporting journals and a Labour publication [the *Daily Herald*], of which I know nothing, there is a multi-millionaire ... a Shipping King, a Cotton-waste King, Coal Kings, an Oil King, and the rest of them ... capitalists ignorant of Fleet Street [who] dictate terms to those who have spent their lives trying to understand the complex questions of a newspaper.

The Oil King was Lord Cowdray, owner of the *Westminster Gazette*, of whom Northcliffe wrote: 'His newspaper is about as good as my first oil well and pipeline establishment would be ... [with] ignorance, provincialism, extravagance, mismanagement and muddle written all over it. It was always a "kept" paper. For years it passed from one millionaire to another, and swallowed money in buckets.'

All this sprang from a considerable degree of resentment, for Northcliffe, though unfathomably rich himself, had made his pile entirely through the press. He was an inspired entrepreneur: the Rupert Murdoch of his day. He never stopped reminding people that he was a journalist himself, and a brilliant one at that. He had launched a plethora of publications, from *Answers to Correspondents*, a weekly amalgam of fascinating facts, in 1888, to the *Daily Mail* eight years later. Within three years the *Mail* became the first paper in the world to sell a million copies a day – more than the rest of the British national press put together.

A lot of the strictures in *Newspapers and Their Millionaires* were simply mischief-making, reflecting the kind of childish competitiveness in which the mass-circulation national papers have always engaged, and there was a lot of pot-and-kettle about it. But such strictures stemmed from a deadly serious impulse – the impulse that also drove Northcliffe's apparently paradoxical support for trade unions. The pamphlet was the first open indication of an approach to the management of national newspapers that would stifle competition for decades and lead to dire consequences for journalists and their union sixty years later. Its direct purpose was to counter a movement among employers, during the post–First World War depression, to cut wages. Northcliffe would have none of it: he wanted wages to rise because his paper made so much money that they could afford to pay more. But for his competitors it was harder, and for prospective new entrants to the industry it would be harder still. Lord Northcliffe was protecting his profits. ▶

He reported that an unnamed 'colleague', as he called his rival owners, had said to him: 'The wages are preposterous. Some of these men have motor-cycles and sidecars; more than one of them drives a motor car.' He had replied: 'And why shouldn't they? If we are to retain the best skilled labour we must pay it properly.'

In a letter of 1912 he told the NUJ: 'It is my proudest boast that the changes and competition which I have introduced into English journalism have had the effect of increasing the remuneration of almost every class of newspaper writer.'

The first stirrings of organisation had been in 1884 when a group of reporters who had been covering the Royal Agricultural Show in York met to discuss their common problems – including access to official information, damage caused to journalists' reputations by cases of misreporting, and instances of financial distress involving colleagues and their dependants. The first such meeting was held in Manchester, according to the NUJ's first historian, Frederick Mansfield. The outcome was another meeting, held the following year at the Grand Hotel in Birmingham, where the National Association – later the Institute – of Journalists was formally inaugurated. It was probably no coincidence that the NUJ's origins later followed the same geographical path: disgruntled journalists gathered in Manchester and in Yorkshire and an inaugural conference took place in Birmingham, with London joining in later on.

The Association's aim was 'to promote and advance the common interests of the profession', and its membership, it was decided, would consist of 'gentlemen engaged in journalistic work'. In 1888 it appointed a full-time General Secretary and took offices in Fleet Street; two years after that it became the Institute of Journalists and received a royal charter from Queen Victoria. Its membership included proprietors and editors, and it was their presence, effectively blocking moves for improved pay and conditions, that would inspire disaffected Institute members to form the NUJ.

It was in 1891 that the idea of a journalists' trade union seems first to have been raised. That was when William Newman Watts, who would become one of the founders of the NUJ and its first General Secretary, was chief reporter of the *Darwen News* in Lancashire. At a meeting of the local branch of the Institute, Watts raised the matter of the journalists at the *Preston Herald* who had recently gone on strike for better conditions. The branch chairman, who was also the proprietor of the *Darwen News*, ruled that the IoJ could not intervene in a dispute between an employer and his employees. Watts immediately resolved to try to establish a union, even sketching out a provisional constitution and a set of rules. But he made little progress in the next few years, while not abandoning the hope that the IoJ might be reformed. Having worked for various papers in Lancashire, by 1905 he was on the *Manchester Evening News*. At an Institute meeting that year he moved a resolution that newspaper proprietors and directors should not be members, or should be restricted in future to associate member status. But again Watt found little support, and it seems he now gave up on the Institute.

However, he found a more sympathetic hearing among his colleagues on the *Manchester Evening News* and its sister morning paper, the *Manchester Guardian*. The *Guardian*'s liberal traditions meant that the two papers were known not only for the good pay and conditions they offered – the entire staffs of other local papers would sometimes apply for vacancies – but also for the progressive views of their journalists. It was another paper, though, that published a series of articles putting the case for a journalists' union. In its issue of 27 July 1906 the *Clarion*, a popular and influential organ of the left, carried an article by an engineer turned writer, one Frank Rose, headlined 'A Trade Union for Journalists?' Journalists could only improve their conditions and protect themselves from outside competition, he wrote, if they organised. 'The newspaper men are beginning to recognise that, after all, they are only a body of men who have to live by working in a newspaper factory and that a newspaper factory differs in no essential from any other factory.' In a further article the next month Rose ridiculed those who excused journalists' low pay – an average of £1.50 a week – by maintaining it was a professional salary rather than an industrial wage.

Rose was clearly aware of the discussions going on between Watts and others, for he referred to such plans as were currently under way. That autumn, the talk intensified, and within a few short weeks during October and November moves to form a union of journalists took shape. One of the first meetings was convened at the Manchester Press Club on 13 October; another was held a week later. Out of these discussions came the resolution to call another, larger meeting, at the Albion Hotel (again in Manchester) on 17 November. Henry Marriott Richardson, who would become the union's second General Secretary, recalled the occasion in the *Journalist* nearly twenty years later: 'R. C. Spencer, then chief reporter of the *Manchester Guardian*, was in the chair and W. N. Watts acted as secretary ... The room was soon misty with tobacco smoke. Possibly there were about forty present ... The meeting sprang out of the general discontent with journalistic conditions.'

Out of this gathering came a decision and a declaration. The decision was to call a national conference, in advance of which journalists were urged to hold local meetings and set up embryonic branches. The declaration, addressed 'To the Working Journalists of the United Kingdom', was sent out to newspaper offices around the country. It began: 'The strong conviction that there should be established a new organisation capable of safeguarding and furthering the interests of working Journalists has led us to begin this movement ... we suggest as a title, "The National Union of Journalists".' Its objects would be to defend professional interests by taking action to right legitimate grievances with regard to salary, conditions of employment and tenure of office, as well as to establish unemployment, benevolent and retirement funds. It also proposed 'to deal with questions affecting professional conduct and etiquette'. The Manchester pioneers had defined what the NUJ would become over the next hundred years.

Manchester was a likely focus for early union activity. The city that had spawned Britain's Industrial Revolution had also seen much early trade unionism and the first Trades Union Congress, in 1863. It was also the biggest newspaper centre in England outside London, which helped create a sense of journalistic community as well as a venue for newspapermen to meet and discuss their circumstances.

The idea was not Manchester's alone. In Woolwich and Greenwich in south-east London, in Leeds and in other centres, there were similar stirrings. Frederick Mansfield suggests that around 1890, when Watts was having his moment of epiphany in Darwen, a journalist in far from industrial Torquay had raised the possibility of starting an association in Devon and Cornwall.

In Fleet Street, however, the focus of the new journalism, there was little enthusiasm, but in the nearby suburbs men such as David Berry, Walter Betts and Mansfield himself (then the editor of the *Erith Times*), inspired by Rose's articles in the *Clarion*, were also advocating unionisation. When news reached them of the Manchester initiative, they had

The old Acorn Hotel in Temple Street, Birmingham, site of the NUJ's founding meeting in 1907. (NUJ Collection)

decided to join it. And as journalists began organising around the country in advance of the conference in Birmingham that was to formally found the NUJ at Easter 1907, the first incursions were made in Fleet Street. On 7 March, the first meeting of the Central London branch of the yet to be formed union was held at the Old Cheshire Cheese pub on Fleet Street. Joseph Heighton, a sub-editor on the magazine *Tit Bits*, one of the new publications that were helping to create a thriving journalism industry, was elected secretary.

Across the Pennines from Manchester, meanwhile, Yorkshire journalists had also been exercised by the notion of forming a union. In Leeds, George Lethem of the *Leeds Mercury* was the leading light. Like Watts a disillusioned member of the IoJ, Lethem began to draw up plans, rules and a constitution. When news of the activities in Manchester reached Leeds, Lethem and his colleagues invited some of the Lancastrians to address them. More than 150 journalists crowded into the Hotel Metropole, and after lengthy discussion Lethem persuaded an initially hesitant gathering to establish a West Riding union branch. The ball was rolling. Around the country similar meetings were taking place. All would find their focus in Birmingham at the end of March 1907.

'The first National Conference in connection with the National Union of Journalists was held at the Acorn Hotel, Birmingham, on Thursday, March 29 and Friday, March 30, 1907.' Thus ran the first official minutes of the NUJ. The meeting was comparatively small: twenty-five journalists were sent as delegates from nascent branches, together with William Watts, the acting Secretary; Frank Rose, who had advised the Manchester meeting on drafting the rules, and J. C. Menzies, also from Manchester, who served as the first, acting Treasurer. R. C. Spencer, another Mancunian, was in the chair. The delegates sat at long baize-covered tables in a dimly lit room that quickly became stuffy, even though smoking was banned during the business sessions. Spencer sat at one end, Watts to his right. Speeches were limited to five minutes: there was much to do. 'We journeyed hopefully that Good Friday morning in 1907,' William Small, a Wolverhampton delegate, wrote later, 'little dreaming, however, that the meeting was destined to play such a prominent part in the modern history of British journalism.'

Over two days, these men mulled over the basics of union organisation. In his opening speech, Spencer argued that a union for journalists was not an act of aggression towards employers, or even against the Institute. Indeed, if the union were to succeed in getting the support of British journalists it would mean not only an improvement in conditions but also a better understanding between them and their employers. With such moderate sentiments, then, the union's founding conference began. By the end of the first day, a set of rules had been adopted and a first financial statement had been accepted: after setting-up costs had been subtracted from various contributions and gifts, the new organisation would begin life with a balance of £5 4s 1d (£5 20p).

A proposal from the South East and east London that 'no full member of this Union shall accept any berth [job] for less than 30 shillings [£1.50] a week' was rejected as likely to establish a low rate of pay not as a minimum, but as a norm. As Watts had proposed in 1905, proprietors, managers and directors of newspaper firms were excluded from membership, which was limited to 'working journalists who are and have been for three years members of a journalistic staff or who have been and are dependent on their own journalistic work'. From the outset, freelances owing their living to the trade were welcomed, as were newspaper artists and photographers. And with little fuss, women journalists – not 'lady journalists', as one amendment suggested – were accepted as full members. They would be 'required to pay the same contribution and entrance fee and will be entitled to the same benefits, qualified to hold the same offices, and subject to the same rules and regulations'.

Soon after the delegates began their second day's work, Spencer moved the motion 'That the National Union of Journalists be, and is hereby, brought into existence'. George Lethem seconded the motion, adding: 'I hope and believe that this will prove to be a gathering which in the annals of working journalists will be historic.' Watts, whose brainchild it had been, said simply: 'The youngster we have produced is now the child of the country, and the country will have to support it. I don't believe any of you will regret the time and trouble you have taken in coming here today.'

William Newman Watts: Father of the NUJ

William Newman Watts laid the foundations of the union and worked himself to death for it. He was born in 1868 in London but moved to Manchester as a child. Ink was in his veins: his first job was as a copy boy – sorting and delivering sheaves of news from one department to another – at the *Manchester Evening News*. His first reporting jobs were at Oldham and Bolton, before he became chief reporter of the *Darwen News*. After stints on the *Lancashire Daily Express* and *Northern Daily Telegraph* (both based in Blackburn), he returned to Manchester in 1902, where he became chief reporter back at the *Evening News*. It was an office in which his co-workers were sympathetic to his union aspirations.

Watts carried out his union work in his spare time from his home at Blackley; his address – Fern Lea, Glen Avenue, Boggart-Hole Clough – adorned the heads of early letters and circulars. There, Watts, his wife Annie and their children turned the house into the union's 'head office', first one room then another being converted for the purpose. Some nights he would be away on speaking tours at new branches. His daughter, also called Annie, later wrote:

> I can remember when were living at Blackley … spending many hours each evening addressing envelopes, etc, for Dad. These were sent to journalists in every town in England. The six of us, mother, father, my sister, two brothers and myself, all helped. We folded circulars, put on stamps and at the end of the evening ▶

Far left: William Newman Watts, founding General Secretary and guiding spirit of the NUJ. (NUJ Collection)
Left: Henry Richardson, a co-founder and Watts's successor, and first editor of the Journalist. *(NUJ Collection)*

heaped them into baskets and my brother's toy barrow … We generally managed to fill the post box nearest our home, so that the last lot of envelopes could hardly be jammed in the box … I believe father arranged for a special collection when the work grew heavier.

After the union's foundation and when he became the first General Secretary, Watts's workload increased further, with the opening of a union office in Strutt Street, Manchester, near the *Evening News*. The outbreak of the First World War, with many men leaving for the trenches, left still more work for him, and frequent travel took its toll. By the winter of 1917, his doctor was warning him to cut his workload. By the end of the year, he was confined to his bed, but he continued to work. He underwent an operation in January 1918, and made a surprise, and moving, appearance at the union's annual meeting in Leicester that year, where the delegates re-elected him. But his ill health was apparent, for the conference also appointed Henry Richardson as acting General Secretary.

Watts's daughter recalled. 'We knew he was fighting a losing battle. We hoped against hope that he would be spared to carry on his good work. Amid all his pain, his beloved Union was never far from his thoughts. Suddenly, early on May 23, 1918, at the height of a thunderstorm came the end of the earthly stage of Dad's life.' He was only fifty.

Tributes to Watts recalled an amiable, humorous man, with a sensitive side to his nature; an 'all-round pressman' and a convinced trade unionist. On the wreath of red roses intertwined with evergreens that was the official tribute at his funeral was a note that read simply: 'The Union he cherished will never forget.'

A sense of community

Democracy: organised chaos

> We need to cherish any scrap of independence we possess and
> can secure. We are not mere hirelings; our work is creative and
> responsible work. The activities of rich adventurers in buying,
> and directing the policy of groups of newspapers is a grave public
> danger. A free-spirited, well-paid, and well-organised profession of
> journalism is our only protection against the danger.

So wrote H. G. Wells, one of the union's prominent early members, in a
message to the NUJ in 1922.

H. G. Wells

H. G. (Herbert George) Wells (1866–1946) received a basic education
at a local school in Bromley, and was apprenticed as a draper. He
escaped from drudgery with a scholarship to the School of Science,
where he founded and edited the *Science Schools Journal*. In 1891 his
major essay on science, *The Rediscovery of the Unique*, was published in
The Fortnightly Review, and he established himself as a novelist in 1895
with his science fiction story, *The Time Machine*. He joined the NUJ
in November 1921 and remained a member for the next seventeen
years.

These words have been a rationale for the union's activity since its
inception. Trade unions are not just industrial organisations, concerned to
extract the highest price for labour. They have always been cultural organisations too, set up by working people as alternatives to the order of society
ordained by the establishment. There are not many activities whose independence from the state, Church, political parties and big business matters
more to society than journalism. Everyone agrees, whether they mean it
or not, that a free society needs a free press, that democracy depends on
free information as well as on opinion and that it's the journalists' job to
provide it. The NUJ is their community organisation. Its role in helping

to sustain democracy in the UK and Ireland has required it to be a demo-cratic body itself. It has developed an elaborate structure of accountability that is wholly elective, which it works hard to maintain.

With democracy comes politics and with democratic politics come occasional crises among the leadership, but they have never seriously undermined the union or its ability to function. The general reaction among members when the leadership have fallen out has been: pull your-selves together and get on with it. Whenever the union has had its back to the wall it has held together superbly. It is the journalists' sense of community that will always hold it together.

An intense level of debate has driven the union's activity. The supreme policy-making institution is Annual Delegate Meeting, which has the authority to determine everything the NUJ says and does. Each year it gets through a phenomenal amount of business. The ADM in 1980, held in the Northern Ireland seaside town of Portrush, debated a record 382 motions in four days, ranging from a bid by Irish members to change the union's name to the International Union of Journalists (which failed, motion 1) to applause for branches supporting local community radio stations (motion 382, carried). At times it seemed to be getting a bit out of hand. After the 1965 conference (only 176 motions) the chairman of the ADM Standing Orders Committee (SOC), Lawrence Kirwan, wrote that it was all 'too democratic'. Branches were abusing their unlimited right to table motions: if they had been sensible, he continued, there need have been no more than fifty-seven to cover all issues. But nearly all attempts to tighten the procedures have been knocked back, though the right to bring last-minute 'emergency' motions was restricted in 1980 to absolutely vital matters; before then there had sometimes been more than fifty of these, dealing with such questions as the quality of the hotel cuisine as well as genuine emergencies.

Annual Delegate Meeting and the
National Executive Council

There are two groups of people that take the big decisions in the NUJ:
the Annual Delegate Meeting and the National Executive Council.
The basic structure has remained unchanged for 100 years.

ADM is the supreme body, a four-day frenzy of democratic activity.
Invariably staged at Easter time, it consists of a couple of hundred elected
representatives of all the branches in the union – all of them working
journalists. The national executive and the union's officials have no
votes, and ADM can be uncomfortable for them at times, as the delegates
subject the leadership to rigorous scrutiny and chew over the whole
range of union activity. So regular have criticisms of the NEC been
at times that there is sometimes ironic surprise when its view prevails.

ADM gives instructions to the NEC, which runs the union between
conferences. In turn the NEC instructs the General Secretary who
runs the union day-to-day. The NEC also comprises elected reps of
the membership – around a couple of dozen of them – who give their
time to the union voluntarily. If a thorny question comes up on which
the union rules are unclear they can 'interpret' them – but they must

*Delegates, all male, at the 1915 ADM in Sheffield, the earliest ADM of which a
photograph survives. (NUJ Collection)*

Delegates at the 2004 ADM in Liverpool. (Paul Herrmann)

secure the endorsement of the next ADM. Only ADM can determine the union's rules – and these rules put some restrictions even on ADM. For the union to affiliate to outside organisations, like political parties, there must be a vote of the whole membership. And ADM cannot instruct the editor of the *Journalist*, the union's magazine, who enjoys editorial independence.

The conference is a lot more than a talking shop. Equally important for the activists who take part is the get-together with colleagues. The atmosphere is hectic and the debates are leavened by frequently uproarious socialising. There is much activity on the fringe, with meetings and debates. In the 1960s a group of delegates began to stage what was then called a 'ceilidh', a booze-up with jokes and a satirical song about conference personalities. In the 1970s broadcasting delegates began to hold a (rather exclusive, invitation-only) dinner at which satirical sketches were performed, and in the 1980s the events merged into a late-night show that at times achieved a high standard of comedy. Such things do not last well, let alone in print, but a sketch at the 1992 ADM gives something of the flavour: this was the conference where sacked NUJ General Secretary Steve Turner made an unsuccessful bid for reinstatement, and the revue had a version of the Monty Python 'dead parrot' sketch – rather fresher then than it is now – in which a man takes a hapless General Secretary back to the shop where he bought him to complain he has been sacked ('been let go', 'got his cards', 'joined the unemployed million' etc), only to be told 'no he hasn't, he's on leave' and so on.

For a full breakdown of the NUJ's working structure as it stands in 2006, see Appendix 2 on page 341.

The mechanism for imposing order on this state of commotion without infringing democratic rights is finely balanced. The SOC is independent of the executive and takes its instructions from the conference itself. It cannot decide anything: all its decisions are open to challenge and must be ratified. In practice the system runs smoothly. It survived its greatest test at the dramatic ADM in London in 1992 when two top officials who had been sacked made bids for reinstatement: General Secretary Steve Turner,[2] dismissed by the executive, and finance controller Daniel Stafford, dismissed by the Acting General Secretary Jake Ecclestone after Turner's departure. The 'order paper' drawn up for the debate by the SOC

'The delegate who thought the NEC was right.'
One of the cartoons contributed by the great cartoonist Carl Giles to the Journalist *during the Second World War. (*Journalist*)*

Ken Ashton, General Secretary from 1977 to 1985. (NUJ Collection)

was thrown out by the conference: it looked as if anarchy had finally triumphed. The SOC chairperson Pauline Norris recalls: 'We had recommended that the motion to reinstate Turner was out of order because he had signed a settlement not to have his job back so had no right to claim it. There was a challenge and we were rolled over. So of course none of the amendments … had been composited into motions because we said they shouldn't be discussed. We would have to start all over again.' But she was one step ahead. 'As it happened I had anticipated this and prepared an alternative paper with everything in order,' she says, 'and I was able to have it circulated.'

Toppling leaders

Steve Turner was not the only NUJ leader to be forced out of his job. In 1985 General Secretary Ken Ashton was subjected to an inquiry over allegations, raised by a trustee of the union's pension fund, that he had conspired with senior executive members to grant an augmented pension to himself and the financial controller Niranjan Paik. There was a hugely bitter row, with counter-accusations of a conspiracy to get rid of Ashton, who was not an effective leader and was having a miserable time anyway. He was one of the old school, a former sub-editor on the *Daily Mail* in Manchester – the sixth successive Mancunian in the union's top job – and he had faced constant criticism from the union's more militant elements.

The charges against him were never properly tested because a severance deal was secretly negotiated which Ashton accepted on the eve of the 1985 conference. The inquiry into the conduct of the six executive members allegedly involved did go ahead, however. Matters were complicated by the fact that the executive meeting at which the pensions decision had supposedly been ratified had not been minuted: the NUJ was in the throes of a potential catastrophe at the time, with the sequestration of all its assets threatened over an industrial dispute, and to protect the union from the courts it had been agreed not to record the decisions taken.[3] Charges were initially found proved against one, former President John Devine, but they were dropped on appeal. 'Nobody dunnit,' the *Journalist* reported. Niranjan Paik left the union two years later.

Number two in the union when Ashton and Turner departed was Jake Ecclestone, a man whom controversy stalked like a shadow. Supporters of those who lost the top job (Ashton, Turner, and Harry Conroy) during his sixteen years as Deputy General Secretary – including three spells as acting GS during interregna after the departure of the three men – accused him of plotting against them. So events took an almost Shakespearian turn in 1997 when Ecclestone himself fell to a coup and the NEC, urged by a fourth General Secretary, John Foster, unceremoniously sacked him. Foster maintained that Ecclestone and his friends were plotting against him – and the Deputy had certainly made his criticism of a plan by Foster to devolve a degree of financial autonomy to the Irish section of the union very public. Accusing Foster of destroying the NUJ, 'something that not even Margaret Thatcher could achieve', was not going to endear him to many. Ecclestone went to law to force the union to let him stand in the subsequent election for his old job. He came second, to John Fray – a former broadcasting organiser who was backed by Foster – and then successfully sued the union for libel over a document Foster had produced. Ecclestone could ultimately have been the victim of his capacity for moralising overstatement. He had indeed, as he claimed, achieved a lot for the union – as much as some of those he saw depart. ▶

But as it approached its centenary, the union was, it seemed, outgrowing its tendency towards fratricidal strife. Foster's successor Jeremy Dear, elected in 2001, was re-elected unopposed five years later. He was not only the first in union history to win the job without challenge, but the first to be re-elected since the requirement for five-yearly elections had been introduced in 1982.

Pauline Norris's accession to the chair of the Standing Orders Committee in 1975 was a remarkable instance of the changes taking place within the union at the time: a woman of twenty-eight heading a committee that had hitherto consisted entirely of men well into their middle years – only two other women, Rosaline Kelly and the Wapping 'refusenik' Pat Healy, have made it since.[4] Norris and Kelly were both prominent in the Magazine and Book branch in the 1970s when the union's democracy received a massive shot in the arm with the arrival of the '68 generation'. NUJ politics have always been fairly radical – though never dominated by any one group – but this was a revolution. Activists from the new left in magazines combined with militants from provincial newspapers to mount a challenge to the established leadership that left it reeling.

The Magazine and Book branch was formed in London in 1968, bringing together the Trade and Technical (dating from 1924) and the Periodical and Book branches. It had more than three thousand members from the start and added another five hundred in its first year, making it the union's biggest branch; there were then twenty-one thousand NUJ members all told, and numbers were rising fast, increasing by more than 50 per cent in the 1960s. The IPC (International Publishing Corporation) magazine and book group was the biggest employer of journalists, with eighteen hundred on the payroll. The IPC group chapel proved itself tough and resourceful. It held its first strike in 1972, winning 33 per cent pay rises – a huge amount even in those inflationary days. The deal was accepted by 703 votes to 283, with 28 abstentions; more than a thousand members attended what was possibly the biggest NUJ meeting ever. But this was only a rehearsal for one of the most astonishing disputes in the union's history: the upside-down IPC work-in of 1979.

Again pursuing a pay claim, the journalists started 'working to contract'.

The IPC managers suspended the whole workforce. 'they sent letters telling us all to go home,' Norris recalls, 'but nobody did. They wanted us to go on strike but we carried on working. They said we were all trespassers in the building, but we wouldn't leave. The company stopped paying us. They stopped our post so we couldn't get any material' – no fax or email then.

This went on for five weeks. Somehow, some journalists on some of the publications managed to produce pages. 'When the pages came back from the typesetters we had to intercept them at reception to stop editors getting them,' says Norris. The then Father of the IPC group chapel, Colin Bourne, recalls that they actually got a few titles printed, against management instructions, through contacts with the print unions. 'The company couldn't believe it and agreed to negotiate.'

Norris looks back: 'We were near to agreement when there was trouble at *Melody Maker* [then one of the top music magazines]. Their office was in a hut in the car park because they tended to work at night when they couldn't get into the building. One of them had just thrown a typewriter out of the window of the hut. Colin Bourne said to management: "Perhaps now you will believe our members are working normally".' What had happened on *MM*, according to Bourne, was that a 'non-strikebreaking' edition had been secretly produced with management connivance and without the knowledge of the editor, and he, Bourne says, 'went spare'. By now matters were so confusing that the dispute had to be ended so as to preserve people's sanity. The journalists ended up with salaries 21 per cent higher – and back pay for the whole work-in period.

Not all the magazine activists were radical leftists, of course. The Mother of the Chapel on the big IPC women's weekly magazines – *Woman, Woman's Own* and so on – was Wendy Forrester, well known as a Conservative. 'At every meeting,' Bourne recalls, 'she always declared an interest because she was a shareholder. At one of the mass meetings she stood up and said, "The company not only wants the spoils of war but they want to drag the corpse round the battlements." The effect on the nervous members who had all been sacked was electrifying.' Another of the magazine women activists, Barbara Gunnell, remembers Forrester standing out among 'a lot of self-conscious scruffiness, baggy jeans and old fur coats. Wendy Forrester wore a twin-set and had her hair styled, a Tory cast among the various ultra-left types … You'd think, what on earth makes someone like that turn up to a meeting like this?'

Wendy Forrester, London magazines activist of the 1970s, receives her NUJ Membership of Honour at the 1994 ADM from executive member Colin Bourne. (Lesley Smith)

Forrester may have been tolerant, but elsewhere there were some angry confrontations between the old guard and the new left. The most dramatic happened at the 1974 annual conference in Wexford, Ireland, when an attempt was made to sack another General Secretary, Ashton's predecessor Ken Morgan. The attack came not from the left in the big London branches but from the leaders of the 'chapel power' movement that in the late 1960s had launched the crusade for decent wages and conditions for the grossly underpaid members on local newspapers.[5] Mike Bower, journalists' leader on the *Sheffield Star*, and Peter Dodson, his counterpart on the *Middlesbrough Gazette*, accused Morgan of conniving with the employers to undermine the prosecution of a national wage claim. Morgan emphatically rejected any accusation of dishonesty.

The debate got heated and the President, John Bailey, decided not to hold the vote but to adjourn overnight and vote in the morning. Morgan, a mild, courteous and very clever man, had brought his wife and daughters to the conference. 'They were sitting there while I was assassinating their father,' Bower recalls. 'No one would speak to us,' says Dodson. 'We had become pariahs. Next day we were hammered in the vote.'

That adjournment could have saved Morgan his job. He quit three years later to work for the Press Council. Was he driven out by the contin-

Ken Morgan, General Secretary from 1969 to 1977, with Deputy General Secretary Charles Harkness to his right. (Christopher Davies/Report)

uing criticism? With characteristic understatement Morgan says: 'I must have been a bit fed up at the NUJ but I wanted to do the PC job.' It was a great loss to the union; Morgan had tremendous forbearance and an ability to weather storms sadly unmatched in many of his contemporaries. For he was not the first official to leave at that time: his former deputy, Eric Blott, and North of England organiser Geoff Heighton had already gone, the latter citing the 'denigration of officials' as the reason. Bower was appointed to the northern job.

Both Bower and Dodson say that personally they got on well with Morgan, and generally at ADMs the comradely atmosphere has overridden political hostility. But on the NEC the divisions were often tense. Francis Beckett, who joined it in 1976, says: 'During most of my time on the NEC, the union's internal politics were poisonous. It had turned into two armed camps, "left" and "right". It was a division filled with distrust and dislike. The two sides drank in different pubs and held caucus meetings to decide their view on the main agenda items.' On occasions these gatherings were by chance held in the same venue and people blundered embarrassingly into the wrong one.

From 1971 the far left were grouped around Journalists' Charter, a rank-and-file organisation of the kind promoted in many unions by the Trotskyite International Socialist (IS) group, which in 1975 became the

Socialist Workers Party (SWP). It was not an exclusive or membership group and it was by no means controlled by the IS, but it formed a basis for networking. 'It was tremendously effective at connecting members from different sectors and areas,' says Gunnell, who was an IS member. 'We organised slates of candidates for union elections and wrote pamphlets which did influence union policy.' There was a huge rumpus when a Charter bulletin read out at the 1972 ADM allegedly libelled Heighton. He immediately initiated legal action, financed by the union, but the next year's conference put a stop to it. The Journalists' Charter organisation petered out in the mid-1980s, and in 1990 a split in the left saw the SWP heading off on its own. But the left network lasted until the early twenty-first century, even though there was little industrial action to agitate around and it functioned only at the ADM.

New NEC members tended to get wooed by both sides. Denis MacShane, who went onto the executive in 1974, recalls arriving at the hotel where the meetings were to be held and being approached by a member who said he was 'the whip for the left faction' and that he, MacShane, had been put down for the finance committee. That whip was Jimmy Cox, Father of the NUJ Chapel at the *Daily Record* in Glasgow, who as James Cox later became a thoroughly respectable BBC radio news presenter. Some managed to remain impartial; some, like the virtuoso political operator Vincent Hanna, another BBC heavyweight, liked to flirt with both; but voting was on party lines and heavily canvassed. The executive developed an eerie compulsion to decide really major issues by knife-edge votes. In 1992 Steve Turner was sacked by 10 votes to 9. The same figures had defeated three successive attempts during the Wapping dispute of 1986–7 to order all the NUJ members at Rupert Murdoch's Docklands plant out on strike.

If discussions in Magazine and Book followed the new left line in an untroubled way, those of its nearest rival, the London Freelance branch, did anything but. The three-thousand strong LFB was the scene of the most rancorous political strife. This was where the right wing fought back, following the standard of the celebrated *Times* columnist Bernard Levin. Levin was a forerunner of Thatcherism, one of the early Labour-supporting journalists to veer to the right; as a star columnist of the time he had quit the *Daily Mail* in protest after a pro-Labour article was censored. Like Magazine and Book, the LFB had come under the sway of the far left, and in 1976 Levin set about stopping them in their tracks. He was well connected, and he assembled a galaxy of journalistic notables, among them Michael Frayn, Marghanita Laski, Woodrow Wyatt and Ferdinand Mount. Laski, a renowned writer and critic, reduced one meeting to helpless laughter when she remarked: 'One could never understand what the union could do for one that one's agent couldn't do.' Levin used to produce a circular for his supporters before each meeting with instructions on how to vote: basically, to raise their hands when he did.

Levin's more powerful weapon was his thrice-weekly column in *The Times*, which he persistently exploited to grind his union axe, attacking not just the foes in his own branch but the union in general. At the time of NUJ elections he would print lists of the candidates that enjoyed his approval. Quite what *Times* readers made of it was a mystery, but the NUJ didn't take it lying down. In 1985 he was formally reprimanded by the NEC over a spiteful attack on a woman who had brought a complaint to the NUJ Ethics Council[6] over a feature in the *Sun* that began 'Which is a woman's sexiest bit of all?' 'There may indeed be a woman so priggish, stupid, humourless and hysterical that she did indeed experience what she claims to have felt,' Levin wrote in his *Times* column, 'but [her] problems, whether physical or psychological, are not, thank God, my concern.' The union did not discipline the great stylist for his language, however, but for the offence of deterring members from using the union's procedures – a slightly shaky charge perhaps, but after ten years enduring his sniping there were few to complain.

The 1970s were not the first time that left-wing politics had stirred controversy in the NUJ. There were many radical socialists among the founders, including Henry Richardson, who became the union's leader in 1918 and earned the benign disapproval of Frederick Mansfield as a 'pronounced left-winger ... a "Red", a revolutionary, a "Bolshie". Everyone knew of course that he was a Socialist,' Mansfield wrote, 'and he was very popular on the ranks of the Left ... It was only in times of real crisis, like a general strike or a move to affiliate with organised labour, that there was any great fear of the secretary's tendencies.'

Richardson's successor, Clement Bundock, was the cause of some agitation when he was appointed the NUJ's first full-time organiser in 1923, since he had been a conscientious objector during the First World War. The South Wales branch ran a campaign against him but the 1924 ADM overwhelmingly endorsed the appointment.

From the Second World War until the mid-1950s there was a more

Two brave men

In 1950 there was outrage when two leading journalists fell victim to
the Cold War pressures that gripped the press and much of the NUJ
with it – though neither man, it must be said, was a communist nor
anything like one. The great foreign correspondent James Cameron
quit the *Daily Express*, and the great editor Tom Hopkinson was sacked
from *Picture Post*. Both were NUJ members, both were brilliant journalists, both lost their jobs under political pressure and were precisely
the kind of journalist the union would have been anxious to support;
but the union could do little for them. Cameron, who walked out
of the *Express* in protest at 'red-baiting' articles in the sister *Evening
Standard*, appealed to colleagues for support – of which he received
a considerable amount together with more than 260 letters. At the
union's 1950 ADM there were 'loud cheers' for him, but delegate Frank
Lloyd commented:

> It is not enough to pat Cameron on the back for heroism. It is a
> shame that it is left to the individual conscience of a journalist to
> raise issues of this magnitude. It is a shame that the only recourse
> Mr Cameron had to draw attention to his stand was a letter to
> *The Times*. There should be a statutory body which should give
> the fullest protection to a man bringing a proper complaint of
> this sort.

This was a reference to the Press Council, yet to be set up, in which
the union was then banking all its hopes for a fairer and more responsible profession. Quite what the Press Council could have done about
these departures is far from clear.

Hopkinson was sacked from the editorship of the most popular news
magazine ever published in Britain for running a story by Cameron
that told some uncomfortable truths about the treatment of prisoners
by Britain's allies in the Korean War. He too attracted sympathy, and
was invited to a meeting of the Publications and Book branch. But
when the matter came to the NEC, all it could do was 'deplore' the
fact that normal procedures had not been followed in the dismissal.
The executive went on to recommend that, since 'assurances had been
received from the proprietor, the matter be regarded as closed'.

*Clement Bundock, General Secretary
from 1938 to 1953 and author of the
50th anniversary history of the union.
(Picture Post/Getty Images)*

serious political backlash: a witch-hunt against communists active in the
union. In the late 1940s the *Journalist* had been printing regular calls from
branches to bar communists from union office. It was ironic that there
seemed to be much more antagonism towards communists then than there
was twenty years later – London Freelance branch apart – towards people
a long way to the left of them. There was a second irony: the editor
printing these diatribes was a communist himself.

The book trade union

It was the growth of the media conglomerates that brought the editorial
staff in book publishing into the NUJ's domain. What had been principally a small-business industry became part of the global media as
magazine publishers – notably IPC and Thomson's – bought companies
up. So successfully did the members organise that they established a
strong foothold and the union was pleased to have them, whether
they counted as journalists or not. Activists in books have sometimes
had to remind the union that not all its members are journalists,
but the union prefers to say that they are: they produce editorial ▶

work for publication. The Book branch was hived off from Magazine
and Book in 1973.

Book members injected imaginative and novel elements into industrial activity. The first instance was the occupation by its staff in 1974 of
the office of a small north London publisher called Education Audio
Visual. The Mother of the six-strong chapel, Hilary Horrocks, recalls:

*Members of the Educational
Audio Visual chapel who
conducted the union's first office
occupation in north London in
1974. (Phil Franks)*

*Annabel McLaren (left) and
Jenny Golden, two of the
members occupying Robert
Maxwell's British Publishing
Corporation offices in central
London over Christmas 1981,
being presented with a brace of
pheasants by* Journalist *editor
Ron Knowles. (Andrew Wiard/
Report)*

I was delegated, as the MoC, to stand outside the street door of
the office early one wintry morning and inform the arriving
directors that the chapel had occupied the building and they
couldn't come in. The other NUJ members had their shoulders
against the door behind me, and tense seconds passed before
our bosses decided against a trial of strength. Apoplectic, they
retreated.

The chapel's half-dozen members were young, and most of
them very new trade unionists. We had debated long and hard

most of the previous night, angry at the news we'd just received from the New York-based employers that they had decided to close their London editorial office, and suspecting that an occupation was the only effective weapon at our disposal, but worried that the union would not back a potentially illegal action.

In fact they got strong official support. The occupation, sustained by other NUJ members, lasted three weeks. 'It was one of those intense interludes in your working life when you felt vividly "alive",' Horrocks says.

There was a longer occupation at the British Printing Corporation (BPC) office in the City of London, part of the empire of the notorious publisher Robert Maxwell. Again the issue was jobs: ten were to go from the MacDonald Futura imprint. As invariably with Maxwell, talks dragged on for weeks and the familiar pattern followed: the sixty-five NUJ members held lengthy meetings in the office and were sacked, but instead of going, they stayed – for three months, including Christmas and New Year 1980–1. A quasi-military support operation was implemented, with carefully monitored admission via the back stairs to the tenth-floor office and a rope hoist to pull up supplies at the front. A TV, food and drink were brought in by NUJ members from all over London. There was a Christmas tree and gifts, and *Journalist* editor Ron Knowles, who lived in the Cambridgeshire countryside, brought a brace of fresh pheasants – too fresh for the city-bound members, who said they had 'gone off' and wouldn't eat them. Eventually the threat of job losses was withdrawn, pending further talks.

Book members devised novel ways of highlighting the notoriously low levels of pay in publishing houses. In 1983 they held a 'Not the Booker Prize' dinner, with writers, including prizewinners, as speakers. The 'Not the …' prize was awarded to Fay Weldon, who had chaired the judges at the real thing two weeks earlier. They gave her a book with completely blank pages, which she said 'was no doubt the book produced this year which in 1983 most nearly reached perfection'.

In 1998 the Book branch celebrated its first twenty-five years of NUJ membership with a poetry competition, for twenty-five lines of verse.

The biggest book chapel, at Penguin, has used its strength to good effect to win what has been claimed as the model agreement for the industry, in terms of pay, working conditions, hours, holidays, parental

▶

leave and redundancy provision. The chapel had fought for it with a number of disputes over the years, taking strike and other actions such as picnics in the building, go-slow queues to clog up security on arrival at work, and in one instance a 'democracy wall' where members posted propaganda in the office. Most significantly, they were able to keep the agreement and all its terms through the period of 'derecognition' during the 1990s (see Chapter 3), and even to secure their application to all staff when Penguin merged with the giant publishing group Dorling Kindersley in 2000. The union had not been strong at DK, but a joint ballot of the two staffs resulted in a 98 per cent vote in favour of the NUJ – a clear vote of confidence in the work of the Penguin chapel over the years.

Working women, union women

'Should reporters marry? Of course they should. But lucky the reporter who marries a woman who does not expect Civil Service hours. And lucky the office whose reporters marry such women.' Sentiments such as these expressed by a *Daily Mail* reporter in 1963 would later have raised indignation at their casual acceptance that a man's place was in the newsroom, a woman's in the home. But they figured in *The Practice of Journalism* (1963), a book intended as both a training manual and an inspiration for aspirants to the trade, jointly produced by the National Council for the Training of Journalists (the NCTJ) ... and the NUJ.

Even as the book was being written, increasing numbers of women were entering journalism. They had been doing so since the late nineteenth century. A study of white-collar (or 'black-coated') workers at the turn of the twentieth suggested that of some 12,500 journalists thought to be working in Britain, perhaps 10 per cent were women, most working as writers for the magazines that sprang up in the last quarter of the previous century as such proprietors as Alfred Harmsworth began to cater for women readers. Women did find their way into newspapers too. The *Daily Mirror* was launched in 1903 as a newspaper for 'gentlewomen', and its largely female staff was headed by a woman editor, Mary Howarth. When sales slumped, however, Harmsworth installed a male editor, who sacked most of them; 'it was like drowning kittens', he said later.

Women were similarly a minority within the trade union movement as a whole, but would become gradually more important, and vociferous. It is to the NUJ's credit that, from the beginning, it took equality – at least in terms of pay – as an issue for which it would campaign. The first pay agreement with the Newspaper Proprietors' Association in 1917 covered men only, and there was so much anger from the few women then working on Fleet Street that officials were shamed into getting them included a year later. Since then, all union agreements have covered men and women alike, without distinction.

On the other hand, women have been poorly represented in the union's structure. Only three times in the first hundred years was a woman elected to the presidency, the highest office for voluntary members, and among the staff of full-time officials none was appointed until 1978.

In the *Union Journal* of November 1909 a correspondent, 'ES', noted that while 'with the single exception of the Stage, no career is invested with more glamour by the ambitious girl than Journalism, there is but a poor outlook for women, be they ever so energetic and resourceful among the ranks of purely news-gathering journalists'. Women reporters, ES complained, might be as technically competent as men, but would suffer from the prejudices they faced in general as well as those within the profession. And when it came to 'indoor' – office – work, women subeditors faced other, cultural pressures, ranging from the assumption that they could not work late or antisocial hours, to the notion that they would not be able to tolerate the coarse male-dominated environments. While this might for the time being force most women journalists to concentrate on working for 'women's interest' titles, ES concluded, it would not stop them eventually conquering the male bastions: 'The arrival of the woman journalist is in itself a sign that the interests of the sexes are becoming more and more alike.'

It would be almost a century, however, before the numbers of women entering journalism would equal those of men.

In 1917 Alice Chalmers-Lawford was elected the first woman delegate to the union's Annual Delegate Meeting. Describing the experience as the 'two happiest days I have spent since I reported my first engagement eight years ago', she said:

> Another illusion of mine has vanished. It was that in the main the
> intrusion of women in the Union was regarded as a necessary but
> regrettable evil by the main part of the menfolk. I hope that in

future there will be no ADM without a woman delegate. I hope that
before many years pass a woman will enter the charmed circle of the
Executive. To be frank, I have even dreams of the days in the dim and
distant future when delegates will rise to address 'Mrs President'.

Fifty-eight years would pass, though, before Rosaline Kelly, a magazine
journalist from Ireland who had made her career in London, became the
NUJ's first woman President. The union presidency is an annually elected
position from among the national executive, consisting of voluntary
officers, all working journalists; by custom, nobody serves for more than
a year. Then, as Kelly recalls: 'I told people not to address me as "Madam
President" just "President", but a few of them took a while to get out
of the habit.' Within the NUJ hierarchy women made slow progress
generally, and only three had by the 1970s found places on the executive
– Chalmers-Lawford representing the south of England in 1920, Nora
Wiles from Manchester in 1948 and Diana Hutchinson from magazines
in 1969. Increasing numbers of women became active in union work,
mostly in the chapels and branches, though some, such as Katie Doyle,
another Manchester activist who worked to reform the union's organisation during the 1960s and early 70s, achieved higher profiles.

In the 1950s it was still possible to find in the *Journalist* reports about
women joining the union, or taking up chapel or branch posts, that
included references to their marital status – or even on occasion to their
having received a 'welcoming kiss' from the branch chairman.

In 1966 it wrote of a woman who was 'cherished by her colleagues
as a superb coffee-maker and as senior vice-chairman of the Plymouth
branch'. She was 'elegant', she wrote the 'Pop Parade' column for the
Sunday Independent and had 'won fame as a local actress'. And she would go
on to become one of Britain's best-known TV journalists. Angela Rippon
was twenty-one when she became 'Father' of the NUJ chapel on the
paper, as the *Journalist* reported.

From the mid-1960s, however, developments in the wider world challenged the way the union regarded women. The influence of feminist
thinking, the rise of the women's movement and the growing numbers
of women entering journalism and the NUJ brought about changes both
in attitudes and in the structure of the union. Such questions as equal
rights and work opportunities, maternity (and paternity) rights, childcare
provision and job-sharing assumed more importance in union discussions and campaigns. So too, as the union took its part in wider debates,

Rosaline Kelly, the first woman to become President of the NUJ, was made NUJ Member of Honour at the 1979 ADM. President Denis MacShane applauds. (Andrew Wiard)

came questions about sexism in the media, how their images of women were created, and the effects they had. As part of this process, the increasing influence of women in the NUJ had its impact, not just in terms of numbers but in the roles they filled and the structures they helped create.

Rosaline Kelly took her seat on the union's national executive as a representative of the magazines sector in 1972. It was an important year for the NUJ's evolving attitude towards women in journalism, of whom some four thousand (out of 25,000) were now members. At the Annual Delegate Meeting that year, at Tenby, it was decided to investigate discrimination against women. The *Journalist* would begin its report on the ADM: 'The cause of Women's Lib triumphed ...'

The decision to look into the conditions under which women journalists were working came amid growing complaints about unfair practice. Margaret Hignett, a member from Cardiff, said that, while women had better work records than men, they found it harder to get jobs. A pilot survey showed that 37 per cent of women journalists were earning union minimum wages, as opposed to 20 per cent of the NUJ's overall membership.

'I did my job on equal terms'

Alice Chalmers-Lawford began work on the *Mid-Devon Advertiser* at the age of thirteen and a half, having already acquired a shorthand speed of 120–40 words per minute. She joined the NUJ as a probationary member in 1913, aged seventeen, and within four years became the first female delegate to the union's Annual Delegate Meeting. In 1920 she was elected to the national executive, but served only one year. In 1968, as Betty Pope (she had married in 1931), she received a standing ovation when she was presented to that year's ADM. She recalled that she had eventually agreed to write a 'women's column' after some two decades as a reporter. Previously, she emphasised, 'I did my job on equal terms with my male colleagues – including the district reporting and night staff turns.'

The union itself came in for criticism. Mary Holland, an Irish reporter highly regarded particularly for her work on Northern Ireland for British papers, complained that while the NUJ had been committed to a policy of equality, women had received neither equal pay nor equal opportunities. Among the targets the union set itself were to abolish the limits on the numbers of women accepted for NCTJ courses, equal opportunities for promotion, an end to the policy of paying women the lowest possible rates, improved maternity leave and benefits in union agreements, as well as an end to discriminatory conditions in pension schemes and different retirement ages from men. It would prove a long struggle, and one that is still far from over as the union enters its second century.

However, within four years of the Tenby debate, as mentioned earlier, the union elected its first woman President. Rosaline Kelly has always insisted: 'Don't call me the first woman president – I am the first president who was a woman.' Her career was in magazines, where employment and promotion prospects had long been better for women than in newspapers or broadcasting, and where women played a greater role in chapel and branch activities. Pauline Norris, too, who would become a familiar figure at the union's annual conferences, smoothing its procedures, was drawn into NUJ activity at IPC in the early 1970s. Barbara Gunnell, who with the broadcast journalist Scarlett MccGwire was elected jointly to the union presidency in 1988, also began her NUJ involvement as a magazine journalist in the same era. The influence of women was prodigious, she says: 'Women ran the branch. Their organisation at IPC was utterly brilliant.'

Barbara Castle

Barbara Castle (1910–2003) joined the NUJ in 1944, the year after Ted Castle, her future husband, then the night editor of the *Daily Mirror*, made her the paper's housing correspondent. 'My Ted should be here now,' she said when presented with her NUJ life membership in the 1980s, 'because he absolutely loved the NUJ.' She was elected to Parliament in the 1945 Labour landslide and joined the cabinet as Minister of Overseas Development in 1964, moving to Transport the following year, where she introduced seat belts and the breathalyser. In 1968 she became Secretary of State for Employment and Productivity, and introduced the white paper on trade unions, *In Place of Strife*, which sought to regulate industrial disputes. Her proposals were abandoned in the teeth of fierce trade union opposition, including from the NUJ, but she did get through the 1970 Equal Pay Act. When Labour returned in 1974 she became Health Secretary, achieving the best-ever pay rise for nurses and phasing out pay beds from the National Health Service. But when James Callaghan replaced Wilson as Prime Minister in 1976, he fired her. She was an MEP from 1979 to 1989, and remained in the NUJ until her death.

Kelly's vigour – and her sharp eye for procedural nonsense – made an instant impact on the union's executive, and she became President within four years. Even so, the union's male bastions still proved suspicious. 'I went on a tour of the country, but I was not allowed to put a toenail in what was then Fleet Street,' she recalled. 'I set out to visit as many branches as I could, but I was never invited to Central London.' Pauline Norris also recalls resistance, even outright antipathy, towards women in the union. 'The NUJ was very old-fashioned and sexist in those days,' she says. 'At ADM, the Magazine and Book branch delegation had as many women on it as all the other branches put together. Sometimes when we went to the microphone, some men would shout things like "Get 'em down."'

Joint Presidents 1988–9, Scarlett MccGwire (left) and Barbara Gunnell (right), with union member and former Labour minister Barbara Castle. (Andrew Wiard)

In November 1978 the NUJ appointed its first female full-time official when Linda Rogers, previously a banking union organiser, joined as a national organiser. The following year, Peta van den Bergh, a former local newspaper reporter and radio journalist, became the second, with responsibilities for the union's freelance members. These were the only two appointed as national industrial organisers until 2006, when Sue Harris became a third; other women have been employed as assistant organisers or as legal, regional or equality officers.

To some extent the possibilities for women were enhanced by the introduction in 1984 of job-sharing for union posts, to help women with childcare responsibilities. Gunnell and MccGwire were job-sharers as joint Presidents. Gunnell had joined the NEC as a job-sharer with photojournalist Angela Phillips the day the rule came into force (an all-male jobshare was formed at the same time). That year the NEC attained eight women members; the all-time high of ten (out of 44, including eight job-sharing) came in 2003.

Campaigns to address the problems of sexism in journalists' use of words and images proved influential, while the union also strengthened its Code of Conduct to this end. But though it would establish an equality

Pauline and Bob Norris, both prominent NUJ members for 40 years, with son Drew at the 2001 ADM where Pauline joined her husband as a Member of Honour. (Martin Jenkinson)

working party, which became the Equality Council, to encourage women members to play a greater part in its activities and improve their working conditions, by the end of the century there was still much to be done. By then there had been a third woman President: Anita Halpin, a veteran communist from the public relations sector, held the position in 1994–5 – and was, like Kelly, the only woman on the executive at the time. 'Of course more women should stand for union positions,' she said, 'but the union itself should look at the difficulties we face. The pressures on working women are getting greater all the time and people have to put earning a living and caring for their families first.'

Domestic pressure has certainly kept women out of top union positions. One of the key activists of the 1970s and 1980s, Linda Piper, says it was 'having kids that prised me out of NUJ activity'. Her employers, the Westminster Press group of provincial papers, wouldn't pay her for time off on union work. 'I had two children: there were weeks when my whole salary went to pay childminders. I used to take my daughter Morrigan, the oldest, to meetings with the Newspaper Society [the provincial news-papers' employers' association]. The NS bosses were revolted.' The job of full-time NUJ organiser for the provincial sector came up in 1983 and

Piper was invited to apply. 'I was pregnant at the time,' she says. 'I didn't feel I could take a union job so I didn't apply.'

In 2003 women outnumbered men among new entrants to the union for the first time, and comprised 40 per cent of the membership. In 2007 – assuming that, as is customary, the Vice-President elected the year before assumes the top position unopposed – the NUJ was expected to elect Michelle Stanistreet of the *Sunday Express* as its fourth woman President in 101 years.

Mary Stott

Mary Stott (1907–2002) was the first and longest-serving editor of the *Guardian* women's page, using it as a platform for women's voices and concerns from 1957 to 1972. She started work on the *Leicester Mail* aged seventeen as a temporary copyholder, not allowed to join either the Typographical Association or the Correctors of the Press Association because neither accepted women. When, at nineteen, she was asked to take over the women's page, she said: 'It nearly broke my heart – I thought my chance of becoming a real journalist was finished.' She worked on the *Bolton Evening News*, and in 1933 moved to the Co-operative Press in Manchester, where she edited two pages of the weekly *Co-op News* devoted mainly to reports of the women's cooperative guild, and children's publications. In 1945 she became a sub on the *Manchester Evening News*, but was fired five years later to protect the male succession to the post of chief sub-editor. She was never an orthodox feminist. But she was an active member of Women in Media, and led their march to Downing Street in February 1973. Nor was she orthodox in union matters. She believed in the special authenticity of amateur contributors, arguing that readers could often identify more closely with a non-professional writer. But her pages were influential.

The *Journalist*: the union in the mirror

The dashing, dark-haired socialist Henry Marriott Richardson was editor of the *Union Journal* for ten years from its first edition in November 1908. He didn't have an easy ride, but editors seldom do. Just what kind of journal journalists should use to communicate with journalists was the subject of much early debate, but the outcome was not decisive. Members wanted it to be both independent and official, authoritative and free ranging, informative and propagandistic. The way the journal swayed one way or the other has varied with events and with the ability of successive editors to navigate the currents of union affairs. The editor of the *Journalist*, as it was known from 1918, is a lone sailor, studying the wind and the stars, ever on the lookout for the next storm.

The editor has always been elected, not appointed. Until 1973 the job was a voluntary one, elected at the annual conference and carried out for a modest annual payment. Then it became a salaried job, elected from 1982 by the whole membership (from 1973 it also enjoyed constitutional independence from the executive). As far as the union knows this is a unique arrangement: an editor elected by his or her readers, with no control from the owners – an almost utopian institution. It doesn't suit everyone: there have been those on the NEC who cannot abide it, but if anyone was going to try it, it was going to be the NUJ.

At heart is the question: should the journal be journalism or PR? A publication produced according to journalistic values or a propaganda tool under the direction of the executive? The distinction need not be absolute: there is more than one kind of propaganda. Richardson wrote:

> The *Journal* is a dull rag ... We wish it was not a dull rag. We would like it to scintillate with wit and humour, and be a thing of jokes and personal jottings. But there are reasons why it cannot be. For one thing, the journal was meant to be a dull rag. It is the organ of a dull organisation – an organisation dealing with the dullest of mundane subjects, the remuneration and hours of labour.

At the 1915 ADM a proposition from Tom Foster of the Central London branch that the *Journal* should 'express the views of the National Executive' was accepted, despite the doubts of revered General Secretary William Newman Watts. Watts pointed out that the executive 'was not united. Some resolutions are passed by a majority of one, and is such a snatch majority to say what was the policy of the union?' In response,

R. C. Spencer of Manchester sarcastically proposed 'the appointment of a jellyfish. If we are to have an editor, he must edit the paper. He would never bring out a paper with which everybody would agree.' The next year Central London was back with a demand that the *Journal* be 'remodelled. The make-up is wrong. The whole thing is wrong from title page to imprint. This title is misleading. A better title would be "the Journalist", for it would then appeal to all journalists. We must also see that it is organised on business-like lines, in order to make it more interesting to journalists ensued.'

The title was indeed changed, and before long the editor too: in 1918 Richardson was elected General Secretary and moved up, to be succeeded as editor by one of his Fleet Street critics, Frederick Mansfield, an urbane establishment figure who tended to patronise northern radicals such as Watts and Richardson. He was a prolific and authoritative writer and highly influential in the union's beginnings in London. After two years he stood down, giving way to another Fleet Street hand, C. P. Robertson, who straight away asserted his independence, beginning his first editorial: 'The General Secretary was not quite correct when he said last month …'. The GS, of course, was Richardson; at his election, Robertson had been runner-up.

Editors tend to last either a very short or a very long time. There were half a dozen more before 1942, when a tussle over independence cost Owen Rattenbury the job. He wrote a leader saying: 'The editor should be absolutely independent, so long as he does not use his independence as a partisan.' At the ADM that year he stood down: it had been revealed that a leader written by Rattenbury had been stopped by the President, who that year was Tom Foster. Rattenburg's successor, Gordon Schaffer, a one-armed left-wing Labour activist on *Reynold's News*, the Sunday paper owned by the Co-operative Movement, was an adept political operator who had no difficulty maintaining an equilibrium with the NEC. In 1948 he too stood down and the position went to his friend and *Reynold's News* colleague Allen Hutt, who edited the *Journalist* for 23 years.

In the Cold War days Hutt's communism was divisive but the leadership always stood by him, for he was totally embedded in the bureaucracy. He was on the NEC and would become NUJ President for 1967–8; in one issue that year he included eight pictures of himself. He became chief subeditor of the *Daily Worker* and was a great authority on newspaper design, devoting pages to articles dissecting the design of other papers and to stories of himself receiving design awards. He covered extensively fraternal visits to and from the socialist countries of Eastern Europe. Incongruously, he peppered the paper with cheesy pictures of beauty queens at press balls around the country – not union members but young women setting out on the beauty circuit. He liked his pretty girls, did Allen Hutt, invariably captioning them as 'attractive'. From 1963 he turned the *Journalist*, until then a busy if formalistic quarto newsletter that had varied little in fifty years, into an A3 tabloid newspaper. From then on it was to change dramatically every time the editor did, as if it were an assertion of independence.

Hutt's *Journalist* ignored activity outside the NEC's control, such as the rise of political activity and the wave of unofficial strikes in the late 1960s. Rows blew up over his policy of not reporting the ADM in detail: he used to write just a witty and highly personal 'sketch' of the proceedings and list the decisions taken. Members started to complain, and there was a storm of protest at the 1969 ADM over an Editor's Note he had inserted under a letter complaining about the reporting of the previous year's ADM: 'The *Journalist* feels no obligation to give space to speeches contrary to long-established union policy,' Hutt wrote. The conference passed a motion that members' views should be reported 'whether or not they accord with NEC or NUJ policy'.

In 1971 it all caught up with Hutt. For the first time in fourteen years he faced a contest for the job – still nominally elected annually at the conference. A young man called Ron Knowles, a militant from the North of England, barely known at national level, had the presumption to run against him. Hutt won – by ten votes, 167 to 157; the front page account of this 'sensation' appeared alongside a story of the editor winning yet another design award. But Captain Hutt had run aground and would not stand for election again.

In the changed spirit of the time it was decided to make the editorship a full-time job, to be elected every three years, and to grant the *Journalist* editorial independence. It was as much a reaction to the stifling arrogance of Hutt as it was an ideological move. For a year the job went to his long-serving assistant, Ted Simpson of the London *Evening Standard*, and he was put up to stand for the full-time job, against Knowles, when it was established in 1973. At the last minute Simpson pulled out, unwilling to put his livelihood at the risk of regular re-election, and Knowles the militant had the paper in his hands.

The longest-serving Journalist *editor, Allen Hutt (1948–72). (NUJ Collection)*

Knowles's *Journalist* was almost as egotistical as Hutt's: pugnacious and aggressive – at times almost brutal – and rough and ready in design; the journal of a very much changed union. He received shoals of angry letters that he revelled in publishing – in response to which letters of support came flooding in. 'Militants in Power' was his splash headline when the NEC, likewise transformed by a new intake of radical activists, scrapped its Administrative Committee, the *ancien régime*'s secretive decision-making core. But while it crowed over triumphs and fulminated against bosses and scabs, the *Journalist* was open to all and ran a wide range of debate. There was a lot of it about at the time.

The next change veered just as drastically in the opposite direction. Knowles decided to become an NUJ industrial organiser, covering his home turf in the English provinces, and the new editor – the first elected by a ballot of the membership – was Tony Craig, formerly of the *Daily Express* and an ally of Bernard Levin in the London Freelance Branch.[7]

Craig was much maligned and didn't last long, but his paper was admired by many. He adopted an elegant but rigid modular layout with restrained headlines, every single word in Century typeface (Hutt had used Times with Bodoni heads, Knowles Century and Univers). He filled the pages with acres of reports, transcripts of meetings and other documentation; it was the NUJ newspaper of record, very formal, with a pompous leader column. But it had a certain style, and included columns from heavyweight journalists, contacts from his Levin days, such as Katherine Whitehorn, James Cameron, Michael Foot, Selina Scott, Mike Molloy and Magnus Linklater.

Baptism of fire

Ron Knowles was the embodiment of NUJ chapel power in provincial newspapers, and his editorship drove some of the more traditional members to almost speechless rage. He had become a kind of flying militant, travelling provincial England stirring up action in local chapels, while raising a family of, eventually, five children. He calculated that when, at the age of thirty-four, he took the editorship it was his fifteenth job. He was never fired, though. Knowles was a skilled sub – and a witty and scathing writer – and left jobs either in protest at some management stupidity or for better money elsewhere.

He had begun this peripatetic career on the *Evening Sentinel* in his home town of Stoke-on-Trent – where Henry Richardson also started – and had experienced an uncanny introduction to trade unionism when his father, a printer on the paper, went out on strike. Young Ron was then an indentured trainee and, though seniors struck in support, trainees were instructed by the NUJ to work. This was routine, since the union did not want youngsters to break their indentures and lose their careers.

'I felt excluded by this from my colleagues who had been so good to me,' Knowles recalls. His father was the National Graphical Association representative on Stoke trades council, the local union federation, which Knowles had to cover – and he got his first front-page story reporting his father's strike speech. But it was other stories that made him militant, he says. 'I was reporting inquests of miners and pottery workers killed at work. I saw their widows given measly amounts and it woke me up to reality – because the employers were being niggardly to us too.'

What put paid to Craig was a relatively frivolous matter. He had decided to revive a cartoon strip, 'Varoomshka' by John Kent, which the *Guardian*

Cartoonist John Kent with a sample of his 'Varoomshka' cartoon, the 'sexist' nature of which put paid to the Journalist *editorship of Tony Craig. (Andrew Wiard/Report)*

had dropped shortly before. It showed the adventures of a glamorous and lightly clad ingénue making naïve comments on current affairs. But it wasn't funny, and Craig must have wondered whether it was worth the trouble, because it brought a torrent of condemnation for what radicals in the union – not just women – saw as the sexism of the drawings. His own branch, London Freelance, which had seen off the Levinite counter-insurgency, stopped distribution of the *Journalist* to its members for a time, so Craig had it mailed direct from union HQ.

After a few months he dropped the cartoon and shortly after that left the job for reasons unconnected with the editorship. But according to his successor, Bernie Corbett, he was doomed anyway: 'He would have been got rid of, because he exercised his independence from the NEC of the time.' Despite editorial independence, *Journalist* editors can't sail against the prevailing wind; they have to tack.

Corbett came from the left – though not the ultra-left – but his strength lay in his editing talent. He was a former sub and NUJ activist on the *Birmingham Post* and the *Guardian* with a strong focus on story angles and a mordant genius for headlines. Journalistically his paper was outstanding, but after eighteen months he returned to the *Guardian*; he was more at home on the subs' desk. For a year the *Journalist* was edited temporarily basis by Eric Butler, the sixty-three-year-old sports sub on the *Sun* who

Bernie Corbett, editor of the Journalist *from 1985 to 1987. (Lesley Smith)*

had refused to join Murdoch's move to Wapping and whom Corbett had dubbed the 'Hero of Wapping'.

After three short editorships came another long one. Tim Gopsill was elected in 1988 and re-elected in 1993; in 1998 and 2003 there was no contest. He too came from the left as a former associate of Ron Knowles, though with a less combative style. In 1993 he converted the paper back to an A4 magazine, and with full colour from 1996. Relations between the *Journalist* and the leadership were regularised by the establishment in 1989 of an editorial advisory board, elected at the ADM every year, but this did not mean controversy had died. During the short general-secretaryship of Steve Turner (1990–1) the new leader was granted a column in the *Journalist* that he employed to lambast all and sundry – including the editor. 'Terrible Tim's political toy' he called the paper. The column became something of a cult item in the trade union movement: miners' leader Arthur Scargill told Gopsill he was an avid reader.

Freelances: servants without masters

When NUJ freelances opened an email discussion group they called it
CatHerds. Trying to organise individual self-employed journalists into a
trade union, it was felt, was like trying to herd cats. CatHerds bulletins
are full of ideas for assembling the combined effort of freelances into an
industrial force, a task that has preoccupied the union since its early days.
The problem is that it is not the people that are freelance, but the work.
The industry casts its net for material much wider than among the journalists it directly employs and its suppliers are often impossible for the
NUJ to identify, let alone represent. A huge amount of published material
originates out of house: probably, for most magazines, most of it.

There are bona fide self-employed freelances; staff journalists who
work shifts or write for or sell stories to other publications; there are
agencies of all kinds, and wannabes and plagiarists trying to crash into the
trade. There is syndicated material, there are articles from non-journalist
experts, and stories and pictures from just about anybody. Journalism in
Britain and Ireland is not a closed profession – and it shouldn't be – yet
the union has to try to exert some kind of leverage over the business to
maintain both decent rates of pay and professional standards.

In 1909, ninety-five years before CatHerds went on line, the union
executive contemplated a report on the thorny question of freelancing.
'The possible varieties of free lances are many,' wrote executive member
J. H. Harley, 'and by permutation and combination of these many varieties
you may reach an infinity of possible problems.' The executive resolved
that 'the matter was not yet ripe for a decision'.

Freelances included, according to Harley, the 'gentleman who may be
described as "one who was once a reporter but now only works when
the right thing tumbles his way and he has no beer into which to dip
his beak"'. Such stereotypes have always hung round journalists' necks.
Many of the union's best-known members – George Bernard Shaw, G. K.
Chesterton, H. G. Wells, George Orwell, Bernard Levin – were freelance
writers, but much more numerous were the 'linage' merchants who sold
stories for payments that were traditionally calculated on the number of
lines of type the stories made, articles being set in separate lines of lead on
Linotype machines.

G. K. Chesterton

G. K. (Gilbert Keith) Chesterton (1874–1936) is remembered today mostly for energetic poetry, for his paradoxes, for novels like *The Flying Inn* and *The Man Who Was Thursday*, and for his fictional detective, Father Brown. But in his lifetime he was better known as a journalist and controversialist who converted to the Catholic Church in 1922. A year later he founded a magazine called *GK's Weekly* which promoted a political creed called distributism, an attempt to take the best from both socialism and capitalism. In April 1909 Chesterton addressed an NUJ dinner at Anderton's Hotel, Fleet Street, held to launch the union's drive into national newspapers. His speech, according to someone who was there, began with 'some characteristic paradoxes and homilies', but he also advised every journalist in London to join the union, and set an example by joining it himself that very night.

In its mission to establish minimum fees for freelance work the union did manage in the 1920s to secure a scale of rates with the Newspaper Proprietors' Association, representing the national papers. These rates, which remained unaltered for twenty-five years, were 12.5p (2 shillings and 6 pence) for up to sixty words and 1p (two and a half old pence) for each eight words thereafter. In 1947, in recognition of their inadequacy, the union negotiated an increase that doubled them at a stroke. It also won photographic rates for the first time, pricing pictures at between £1.12 and £7.35.

The Newspaper Society, representing provincial papers, refused to negotiate a rate at all until 1952, when they conceded a magnanimous 0.6p (one and a half old pence) a line for weekly papers and up to one whole penny a line for the bigger dailies. Three years later the NS also conceded photographic rates of between £1.05 and £7.87. The definition of rates by the line continued in NS freelance agreements right up until they were terminated in the late 1980s, by which time electronic photosetting had long replaced the Linos.

The linage system, said Clem Bundock, General Secretary from 1937 to 1952, caused 'formidable problems, which at all stages of the union's history have provided enough trouble to keep Solomon himself, were he on the NUJ staff, in full-time employment'. Linage was paid not just to freelances, but also to staff on local papers who sold on their best stories to the nationals and to agencies. It pitted journalists against each other. Senior reporters on the bigger assignments and those who covered the courts would have more stories to sell, and sub-editors would have none – at least, none of their own. It was common for senior journalists with contacts on national newsdesks to hog the linage for themselves, robbing the juniors who had often done the work. Another problem was that employers, aware that the system supplemented the journalists' incomes, used it to keep salaries down. When union negotiators pleaded the poverty of members, editors would reply, 'But look at the linage they can earn!'

Linage was handy extra income for the staffers then, but the penny-a-line (or lower) rates were so pitiful that a freelance could hardly live off them. 'Let's do away with linage' was a call from the *Journalist* in 1934. 'It has done incalculable harm to the Union, especially to the free-lance section of it. The free-lance men have a natural and perfectly healthy objection against being underpaid. No, you should be paid price rates, to secure an adequate return for your free-lance labours for the modern newspaper.' But it was to be decades before the industry adopted a system of commissioning work in return for properly agreed rates. In the meantime the NUJ promoted the 'linage pool' system, whereby all outside earnings that came into a newsroom were totted up and divided among the staff.

Then there were the amateurs – what Bundock called the 'motley crew of outsiders, magistrates' clerks, newsagents, relieving officers, clergymen, officials of football associations and many others' – who ply the media with material and have bothered the union throughout its history. In the early 21st century they became known by the strange name of 'citizen journalists'. As mobile phone technology allowed pictures to be taken and transmitted, the media were flooded with newsworthy digital images from members of the public. At the same time the internet allowed virtually anybody to set up websites and publish their own material. Concerned at the implications for professional standards as well as for its members' work, the union in 2006 drew up guidelines to control their use.

For decades, non-journalist sports writers have been the subject of particular complaints; not for writing specialist articles, which the union regards as legitimate, but for producing reports of events that could have been covered by freelances. In 1950 the Swansea branch complained that the press boxes at South Wales rugby matches 'resembled a convention of ex-Cardiff rugby footballers'. Even more objectionable was the practice that developed after the Second World War whereby sports personalities put their names to columns that had been 'ghosted' for them by sports subs or reporters. Feeling was so strong – especially in Manchester where the northern editions of the popular papers were produced – that the 1948 ADM decided, against the advice of the executive, to instruct members not to handle them. The union could not enforce this decision, but matters came to a head in 1951 when members in Manchester decided to boycott the sports reports in the *Sunday Times* of a certain Brigadier Smyth. The issue went to a joint committee with the NPA, which took three years to produce a grandly titled 'concordat' under which it was agreed that preference in sports commentary should be given to staff or freelance journalists and that non-journalist articles should carry 'reasonable accreditation': in effect, a note that X (the name) was talking to Y (the journalist).

But since big names are important for selling newspapers, Fleet Street editors largely ignored the concordat. In 1974 the NEC repudiated it and called on chapels to act on their own cases. NEC member Alan Lofts, a sports journalist with a long record of campaigning against the press-box sport stars, said it was a 'stinking cesspit that needs cleaning up'. A report to the executive said the 'mass use of journalists to "ghost" big sporting names is clearly handicapping the development of sports journalists as commentators in their own right ... The use of an 8-point italic line at the end of a ghosted piece is hardly "reasonable accreditation" if the personality's name is displayed in 30 point at the top.'

But the practice continued, and even the credit line fell into disuse by the end of the 1990s. Readers would have no idea that the most the personality concerned had contributed to the article was half an hour's chat on the phone. It must be added, though, that many celebrity sports commentators, especially in the upmarket papers, did write their own words, and that many, including cricket legends Freddie Trueman, Trevor Bailey and Jim Laker, joined the NUJ.

Treat them fairly and squarely

When the union adopted its Code of Conduct in 1936 no fewer than three of the thirteen clauses covered the question of fair treatment for freelances: members were not to take work intended for freelances or to appropriate the work of others for linage purposes, and they must be prepared to give up linage so as 'to provide a free-lance member with a means of earning a living'. At the same time the union decided to launch a Freelance Directory, listing freelance members by their skills and availability. Response, however, was poor, and the first edition did not appear until 1951. It then continued in print until it was put on line in 2002. A Freelance Fees Guide, setting recommended rates for all kinds of work, was published biennially from 1978, and went online in 2004.

A backlash in books

On one occasion when a chapel's action against a non-journalist contributor was effective it was to rebound in the union's face.

It has always been common and generally acceptable for prominent political figures to write columns, but in 1969, at the height of the NUJ 'chapel power' movement, the *Daily Mirror* chapel in London decided to boycott one by Clive Jenkins, the leader of the white-collar Association of Scientific, Technical and Managerial Staffs. The chapel had a de facto 'closed shop' and the column was stopped, but Jenkins took his revenge. ASTMS was an aggressive expansionist union and, according to Bob Norris, an NUJ official who worked with the book sector for thirty years, it was beginning to recruit actively in book publishing, and for years the NUJ suffered from this rivalry on the book front.

Contributed words and pictures are only a part of freelance journalism. There is also work done inhouse, on shifts, paid by the day. From the union's first national pay agreements at the end of the First World War there were rates for what in pre-astronautical times were called 'spacemen' – that is, freelances hired as reporters by the assignment or by the day. In the union's first agreement with the Newspaper Proprietors' Association (NPA) in 1917 the rate was 25p for a story or £1.05 for a day. Casual shift working became more prevalent, notably in sub-editing, as newspapers from the 1950s onwards became more 'edited' with the growth of the tabloid press, and fewer articles reached print as written by the reporter. The increasing multiplicity of source material also required subbing skills to pull it all together.

At times chapels have set out to 'decasualise' – that is, to achieve staffing levels high enough to eliminate the use of freelances except to cover holidays, sickness or parental leave. But casuals are so attractive to managements, since they are entitled to none of these benefits, that they keep using them. The increase in casual shifts brought the scourge of the 'moonlighters', staff journalists who work for other papers on their days off. In the 1960s, when papers were prosperous and expanding and when powerful chapels in London and some big provincial cities negotiated four-day weeks, moonlighting – 'double-jobbing', as it is known in Ireland – was rife, as journalists worked their extra days elsewhere.

This created problems when work was short. In 1971, when the *Daily Sketch* closed down and 271 journalists were made redundant by the Daily Mail group, which owned it, appeals were made to the moonlighters to give up their work. The Central London branch rejected a motion to ask staffers to give up their extra shifts, which led to the resignation of the branch chairman Jim Manning and to a major row at that year's ADM. The union was instructed to do all it could to find work for the victims, and the ADM howled down a Central London motion that instead of giving up their bunce the moonlighters should pay a levy of £1 per shift for the unemployed. 'Our colleagues want work, not charity,' said Keith Blogg of the *London Evening News*, also part of the Mail group. 'It is disgusting to hear speaker after speaker arguing in favour of retaining their own Saturday extras.' Blogg was referring to the widespread use of casuals by the Sunday papers, which with relatively small staffs have always needed large numbers of them on Saturdays.

In 1980 the NUJ London Freelance branch (the LFB) decided to launch a frontal attack on the moonlighting system, which was not only depriving freelance and unemployed members of work but was actually holding freelance rates down. The rates were low because those doing the work did not depend on it for their livings. Had they been higher, publishers would have employed more staff and there would have been fewer shifts to exploit. Freelance NEC member George Findlay, owner of a news agency in Cumbernauld, wrote in the *Journalist* that the moon-lighters were 'motivated by greed, not need ... the union exists to protect the interests of all its members, not to make the fat cats even fatter.' This allegation was substantiated from the horse's mouth, as it were, when fellow NEC member David Thompson, Father of the NUJ Chapel at the *Daily Mirror*, admitted to LFB representatives at a meeting they called to discuss the problem that his members were 'caught in the wealth trap', with school fees and private health premiums to pay, and could ill afford to drop their shifts.

The campaign involved setting up a freelance casuals' register for editors to draw on – it was noted that a shift on the *Willesden and Brent Chronicle* in north-west London paid more than a shift on the *Sun* – plus discussions with chapels, the toughening of union policy, and the targeting of individual moonlighters for complaint under union rule; taking work off freelances was, after all, against the Code of Conduct.

To begin with the campaign had some success. The LFB narrowed its sights on one Sam Benest, a sub on *The Times* who had two other jobs, and branch chairman Terence Kelly laid a formal complaint against him. At the NEC hearing into the case Benest, somewhat to his accusers' surprise, agreed to cease his outside work and the case was dropped, a joint statement declared that 'staff journalists have a duty to ensure that freelance colleagues have first call on casual work'. The Father of the *Times* chapel, Paul Routledge, pledged to advance the policy.

But in the long run nothing came of it. In 1980 there was a near repeat of the *Sketch* closure when the *London Evening News* went down, with the loss of 142 journalists' jobs. The LFB passed a motion calling on the NEC to instruct chapels to stop the moonlighting 'in order to provide more staff vacancies and casual shifts for unemployed members'. The NEC rejected the motion by 13 votes to 3. General Secretary Ken Ashton went to the next branch meeting, where he received a 'cool reception', according to the *Journalist* report, after telling the freelances that they should give up their own work for the unemployed.

The LFB, founded in 1951, was the first of its kind; others followed in Edinburgh and Manchester within a year. By 1980 the LFB had three thousand members and was the second-largest in the union. The biggest was the London Magazine branch, with nearly four thousand; the growth of the two was related. The nature of the business had changed; there was now an abundance of work in consumer and business magazines. Writers and photographers alike were working to commissions, in particular for features, that paid more than most newspaper work but brought a new set of problems, to do with the issue of copyright. While news was ephemeral and no one bothered about it once it was gone, features were different. Freelance photographers had always worried about copyright, because pictures can be reused indefinitely. But now writers were seeing their

work widely reused by the big publishing groups, which were determined to take possession of all rights – especially after the 1988 Copyright
Patents and Designs Act came into force.

The Copyright Act was one of the NUJ's shining legislative achievements. Working through the British Copyright Council the freelances
lobbied MPs and peers with the aim of securing the right of all freelance
'creators' to own all the rights in their work, and ensuring further payments
when it was used again. The leading advocates were two freelance photographers – Anne Bolt, long-time chairperson of the LFB and of the union's
Freelance Industrial Council, and Andrew Wiard, who also spearheaded
the campaign for police recognition of the press card – together with Bob
Norris, the full-time official then responsible for freelances. When Bolt
died in 1997 Wiard wrote in the *Journalist* obituary: 'Anne left a little time
bomb ticking under the publishing world, in the photographic sections of
the 1988 Copyright Act, which has now exploded with such force that a
small army of corporate lawyers is employed to limit the damage.' In her
memory the union ran an award for young photographers for a couple
of years.

It was this very success that compelled the NUJ to constantly fend off
publishers seeking to cajole freelances into surrendering their rights – or
if that failed, swindling them. Some, including the biggest magazine group,

*Anne Bolt, whose work on the 1988
Copyright Act brought major benefits
to freelance colleagues. (Anne Bolt
estate)*

IPC, used to print on the back of payment cheques the requirement that the freelance assign all rights to the company before the cheque could be banked or cashed. It had no legal force, but it worried some people and they signed.

The hunger for rights intensified with the expansion of the internet and the proliferation of outlets through which publishers could sell work on. Many told freelances they must sign over their ownership before being commissioned, among them another big consumer magazine group, EMAP, which in 1995 informed contributors in an astonishing letter that they must surrender 'all rights, throughout the universe, in media yet to be invented'. Some loyal union members lost work by refusing to comply, but others by being persistent and producing work of high quality managed to retain both the copyright and the work.

The union prepared a number of legal cases to win payment for the unremunerated reuse of material online and confirm the authors' continued right, but none came to court. The first was dropped in one of the NUJ's financial crises in 1990, and others have been settled by publishers anxious to avoid a legal precedent. These gains were welcome, especially one made by the chair of the Freelance Industrial Council, Phil Sutcliffe, a music writer, who proved that union activists can practise what they preach when in 1998 he won £2,500 from the *Sun* for their pirating of an article on Oasis he had written for *Q* magazine under an agreement with the band that prevented use of the material elsewhere. Sutcliffe pointed out that he owned the copyright largely because freelances working for EMAP, *Q*'s publishers, had fought for it when the company tried to impose the 'all rights throughout the universe' contracts.

NUJ freelances have made sacrifices too by withholding their work from companies where staff are on strike. The union asks for this support – in law it cannot instruct them – because strike action is easily undermined by the supply of outside material and because raising salaries leads to a general uplift of rates; but in a long dispute the sacrifice can be considerable. In the 1980s, when there were protracted NUJ disputes, freelances were paid compensation under the 'Findlay formula', a complicated scheme invented by George Findlay, under which the proportion of the freelances' incomes derived from the publisher concerned was taken into account. In the year-long Wapping dispute of 1986–7 tens of thousands of pounds were paid to freelances via this scheme.

London freelances maintained solid support for the strikes at the big magazine groups, and this solidarity worked both ways: in 1981 the thousand-plus staff at IPC Magazines backed the union's first and only freelance strike by refusing to handle all freelance material that came in – leading to a hike in the rates of over 20 per cent. Two years later the forty-strong freelance chapel at Independent Radio News in London – an NUJ closed shop of freelances as well as staff – won huge rises by coming to within two hours of a strike that would have closed the station.

From the 1970s the union had agreements on freelance rates with most big publishers, as well as the longstanding ones with the newspaper employers' associations and the BBC. It was union policy that chapels should not conclude house agreements without covering freelance rates, and some did manage this feat, the first being the *Manchester Evening News* in 1973. But as chapels lost their agreements in the 1990s, so did freelances – and theirs were to prove a lot harder to win back.

PR: Absolutely organised

Combining journalists and public relations officers in the same organisation is like having to accommodate both lawyers and police: both are in the same basic line of business, but at times their work pits them against each other. Journalists like to mock public relations; the *Journalist* has often carried letters critical of their trade. In November 1949, for example, the Fife branch called for PRs to be drummed out of the union – or at least, defined as ineligible for membership. Many journalists who were union loyalists and had switched to PR remained in the union, sometimes actively. 'The PRO is not a bona fide journalist,' wrote Fife branch secretary David White, 'but a publicity agent working for the interests of his employers. The system we regard as a menace to our profession and to the freedom of the Press.'
The response in the next issue was more than tit-for-tat.

It is of supreme importance both to PROs and to the Press there should be close co-operation between them [wrote R. S. Forman of the Central London branch, a Whitehall PR]. What better foundations for such a relationship than that PROs and journalists share membership of the NUJ? There is a most regrettable move by the Authorities to limit appointments in PR sections of the ▶

Civil Service to the ordinary rank-and-file of the department. They seem to think, most erroneously, that a PRO needs no training or experience other than the Civil Service affords. I am hoping the NUJ will back us in our endeavours to correct this error.

The idea of the NUJ becoming involved in public relations took hold. In 1951 Ted Jones of London Radio wrote:

> Scattered among branches of the NUJ are many journalists who like myself have left Press or radio journalism for Public Relations. Unfortunately, owing to the too generous exodus into PR of non-journalists whose dealings with the Press are so often mischievous, PR has become a calling which, I fear, is often unjustifiable [*sic*] maligned. Yet PR is here and – let's face it – is here to stay ... Surely then a case exists for the formation of a PR section of the NUJ. Will any Union member interested in a PR section please contact me.

Clearly people did, because in 1952 a PR section was founded and in 1957, in London, the Press and PR branch. The core of the branch was the public sector: the big expansion of UK government PR happened during the Second World War, when, in a completely new approach to public information, the newly founded Ministry of Information employed more than three hundred press officers. The NUJ established a Whitehall branch to represent these members in 1948. The trend continued after the war with the Labour government's nationalisation and social welfare programmes. Providing accurate and useful information about public service and industry was a central aim and required substantial press and information offices. Many industrial and business journalists went to work in them, not for the salary or for an easy life but from a genuine commitment to inform. It is an element of PR that has been progressively undermined by commercial pressures ever since.

Keen to expand NUJ representation in the burgeoning industry, the union agreed after lobbying from the branch to change the rules to allow membership to PRs who were not trained journalists. Before 1961 the union had been open to 'journalists engaged as public relations officers'; the definition then became 'men and women engaged as journalists in public relations'. By 1978 the PR sector had a thousand members. In 1993 the rules were changed again to allow the admission of advertising copywriters. The ADM that year was told that PR was a sector that 'badly needed organising'; no doubt it did, but few fitting the new definition were actually recruited.

From the 1960s the membership of the PR section widened to bring in the voluntary sector: charities, non-governmental organisations and other unions. (The *Absolutely Fabulous* strain of public relations is not well represented in the NUJ.) In 1965 a Trade Union Press Group was formed from members working for other unions, which persuaded the TUC to launch an annual award scheme for union journals – an award the *Journalist* has never won. For a time the group negotiated the freelance rates paid by union journals with the freelances themselves, until they broke off the agreement in 1996.

In the 1970s local authorities also expanded their press offices, and when there were disputes on local papers the NUJ was able to call on them to stop supplying news to the publications involved. In 1975 the Press and PR branch published a set of guidelines for PRs in disputes. All members, not just those with the local councils, were asked to stop the supply of releases and to decline to respond to queries. A large number of Labour-controlled authorities, whose leaders often had little love for their local papers, did comply. Islington Council in north London boycotted the main local paper, the *Islington Gazette*, in 1981 when the group that owned it closed the nearby *Camden Journal* and the NUJ got into a dispute over the closure. Because of its hostility to the paper the council, led by Margaret Hodge (who became a government minister after 1997), maintained its boycott when the dispute ended. But this proved damaging to the council itself, since the *Gazette*, now a non-union paper, rapidly worked up a formidable bank of contacts and received an endless stream of leaks, often embarrassing, which the council's press office, officially banned from talking to the paper, could do little to parry. The press officers were driven almost to distraction by the perpetual damage limitation they found themselves involved in, and the NUJ eventually sent a delegation to see Hodge to persuade her to lift the boycott.

For all the fragmented nature of the industry, with no large work-places to anchor it, the union's PR sector did succeed in negotiating agreements with some organisations. First was the National Coal Board in 1954, followed by the PR agency Infoplan and the British Travel and Holiday Association; in Ireland an agreement was reached at the Bord Failte, the national tourist agency. During the 1970s the press and PR branch even had a negotiations officer. But the members best ▶

The five members sacked during the Haringey Council strike in 2004: from left,
Ola Ontatade, Marie Sterry, Dan Ward, Elliott Spiteri and Jim Boumelha.
(Stefano Cagnoni)

protected were those covered by agreements made by the big public
service unions that organised their workplaces. The NUJ arranged
'linking agreements' that allowed staff to be members of two unions
for the price of one: the main union would negotiate pay and conditions, while the NUJ would represent them on professional matters
– an area the other unions were often happy to cede. NUJ members
in local government, for instance, have been members of NALGO and
later Unison, and have joined in their strikes. Journalists who went
into universities and colleges to teach on the journalism and media
courses that spread so quickly in the 1990s were joint members of the
lecturers' unions.

There have been NUJ strikes in PR as well. In 1989 there was a
two-week stoppage at NALGO itself, which had a twenty-five-strong
NUJ chapel, over the sacking of a member accused of leaking union
information to an employer. In 2004 there was a long strike at the
London borough of Haringey, where consultants had been brought
in to revamp the communications departments and jobs were to go.
Father of the NUJ chapel there was Jim Boumelha, one of the union's
most prominent militants of the 1980s, who led the three-year dispute
at Robert Maxwell's Pergamon Press in Oxford.[8] Haringey was one

dispute that Unison, who represented the bulk of council staff, unfortunately decided to keep out of, and all five members concerned lost their jobs.

The fragmentation of PR in the public sector became a growing concern. More and more work was farmed out to consultancies, whose practitioners were more susceptible to political direction than were professionals with their commitment to public service standards. This was the age of spin, as the straightforward provision of information gave way to the techniques of news management and persuasion. It was happening, of course, in central as well as local government. The union's Whitehall branch had been folded into Press and PR in 1984, and little restraint was being imposed on what the union saw as the corruption of the trade of public information.

In 2005 the NUJ produced another set of guidelines setting parameters for public service PR. Getting it applied was the task of the new century for the Press and PR branch.

Race in the union

In November 1968 Lionel Morrison, a journalist with extensive experience, applied for a sub-editor's job on the *Guardian*. Summoned for an
interview, he arrived at the paper's office, and the receptionist asked him to
take a seat while the night editor was called. After a few minutes, Morrison
recalls, the night editor walked into the otherwise empty foyer … and
right past him, three times, as if he were invisible. After a few embarrassing
moments when the editor asked where Mr Morrison was, the receptionist
'had the grace to blush' and pointed out the editor's mistake. 'As I got up
to follow him,' Morrison wrote later, 'I pondered the problems of having
a Scottish surname and an "unblack" accent, and of not having informed
him that I was a black journalist.' [9]

Despite a good interview, 'handshakes all round' and an agreement that
he should start in a few weeks' time, Morrison heard nothing further. A
few weeks later, he saw the *Guardian* was advertising a similar position.
'There was and still is no doubt in my mind that I did not get the job
precisely because I was black,' he wrote.

Morrison was a South African journalist who had been repeatedly
arrested for his anti-apartheid activities. He came to Britain and worked
as a freelance for national papers and magazines and became principal
information officer for the Commission for Racial Equality. In 1987 he

*Lionel Morrison, NUJ President
1987–8. (John Smith/Profile)*

was elected the first black president of the NUJ. In an interview with the *Guardian* (which to its credit, alluded to the incident mentioned above) he stressed that during his presidency he wanted to raise, among other issues, the question of race and the British media. It is an area in which the NUJ has now been formally active for more than thirty years.

Black and Asian journalists were working in Britain well before the NUJ was founded. In London in the 1890s, Celestine Edwards, born in Dominica in 1858, edited two magazines including *Fraternity*, the monthly journal of the Society for the Recognition of the Brotherhood of Man. In 1912, what is thought to be the first black magazine published in Britain, the *African Times and Oriental Review*, was founded and edited by Duse Mohamed Ali. After the First World War Claude McKay, a Jamaican writer, reported for the *Worker's Dreadnought*, a radical paper edited by Sylvia Pankhurst.

The increase in immigration led to new publications, with titles such as the *Caribbean News*, the *Gleaner*, the *West Indian Gazette* and the *Afro-Asian Caribbean News*, all established in the 1950s. A second wave appeared from the 1970s, including the *West Indian World*, the *Nation*, *Caribbean Times*, and the *Voice*. A further development was the emergence of local radio programmes, and later local community stations, aimed at black and other minority ethnic communities. Few black or Asian journalists were finding jobs on mainstream publications or in broadcasting, however, and when they did their experiences could be difficult: the broadcaster Alex Pascall, for instance, complained of persistent management obstruction during his period presenting the *Black Londoners* programme on BBC Radio London during the late 1970s and 1980s.

Yet already in the 1950s questions of race had begun to be raised within the NUJ. Postwar independence movements, the increase in immigration and a sense of greater internationalism were probably all contributing factors. Not that the union was free of the casual racism of the times. In August 1952, a front-page pocket cartoon in the *Journalist* joked about the increase in PR handouts arriving on journalists' desks – but in this case, the journalist was depicted as a crudely drawn black editor underneath a palm tree, instructing a drummer to 'knock it down to 200 bangs'. And in October 1963 a *Journalist* caption story about a group of coaldust-grimed NUJ members visiting a coalmine observed that only one, a West Indian, 'showed no change in his complexion'.

Ten years earlier, more progressive sentiments had been expressed. At a north London branch meeting in 1953, Bob Pennington of the *North*

London Press had pointed out that the use of the term 'coloured man' was distasteful. The branch passed a motion that seems remarkably prescient. It urged that 'journalists should no more make a point of stressing the colour of a man's skin where it is completely irrelevant to the case they are reporting than they would, in similar circumstances, stress his religion'.

Even so, race did not feature centrally in union debates until it surfaced in British national politics, notably after Enoch Powell's 'rivers of blood' speech in March 1968 and the arrival of East African Asians in the early 1970s. Then came urban riots in Bristol, Liverpool, south London and elsewhere, and the rise of the far-right group, the National Front, and its successors. All of this led to the question of media coverage of race. NUJ activists were involved in groups such as the Campaign against Racism in the Media, which sought to further the debate through a series of pamphlets such as *It Ain't Half Racist, Mum*, and interventions in various NUJ forums.

In 1974 delegates at the ADM held in Wexford, Ireland, voted to establish a Race Relations Working Party. This committee, initially chaired by Lionel Morrison, was charged with 'monitoring the progress of relevant legislation and campaigning for improvements where necessary; opposing and publicising where possible cases of racial discrimination within the Union and promoting equality within the Union; campaigning against racism in the media'. The working party would become a focus for much of the union's work in the area of race, though more militant members criticised it as ineffective.

Over the next sixteen years such criticisms would gain ground, and in 1990 the ADM held at Loughborough voted to replace the working party, whose members had been elected at the ADM, with a Black Members' Council and an annual conference of black NUJ members. Among the leading early activists on the BMC were Marc Wadsworth, a television journalist and campaigner for black sections within the Labour Party, and Jim Boumelha, who would later become the union's second black President.

A year after the Race Relations Working Party was set up the 1975 ADM approved a new clause in the NUJ Code of Conduct, which called for members not to 'originate material which encourages discrimination on grounds of race, colour, creed, gender or sexual orientation'. Later that year the union, together with the Community Relations Commission, produced a reference card, designed to be distributed among journalists. In addition to exhorting journalists to mention race or nationality only when relevant and to resist sensationalising stories that could harm race relations, it also called on them to press for equal opportunities for black and Asian staff and for better coverage of black and Asian affairs, as well as to expose the activities of racist organisations. The 1977 ADM went further, passing a motion to 'instruct every branch to set up a watch-dog committee to monitor racial stories and report any instance of a breach of the NUJ Code of Conduct to the Race Relations Working Party'.

A conference jointly organised by the NUJ and the Community Relations Commission (CRC) in 1975 brought together journalists, employers and activists. Jim Rose, chairman of Penguin Books, told a discussion on employment opportunities – or the lack of them – for black journalists that 'employers have behaved lousily in this field'. A young Greg Dyke – then a CRC press officer and later, as Director-General of the BBC, to agree that the corporation was 'hideously white' in its employment practices – argued that it was the prevailing traditions and values of many newsrooms that led their journalists instinctively to regard blacks as 'a problem'.

One financial initiative taken by the union would prove of lasting worth. In the late 1980s it established the George Viner Memorial Fund, named after a former training officer, specifically to offer assistance to trainee journalists from ethnic minorities. By 2006 it had made awards of more than £100,000 to more than a hundred students.

While Morrison and others continued to argue for increased employ-ment opportunities for black journalists, it was the reporting of race, and in particular the reporting of racist and far-right groups, that exercised many on the left within the union during the 1970s and 80s. In some cases, the issues exposed tensions within the NUJ, especially over the union's stance on press freedoms. In the spring of 1975, for example, the decision by the *Camden Journal* chapel in north London to refuse to work on an issue of the paper that carried an advertisement for a National Front rally led to divisions on the union's executive. For General Secretary Ken Morgan the chapel's action was embarrassing, coming as it did a few weeks after a recent declaration by the union opposing censorship. But for *Journalist* editor Ron Knowles, it was a 'bold, imaginative and proper' response. The decline of the National Front in the 1980s reduced some of the potential for conflict, though the rise of the British National Party in the next decade presented similar dilemmas for journalists. And by the beginning of the twenty-first century press coverage of Islam, and of British Muslims, was also emerging as an issue for NUJ debate.

In 1991, the NUJ's Black Members' Council had began to work for

*Student recipients of George Viner Memorial Fund grants at a reception in 2003.
(Stefano Cagnoni)*

changes within the Trades Union Congress. The NUJ's delegates successfully moved a motion at that year's TUC calling for an annual TUC black
workers' conference. Abroad, the BMC was also instrumental in establishing the International Federation of Journalists' working group against
racism and xenophobia. And at home, it sought to reclaim the memory
of many forgotten or little-recalled black journalists when, together with
the *Guardian*, it launched the Claudia Jones Memorial Lecture in October
2002, designed as an annual event during Black History Month.

The BMC's leading figures in its first decade were often critical of
the union's leadership on race and diversity issues, as well as that of the
TUC; symbolically, in 1994, its newsletter *The Black Journalist* noted that
of fourteen pictures in the union's annual report, none was of blacks. The
criticism had little apparent effect: there were no black faces in the 1995
annual report, either. While some black and Asian journalists had achieved
success in British journalism by the new century – and the NUJ by 2006 has
1,700 ethnic minority members, a majority of them women – they were still
under-represented in British newsrooms, and, arguably, within the union.

2

SETTING THE RATES

Not just bread, but jam

The General Secretary stood like a Victorian patriarch with his hands clasped behind his back, looking out of the window. The young man in the Glasgow hotel room with him was not of a nervous disposition, but today he was apprehensive. Both knew their meeting was a clash, not just of two generations, but of two union cultures. Both realised that momentous change was beginning to transform the NUJ. Neither could have suspected that twenty years later the young man would be leader of the union, and no one could have guessed that his leadership would see the collapse of the dynamic process that was just beginning.

Harry Conroy was twenty-five, a 'wee boy from Pollok' who had started in time-honoured tradition as an editorial messenger and was now a tenacious crime reporter on the *Scottish Daily Record*. He had also become deputy Father of the NUJ Chapel, and since the Father, Jimmy Cox, was away, it was Conroy who had been summoned to meet Jim Bradley at the Saint Enoch Hotel. 'As I walked into the room my knees were knocking,' he says. 'I was in awe of this man. He was an awesome man.'

It was 1968, and Jim Bradley held more authority than any leader of the union since the founding generation gave way in the 1930s. He had a quiet but formidable manner that in sixteen years as General Secretary – he was now twelve months from retirement – had made his leadership unassailable. But the *Daily Record* chapel had recently embarked on

Harry Conroy as he took office as General
Secretary in 1985. (Jez Coulson)

The union's greatest leader, Jim Bradley,
General Secretary from 1953 to 1969.
(NUJ Collection)

a course that challenged not just the union's leadership but its entire
approach to relations with employers over the last fifty years. The journalists had been holding disruptive meetings to back their demand to
negotiate their own salaries rather than accept those fixed at national level
with the employers' associations. They had a powerful chapel and enjoyed
the even more powerful support of the print unions in pursuit of a local
or 'house' agreement. The unions had stopped production of the paper on
several occasions.

Since the NUJ's first pay deal with the Newspaper Proprietors' Association, representing the Fleet Street papers, in 1917, pay scales had been
carved in stone in the national talks. There were reasons for this, on both
sides. For the NUJ, it kept the rogue employers in line; those who would
have nothing to do with the union and were determined to impose the
lowest wages and the worst conditions they could get away with were
obliged to stick to the rate. For the employers, it blocked the journalists on
the most profitable papers from exercising their muscle to secure higher
salaries; individuals could win more through 'merit money', but the basic
scales were kept in check.

The dam held until the late 1960s, when great cracks began to appear. That period, described as a watershed in many social fields, saw in the NUJ the start of what became known as 'chapel power'. It was about a lot more than the procedure for negotiating pay rates. Over the next ten years a new generation of activists would turn the organisation on its head. As journalists in offices around the country started to feel their strength, the NUJ became more vociferously militant and political. Journalists were fighting for better pay, better conditions, a better profession and a better world. They might not have seen it then, but in retrospect it would look like a union golden age.

In Scotland, the umbrella salary agreement was with the Scottish Daily Newspaper Society (SDNS). But the *Daily Record* and the sister *Sunday Mail* were in an anomalous position: they were owned by the giant International Publishing Corporation, which also ran the Mirror group in London (and papers around the world) as well as Britain's biggest magazine group. Pay scales on the *Mirror* were set by the Newspaper Publishers' Association agreement in London. The result was that the *Record*'s salaries were much lower than those in Fleet Street and even in the national papers' Manchester offices. The union had been striving for decades to get the Manchester and Glasgow journalists into the NPA agreement. The Manchester offices, whose salaries had been limited by the Newspaper Society agreement (covering provincial papers), had been incorporated back in 1944. Glasgow's never had been. The SDNS rates were held down so as to accommodate smaller papers, but now the *Record* journalists didn't see why they shouldn't go for more – especially when the skilled picture engravers' union SLADE secured a landmark rate of £2,000 a year in Manchester. For *Record* journalists the minimum rate in 1968 was £1,500. In pursuit of their claim, Conroy recalls, 'We stopped the paper two or three times. It was a running guerrilla war. Managers were getting very angry.'

And so were union chiefs, which was why Bradley had come up from London. After clearing the air, the General Secretary agreed that the chapel could formally present a claim, which required executive consent under union rules. At least, that is what Conroy believed. When the chapel presented its claim for a £1,750 minimum, the *Record* managers told Cox and Conroy that they couldn't go ahead with it – because it was against union policy. 'I told them Bradley had cleared it,' says Conroy, 'but they didn't believe me. They picked up the phone and called the General

Secretary in London. They handed the phone to me, and Jim Bradley told me he had done nothing of the sort, young man.'

Such was the relationship between union and employers. The whole machinery of industrial relations was centralised. Not only was the negotiation of agreements a national matter but so was their enforcement: to sort out snags that arose locally, they encompassed mechanisms that involved joint committees at national level; and there were always clauses forbidding disruptive action while the procedure was under way. This last was an increasingly sore point between the union leadership and local activists. Given the complexity of the agreements, it was hardly surprising that companies were constantly failing to adhere to the terms; and chapels with members who were being underpaid were expected to sit and wait for the decision of a national committee that could deliberate for weeks and was more than likely, in the end, to turn them down. As chapels became more militant, accusations that it was all just too cosy and complacent proliferated.

The *Record* chapel had to settle for a 'mini-agreement' – a deal that covered terms and conditions but not pay. Then in 1969 the union executive agreed a new deal with the NPA under which individual house agreements would be permitted. Everything had changed. The *Record* chapel had agreed on Christmas Day as the deadline for the end of negotiations. Conroy recalls: 'By Christmas Eve we had got up to £1,700 but the chapel rejected it and wanted the full amount. It was my first Christmas with my new baby daughter Lynn so I asked the chapel to extend the deadline to Boxing Day to allow me to be at home. They reluctantly agreed to put it back a day.' On 26 December the two sides agreed, in the Christmas spirit, to split the difference and the chapel accepted £1,725 – though not without some grumbling from the back of the room.

It was the beginning of the end of fifty years of national agreements. Ironically, the factor that had forced the union into such an arrangement in the first place was the very weakness of journalists in local offices, who had been striving with limited success to strike local bargains. It was bound to take time for the NUJ to marshal its strength for a national confrontation, and the cautious founders adopted a step-by-step approach.

In 1909 the union had set up an Employment Bureau to collate data on just what was being paid around the country. It sent out 'census' forms to every office – though only in the provincial press. It was discovered that there was no pattern to the pay rates: a comprehensive report by the bureau in 1916 revealed no fewer than seventy-one different rates. While the lowest were pitiful, it was noted that in each district there were better employers, and the strategy was for branches to tackle their bad payers by using the better ones as examples. It was argued that if the union were to go for flat-rate increases, the good bosses would have to pay more and their employees' jobs put in jeopardy. Likewise, percentage increases would benefit more the better off, and it was the lowest paid that needed help.

In fact the increases added up to very little, and major arguments resulted. A hard line was pushed by Henry Richardson, one of the Manchester founders and now editor of the *Union Journal*. In a signed article he wrote: 'The scandalous conditions must be faced and fought. Those who hold aloof are the slaves of appalling indifference and still more appalling snobbery allied to wilful ignorance.' Some members, seeing this as a call for strike action, threatened to resign. Richardson reassured them that not even he would dream of advocating a strike – 'save in the last emergency'.

It was not long before circumstances turned the union's head in the right direction. Six months after the 1914 ADM came the cataclysm of World War One, and by the time it ended four years later the union had national agreements in place. Of the NUJ's 3,200 members in 1914 – only thirty of them women – 1,300 went into the forces, putting greater pressure on those remaining at home. This resulted not in higher pay for them, but simply more work. Advertising fell drastically, papers cut back on production, and many started to cut wages: it was announced at the 1915 ADM that some members had lost up to a quarter of their salaries. At the same time there was a steep rise in the cost of living: prices rose by more than 30 per cent in the first year of the war. Tales of desperation reached the union HQ and a campaign grew for the payment of a 'war bonus'.

The 1915 ADM supported a call from the Central London branch – representing the highest-paid, of course – to approach the national and regional employers' federations with a demand for 30 per cent pay rises. The NEC decided this was beyond achievement, and instead wrote to the various federations of newspaper owners – there were then seven – seeking increases on a precise scale that gave proportionately much more to the lower paid: the amounts ranged from a rise of £1 (an average of 66 per cent) for those on £1.50 a week or less, to 7.5 per cent for those earning £5 or more. The only one to bite was the Northern Federation, representing dailies and some weeklies in the North of England. They agreed a scale with six grades only slightly inferior to the union claim. This was a great step – the NUJ's first wages agreement – but a greater one was soon to be achieved, when the Central London branch decided the time had come to take on the most powerful employers of all.

The NPA had hitherto spurned NUJ approaches but now agreed, somewhat disingenuously, to receive a joint deputation of the NUJ and the Institute of Journalists. For all its keenness to make progress, the union couldn't really agree to that, and the NPA then agreed to meet the two bodies separately. Central London representatives had their ammunition ready. In accordance with the official policy, they had drawn up their claim to establish what Fleet Street leader Tom Foster called a 'Plimsoll line' for pay. This set down for the first time the principle of a 'rate for the job'; in other words, a single minimum rate.

To everyone's amazement, including most of the bosses themselves, the NPA readily agreed to the scheme. They undertook to pay basic rates of 5 guineas (£5.25) a week to reporters and photographers and 6 guineas (£6.30) to subs, with other rates for sports and city staff and parliamentary and court reporters. The basic rates would rise for two years by half a guinea a week. The great fault in the agreement was the exclusion of women journalists, but a year later the negotiators would be shamed into getting that reversed.

The guinea

Between the two world wars salaries on national papers were expressed in 'guineas' – multiples of one pound one shilling (£1.05), in the sterling system of 20 shillings (240 pennies) to the pound.

The guinea was already archaic, and its use in Fleet Street was the consequence not of some quaint tradition but of the quick response of some smart thinker on the Central London branch committee who, when the amounts were originally drawn up in simple pounds, apparently remarked: 'Why not go for guineas? They don't sound as much as they really are.' That suggestion – with its agreeable echo of professional status – won 5 per cent more on salaries for years to come.

How did such a landmark agreement come about with such apparent ease? Partly it was due to the wartime conditions and the employers' appreciation of the hardships that journalists were suffering; in the Fleet Street village of the time, some of the NPA bosses and union leaders were friends. Or was it simply the result of the long years of patient, painstaking and – for the activists – arduous preparation? The union had no full-time officials at that time, its head office was still in Manchester, and the burden of organising Fleet Street had fallen on three men in particular: Tom Foster, the burly and ebullient branch secretary, was a parliamentary reporter for the *Daily Chronicle*; F. J. (Frederick) Mansfield was a writer on *The Times*, as well as being a member of the union executive and during 1918–20 editor of the *Journalist*; and Walter Veitch, chairman of the Parliamentary branch, was London correspondent of the *Aberdeen Daily Journal*.

Then there was the union's secret weapon: the sympathetic intervention of the most powerful press baron of the time, Lord Northcliffe, owner of *The Times* and the *Daily Mail*. Just before the crucial meeting with the NPA, he was tracked down abroad by Foster, and sent the union this message: 'You know that the union will have my support in any reasonable negotiations with the newspaper proprietors. I am one of the few newspaper owners who have been through the mill of reporting, sub-editing and editing, and I have very vivid and resentful recollections of underpaid work for overpaid millionaires.' Lord Northcliffe's motives were not as altruistic as they might have appeared, as journalists were soon to find out, but they did the trick for now.

The other federations soon gave way and the principle of the universal minimum rate figured in all the agreements. The Newspaper Society, representing provincial papers, conceded in 1918 a £3 minimum for weeklies and rates from £3.68 to £4.20 for dailies. The rates were low and not everyone was pleased, but the very poorest reporters had their incomes doubled at a stroke. Within a year the London news agencies, the Association of Press Photographic Agencies and the Weekly Newspapers and Periodical Proprietors' Association, covering magazines and other periodicals, all fell into line.

So quite suddenly and almost by stealth the NUJ in 1919 found it had established national minimum rates for the entire industry. There were then 4,300 members – more than a thousand had joined or rejoined in the two years after the war. It was as if, like an infant Hercules, the union hadn't known its own strength. In theory at least every workplace in

Britain (though not Ireland) was covered by these agreements; Scottish employers were paying NS rates.

It was a position that later generations might envy, for it was never to be repeated. To start with, the periodical publishers soon had a change of mind: in 1920 they reorganised themselves as the Periodical Publishers' Association and broke off agreements with the union, a stance it has held to ever since. The NUJ has always had to negotiate rates separately with magazine publishers. Then, in late 1919, progress stalled in dealing with the newspaper publishers. The NUJ went back to the Newspaper Society to negotiate improvements to the rates and was sharply rebuffed. No money was on offer, but the two sides did agree to go to arbitration. The union put a huge amount of work into presenting evidence, producing witnesses from all round the country and tables of statistics to back its case for a £5.52 minimum for weeklies and from £5.87 to £7.50 for dailies. Henry Richardson, by now the first full-time General Secretary, made what by all accounts was a brilliant presentation. But the outcome was poor: rates ranging from £4 to £5.20. The only positive point was the scale itself, with the weeklies and dailies broken into categories by size of town, setting higher rates for the bigger centres. This formula survived until the 1980s.

National paper journalists also succeeded in getting their rates up, with a minimum of eight guineas a week agreed in December 1919. This, for the first time, was for a working week limited to 44 hours, or 38.5 for night staff. There was also a 'one paper, one staff' rule, stipulating that papers in the same group must have discrete staffs. But the next claim, a year later, ran into a wall: the union put in what Mansfield conceded was 'something like the by-laws of a Fleet Street Utopia'. It contained thirty-five clauses that included a weekly minimum of eleven guineas, overtime pay, four weeks' holiday, a three-month notice period, a grading scheme with fixed proportions in each grade, a limit to the number of juniors employed and employment preference for union members. There was also a new and significant feature, the NUJ's first foray into the business of editorial standards: a claim for a distinction to be made between editorial matter and advertising, with advertising material clearly marked.

For the first time journalists discovered what it was like to have the power of the press turned against them. The NPA contemptuously tossed the claim aside, declaring that they would talk about nothing but salaries and minimum conditions. The Central London branch called a rally to decide what action to take, and the day before it was to be staged Northcliffe's *Daily Mail* launched its first attack. The demands would 'render the position of almost every newspaper financially impossible,' it said. They amounted to 'interference with the conduct of newspapers. The reply of the *Daily Mail* to these demands, if pressed, will be a complete shut-down.'

In later years this might have been regarded as a routine response, but in 1920 it came as a genuine shock – and it had some effect. At the union meeting, which had to be moved to a larger venue to accommodate the numbers, opinion was divided. There were those full of indignation and up for a fight, those who felt the demands should be modified, and a few, Foster said, who had already got cold feet. But the discussion was business-like and the outcome was to lop a few clauses from the document.

But the *Mail* had scented blood. Next day it headlined: 'Jam Factory Journalism – Extremists Outvoted – Many Demands Dropped'. This was substantiated in a leader saying that the proposed grading system was 'better suited to a jam factory than to editorial staffs of newspapers'. Outraged members wrote to the *Journalist*: one signing himself 'Pip-maker' protested that the *Mail* did not 'live by bread alone – there's jam as well. Do the £2,000 and £3,000 a year men fear their salaries will be reduced if others get jam-factory justice?'

The NPA now offered a one-guinea rise (bringing the weekly rate

Tom Foster, early leader of the NUJ in Fleet Street. (NUJ Collection)

Frederick Mansfield, author of the first history of the NUJ in 1941. (NUJ Collection)

to nine), but to be paid to reporters with four years' service instead of the former two; there would be no increases on other rates, and higher earnings would be entirely discretionary. Overtime was refused. The 'one paper, one staff' rule would go. Another mass meeting was called, which rejected the NPA offer (only two voting for it) and went on to carry to acclaim a call for a ballot for strike action.

But the NPA would not budge. Individual journalists were put under pressure and staff on the *Mail* were made to declare they would not strike. The militancy evaporated and the offer had to be accepted – though Foster, bitterly disappointed, refused to be a signatory, saying he was 'not proud of Fleet Street'. The journalists' bluff had been called and they had backed down.

The salaries and conditions in that 1921 agreement would stand unchanged for the next twenty years. After an uplift in 1921, the same went for the Newspaper Society rates. At least, though, wages did not fall, as they did in many industries during the decade; and with the deflation of the late 1920s, when prices fell, they were worth a little more. In 1923 and again in 1932 the Newspaper Society did try to cut wages, but the NEC declared its resistance and the proposals were dropped as, both times, the economic circumstances of the papers improved.

Annual Delegate Meetings in the 1930s produced updated National Programmes, aspirations that were never to materialise. Industrial action was not an option. For one thing, during the slump, unions were on the retreat. For another, after the General Strike of 1926, those working in the press had agreed not to take action under the no-victimisation agreement reached between the Printing and Kindred Trades Federation, of which the NUJ was an affiliate, and the employers.

In fact it took another world war to break the deadlock, and it needed official arbitration. Again in 1939 there were job losses, despite the military call-up, as papers slashed production and some in the provinces even closed. In 1940, when the NS refused a 50p a week hike in the basic rate, the unions, working through the Printing and Kindred Trades Federation, took their claim to the National Arbitration Tribunal set up as a wartime measure to handle problems without resorting to industrial action. The tribunal awarded 25p. Next year the NS conceded another 25p, and in 1942, after the union had claimed a guinea a head, a further 30p, bringing the provincial minimum now to £5.16 a week. A further PKTF application to the tribunal, in 1943, proved fruitless and after a long wrangle the NS agreed to an extra 38p a week, with the condition that there would be no further rise until a year after the war ended unless there was 'an appreciable' increase in the cost of living.

With the war over, the unions began to flex their muscles. The printers launched an overtime ban over hours and holidays – there were still no guaranteed holidays on NS papers at all, and hours were governed only by a 'memorandum' exchanged with the NS in 1930 saying journalists shall 'be entitled normally to one and a half days a week free'. Now in 1947 the NS finally conceded holidays – three weeks a year on dailies and two weeks on weekly papers – and limited hours: 160 hours every four weeks on morning papers, 168 on big weeklies and 176 on the smaller ones. 'The accomplishment of an hours and holidays agreement for the provinces has proved to be one of the most difficult tasks we have ever undertaken,' the NEC said in a report to the 1947 ADM.

Four years later, national papers won four weeks' holiday. There had been rises in 1941 and 1943, and in 1944 came the breakthrough for staff in Manchester, who had been seeking NPA rates since 1936. Now they were included in the agreement, with a rate of £8.77 a week; the London minimum then was £10.32. With a mind to improve their position, and lacking the inhibitions of their London colleagues, the Manchester journalists had built up the most powerful chapels in the union – in particular that at Allied Newspapers, the Kemsley group, publishers of the *Daily Sketch* and no fewer than four Sunday papers — the *Sunday Dispatch*, *Empire News*, *Sunday Graphic* and *Sunday Chronicle*. Known as the Withy Grove chapel from the street it was on, it had what Ken Morgan, a Manchester journalist who became NUJ General Secretary in the 1970s, calls 'an awesome reputation, not only in the union, but among the employers, as being a bunch of people that you didn't want to tangle with if you could help it'.

In the mid-1940s the Withy Grove chapel had a brilliant and determined young leader: Jim Bradley. He had come to national attention in 1939, when after the outbreak of war publishers had started laying people off. Like Harry Conroy thirty years later, he cut his union teeth as part of a well-organised workforce. The union had negotiated a deal with the Newspaper Society that job losses could be absorbed by staff going on to short-time working. Kemsley's Manchester managers, however, announced that forty jobs were to go, without negotiation, and the chapel retaliated by announcing it would strike. Tough negotiations led to a much praised deal to cut everyone's hours by 10 per cent. The *Journalist*'s 'Manchester Notes' column reported in November 1939: 'The branch heard from Bradley, the clerk of the chapel, the full story of the remarkable negotiations … and the warmest admiration was expressed.'

Manchester journalists had a pragmatic approach, which profited them further ten years later in 1949 when an NUJ claim on the Newspaper Publishers' Association for sixteen guineas a week was knocked back by arbitration, and the employers refused to increase a 60p offer. London members immediately rejected this in a ballot, and with no prospect of further negotiation the union asked them to vote on taking strike action. The result was 514 to 448 not to take action. They were thus left high and dry, and had no rise for two years. As in 1920, Fleet Street journalists had marched up the hill, only to march down again. Meanwhile Bradley's colleagues in Manchester, now firmly part of the NPA pay structure, had accepted the offer and pocketed the cash.

The long-standing claim to achieve parity with Manchester for the Glasgow offices, however, came to nothing. At the end of the war the

Scottish Daily Newspaper Society was paying NS rates and the most they could be persuaded to do was to add a little extra to the top NS daily-paper bands. Weekly papers in Scotland had their own employers' group, the Scottish Newspaper Proprietors' Association (SNPA), which had agreed to stick to NS rates. Journalists in Ireland did not have their own agreements until after the war.

Next to enter the London fold were the news agencies – there were just three in those times: the Press Association, Reuters and Exchange Telegraph (Extel). Their rate too had been stuck, at a guinea a week less than the nationals, since 1920. After the war the union set out to eliminate the discrepancy, and finally achieved it in 1955. That left just the photographic agencies with no agreed salaries at all – the employers' association had abrogated the original agreement in 1923. To back up a claim the union balloted agency photographers in London on the possibility of industrial action and was pleased to get a 43–5 yes vote, which shook some sense into the employers and a deal was quickly reached.

There were further small pay increases in all areas but as the economy grew in the early 1950s journalists' salaries began to fall behind and in 1955 it was felt that the time had come for the NS agreement to be comprehensively renegotiated – for the first time in thirty-six years. By now Bradley was General Secretary, and in presenting the union case he demonstrated just how far behind journalists had fallen. Before the war, he said, the average weekly earnings in industry had been £3.48 (£3 9s. 6d. in old money). At that time the lowest NUJ rate was £4.38, a positive differential of 90p. He went on: 'In 1954 average earnings in industry were [£9.88]. Our rate is [£9.35]. In other words, our position has been drastically reversed. Do you wonder that our members say – as they have said for years – that the status of journalists is falling? Do you wonder that they are dissatisfied?'

The negotiations were long and difficult but a restructured agreement was endorsed by a ballot, granting rates from £11.13 to £14.38. A more complex series of grades was established, as well as higher percentage rates for juniors.

The birth of chapel power

The *Journalist* of October 1967 carried a short report, tucked away on page 8, stating that during July the chapel at the *Middlesbrough Gazette* had been on strike. It did not say how long the stoppage was, but it did quote the Father of the Chapel, Ron Knowles: 'The chapel members stood united, despite the knowledge that we did not have official union backing.'

This wasn't the first NUJ pay strike: there had been a long and successful one at Radio Eireann in Dublin in 1963, and a number of little disputes over the payment of the annual increases. Doug Lawson, who was an NUJ Father of Chapel in several provincial offices during the 1950s–80s, recalls: 'What often happened was that people earning above the minimum didn't get the rise because they were already earning the new rate. You didn't want to go to a formal national dispute over it so you just sorted it out.' The Middlesbrough stoppage started the same way, but what had been a ripple expanded into a wave of militant action that swept through the press over the next fifteen years. Knowles was one of the key figures in the 'chapel power' movement, and clashes between the militant chapels and the national leadership were a feature of its early years. The movement reflected both the industrial and social changes of the times, and the growth of a new breed of journalists – less deferential and more inclined to put up a fight to realise their aspirations.

● ●

First strike was the longest

The NUJ's first strike was also its longest. It began in 1911 and went on for eleven years.

It was not about pay, but working hours: the reporters at the *York Herald*, a morning paper, were 'the hardest driven of all the daily papers in the country', working from 9.30 a.m. to midnight or even 2 a.m, seven days a week. The chief reporter, Clifford Nixon, was sacked for 'misconduct', after two years of cautious NUJ attempts to alleviate the Dickensian conditions; his offence had been to suggest ways of doing this. The union-approved plan included allowing each employee one day off a week and employing two new reporters; by now so many had become ill from overwork and had left that there were only four to cover the whole of east Yorkshire. No formal NUJ chapel had been formed, but Nixon had been acting as a spokesman for the staff. He became the union's first 'martyr' and it looked after him, quickly finding him a better job in Fleet Street.

All the other reporters quit – one of them even offering the company his month's notice money to get out; it was accepted. The union then blacklisted the paper, announced that any journalist who took work there would be expelled, and went to some lengths to stop young reporters filling the vacant jobs. It was only in 1922 that the ban was lifted. Henry Richardson later wrote that the action was 'both effective and ineffective. It did not improve conditions in the office at the time but it improved them in many another bad office'.

Knowles recalls the Middlesbrough strike:

I had an assurance from the editor that an increase would be paid all round, but some people didn't get it. We called a meeting and I said the only way you are going to get it is a strike, and we just walked out. I had a call to meet the management who said they would clear it up, so we went back, not to work, but to a meeting in the canteen. The managing director came in and said there were just two or three special cases [among the workforce]. I asked people who hadn't had the rise to put their hands up, and twelve of them did. It was obvious managers were lying so we went out again, and were out for three days.

The management called us in and said it was a clerical error and everyone would get the rise. But that wasn't the end of it. We demanded an apology and full pay for the time we were out; no-one should lose pay because of a clerical error. We won everything. I reported this to the chapel and a member stood up at the back and said, 'We're not going to let them get away with that, are we, Ron?'

After that the chapel was rampant. We didn't wait to get backing from Acorn House [the NUJ HQ] because we didn't need it. They would send officials to tell us to go back to work and we would ignore them. We had strikes over various issues but they never lasted very long because management were gun-shy.

The Middlesbrough chapel produced a number of able trade unionists; several went on to higher union office, including Knowles and his successor, Peter Dodson, a shrewd and level-headed character. 'We had disputes and they were all about pay, and for a time we were the highest paid regional paper in the country,' he says. 'We won lots of awards, and while we were

portrayed as a bunch of mad people we were producing a good paper and
the chapel took the view that we should be properly rewarded for it.' The
Gazette was part of Thomson Regional Newspapers, a prosperous group
that, Dodson says, were 'relatively easy to deal with. We didn't always get
great settlements but they weren't bent on destroying the union. They
took a tough line, but they were making money and they were prepared
to do a deal. That's what was different from managements later on.'

The fire spread through the region and then more widely within the
TRN group, which owned the *Newcastle Chronicle and Journal* as well
as papers in Edinburgh, Cardiff, Belfast and elsewhere. Within a year
of Middlesbrough's first stoppage the union had negotiated a group
agreement with TRN on pay – the NUJ's first with a single newspaper
employer – and house 'productivity' deals followed throughout the group.
The Father of the Chapel in Newcastle was for a time Greg Dyke, on his
way from being a reporter on a west London weekly to Director-General
of the BBC. The Newcastle chapel was once disowned by head office
when it walked out unofficially, and there were acrimonious exchanges
in the *Journalist*. Newcastle branch chairman John Dougray thought the
executive was 'too busy trying to assure the employer they are reasonable
men trying to keep the hotheads under control'.

In June 1969 Ron Knowles wrote an angry article in the *Journalist* on
the 'bitter frustration' of provincial militants: 'Officers of any chapel that
initiates industrial action in pursuit of a house agreement find themselves
in a procedural no-man's-land, under fire simultaneously from the NUJ
hierarchy and the employers.' He complained about the clause in the NS
agreement that imposed a twenty-eight-day moratorium on any proposed
action while a national-level joint committee, on which the chapel was
not represented, investigated the position. 'Chapels do not have faith in
our executive or officials and are afraid they will be betrayed, that the
union will accept a cheap unsatisfactory compromise.' Even if the NS
agreement had to be honoured, he said, chapels should be guaranteed
official support for industrial action if the outcome of the joint committee
was unsatisfactory.

In the next issue of the *Journalist* Jim Bradley wrote in reply that the
NEC 'cannot contemplate a future of anarchic house bargains in some
offices and failure of unplanned local assaults in others. Chapels must
not abuse the Union for requiring observance of its rules.' In November
that year the NEC censured a number of chapels for breaches of the rule

requiring them not to enter negotiations or reach agreements on wages without the clearance of the executive.

They're so mean

The miserliness and vindictiveness of the Newspaper Society had long been a fixed star in the NUJ firmament. In 1966 an ADM delegate from the Magazine and Book branch, Chris Price – who from 1974 became a strong NUJ voice in Parliament as a Labour MP – declared that the NS 'would take a dead fly off a blind spider'. In September 1978 a provincial member who won a fairground shooting competition was quoted in a diary story in the *Journalist* as saying: 'I just thought of the Newspaper Society and everything went blank.'

National agreements negotiated with the NS and the NPA were still the order of the day, but they were changing. The great breakthrough came in 1969 when the NPA conceded that house agreements could be concluded to top up the national rates. First in the queue for talks was Rupert Murdoch's *Sun*; after buying the ailing title from IPC in the September, he immediately began talks with the NUJ and within a year there was a house agreement. Murdoch was also to be the first national employer to tear up his NUJ agreements twenty years later. The other national papers followed his lead – just as, similarly, most of them were to do in the 1990s. The Telegraph group signed a 'model' agreement, with percentage increments on top of the NPA rates, plus others for length of service. The immediate average rise was around 10 per cent; for some it was 30. Five weeks' holiday was awarded, and sabbaticals after five years.

While the London deals (covering staff in Manchester too) were being reached by negotiation, in Scotland there was turmoil, and not just at Conroy's *Daily Record*: journalists on the morning *Glasgow Herald* had discovered that their compositors had been given a £7 a week rise. When management refused to match it for them, they walked out, despite attempts by NUJ officials to stop them. In response the employers – acting in concert – shut down all the papers in the country and laid everyone off. A day later production was resumed, but journalists on the *Record* and the Scottish *Daily Express* refused to go back, in solidarity with their *Herald* colleagues. The Glasgow branch held a special meeting: the three hundred journalists present were told that the company had now offered an increase equivalent to the printers'. Everyone went back to work. The outcome was hailed as a triumph for the *Herald* chapel, but once again there was backbiting, branch reps accusing the union's national officers of being 'ill-informed' and showing 'solidarity with the employers'.

In 1970 Jim Bradley retired. Among the tributes to his 'Churchillian' stature in the union was one from the chairman of the Central London branch, Owen Senior, praising him as 'a pioneer of chapel power'. And so, despite the disputes of his last couple of years, he was. Bradley was a brilliant organiser during his days in Manchester at Withy Grove, which can be regarded as the first 'chapel power' workplace. He was often at odds with the national leadership, and as the union boss himself he was faced with an unprecedented upheaval in union activity. But he retained the respect of all sides and, unlike some former leaders, maintained his NUJ connections and friendships right to the end of his life, in 1993.

The actions taken by the militant provincial chapels were not an end in themselves: they were aimed at improving the pay and conditions of the most exploited people in the industry. This was understood through-out the union, and the ADM in April 1970 unanimously rejected an offer from the Newspaper Society and resolved to back the members fighting for more. At that time the NS scales ranged from £1,183 to £1,417 a year; the average national wage was £1,650. ADM rejected as impractical a call from provincial branches for a minimum of £2,000 a year for senior journalists, but ADM was too cautious. It was only three months before journalists at Sheffield Newspapers would hold a marathon forty-eight-hour mandatory meeting to win an acclaimed house agreement achieving that £2,000 target for the first time. The union then reached a two-year national deal with the NS that lifted rates by 30 per cent, from £1,300 to £1,847, and a senior journalist with more than five years' experience on the biggest dailies could now earn £1,898.

Sheffield's tactic, the lightning mandatory meeting – essentially a strike without leaving the office, which all NUJ members are instructed to attend – became widely used, and in 1972 a chapel's power to order one was written into union rules by the ADM. One of its proponents was the Father of the Sheffield Chapel, Mike Bower, another cool customer and a leading figure in the grassroots rebellion that swept through the union in

Mike Bower, chapel power leader on the Sheffield Star *in the 1970s. (Christopher Davies/Report)*

the 1970s. 'If you do it at the right time a short stoppage can do a hell of a lot of damage,' he says. 'A half-hour meeting can make a mess of a lot of things. They lose a lot of revenue and we hardly lose anything. We had to be more militant than we needed to be, to show the employers we could; they had always believed we would never do anything.'

There was a popular union joke at that time: the NUJ had acquired an answerphone – a new-fangled device – at Acorn House, its London HQ since 1966, and the recorded message said: 'You have reached the NUJ. If you are Mike Bower, Ron Knowles or Peter Dodson, get back to work.' This was too close to home to be really funny.

Bower recalls a mandatory meeting during which he received a phone call from Ken Morgan, then General Secretary, who asked: 'What are you doing?' Bower said he was sitting in the office.

'Are you working?'

'No, we are in a chapel meeting.'

'Tell them to go back to work,' said Morgan.

Bower held the receiver in the air and shouted: 'It's Ken Morgan! He wants us to go back to work. What do we say?'

There was a volley of abuse and Morgan rang off.

There are similar accounts from the other end of the line. Bob Norris, who was the full-time organiser for newspapers in the 1970s, recalls that

Bower once rang him and said: 'We are on strike and if you tell me to go back to work I will put the phone down.' Bower explains:

> Ken Morgan always wanted to do the decent thing, but there are times when you can't. If the national agreement says you can't take action over this or that, you can't accept it. On a number of occasions we tried to get union support to improve our lot and the union kept telling us what we couldn't do. So we thought, we will have to ignore the union. The difference between us and the previous generation was that they thought that winning the debate was enough. They were decent guys but they thought that the weight of the argument alone was enough to convince the employers. In a perfect world it might be, but it wasn't our experience.

Now that there was a group house agreement at Thomson Regional Newspapers, its chapels followed a three-tier strategy to boost their rates: national, group and local, each leapfrogging the one that preceded it. But the other groups wouldn't play the game. Another big North of England title, the *Northern Echo* in Darlington, was the scene of a dispute in 1971. It was owned by the Westminster Press chain, which refused even to talk to the NUJ at group level, so the *Echo* chapel struck out on its own. It got official backing for strike action, but after seventeen days, even though it had rejected a slightly improved offer on pay grades, the union ordered it back to work. Managers had brought in strikebreaking journalists from other offices, and in solidarity the militant *Gazette* chapel in nearby Middlesbrough 'blacked' the copy of freelances who had worked through the strike. But it was not the end of trouble in Darlington, where one of the most fractious of the union's closed-shop disputes was fought six years later.

Next to break the £2,000 per annum barrier were the Scottish daily papers, which concluded a 35 per cent rise in September 1971 in which the minimum rose from £1,600 to £2,100 overnight. The *Herald* in Glasgow succeeded in getting an extra £500 across the board in its first house agreement. For the first time in fifty years, salaries were rising fast. As provincial papers hit £2,000 for the highest paid journalists, in January 1971 the nationals passed the £2,500 minimum – a staggering 35 per cent increase over the previous rate of £1,700. Now the NPA, daunted by what the power of the chapels might achieve, tried to reverse the tide: preferring to deal with the national union, it offered big rises on condition that house deals would be frozen for eighteen months. There was a furious reaction.

The *Mirror* chapel went on unofficial strike. It advised its members to stop paying their NUJ subscriptions and took out an injunction against both the employers and the union, on the grounds that by preventing them negotiating in-house they were breaching the terms of their agreement. Chapel Father Bryn Jones said: 'The freedom of journalists on individual newspapers to negotiate house agreements is not for sale.' His chapel colleague Paul Carden explained in the *Journalist*:

> Until 1968 we accepted, with increasing reluctance and resentment,
> postwar settlements that enabled financially stronger papers to
> shelter behind weaker ones. The outcome was artificially depressed
> wages, with negotiated minima geared to the financial position
> of the weaker papers ... Before the current ill-fated negotiations
> with the NPA began, we extracted from [union leaders] categorical
> assurances that ... chapels would be able to try and improve on the
> terms in house agreements. It is because we feel we have been grossly
> betrayed ... that the whole of Fleet Street is in uproar.

The *Mirror*'s application for a High Court injunction failed.

The *Sun* went on strike as well, and it took the intervention of the TUC to get the two offices back to work, on the agreement that all conditions could be negotiated in-house except basic rates of pay. The NPA came to its senses and dropped its 'no house deals' condition – and agreed a basic rate of £2,900; it had doubled in six years. National average earnings in July 1972 were £1,860. Bryn Jones exulted in the *Journalist*: 'For the rich and powerful chapels this will mean further big rises, setting the pace for the rest of Fleet Street.' The average national paper salary, he added, was £3,800 a year.

August 1972 was headlined in the *Journalist* as 'bonanza month'. Journalists in every national chapel received big increases. The Mirror group came top of the league with its award of £750 a year extra over eighteen months, and the Express group followed close behind with £725. These were times of relatively high inflation – in 1971 it was 9.4 per cent – but they were also fat times in Fleet Street. Printing unions, enjoying their closed shops, were pushing up rates ever faster, and the employers found themselves competing in a bizarre wages auction in which the strongest paid more and the weak went to the wall. It was the survival of the richest, and for a time journalists were enjoying a slice of the action.

In the provinces, the activists liked to see it slightly differently: they

were intent on helping not just themselves, but the whole sector. Mike
Bower, whose Sheffield chapel was one of the strongest, explains:

> The national agreement meant very little to us. It was mainly for
> the weekly papers. The strategy was that we will strike local deals
> in the strong offices that will drag the rest along and capitalise on
> good local agreements. We were definitely not saying 'I'm all right
> Jack, sod the rest of you.' That's not what trade unionism is about.
> We were looking at the nationals where the strongest chapels did
> just look after themselves and we decided we didn't want to be like
> that.

But the right to negotiate provincial house agreements, though practised
in the strongest offices, was still not permitted by the NS agreement and
it took the NUJ's biggest campaign of industrial action to date to win it.
In October 1973, at the annual talks, the union claimed this right, and
the executive ordered mandatory meetings in offices round the country
with a view to firing a shot across the NS bows. A ballot on possible strike
action returned a 6:1 yes vote and the union decided on a three-day
programme of lightning stoppages.

To the delight of the young radicals, the first day was 14 November,
the wedding of Princess Anne and Mark Phillips – 'Too good a target to
ignore,' said the *Journalist*, now under the editorship of Ron Knowles. But
editors just rolled up their sleeves and produced papers single-handed.
One major disappointment for the NUJ was the lack of support from
the print unions. The most powerful, the National Graphical Association,
representing compositors, had a policy of accepting only work written
or sanctioned by editors, which the NUJ had always accepted. But now
NGA members were setting anything the editors put through – in this
case, screeds of material from the Press Association, the national news
agency that supplies all dailies in the UK. Repeated phone calls from the
NUJ's tireless Assistant Secretary Ron Hallett to the NGA headquarters
in Bedford failed to secure a tightening of the practice, and if the NGA
wouldn't black copy, then the other print unions wouldn't either.

For dozens of newsrooms this was the first strike in their history.
Their action had its effect and the ban on house bargaining was lifted. In
addition a 7 per cent pay rise was agreed, the maximum under government wage-restraint laws, plus an element for 'unsocial hours' so as to get
more without exceeding them: the previous year's rise had fallen foul of

the wage regulations and the NS had held back the difference, leading to a dispute over when it could be paid.

Now the best-organised offices got going. The *Jersey Evening Post* negotiated a 40 per cent rise. The *Birmingham Post and Mail* secured a £585 a year rise for subs based on 'extra duties', a ruse that cleverly circumvented the wage-restraint law; the *Journalist* report cited the Birmingham chapel clerk, one 'Aiden' White, for his endeavours. Aidan White was to become a leading light of the next generation of chapel militants, later NUJ Treasurer, then General Secretary of the International Federation of Journalists.

In fact that 7 per cent rise, even with the 'unsocial hours' payments, was in real terms a loss. The maximum for any individual worked out at 10 per cent, and inflation was 12 per cent at the time. Despite all their heroic efforts, provincial newspaper journalists have never really escaped the ghetto of low pay. Even the most handsome gains have compared poorly with salaries in comparable occupations such as teaching or advertising – and with other areas of journalism.

In the second half of the 1970s the NUJ was involved in more or less constant disputes. Charles Harkness, who was NUJ Deputy General Secretary from 1975 to 1981, says that during those years there were only three or four strike-free weeks: 'There were days when we started with a dispute at a radio station and then a provincial paper or a magazine or book house and ending up in Fleet St at midnight.' Harkness was another graduate of the Middlesbrough militancy academy: he succeeded Dodson as Father of Chapel at the *Gazette*, emerged to challenge the old guard at national level and enjoyed a rapid rise to union office – he was elected union Treasurer at the dramatic ADM at Wexford in 1974 and DGS a year later.

The militancy virus endemic in the local papers spread from the North of England to the London locals with the case of the 'Sidcup 63' – journalists on Westminster Press's *Kentish Times* who were sacked in 1974 for imposing sanctions over the next round of NS pay negotiations. Offices all round England were refusing to handle copy from non-union journalists and at the *KT* the whole chapel was suddenly dismissed for it. Next day a sub was sacked from the *Slough Evening Mail* – another WP title – for refusing to receive copy from a chief sub who was a member of the Institute of Journalists and who was breaking the union action. It seemed the company was taking the union on, especially when it was revealed

that the group had told editors two months earlier to pick out journalists
who might break an NUJ strike. Members on other London local papers,
already imposing sanctions, pushed to come out on strike in solidarity. A
London action committee was formed. The executive gave the go-ahead,
with astounding results. There was so much bottled up resentment against
the Newspaper Society that more than eight hundred members walked
out and in just three days twenty-six weekly paper editions were lost. The
NS then agreed to talks and the sacked staff were reinstated.

The leading players were not young hotheads, but two sober middle-
aged senior journalists on the executive: Eric Gordon, who was editor of
the *Camden Journal*, and Selwyn Evans, a reporter well into his fifties on
the *Acton Gazette*. But new activists also emerged, notably Aidan White,
who had moved from subbing on the *Birmingham Evening Mail* to the
weekly *Stratford Express* in east London, and Linda Piper, a reporter on the
Kentish Times. She recalls the end of one strike, which won them a house
agreement. One of the chapel committee just couldn't sign it, such was
his hatred of WP. 'He couldn't speak. He could only shout "you bastards!"
With Westminster Press it was appalling. It was just gratuitous insults. You
could not have a reasoned discussion with them.'

Westminster Press – which sold its titles to the US-owned Newsquest
group in 1995 – had a loathing of unions apparently rooted more in
genuine class hostility than simple business interest. Charles Harkness,
who had worked at WP's *Northern Echo* before joining the *Middlesbrough
Gazette*, explains:

> A lot of the battles in the 1970s were because the proprietors
> felt they were under attack, not just from the union but in the
> world at large. The papers were owned by dignitaries, they were
> the establishment, like the Duke of Atholl, who was chairman of
> Westminster Press. People used to bow in front of the Duke and
> call him 'Your Grace'. But the journalists had a better education
> than before, they were graduates yet were being treated like family
> retainers. Westminster Press offered discounts for staying in a cottage
> on the Atholl estate. We didn't want a discount at Atholl's cottages
> but a decent pay cheque.

The *KT* was said to be Britain's biggest weekly paper, yet pay was as
low there as anywhere. Piper recalls 'a trainee with us whose mum sent
him money for a pair of shoes, for Christmas. The kid couldn't afford
shoes, he just wore plimsolls' (there were no trainers in those days). But

Aidan White, one of the second generation of 'chapel power' leaders in the early 1980s. (John Smith/Profile)

the chapel had a precious gem: the support of the National Graphical Association. Piper says:

> The company settled with us because the NGA said they would support us. The FoC Bernie Laroche came to a chapel meeting and promised support. He stood on a table and everyone cheered. We had very good relations with the NGA and SOGAT [the Society of Graphical and Allied Trades]. They couldn't actually stop the papers – they did close our printworks but the company printed in Uxbridge [WP's big publishing centre in west London].

After that there were frequent disputes on local London papers: three strikes in eight months during 1975 at White's *Stratford Express*, and another at the *Slough Evening Mail* over the victimisation of the Mother of Chapel by a vindictive editor; plus two-week stoppages at the Hornsey Journals over job cuts and at the *Middlesex Chronicle* in Hounslow over a management breach of the NS agreement. All this was part of the build-up to the great all-out Newspaper Society strike of 1978–9 – and to an equally successful battle for London weighting on the weeklies a year later.

The suburban unrest in London spread to Fleet Street and there were

Linda Piper, leading activist in local newspapers in the 1970s and 1980s. (Andrew Wiard)

several disputes in the second half of the decade. In July 1975 journalists
at the *Daily Telegraph*, after three days of mandatory meetings, stopped
production of the paper for the first time in 120 years. There were urgent
talks at the Advisory, Conciliation and Arbitration Service, which produced
a pay settlement at 10.30 the next evening, and the journalists returned
to work and brought the paper out that night. The result of the talks was
an 11 per cent rise instead of the 7 per cent on offer. Heartened by this
the *Telegraph* chapel came out again in July the next year with the aim of
breaking the log-jam in the ongoing talks on staffing levels under the new
technology. This would be a double landmark: the NUJ's first dispute over
technology and the first officially ordered strike in Fleet Street's history.
The *Telegraph* enjoyed a reputation as one of the most militant offices,
despite the presence of a sizeable IoJ chapter and the rather anti-union
tenor of its editorial line. The picket line of these respectable gents in their
city suits – some wore bowler hats, just for fun – was a much enjoyed Fleet
Street spectacle.

The trouble had begun in Manchester, where *Telegraph* staff were to be
laid off and new rotas imposed on the rest, without consultation, on the
introduction of computerised setting. There were long chapel meetings,
for which the managers had docked the members' pay, and when they
refused to work the new rotas they were locked out.

General Secretary Ken Morgan instructed the London office to strike. After four days they were again able to stop publication, thanks to the solidarity of the SOGAT electricians who declined to cross the besuited picket line. To add to the pressure the union then ordered out the whole of Fleet Street in support. At talks at the TUC the company gave in. There would be extra casual staff to cover any shortfalls and the Manchester members got their jobs and all their pay back. As a letter in the *Journalist* in July pointed out, the all-out order seemed to have done the trick; but what would have happened had the bluff been called might have been another matter. A strike, the letter said, would have benefited only the *Telegraph* management, 'who would have seen their rivals similarly silenced'. The writer was the Father of Chapel at *The Times*, Jacob Ecclestone.

All the action over pay in the late 1970s took place under the shadow of the Labour government's pay restraint policies. Between 1975 and 1979 there were continuous limits on wage increases, ostensibly to control inflation. All pay agreements had to be reported to the Prices and Incomes Board for approval. The system had the support, as those of Labour governments generally did, of the TUC, which made attempts by unions to win big increases for the lower paid extremely difficult. The system was chronically unfair: higher-paid employees with more clout were able to dodge around the regulations, while those dependent on nationally set minima could not. A set-up supposed to benefit the poorest in fact worked against them, and it was the mounting anger and frustration of low-paid public service workers that brought about the 'winter of discontent' of 1979–80 – and that of the worst-paid journalists that triggered the Newspaper Society strike of the same time.

For the better-off this was the 'age of the allowance': powerful NUJ chapels concocted all manner of schemes to disguise above-the-limit rises. Because salaries were tied to defined jobs, people were given new titles: false promotions left national papers with tiers of underemployed executive associate managing consultant editors for years. Some of the new terminology stuck: this was when specialist reporters became correspondents and correspondents became editors. There were allowances for purchasing newspapers, late working and early working, for special duties and extra responsibilities. The only limit was the scope of people's ingenuity.

The champions at this game were the chapels in IPC's Mirror group – the *Daily* and *Sunday Mirror*, the *Sunday People* and the *Daily Record* and *Sunday Mail* in Scotland (now covered by a group agreement). In February

1974, when everything was up for grabs during a general election campaign and the union was trying to get a deal with the NPA, they engaged in some particularly fancy footwork. The outgoing Conservative government had a pay policy that allowed only one rise a year, and the Mirror group house agreement had given a rise the previous July. The NPA was trying to spin out national negotiations until after the election in the hope that the winners would slap the restrictions back on, and Mirror managers who had promised to negotiate now said they wouldn't. The chapels went on strike. After two days IPC pulled out of the NPA altogether and settled. With the *Guardian* already outside the group and other employers under pressure to talk, it looked as though the NPA agreement was finished. That year (1974) the rise was the 7 per cent maximum under the pay policy. The next year it would be 20 per cent – plus allowances.

The emphasis on expenses and allowances was not without risk and the union was generally suspicious of relying on them. They are a poor substitute for pay rises, since if they are not consolidated into salaries they do not attract future percentage increases. Further, if overclaiming is widespread it gives managers a hold over staff. Down the years dozens of journalists have been sacked for overclaiming. This has sometimes been a pretext rather than the true reason: journalists that editors want to get rid of are at risk if they fiddle their expense or allowance claims. For this reason union activists tend to be careful with their exes.

But in the 1970s it was a case of needs must. The most notorious Mirror scam was the 'hot weather allowance', supposedly for working on summer days. This raised laughs when it transpired that the Africa correspondent wasn't entitled to it, and anger when it was publicly criticised by one of the group's own militant union members. For while Fleet Street members were looking after themselves so handsomely they were supporting the union leadership in its official endorsement of the Labour government's pay policy, effectively denying local paper journalists the ripe fruits they were plucking for themselves. At the 1977 ADM this policy was narrowly approved – by only eight votes, fewer than those cast by Central London alone, and that branch's delegates erupted when a freelance delegate, Roy Greenslade, stood up to accuse them of hypocrisy.

Greenslade was a casual sub-editor on the *Sunday Mirror*. It was a sign of the industrial confidence of union members that *Sunday Mirror* casuals had their own NUJ chapel and even stopped the paper on occasions. 'London Central members are winning while you are losing,' he told

Sunday Mirror *activist Roy Greenslade upset the Fleet Street 'fat cat' leaders at the 1977 ADM. (Angela Phillips/IFL)*

ADM delegates, and listed some of the perks they were getting: inflated expenses for evening wear, TV licences, newspaper allowances, very high mileage rates … and that £2.50 a day hot weather allowance. One London delegate shouted: 'You took it!'

'Yes I did,' Greenslade retorted, 'but I am against the pay policy.'

The big branch votes carried the day in 1977, but this was when 'the fat cats of Fleet Street' became a familiar derogatory expression among union members – and stuck for longer than was really justified. Their branch chairman and in some ways their personification, David Ross, who was Father of the Chapel at the *Express*, wrote to the *Journalist* complaining that they had been 'under consistent attack from our union colleagues', warning the union 'not to strain our loyalty too far' and threatening 'civil disobedience' on national papers if the union did not pay heed to their concerns. These were principally resentment at being underrepresented in union decision-making and at being called on to support provincial actions.

The 'fat cats' took a fair amount of stick in union debates. Barbara Gunnell, one of the leading magazine militants of the 1970s, recalls a conference at which Ross, a short man, was having trouble speaking into the microphone. One magazine delegate called out: 'Why don't you stand on your pay packet?' Gunnell says: 'At the time we thought it was the funniest thing in the world, but on reflection it was really awful. I can't believe that we felt that people who were successful in their careers should be jeered at. What were we trying to do – drive them out?'

One focus of Fleet Street discontent was the Press Association, the national news agency whose copy was used to fill out the columns of provincial papers when journalists were on strike. The 1977 conference took another contentious decision: that PA journalists must take action to stop this supply. The chapel at the PA was split down the middle: half of them could see that their work was undermining their colleagues' attempts to better their lot; the other half fretted that they could find themselves more or less permanently in dispute. The chapel's attempts to negotiate an arrangement with managers to cut off the supply to offices in dispute had already been blocked on the grounds that the PA's contracts with client papers would not allow it. In the face of this the chapel was unwilling to comply with NUJ requests for the subs to slug copy 'not for [the office concerned]'. This was all that was required of them, since the NGA operators in the wire room at the receiving end would obey the instruction and refuse to tear the copy off the machines. The NUJ would naturally have preferred it if the print unions had been supporting the action, but one argument used by the other unions was that they could not reasonably be asked to put their members' livelihoods at risk if the NUJ could not stop the supply of strikebreaking material from its own.

This became a major issue for the new militant leadership of the NUJ. If the PA members couldn't or wouldn't halt the flow of copy, the reasoning ran, they would have to be told to stop work altogether. In May 1977 the union ordered a twenty-four-hour stoppage throughout the provincial press in support of the chapel at the *Northampton Evening Telegraph* in Kettering, which had been locked out in a long-running dispute over a house agreement. The provincial members came out en masse. The union formally asked PA bosses to cut their service to all NS titles.

When unsurprisingly they were rebuffed, they ordered PA members to stop work. President John Devine went to a PA chapel meeting to persuade members of the importance of the action, but the Father of the Chapel, Harold Pearson, spoke against the instruction and urged the chapel to ignore it. Pearson, who was a member of the national executive and had been NUJ President himself four years earlier, threatened to resign from the union. The chapel voted by 100 to 65 not to strike. On the day, the loyalist minority set up a picket line, which about half the members respected, and Pearson led the rest across it. Despite the fury on the national executive, he ignored a 13:7 vote calling on him to resign. Eventually, and humiliatingly, he was disciplined by the executive under union rules and fined £30.

The chapel at Kettering won a triumphant victory after twenty-four weeks on strike, securing their house agreement. They were boosted not just by the nationwide NUJ action but by the fact that members of the NGA broke with their own union and came out on strike in support. Shortly afterwards the PA chapel took industrial action over its own pay and conditions: in July 1977 the agency service was closed completely on the day of the Queen's silver jubilee by an all-union strike over the extra pay offered to work on that day. A year later, in August 1978, PA journalists staged a work-to-rule over their expense and allowances, just like other Fleet Street chapels. They were pursuing the goal of pay parity with national paper rates; the dispute was over how far allowances could be pushed to bump up the total. In the event, the managers agreed the maximum increase allowed by law (10 per cent).

Close to home

The NUJ's own full-time officials boarded the expenses and allowances gravy train in late 1976 when they embarked on a work-to-rule to get their meal allowances raised. But they could hardly be called voracious in their demands. The only permanent allowance they achieved was for buying newspapers, which didn't increase for years and was finally, in the 1990s, absorbed into salaries. In the early 1980s there was, however, a running dispute over officials' pay, and at the 1982 ADM they all went on strike, rejecting an offer from the NEC and appealing to the conference delegates for support – which they got. The move so angered two of the top voluntary officers, the President and Treasurer, that they resigned from the executive, though the President, Harry Conroy – the great chapel power advocate and militant leader at the *Scottish Daily Record* in the 1960s – did later return, and indeed became General Secretary. The Treasurer was John Bailey, generally regarded as a pillar of honesty and principle in the union, who never again took national office.

The Institute's last chance

Members of the Institute of Journalists working through NUJ strikes presented the NUJ with a big problem. In 1966 – not for the first time – the union's solution was to attempt to merge the two organisations.

There had been three previous attempts to bring them together: the first, in 1921, had made little progress. Then, in 1927, meetings were held from which emerged a scheme whereby joint membership would be introduced, the union concentrating on pay and conditions and the Institute on professional matters. But the legal advice was that the Institute's royal charter would preclude such an arrangement, and it wasn't prepared to surrender it. Then in 1944, the Newspaper Society tried to bring the two together. A joint Association of Journalists was proposed, which would include editors as members, and the union voted overwhelmingly in support. A parliamentary bill was drawn up to revise the IoJ's royal charter, but when the final plans were put to the vote the NUJ achieved over 96 per cent in favour while the Institute managed only 50.7. A figure of 75 per cent was the necessary minimum.

The scheme was dead in the water. Leslie Aldous, the NUJ president, furiously declared: 'At least the Union, open and consistent in its purpose to the end, has emerged from these abortive negotiations with its credit enhanced. Not so the Institute. Hopelessly split in the moment of crisis, it has shown itself weak, wavering and fainthearted, with no reason or will of its own.'

In 1966 a fourth and final attempt was launched. This was a 'trial marriage' in which all would be members of both unions but each would continue to function separately. The plan was massively endorsed by NUJ members in a national vote by 7,942 votes to 523, and by IoJ members by 763 to 177. An NUJ Special Delegate Meeting voted by 204 votes to 5 to make the necessary rule changes. It seemed the deal was on.

Enthusiasm was strongest in magazines. NUJ magazine members went to meetings of the IoJ Trade, Technical and Periodical section and, in effect, took it over. The chairman was Lawrence Kirwan, the full-time NUJ organiser in the field. A number of NUJ representatives were elected to the IoJ national council, including Bob Norris, who in 1965 at the age of twenty-five had become the union's youngest NEC member; Rosaline Kelly of IPC Magazines; and Robin Corbett, the political editor of *Farmers' Weekly* (who later became a Labour MP and a life peer and one of the union's strongest voices in Parliament). 'We very nearly had a majority on their council,' Norris recalls.

From the start, NUJ members were elected as delegates to the IoJ annual conferences. The Institute liked to hold these in exotic locations – a far cry from the out-of-season seaside resorts and university campuses frequented by the NUJ. 'We had about twenty out of sixty people at each conference for three years,' Norris recalls. 'We went to Jersey, Malta and Cologne. The whole periodicals delegation was NUJ members.' It was ironic that the Magazine and Book Branch, a centre of left-wing radicalism in the union, was the most active in engaging with the conservative IoJ, but Norris goes on: 'We were playing the long game. It was a shame that most branches ignored it. We could have taken over every IoJ branch if we [had] wanted to. The best tactic would simply have been to take them over. If all branches had done that it would have succeeded.'

In 1971, five years after the arrangement was implemented, there was a special joint conference in the more mundane venue of Southend-on-Sea to tie the final knot. Despite all the headway made by the NUJ, the terms reached in the long years of negotiation were seen by its members as heavily favourable to the Institute. There were three bones of contention that stuck in the throats of many: a change of name to the National Association of Journalists, dropping the word 'union'; the establishment of a new grade of 'employing member' to include proprietors and editors; and the setting up of a National Professional Council which would be outside the control of both the executive and the annual conference. The NPC would be responsible for all 'professional' – as opposed to 'trade union' – matters and would consist of three employer members, together with representatives of the new executive and of seven 'specialist committees' lifted wholesale from the Institute's existing structure; plus others chosen by the NPC itself. Effectively, it would have put complete control of all professional matters into the hands of the old IoJ.

There was much opposition in the NUJ. 'We are giving the Institute the kiss of life,' said Ralph Ravenshear of the South Eastern Area Council. 'I think the whole thing is a confidence trick to prop up their organisation.' Glasgow branch said: 'Those of us who have been fighting battles on two fronts, both trying to improve the wages and conditions of our members and raise their status – "professional" if you like – within the community, strongly object to being relegated to playing a minor role.' The letters pages of the *Journalist*, likewise, were full of indignation. Clarence Wilkie of the Whitehall branch wrote: 'I am grateful [to the Institute] for reminding me that – although I have been an NUJ member all my working life – I am not and never have been a "professional" journalist.'

The resentment was about more than the detail. Union members had long regarded the Institute's pretensions as a 'professional' body as a delusion. To the NUJ the distinction emphasised by the IoJ between 'professional' and 'trade union' matters was not a real one, and the feeling was that the IoJ talked up the first to mask its lack of interest in the second. Yet at the 1971 ADM a call to break off the agreement – made by Greg Dyke of the Uxbridge branch – was defeated. Whatever its distaste, the union was determined to go through with the merger.

But six months later, in Southend, it all came to an end. Delegates from the NUJ and IoJ met in joint conference, but their votes were tallied separately. The draft rules for the new Association were debated one at a time: they had to be agreed by both parties, and all the contentious ones were either amended or deleted by big majorities. Even the long-gamers from the NUJ magazine sector had to give in. Their leading speaker, Paul Foot, made a fervent plea to the IoJ delegates to change the plan for the proposed National Professional Council so that it could be an integral part of the new union. 'If agreement on the merger is to be reached,' he said, 'concessions have to be made. The Institute should be tested on that one concession to see if they would agree to it.' No one from the IoJ spoke in reply, but when the vote came the NUJ delegates voted overwhelmingly to make the change and the Institute voted heavily against. Bob Norris – a delegate for both the NUJ and the IoJ! – said he 'would have liked to have heard some fighting talk from the IoJ delegates, but they had said nothing'.

The marriage was annulled. It might appear in retrospect that a major opportunity was missed, but the truth was that the differences were too great.

Again the *Journalist*'s pages overflowed with angry reactions. One IoJ member wrote to say she had resigned from the organisation: 'Perhaps if the union dropped its large-scale campaigns for better pay and conditions and held genteel conferences in sophisticated tourist spots instead, it too would win the proprietor's smile of approval and would want to hide the "union" tag.' She added: 'The negotiations all along should have been for a takeover and not a merger.'

At the 1973 ADM the NUJ added a new rule: the Institute was to be 'proscribed'. Since then it has been against union rules to be a member of the IoJ; no one can belong to both. There has been no more talk of merging, but tentative contacts were resumed in the 1990s, when John Foster was NUJ General Secretary. He and Norris, then the union's number three as Assistant Secretary, had regular lunches with IoJ leaders to see what, if any, agreement might be reached. At that time the Institute was keen to join the International Federation of Journalists (which also, of course, holds its meetings in far-flung locations). Norris says: 'They wanted our support to get into the IFJ. They saw the IFJ as a club they wanted to join. The talks never came to anything because that's all they were interested in.' The IFJ, headed now by the former NUJ activist Aidan White, turned them down; but they kept coming back, even flying a delegate to Athens for the IFJ's triennial congress in 2004. She came away empty-handed. As Norris reflects: 'We wanted to gobble them up but they are not a tasty morsel any more.' After ninety-nine years, for the NUJ, the IoJ finally didn't matter.

The mice that roared

On UK local papers in the late 1970s the pressure for an explosion was about to blow. The strategy articulated by chapel-power advocate Mike Bower, leader of the journalists at Sheffield Newspapers, was working. The stronger chapels in daily paper offices had been throwing their weight around for ten years, and had succeeded in winning national agreements weighted in favour of their colleagues on the weeklies. Now the smaller offices were feeling their strength. In 1977–8 there were victorious first-time strikes in weekly offices including the *Somerset County Gazette* in Taunton, the *Surrey Herald* in Chertsey and the *Warrington County Press*, and in early 1978 there was more nationwide action over the payment of the annual NS rise.

The Newspaper Society was mean towards the low paid, but the Labour government proved itself even meaner. The NS agreed a £7.35 a week flat rate rise with the NUJ, to help the weekly staff, and submitted it to the Department of Employment for approval. The ministry pronounced that this represented 10.36 per cent of the wage bill, thus breaching the 10 per cent limit, and vetoed it. Thereupon the NS cut the offer to £7.09. This was accepted by the members in a ballot – on condition that there could still be bargaining to top it up at house level – but by now it was February and the deal had been due at the beginning of the year. The employers wouldn't backdate the increase and, relying on the government restrictions for justification, neither would they agree to house bargaining. The

NS was 'fighting to the last drop of other people's blood,' was one NUJ official's comment.

Sanctions were imposed by NUJ members around the country – effectively a work-to-contract, withdrawing the unsolicited extra work and goodwill on which local paper production depends. Some employers agreed to pay up. Others reacted badly: the journalists at Berrows Newspapers in Worcester and Hereford – owned by Rupert Murdoch, of all people – who described themselves as the 'worst paid in Britain', were locked out. Their managers had refused not only the national increase but also a microscopic rise (£2 a week) due to trainees under the house agreement. After two weeks on the streets they settled for £1. To no one's surprise the Westminster Press group was the hardest to crack, the last three WP weeklies in west London falling to a mass picket at Uxbridge in April when the print unions decided to walk out and thousands of papers were lost.

Journalists on provincial papers had long felt undervalued and exploited; now across the country, they were feeling bold. The NS virtually defied them to fight back when in December 1978 it offered just 5 per cent for the settlement due on 1 January. The employers had reason to like that annual renewal date: it meant any run-in would be over Christmas, a time when no one was thinking of industrial action. And if the negotiations dragged on for a few weeks after that, which they invariably did – well, that was a few weeks they wouldn't have to pay the increases. And in 1978–9 they enjoyed another advantage: it was the coldest winter for sixteen years – no one would want to stand for long on a picket line.

It wasn't just the NS that was thinking along those lines: so were the NUJ national executive, the full-time officials, and even some members of the union's Provincial Newspapers Industrial Council, the body that called the strike by just 5 votes to 4 after a national ballot of the membership in local papers. That call was ratified equally narrowly by the NEC – by 12 votes to 11. Ron Knowles, the *Journalist* editor, says: 'I don't believe the NEC or officials realised the extent of the members' anger. Nor did the employers. They had been given a clear warning that the members were going to take them on but they thought it was just rhetoric.'

The national Newspaper Society strike, from 4 December 1978 to 21 January 1979, brought out more than eight thousand journalists, the biggest stoppage in the NUJ's history. Through seven freezing weeks they stuck to their task. John Bailey, the long-serving NEC member for the north-east of England who had succeeded Harkness as NUJ Treasurer, describes the spirit of the strike:

> The impressive thing was how people who had never been on strike
> manned the picket lines. All muffled around the brazier on bitterly
> cold days, sending people off to find food, they were totally at home
> with it, they accepted it. What comradeship there was! There were
> socials to balance the essential mandatory meetings that were called.
> No one was left out and where there was need people rallied round.

It was a big operation for the union. In Acorn House an office was cleared as a 'bunker' and charts on the wall recorded progress around the country. As a rule the NUJ had handed out strike pay, at least in officially backed disputes, but for eight thousand people it was out of the question. The union had only just launched its Fighting Fund, intended in the long run to finance disputes, but there was hardly anything in it. However, hardship payments were available from central funds and there was vigorous fund-raising by chapels. Big donations were made by the rest of the union, including the entire three-thousand-strong membership at IPC Magazines and Books who gave £7,000 – the first week of a 21 per cent pay rise they had just won in their five-week work-in.[1] NUJ full-time officials handed over part of their salaries. Other unions offered their support too – most usefully the Fire Brigades Union, whose members had been on strike the year before and had appreciated the sympathetic reporting of many local papers. They turned up at picket lines with braziers.

The chapel at the *Yorkshire Post* in Leeds was given a ton of coal to burn in their brazier by mineworkers' leader Arthur Scargill. 'It was marvellous,' remembers Pete Lazenby, a young journalist who would become Father of the Chapel in the 1990s. 'One day a Royal Mail pantechnicon pulled up and pallets started falling out of the back, for shelter and for fuel for the brazier. Council workers brought us a shelter to sit in. On Christmas Day someone brought a piano and we sang carols, and the management sent down a trolley from the canteen with whisky and pies and pasties.'

Perhaps the most heartening support came from a source the provinces wouldn't have taken for granted: the Press Association. The PA chapel was ordered out and all chapels instructed not to handle PA copy. Most national offices complied. Half the PA members came out at the start and others in dribs and drabs, but the chapel had the backing of the NGA, which now insisted on the letter of the agreement with the NUJ and

The 'bunker' at Acorn House in the 1978–9 Newspaper Society strike. At work are, from left, national organiser Noel Howell, executive member Aidan White and Journalist *editor Ron Knowles. (Andrew Wiard)*

Police arrest Newspaper Society strike pickets at Oswestry, January 1979. (NUJ Collection)

A Newspaper Society striker in Yeovil put the journalists' case in personal terms. (NUJ Collection)

Mass picketing at the King & Hutchings local newspaper factory in Uxbridge, west London. (Andrew Wiard/Report)

would handle only copy produced by the *Post*'s editor, David Chipp, in person. After three days he gave up exhausted and the wire service closed down.

An even more contentious blacking action was taking place directly opposite the PA's stately Portland stone pile in Fleet Street, in the shining black glass-fronted office of the Express group, where David Ross's chapel boycotted PA copy and the employers went to the High Court for an injunction to compel them not to. This was the start of Express Newspapers versus MacShane, the first of two long-running legal cases that arose from the strike – Denis MacShane, the name on the writ, being NUJ President at the time.

At first the court declined to issue the injunction but at a later full hearing it did so. The union lost too at the Court of Appeal, where Lord Denning issued a judgement against the union so perverse that the House of Lords readily overturned it. It was, MacShane says,

> a classic of judicial politicised activism not remotely based on the law,
> when it was quite clear the union had authority over its members
> and could instruct them to go on strike. The Lords ruled Denning
> to be wrong and I became a footnote in legal history, as one of the
> first acts of the incoming Conservative government [in 1979] was
> to change the law to make it clear that no such order for secondary
> picketing could ever be given again by a trade union.

But the strike wasn't really about a national confrontation between union and employers – not in the courts, nor over the negotiating table, nor even on the streets. It was a revolt of the downtrodden, a claim for a bit of respect as well as a living wage for journalists on the weekly papers who had been milked dry for decades. 'Provincial pay was so poor and nothing had ever been done about it, year after year,' John Bailey explains, 'and they just took the chance.' The biggest support came from the smallest papers. They made placards for their picket lines: a photographer with a dog – 'No bones for me this Christmas'; 'Your local journalists demand a living wage. Our first strike in seventy-one years'; '*Western Gazette* – the big paper with the small pay'; 'Local news dies if our wages don't rise', and so on.

The NUJ was not alone in saying this: in a report on the strike the *Economist* surveyed both the wages and the profits of the big groups and remarked: 'What is at stake ... is more than low pay. It is whether the loyalty and professionalism that employers have relied on for so long can continue ... Today the unions feel that loyalty has been a one-way relationship; and that the words "relied upon" could be replaced by the word "exploited".' A letter in the *Journalist* in January 1979 put it in a nutshell: 'Militancy is born, not of revolutionary zeal, but of despair.'

The response to the strike call astounded everyone. In the first week a hundred publications were stopped by the action, twelve of them dailies, which tend to run out of copy more quickly. Lists of the participants appeared in the *Journalist*, which was in its element under Knowles's editorship and brought out an extra edition with a strike poster. Fifty-five daily offices reported 100 per cent participation, but in a few there were problems, where the owners had paid the full claim – and more – to keep their employees at work. At the Liverpool Daily Post and Echo, the Birmingham Post and Mail and the *Evening Echo* offices in Southampton and Dorset, local union leaders opposed the strike instruction and kept their chapels at work for a while. But everywhere there were members who did walk out and set up picket lines, and over the weeks more joined them. The loyalists understood that the success of the strike depended on the strong offices staying out.

There were other offices where the money was likewise immaterial but everyone loyally stayed out. Lazenby says of the *Yorkshire Post*:

> We didn't have a dispute with our managers. We had magnificent pay and working conditions then because we had fought for them; we had had several strikes before. Our house agreement said that whatever the national agreement was, we got 10 per cent more. So this strike was not for our benefit; it was using the big chapels to save the weakest. Management invited us to negotiate but we refused. There was opposition within the chapel but we held it together.

The worst problem was Birmingham. The Post and Mail and their sister titles in Coventry had paid the full £20-a-week rise claimed, and on day one of the strike only thirteen journalists walked out. More were to join them, but most of the chapel broke the strike and, even worse, backed the second High Court case against the union, basing their case on a forgotten union rule they claimed rendered the strike unlawful. Rule 20(b) – which is still operative – says: 'No withdrawal from employment affecting a majority of members shall be sanctioned … unless a ballot of the whole of the members shows a two-thirds majority.' The rule had never been invoked before and its unfortunately vague expression – what does 'affecting a majority' mean? – kept teams of lawyers in work for months. This was the Porter–Pritchard case, named after the FoCs in Birmingham and Coventry, John Porter and David Pritchard, in whose names it was brought.

Its impact was to undermine the union's attempts to discipline members who had broken the strike instruction. As the strike drew to a close there had been a drift back to work as employers agreed to pay the increase, and several hundred faced formal complaints. The union instigated the celebrated 'flying assize', a panel of NEC members that travelled around the country holding hearings in upstairs rooms over pubs, doling out fines and expulsions.

The Porter–Pritchard case began as an injunction to prevent the Birmingham members being disciplined. At first the High Court refused to impose an injunction, but in July 1979 the Court of Appeal took the opposite view and two years later the House of Lords confirmed it – in effect declaring that the whole strike had been unlawful because the union had not balloted the entire membership.

By this time the flying assize had expelled some seven hundred members and fined a hundred more. Now it was agreed to rescind all the penalties – though the guilty verdicts remained on record. A compromise was negotiated under which the union dropped the discipline and Pritchard dropped the case; Porter had died of a heart attack while it was under way. But most of those who had been disciplined simply left the union – a lot of them to join the IoJ. There was great anger at the deal at the 1982 ADM. Carol Leach of the West Essex branch spoke for many when she said: 'Scabs who undermine our disputes and pick up the benefits won at our expense should not be allowed to come back so easily.' There was bitterness in some offices for years. The 1978–9 strike was a rough fight and it did leave scars.

For some of the strikers the scars were physical, the result of bruising encounters with police on the picket lines. The violent conduct of police clearing the way to get vanloads of papers off the presses was unprecedented in the NUJ's experience. Ipswich, Colchester, Oswestry, Cardiff and of course Westminster Press's print factory at Uxbridge were the worst flashpoints. The Uxbridge plant was closed down when van drivers in the print union NATSOPA walked out in protest at the heavy-handed treatment of pickets and when WP managers sacked the drivers.

More than fifty union members were arrested; most were acquitted but a few were fined and one, Steve McKenley from Bristol, who had been arrested several times, was jailed for three months for assaulting a police officer. When this particular news came through during the 1979 ADM in Ayr the conference passed a furious motion of protest while NUJ lawyers applied for bail. After six days McKenley was released.

The Flying Assize

The Flying Assize has entered NUJ folklore as a ruthless process of dispatching members who broke the 1978–9 strike, the nickname inviting comparison with the Bloody Assize conducted by Judge Jeffreys in the West of England in 1685, at which hundreds of people alleged to have taken part in a rebellion against the Crown were summarily sentenced to death.

In fact everything was conducted according to union rule, which requires that a panel of national executive members investigate every complaint laid by other members. There was great anger against the strikebreakers among the membership, and it was the accused members' own colleagues who had laid the charges, not union officials.

National organiser Bob Norris, considered an authority on the rules, officiated at the hearings. An enormous amount of clerical and administrative work was involved, handled by the popular office manager David Reece (who died from overwork – he suffered a sudden heart attack the next year). Not all of the accused were found guilty, and some had their sentences reduced after presenting mitigating circumstances to the union's Appeals Tribunal, which conducted its own provincial tour to hear the cases.

Eight years later there was a strange echo of the enforced mass amnesty for provincial members when the union tried to discipline members who worked during the year-long dispute at Rupert Murdoch's Wapping plant in east London. In this case the executive laid the complaints, found them upheld but then allowed the members to appeal – successfully – to the tribunal. The reason it threw the cases out was to prevent unrest within the union rather than to settle litigation, but the painful lesson was the same – that the union could not enforce its rules against members who broke ranks in crucial disputes. In the Wapping case there was an even more serious consequence: the 1988 Employment Act, which outlawed unions expelling their members for defying an instruction to strike – a move reckoned by many to have been influenced by the Wapping journalists' reaction to the NUJ's attempts to maintain support for the dispute.

For all the setbacks, the strike was a triumph: the 5 per cent rise on offer was virtually trebled in the 14.5 per cent settlement. This was not the highest pay rise won that winter though. The same month, local-paper colleagues in Scotland and Northern Ireland won considerably more – 18 and 19 per cent respectively – for their 1979 agreements, and without industrial action. In April the Scotsman group in Edinburgh and the Aberdeen Press and Journals group, both part of Thomson Regional Newspapers, won 25 per cent.

But this was not the point. For the first and last time, journalists on local papers throughout England and Wales had given their masters a bloody nose, and they felt pretty good about it. The Institute, it should be recorded, whose members had cheerfully crossed the picket lines and worked through the strike, now went to the Newspaper Society and demanded the same 14.5 per cent – and got it. Whether it would have done so without the NUJ action is not hard to guess.

Awesome consequences

The NS dispute produced a grim hangover. The hardest of all provincial employers was a company called T. Bailey Forman, publishers of the *Nottingham Evening Post*. TBF and its managing director Christopher Pole-Carew were pursuing a crusade against trade unions and all who belonged to them. In 1973 they had taken on the print unions, moving production to a hi-tech non-union plant on a greenfield site; in the process they had locked out the NUJ after journalists, who were being required to input into computers, refused to work with non-union print staff. A savage dispute ensued. Twenty-two NUJ members blacklegged and were expelled from the union.

Now, when the NS strike started TBF made it clear that they would sack all who took part, and this they duly did, leaving the NUJ with a terrible dilemma. The Nottingham members had been persuaded to join the strike with the promise that they would be protected, but the union found itself unable to do so. As chapel delegates gathered to vote on the final offer, they agonised: should they stay out and thereby risk their solidarity falling apart, or leave Nottingham in the lurch? There was not much doubt which way they would go, and for all the blood and sweat that was spilled in Nottingham and all the rhetoric invoking unity, it was never a dispute that was going to be won.

The fight to reinstate the 'Nottingham twenty-eight' was bitter, frustrating and violent. The city's police had been pretty heavy-handed with the pickets during the strike, but that seemed like a mere rehearsal for the extraordinary scenes that would take place in Forman Street in the spring and summer of 1979. Hundreds of police turned out to meet the regular pickets and rallies outside the building. In well-drilled flying-wedge formations, they charged the crowds. Dozens were arrested and harshly treated by the magistrates, among them the NUJ Deputy General Secretary Jake Ecclestone who was fined the maximum on a first offence – £250 – for obstructing the police. The magistrate said he would have jailed him if he could.

It began to seem as if the union was taking on the whole city. TBF and Pole-Carew were powerful in Nottingham. Pole-Carew was the High Sheriff of Nottinghamshire and used to enjoy parading around in a white silk cravat, dress coat and gaiters at ceremonial occasions. Though he seemed a ludicrous figure, he was anything but.

One morning in June 1979 the NUJ pickets took the company by surprise and entered the building. The chief union official present was Mike Bower, the former leader of the Sheffield chapel who was now full-time organiser for the north of England. He gives his account of what happened:

> We arrived one day and there was only one cop on the door so we
> just went in. Pole-Carew came down and said 'get out of this office,
> you scruffy little man.' He went into a pub across the road and came
> back with a posse and they got hold of me and pulled me from
> behind a desk. I fell to the floor and trapped my nose and split the
> gristle from the bone. There was blood all over the place. A TV crew
> had arrived by this time and filmed us, but nothing was broadcast.

In 1980 the *Journalist* got a leak from a friendly boss of the record of a private seminar that Pole-Carew had given for newspaper managers on how to break a union. He told his apparently spellbound audience of how he set out to humiliate and discredit union officials and institute a 'reign of terror' against staff on strike. Company doctors carrying out medical tests on new staff should report those that might be 'security risks', and once in post they should be 'needled' to test their reactions. Potential strikebreakers, the report of the session continued, should be bribed to stay in work. Perhaps it was no surprise that five years later Pole-Carew

● *The High Sheriff of Nottingham, Christopher Pole-Carew, as seen by Ray Drury.*

Caricature of Christopher Pole-Carew, managing director of the Nottingham Evening Post *during the seven-year dispute, and High Sheriff of Nottingham. (Ray Drury)*

popped up as a prominent adviser to Rupert Murdoch as he planned the move to Wapping.

The twenty-eight sacked journalists took their cases to an employment tribunal, but it refused to hear them. With little prospect of winning back their jobs the members threw themselves into a new enterprise, publishing a weekly paper, the *Nottingham News*. They received a significant boost from the great football manager Brian Clough, whose club, Nottingham Forest, astounded the football world that year by winning the European Cup. Clough was at the peak of his fame and a well known Labour Party supporter. Right from the start he announced that he would not speak to Polo-Carew's *Evening Post* and took a column in the *Nottingham News*. Such was his authority that the rival club, Notts County, felt compelled to follow suit, and they too boycotted the *Post*. The union ploughed thousands into the *News* and launched a £250,000 appeal. It was a highly regarded paper. But it could never succeed commercially and folded. The dispute was settled on meagre compensation terms in 1986. For the NUJ, Nottingham was a glorious defeat. Sadly, there were more to come.

One of the first, and just as traumatic, was consequent on Nottingham. In October 1983 David Dimbleby, the proprietor of a small group of weekly papers in the wealthy west London borough of Richmond, sacked all his printers and took a contract with T. Bailey Forman at its

Joanna Davies, Mother of Chapel at Dimbleby Newspapers in the 1983 dispute. (Andrew Wiard)

non-union print plant. The mother of the twelve-strong NUJ chapel at Dimbleby Newspapers, Joanna Davies, told him that members would not provide copy to go there, to which he responded by securing a High Court injunction against the union. The journalists came out on strike and he sacked them.

Dimbleby Newspapers was a family firm that attracted young journalists seeking to get to Fleet Street, despite its reputation as a sweatshop. The salaries and conditions were Dickensian. Most were not properly employed but paid by the day. They had to buy their own biros and notebooks and even pay for their own shorthand classes. They had no history of revolt, since few stayed very long, but they proved to be a gallant band in 1983 and fought a year-long battle to uphold union policy.

As in Nottingham the NUJ was taking on the establishment, though a rather more refined branch of it than TBF. David Dimbleby, whom the *Journalist* gleefully reported was known as 'Mister David' to company retainers, was the elder son of Richard Dimbleby, a pioneering reporter of early BBC radio and television, and had inherited his father's lofty position in BBC current affairs as a reverential commentator on momentous events and presenter of political programmes. David had a younger brother, Jonathan, who had a rather more radical reputation, and had bought out his interest shortly before the strike.

The chapel too had backers in the BBC: the NUJ membership in BBC current affairs, led at the time by the impressive figure of industrial reporter and wisecracking pundit Vincent Hanna. The Dimbleby fledglings went to meetings at the BBC Lime Grove studios chapel to urge the elite of the industry to show solidarity. The BBC chapels did indeed declare their aversion to Dimbleby's actions and put some pressure on the corporation not to hire him. For a time he lost some of his highly paid contract work, but neither Hanna nor Joanna Davies was able to persuade the BBC journalists to refuse to work with him. For one thing, any industrial action would have been unlawful, since the Dimbleby affair was to pitch the NUJ into the most perilous confrontation with the law it has ever taken.

The union was already in contempt since the High Court granted Dimbleby his injunction, and was in constant fear of the seizure of its assets by the court. 'Sequestration' was the potential punishment set by the 1982 Employment Act for unions ordering what the law calls 'secondary action' and trade unions call 'solidarity' – striking to support colleagues in dispute elsewhere. The Act, as noted earlier, was a consequence of the union's instruction to Press Association members to stop work during the 1978–9 strike. The landmark case Express Newspapers versus MacShane, which began as an injunction during the strike and went all the way to the House of Lords, had ended in victory for the union – a hollow one, though, since the Conservative government had promptly brought in the Act to overturn the Lords' decision. This wasn't the last instance of its kind – at least two more repressive laws were brought in by the Conservatives to reverse NUJ legal victories – but in this one the union had the dubious double distinction of being not only the cause of the legislation but also the first union to be subjected to its terms.

The Dimbleby journalists' action was unlawful since their dispute was judged not to be with their own employer, and the union leadership feared that any further action could have tipped Dimbleby into having the contempt order enforced – which, thanks to a convoluted series of negotiations that involved at various times practically all the NUJ's top officials, he never actually did. Perhaps he worried that BBC journalists really would pull the plug on him if he had their union effectively incapacitated by the courts. But for nearly a year it was touch and go. To be able to appeal against the injunction to the House of Lords the union had to obey it and formally instruct the chapel to stop the strike. This it did, and for a time the action was unofficial, sustained by support from elsewhere in the union.

A Special Delegate Meeting, a rare event, was called in January 1984, which resolved to persist with the action. The NEC went into a panic and, fearing possible sequestration, decided to take the union's money and accounts out of the country; and since the NUJ Treasurer John Devine lived in Ireland, he would have to take them there. Further, to forestall the risk of any official being compelled to go to court to give evidence against the union, no minutes were taken of this or any other decision.[2] The Treasurer was empowered to refuse to disclose what course of action he had taken, lest that put other officials at risk. Devine protested that this move was fraught with danger and put him in an almost impossible situation. He said later: 'The NEC in wimping out of taking proper decisions reassured me that it had faith in me. I was not asked if I had faith in the NEC.'

Devine went home to Dublin late one night weighed down by cases crammed with the union's ledgers and minute books. He was instructed to find a hiding place for £250,000 from a UK account. In case anything happened to him – like sudden death – he had to tell two friends, one of whom was not in the NUJ, where everything was. Other decisions of a similar cloak-and-dagger nature were taken, which Devine says 'came back to haunt me because they were not minuted. More than twenty years later I still have nightmares about that meeting.'

But he did the job well. Harry Conroy recalls the discovery after he had become General Secretary in 1985 that the union still hadn't got the £250,000 back – but it wasn't in Ireland. He says: 'We kept getting these mysterious bank notices of a numbered account we didn't know about. It turned out that the money was in Switzerland.'

By chance the Dimbleby affair ran at the same time as another awesome NUJ confrontation with the law, the dispute at the *Stockport Messenger*, where the entrepreneur Eddie Shah was in dispute with the National Graphical Association. Here too there was a small chapel of young, inexperienced but undaunted trade unionists taking on much mightier forces with great resolve. In the mid-1980s the NUJ fought its way to the front line of the political struggle between the union movement and a rampant Thatcher government, and though it wasn't strong enough to win, and wobbled a bit on the finances, it didn't flinch.

The Dimbleby dispute was eventually called off, and the strikers went off to other jobs to be replaced with other young hopefuls. In 2001, when the union was recovering its confidence after the Thatcherite onslaught, they in turn mutinied again and succeeded in securing recognition for the NUJ. Dimbleby promptly sold the family firm to the American-owned Newsquest chain, and a rather quaint if unappealing corner of the media industry was swallowed into the mainstream.

Elsewhere in the London suburbs the 1980s saw the final flings of chapel power, starting with the fight by the weekly chapels to win, for the first time, the principle of 'London weighting' – extra pay to compensate for the higher cost of London living. Linda Piper says:

> The London weighting strike was fantastic … People were happy to be picketing because it was warm and sunny and not Christmas. We marched down Fleet Street with the NUJ banner. A cop said, 'What's all this about?' I told him and he said, 'You mean you don't get any money at all for working in London?' He was disgusted. We marched to the NS office and demanded that someone come and talk to us but no one would. But we got wonderful suntans on the picket line.

Inevitably there was more picketing at Uxbridge. Piper again:

> We had huge pickets over there, from all the [Westminster Press] papers. On one occasion I was the only *Kentish Times* person picketing. SOGAT drivers used to come to London on a Wednesday night, pick up the papers and drive to Sidcup. I stood at the front because they would recognise me. They saw me and stopped. They said, 'This is too dangerous, we will run someone over, we won't cross the picket line.' Managers were there and the SOGAT FoC said, 'You pay my blokes to go back without the newspapers. We won't cross the picket lines if we have to run over people.' The managers said no, so the drivers just got out of their vans. The papers did not come out.
>   We settled the dispute, but SOGAT were still out. I told them, 'We will support you.' They said, 'No, we don't want you to go out because they are paying you but still not getting the papers out.' They did us a real favour. The sum at issue was the payment to go

to Uxbridge and back, that's all that was at stake. So we carried on working but the *KT* didn't come out, the drivers wouldn't deliver it. Eventually they had it printed in Germany and flown in and gave them away because they couldn't get them delivered. The dispute cost the *KT* more than £1 million over a payment of less than £400.

The strike had lasted three weeks and was a great success. The Newspaper Society offered £9.30 a week extra. 'It was the first time the employers ever contacted us for talks,' says Piper.

> In the negotiations we were on the winning side. We had a meeting of the London members at the Conway Hall. We recommended acceptance of the offer. It was the first and only time we got a standing ovation from the members who were still out on strike … We had established the principle of London weighting. They all got extra pay. People went back to work feeling they had achieved something.

Quick off the mark

An especially ironic consequence of Labour's fall from power in 1979 was a massive pay rise for journalists working in party communications. Labour's staff, more than any other employees during the pay restrictions of the 1970s, had to stick to statutory limits; there was no fiddling round the edges for them. After the Conservatives took office and the restrictions ended Labour's press officers and the journalists on party publications – all NUJ members – went on strike and won 28 per cent rises.

3

STARTING OVER

Hurricane Thatcher

After the union's pay triumphs of the 1970s everything went into reverse. Just as in the 1960s, it found itself in the front line of political and social change, but now things were moving in a different direction. The changes of the 1980s swept through the industry like a hurricane, knocking the NUJ, and the print unions, off their feet. By the mid-1990s there were only a handful of offices in newspapers and magazines where the NUJ could still negotiate for journalists, though it did manage to hang on to a good proportion of its members: enough to survive and begin reconstruction when the devastation eased.

A combination of purpose now flourished between government and employers, both set on weakening and, if they could, on destroying trade unions. Margaret Thatcher's government was on a mission to create a more individualistic society, eliminating such collective institutions as trade unions; the media employers were intent on introducing computerised production, sacking printers, imposing new work and new pressures on journalists – and above all, ensuring that the NUJ did not inherit the industrial muscle of the print unions. The disputes of the 1980s were mostly not about pay: they were about technology, redundancies, the sacking of activists, and the fundamental right of journalists to be represented by the union.

This was the question of 'recognition' that was to vex the NUJ for the next twenty years. The very function of representing journalists, which had been taken for granted since the First World War, was now suddenly in jeopardy. Employers simply announced that they were going to terminate agreements, hire staff on individual contracts, and fix their salaries individually too. Until the law back-pedalled a bit at the end of the century, the NUJ could not in many offices even represent members in trouble, let alone negotiate their wages.

In the autumn of 1978, as provincial journalists were gearing up for action, the union formally terminated its agreement with the Newspaper Publishers' Association (covering national papers), after sixty years. The agreement was now 'meaningless' and 'a dead letter', General Secretary Ken Ashton said. In every office there was by now a superior house agreement. The troublesome arrangement with the Newspaper Society, representing provincial papers, lasted until 1987, when the national executive decided to abrogate that too. The NS had declared it would no longer require all employers to honour the rates – and what, the NEC asked itself, was the point of an agreement like that? More could be gained, and more quickly, by means of strong chapels pushing for what they wanted. It had worked in the 1970s, so why not now?

Each year after the national strike the NS members, in votes in mandatory meetings, had accepted meagre pay offers from the Newspaper Society. Every member was supposed to attend, but the numbers recorded in the votes dropped to a third of the eight thousand involved. In 1984 the new FoC at the *Middlesbrough Gazette*, Martin Gould, who had been in a high-profile picket line arrest during the national strike, noted in the *Journalist* that only about a thousand had voted to reject the latest offer: 'Those of us who didn't think the offer was good enough must accept the decision and get on with the job of setting out a national claim for the inevitable introduction of new technology so we are ready when the big rush comes.'

The chapels' impotence was embarrassingly underlined at a delegate conference in January 1985. The union's provincial chapels had established a practice of deciding their strategy at meetings known as 'Digbeth conferences' (the first was held at Digbeth Civic Hall in Birmingham in 1978). These had begun as highly charged affairs at which their campaigns were planned in the knowledge that the troops were lined up behind them. But now, though members had voted to reject a below-inflation offer of £5.50–£7.50 a week, their leaders were at a loss: every proposal, whether for strikes or for working to rule, was defeated, and all they could do was to ask the members to vote again, which they did – and accepted the miserable offer.

The NS, sensing the weakened resolve, tried to revive the national agreement. They had talks with the General Secretary – by now Harry Conroy – and both sides agreed to discuss renewing it. It was the NUJ's Provincial Newspapers Industrial Council (PNIC) who were opposed. 'The PNIC went apeshit,' Conroy recalls, 'saying I had got involved in PNIC matters without their authority. They came to the NEC meeting with a motion condemning me for interfering.'

In Scotland, for a time, things were different. The equivalent Scottish Newspaper Publishers' Association agreement had been wound up by the employers in January 1980, but there were good house agreements: it was a four-week strike at Scottish Universal Newspapers, the second in twelve months to win a really big pay rise, that had driven the SNPA to stop the national negotiations. These union successes, as well as continued victories on national papers – a thirteen-day strike at the *Scotsman* in Edinburgh, the first in its history, winning rises of up to £1,300 a year, and the stunning successes of the chapels in the big magazine groups – made a fine send-off for chapel power.

The tide was already beginning to turn when in October 1979 the *Journalist* reported a strange phenomenon: 'A new form of attack on NUJ organisation has emerged. A management has offered bribes to members in return for a signed undertaking that they will not strike.' The company was Cheshire County Newspapers (CCN), a chain of weeklies in north Cheshire that was linked with the Messenger group of Eddie Shah, the entrepreneur who five years later launched the first non-union new-tech national paper, *Today*. CCN was asking journalists to sign personal contracts opting out of the union rates – and paying them generous six-monthly rises for doing so. The Father of Chapel at CCN, Tony Curran, said the company was 'bribing its way to the formation of a strikebreaking force which has signed away its right to take industrial action'.

'Bosses Bid to Buy a No-Strike Force' was the *Journalist*'s headline. That was how the NUJ perceived the move: as a handicap to chapels taking action. Few saw that it was the clouds darkening out to sea as Hurricane Thatcher started to spin.

Hardly had the NS agreement been ended than companies began the process of 'derecognition'. The first was the group in which the NUJ militants had scored their earliest successes: after twenty years, Thomson Regional Newspapers now began to wreak their revenge. In late 1987 chapels in TRN's ten centres were reporting to head office that managers had suddenly started to get tough, forcing members in executive jobs onto personal contracts, tearing up agreements and refusing to negotiate pay deals or even meet chapel officers.

At that time the union was negotiating new technology agreements around the country with, among others, TRN. Harry Conroy recalls:

> The talks with TRN were going really well. Suddenly they ended because Thomson's board in New York took a policy decision to derecognise the union. In June 1987, the day of the general election, I met Ridley Thomas, the MD of the *Scotsman*. He said, 'I have to warn you that if your people go on strike it won't be about whatever you think it's about, but about recognition because I am under instruction to derecognise.'

Conroy was particularly concerned for TRN's two big offices in Scotland: the Scotsman group in Edinburgh and the Press and Journal in Aberdeen. In both centres there was trouble. The *Scotsman* was on strike for three weeks. 'We got them back with nothing and the company started victimising people,' Conroy says. 'It was a dry run for Aberdeen.' The year-long strike at Aberdeen, which began in September 1989, was calamitous. Everyone knew it was coming and the chapel fought valiantly, but it came close to ruining the union. In all there were a dozen strikes against derecognition, and only a couple succeeded.

A *Journalist* article in February 1988 had concluded: 'Having introduced new technology and effectively broken the NGA's organisational power, TRN has now turned on the NUJ. They are scared stiff that the NUJ, with its members' hands on the keyboards, will assume the industrial supremacy once held by the printers. The present de-unionisation campaign is a pre-emptive attack.' The NEC, it reported, had been told that 'the union had been slow to respond to what the company was doing ... and a lot of members had signed away long established terms and conditions in return for worthless assurances'.

The NEC put Deputy General Secretary Jake Ecclestone in charge of drawing up a counter-strategy. He said: 'Members are beginning to realise that Thomsons are playing a very dirty game. A lot of ordinary decent journalists are beginning to resist. When Thomson provoke a fight – as they are clearly trying to – they may get a surprise.' A wages survey in March 1988 showed that, almost alone among provincial chapels, TRN offices had had no negotiated increases at all in 1987. The survey reported that 53 per cent of all chapels were covered by house agreements – leaving quite a big shortfall only a year after the national agreement had collapsed. The Northcliffe group was also refusing to negotiate, but it was paying 'quite hefty increases'.

Only TRN, at this stage, was foisting contracts on people, and doing so in a brutal way. It would have been unlawful to change employees' contracts without consent so they had to be bribed, cajoled or simply bullied into accepting them. One of the worst offices was the *Middlesbrough Gazette*, where the chapel power phenomenon had broken out a generation earlier. At first only one of the fifty-two staff took the bait. In fact David Whinyates, the *Gazette*'s features editor, became something of a symbol. Part of the union's response to the attempts at de-unionisation was to instruct members not to sign personal contracts and to make it an offence under union rules to do so. Whinyates pocketed a £3,000 rise for signing a contract and winning promotion, the chapel brought a formal complaint, he was fined £100 by the NEC, failed to pay and was expelled. By that time, September 1988, it was realised that this wasn't a tenable course of action because hundreds or even thousands would have to be kicked out; so the policy was changed, and Whinyates remains the only member ever expelled for signing a personal contract. But the rest of the *Gazette* chapel did give in. One member wrote in the *Journalist* of their having been 'paralysed by fear. Their resolve was worn away as wages remained frozen. From being one of the union's strongholds, we have sunk to a depressed bunch conscious of our ineffectiveness.'

The effect of derecognition on union organisation was summed up by Alan Mitchell, an executive member for Magazines and one of the more thoughtful activists of the time – magazines were affected a couple of years after newspapers – at the 1992 ADM. Employers, he said, were 'forcing journalists into circular firing squads. They are giving everyone a gun and saying, shoot or you will be shot yourself. They are setting journalists against each other using fear, mutual suspicion and greed.'

Not everyone shared this view. Colin Bourne, former chapel leader at IPC Magazines in the 1970s who had become the NUJ North of England organiser, comments:

We should have told people to sign personal contracts. They were
meaningless. We only gave them meaning by telling people *not* to
sign them. If everyone had signed and insisted that the company
signed an agreement with the NUJ, what could the company have
done? But those who signed dissociated themselves from the union.
We divided ourselves and played into management's hands.

He adds: 'I never said this publicly – it would have been too damaging
– but I was saying it in private.' Bourne left the job in 1996 to train as a
lawyer. Perhaps he had a point.

His colleague Gary Morton, who had taken over from Knowles as
national organiser for provincial papers, reported in April 1989 that all
TRN and Northcliffe chapels had lost recognition. The FoC at TRN's
Chester Chronicle penned an anguished plea in the *Journalist*:

Don't trust personal contracts, however attractive they may seem.
We have had a wage cut imposed on us which wipes out most of
the gains we made in our new tech agreement. We were told the
£14 a week we received for accepting computers was conditional on
signing individual contracts, waiving NUJ rights. The package looked
quite attractive but most of us find ourselves substantially worse off.

That month the NUJ's first strike against derecognition began, not
against TRN but against one of the following pack, Westminster Press.
The chapel at the *Bath Chronicle* were out for four weeks and achieved a
stunning success, retaining pay bargaining with a banding structure and
rises of 5.6–12.5 per cent. In May members at United Newspapers' *South
Wales Argus* in Newport retained their bargaining rights on the strength of
just the threat of a strike. Managers there withdrew a plan to abolish the
pay structure and put all staff on a single rate with merit pay.

But these were short-term gains: recognition was lost soon after, and in
any case within months of these successes four more disputes began, spread
across different sectors of the British print media. One was at a journal
publisher, one on a provincial weekly, one on a big Scottish daily and one
in magazines. They were the most protracted in the union's history and
they nearly brought it to its knees.

What's the contract?

Personal contracts were foisted on NUJ members in newspaper offices all around Britain and were everywhere resisted or at least resented, even where no action was taken. But sometimes there was a lighter side to what was a grim business. In June 1990 contracts materialised at Eastern Counties Newspapers in Norwich. Letters were handed out to all staff, who held a snap meeting and decided to return them to management in protest. The chapel then held a meeting in a nearby social club, to consider the threat they posed. When they came to consider the details it was discovered that every one had been handed back and no one had taken a copy. They had nothing to discuss.

Four apocalyptic strikes

On 24 May 1989 the entire twenty-three-strong chapel at Pergamon Press, a scientific book and journal publisher in Oxford, was sacked for staging a perfectly lawful one-day stoppage. Their proprietor was the preposterous Robert Maxwell, a bombastic, bullying financial trickster and fantasist. The union knew what he was like from more than twenty years' experience: constantly changing his mind, he delighted in humiliating people, and officials had found him impossible to deal with. The chapel was well organised and had already had three or four disputes, winning back jobs for the victims of Maxwell's proclivity for sacking people on the spot, as well as a house agreement.

In 1979 the chapel had come out in defence of a member who had been sacked. The strike lasted three days, and involved Maxwell's son Ian who was then a union member. Maxwell agreed to reinstate the sacked employee and to recognise the NUJ to represent all its members. But shortly after the triumphant return to work he refused to recognise the FoC Jim Boumelha and his deputy Simon Collins, then a member of the NUJ executive. The pair were banished to an office ten miles away. For good measure Maxwell took out a libel writ against the NUJ official Gary Morton, who handled this dispute.

Two years later Maxwell sacked the entire Pergamon Chapel, and they were out for seven months. This one was settled at top-level talks at the

The Pergamon 23 defied Robert Maxwell's publishing empire, which included Mirror Group Newspapers, for more than three years. (Debbie Puleston)

TUC conference, the sort of setting that Maxwell, a one-time Labour MP who liked to parade his political connections, revelled in. When the NGA said they would order their members out, Maxwell had grudgingly taken the members back. It was his second – and last – defeat by a trade union, and it rankled. Now in 1989, he had sacked a member in the book publishing department and refused to let the union represent her, saying it was not recognised there (which was untrue – the NUJ had been recognised since 1967). The chapel, aware of what might well happen, had tried everything to avoid a stoppage. They tried negotiating for four months, and had no fewer than three ballots to strike before being left with no other option. The minute they began their twenty-four-hour action they were all sacked – and not only they: an employee in the personnel department who had protested was also fired. What had begun as a personal case, a routine employment matter, was magnified by Maxwell into a full-scale recognition battle, not just for the jobs but for the union's very right to exist at Pergamon. It would drag on for over three years.

A month later, on 26 June, journalists at the *Essex Chronicle* in Chelmsford, a big weekly series in the Northcliffe group, came out. This began as a pay strike, to raise the shockingly low salaries of the trainees that made

Jeremy Dear, leader of the Essex Chronicle *strikers, 1990. (John Harris/IFL)*

up the bulk of the staff, after most of the seniors had been forced on to personal contracts. But after management suspended the whole chapel for holding a mandatory meeting, it became a fight for recognition. Members were told that any further action would lead to dismissal; again, they had little choice but to walk out. The FoC, unusually, was a trainee himself: Jeremy Dear, a twenty-two-year-old punk fresh from college, with spiked hair held up with soap, and wearing Levi's 501s and Doc Martens. He proved himself a born leader. This strike was to last a year.

In the September General Secretary Conroy's nightmare became reality with the long-awaited confrontation at Aberdeen Journals. It was a delayed explosion. The 116-strong chapel went out, came back and then struck again. Again, they had been through months – two years in this case – of trying to negotiate; and again, managers had precipitated the strike so as to give the union a beating. They turned up the pressure on the strikers, targeting the vulnerable. Threatening late-night phone calls were made to people who were off sick, who had elderly dependents or heavy mortgage commitments, and to trainees. Some were reduced to tears. One person on sick leave was given five minutes to decide whether to go back in, or lose their job. One trainee who was threatened by *Press and Journal* editor Harry Roulson that he would never find work anywhere else was tough enough to hold firm; his name was Michael Gove and he became a top political journalist on *The Times* and a front-bench Tory MP.

Such American-inspired union-busting tactics had thankfully been rare in Britain hitherto, and they came as a shock. 'This company is run by moral bankrupts. It is insidious and vile,' Jake Ecclestone stated.

After nineteen days of intensive effort the union managed to get the journalists back to work. They had secured a deal that gave them, on paper, what the chapel wanted: union recognition and a free choice on personal contracts, with no less pay for non-signers – such had been the pressure that all but twenty-one of the 116 had already signed contracts.

But everyone knew it wouldn't be the end of the matter. Thomson group headquarters in New York were not happy. 'They gave the Aberdeen management hell for settling,' says Conroy, 'because the policy was to derecognise the NUJ. They did not want a settlement. So they tried to get our people out of the door again. I was saying, "Don't go out, hold on in there."' The company initiated disciplinary action against a chapel officer for 'sabotage' and started pressuring pro-union executives to resign. Life was so unbearable in the Mastrick office that when they did come out again after another three weeks members said it was almost a relief.

Conroy was livid. He was away at an International Federation of Journalists meeting in Norway, and though the NEC had given the chapel authority to call another stoppage he had not expected it to happen without being referred to him. He recalled:

> When I came home … Iain Campbell [the Aberdeen FoC] phoned and asked me what did I think about it? and I asked, 'About what?', and he said, the strike, and I asked, 'What strike?' He said, 'We walked out yesterday.' I said, 'We are fucked, we are beaten.' He was not expecting that. He was not happy. But I said, 'If you are out you are out.'

The members were sacked and on strike for a year.

The fourth long recognition strike, at VNU magazines in London, began in November 1989. VNU was a Dutch company publishing business magazines, specialising in computing. It operated from a smart new redbrick block in the heart of Soho in central London and had a staff of smart and sassy young graduates – the Thatcher generation of middle-class media folk who were supposed to look on trade unions with disdain. Soho was a new media land, a cluster of broadcast, film and advertising businesses, a world away from Fleet Street.

The revolt of the VNU journalists was brought about by their managers who, like the others, were pitching for a fight, to eradicate trade unionism from their business. Of course, the journalists' resolve didn't come from nowhere: the NUJ's magazine sector had a long history of strong organisation, not to mention the more recent one of militant chapel activity, and it had been the main engine of the new radical political direction the union itself had taken. The VNU chapel, which comprised more than 90 per cent of the journalists employed there, had a year earlier staged a twenty-four-hour strike to secure its agreement and an all-round pay rise. It should have seen what was coming.

Again, the ostensible cause of the strike was a single sacking: a senior journalist had resigned, then was persuaded by his editor to return. Top managers intervened and insisted he leave. To smooth things over the chapel tried negotiating, but managing director Graeme Andrews simply sacked the man, whereupon his colleagues walked out into the street – on to the cobbles, indeed, since Broadwick Street had been tastefully resurfaced. Andrews went down and stood inside the door to stop the journalist coming back in, the staff walked away, and that was that. Shortly afterwards he sacked the rest of them. They were offered a return to work if they would sign individual contracts and forgo union representation, which they declined. They were out for six months.

So the NUJ went into the 1990s with four intractable strikes under way. None of them won union recognition, and apart from five who were taken back at Aberdeen all 250-odd journalists involved lost their jobs. They cost the union a fortune in dispute pay and organisation expenditure: Aberdeen alone took more than £1 million from NUJ funds. Two of the stoppages – Aberdeen and Pergamon – were formally ended with face-saving formulas and meagre compensation for those sacked. The other two were called off and the journalists moved on. With hindsight it is easy to see all four as mistakes, but none were of the NUJ's making and they were valiantly fought. More than that, they inspired many both inside and outside the NUJ who saw the strikers as heroes in the war against Thatcherism, and they were a source of some pride to the union.

All the chapels fought politically as well as industrially, contacting local MPs, mobilising other unions and their local communities. VNU secured the regular appearance of Labour MP Austin Mitchell, a journalist himself and former reporter and presenter with Yorkshire Television, who became chairman of the NUJ Parliamentary group in 2002. The newspaper chapels

Singing out

The Pergamon and VNU strikers did not confine themselves to the routine strike activities of picketing and lobbying for support. Both groups wrote songs with pointed lyrics, which they performed lustily at all kinds of gatherings.

The 'Ode to Solidarity' was the Pergies' version of the European anthem, the 'Ode to Joy', specially written (to music by L. van Beethoven) for the launch of Maxwell's paper *The European*. The first and last verses ran:

> Maxwell says he's European.
> We know better, he's a fraud!
> Smashed our union, sacked our chapel,
> He could not do this abroad.
> [Chorus]
> France and Belgium, Spain and Denmark,
> Shield their workers with the law.
> If he tried it in those countries
> They would soon show him the door.
> …
> Maxwell's launched another paper.
> Who will read it? We don't care.
> He has set his sights on Europe.
> We will chase him everywhere..
> [Chorus etc.]

Not to be outdone, the VNU chapel produced their version of the Monty Python lumberjack song:

> [Solo] I'm a member of the NUJ,
> I drink all night and I strike all day.
> [Chorus] He's a member of the NUJ,
> He drinks all night and he strikes all day.
> [Solo] I shout and sing on picket lines
> And also in the bars
> I'll carry on with striking
> Till we get company cars.
> etc.

in Aberdeen and Chelmsford, now with smaller, lower-paid and demoralised staffs, highlighted the effect the proprietors' action would have on local news – not just during the strikes but in the long term too. This was to be a persistent NUJ theme as the newspaper industry and then local and regional broadcasting accelerated their cost-cutting strategies after the turn of the century. In Aberdeen there was a boycott of the papers by advertisers that cost TRN even more than the dispute cost the union. The chapel mustered top Scottish politicians at its rallies.

For the twenty-three Pergamon strikers – the 'Pergies', as they were known – the thrust of their campaign was political, partly because their industrial leverage was weak but also because Maxwell, a former MP, was, or thought he was, a big wheel in the Labour Party. In truth he was a mighty embarrassment to Labour and held such sway as he did solely on account of the money he gave to party leader Neil Kinnock's personal office. The stream of complaints from local parties and union branches about his conduct forced the party to set up an inquiry, led by the former tax officers' union leader Tony Christopher, which found resoundingly in the union's favour.

No one was brave enough to force Maxwell to back down, however. What he did was to sell the company to the Netherlands-based Elsevier group, which shortly afterwards merged with Reed International, the big UK magazine and book publisher (and former owner of the Mirror group, which they had sold – to Maxwell! – in 1984). The Pergamon dispute now had an international dimension, and teams of strikers set off for Amsterdam (Elsevier's headquarters), Brussels and New York (seat of Maxwell's US subsidiary, Macmillan) to harass such politicians, bosses and bureaucrats as they could find.

'Harassment' is a fair description of what the Pergamon twenty-three inflicted on Maxwell. They pursued him to every event they could with their banners and their songs written for the occasion. In 1990 he launched *The European*, an up-market weekly supposedly for continent-wide distribution, at a power breakfast in London's Connaught Rooms. Pergies and their supporters set up a line outside the door. Robert Maxwell, who won the Military Cross for his daring exploits in the Second World War, sneaked in by a back entrance, while at the front the Pergies were singing their own version of the European anthem. When he was invited to take part in a debate at the Oxford Union the prospect of a Pergie picket unnerved him entirely, and he pulled out.

The Pergies' most telling long-term achievement was to help with the BBC *Panorama* programme *The Max Factor*, broadcast in October 1990; the producer was Mark Thompson, who fourteen years later took over from Greg Dyke as BBC Director-General. The programme investigated Maxwell's business affairs and led to a run on Maxwell Communications Corporation's share price, the calling-in of his loans from the merchant banks, the collapse of his business – which turned out to be a house of cards constructed on false security and lies – and, finally, to his mysterious death at sea. The strikers had built up good contacts inside the Mirror group – though not with the journalists, who despite sharing a criminal proprietor would have nothing to do with them – and supplied the *Panorama* team with a dossier of damning information. After Maxwell's demise (and fulsome tributes to his wonderful life from *Mirror* executives) it all began to come out. It was to the credit of the Pergies that they kept up their attack on Maxwell even as he was being feted, flattered and financed by so many powerful people in British business and political circles for so long.

The Pergamon strike ran the longest – for 1,176 days in all – and could almost have gone on for ever had not the union's exasperated leadership cajoled a majority into settling for a poor financial settlement from Elsevier, in August 1992. Of the twenty-one involved in the campaign – two pulled out early on – all were still there at the end, an extraordinary tribute to their Father of Chapel Jim Boumelha and his partner Anna Wagstaff, the union's Oxford branch secretary. Boumelha was a Moroccan former medical student who had come to Oxford to study and was hired as a French speaker by Maxwell's French wife Elizabeth as one of a team who helped research her PhD thesis. The Maxwells were so impressed with his work that he was given a job at Pergamon Press – a decision that Maxwell must have regretted.

In 1999, ten years after the strike began, the Pergamon chapel came together again for a celebration of their struggle, which they held in Headington Hill Hall, the mansion in Oxford owned by the council, that Maxwell had rented as his headquarters and treated as if he owned it. With his companies all long gone the council had sold the hall to an Oxford college, which lent it out for the day. 'Truly,' said the *Journalist*, 'the prisoners had taken over the jail.' Eighteen months later, on the tenth anniversary of Maxwell's death, three women who had been involved in the dispute went out to the Canary Islands to retrace his final days, including a dip in the sea

Plaque commemorating the Pergamon dispute outside Headington Hill Hall, Robert Maxwell's former HQ, in Oxford. (Janina Struk)

near where he is believed to have disappeared. 'Swimming on His Grave' was the *Journalist*'s headline. When some complained this was in poor taste, the editor, Tim Gopsill, replied, 'That was the general idea.'

The four disputes and the issue of recognition dominated the union's 1990 ADM in Loughborough. Between the ovations for the brave strikers and the indecisive debates on strategy, denunciations were heaped on NUJ official Gary Morton for suggesting in a *Journalist* article that they should all be wound up. 'If there is no realistic possibility of members getting their jobs back then there is no point in continuing the action,' he wrote.

Journalist cartoonist Steve Bell's comment on the death of Robert Maxwell in 1991.

Finance: four strikes but not out

The NUJ's failed strikes for union rights in offices where employers were tearing up union agreements led to a massive financial crisis, but they were not the cause of it. The strikes were attempts to stop the haemorrhage of members that followed the loss of bargaining rights; falling income was the problem. The union's financial crisis was exacerbated by the cost of dealing with the strikes and the redundancies that followed, but there would have had to be spending cuts anyway.

Crisis it certainly was. During 1987–91 the union lost four thousand members. Twice, its bankers threatened to stop honouring cheques; and a third of the NUJ staff were laid off, including ten of the eighteen full-time organising officials. In October 1991 NUJ Treasurer Bernie Corbett asked in the *Journalist*: 'Is this the union's darkest hour?', and it probably was. The NUJ was £1.5 million in debt and its overdraft was £100,000 over the limit. 'Without the disputes this situation might have bumbled on for another couple of years. Instead the union plunged into a huge, unignorable debt.' Spending cuts were the immediate solution but the problem could be solved only by proper budgeting and financial management.

John Foster, General Secretary from 1992 to 2002, recalls:

Within a day of taking the job I had the bankers telling me not to write any cheques. I was very annoyed. I said I had been elected as General Secretary and it was my job to run the union. I told them, 'You don't come and tell me what to do, I have just been elected by the members. If I cock it up you can tell me but don't tell me how to do it.'

We had £1.5 million of bank debt and £500,000 in outstanding bills, on a turnover of £2 million. We had to get control of it. I said, 'We will try to get within tight controls.' In the first year we made a surplus of £400,000. I went to the TUC and said, 'I want to cut the fees by half.' They argued about it so I said, 'OK, throw us out of the TUC then.' What we did was cut the registered membership by half, which came to the same thing.

The budgeting process turned the union round. We got all the union bodies involved, made them feel responsible and they took note of what they were spending. In ten years we paid off all the debts, we had a new building, which we could pay for and still have the old building. That's what I'm most proud of – turning the union round from bankruptcy to a sound financial footing.

Morton had assumed for himself something of the role of a Cassandra, articulating what several in the leadership felt privately; but ending long strikes can be difficult when the union is geared up to support them. Morton was actually bidding for the leadership himself, plotting a run for General Secretary in the election due that summer, on a platform of sorting out the NUJ's chaotic financial and organisational state. He came third out of five runners.

The *Essex Chronicle* chapel in Chelmsford had based its strategy on solidarity action in other Northcliffe chapels so as to put pressure on the company. In a few centres mandatory meetings were held, and in some areas Labour-controlled councils stopped advertising in Northcliffe papers, though in truth it didn't amount to much. But the Loughborough ADM delegates took an early-morning break to hold a mass token picket at the nearby *Leicester Mercury* office, where the chapel came out to greet hung-over delegates and Jeremy Dear climbed on to a wall to make a speech. Standing listening were Conroy and the former chapel-power militant Aidan White, by now General Secretary of the International Federation of Journalists. As the two GSs chatted, White remarked to Conroy: 'Watch that bloke, he'll be General Secretary one day.' He was right.

In July 1990 the strike was called off. Only five of the fourteen strikers remained. The VNU strike had likewise been ended in May. Aberdeen fought on until September, when after intensive negotiations TRN offered compensation of between £2,500 and £12,500 and a return to work for twenty of the strikers. But only fourteen were even interested, and as it turned out TRN was to renege even on this deal. They eventually took back just five.

Only one newspaper chapel secured union recognition by taking strike action: this was at the independently owned weekly the *Rotherham Advertiser*, where a stroppy NUJ chapel struck for fifteen weeks and managed to retain their agreement. They had to take personal contracts, they lost a pay rise and they accepted more flexible working, but they did have pay talks and they still had that piece of paper. FoC Phil Turner, a battle-hardened union veteran, complained that they had let themselves down by voting (8 to 5) for the return-to-work formula after they had all been sacked. In fact they had surpassed the efforts of all other chapels – except one, and that was in magazines.

While the NUJ's right to represent members was being virtually wiped out in newspapers, most magazine groups, apart from VNU, held off. It was four years after the Thomson group began to wreak havoc in its regional newspapers division TRN that it turned its attention to its magazines in International Thomson Publications (ITP) in London. Here it was brought to a juddering halt. The chapel had a closed shop, and it resisted plans to split the workforce in half and withdraw recognition from the group chapel by going on a four-day strike. It even secured a promise in writing that ITP would maintain recognition and not introduce personal contracts, which management stuck to. Instead, two years later, they sold the group to the non-union publisher EMAP. The formidable FoC Mike Sherrington lost his job; he later became a full-time NUJ official.

The other magazine groups were not so lucky and suffered the storm as badly as the newspapers had. The full blast hit in the spring of 1993, when by a strange coincidence four of the biggest groups ended their NUJ agreements within a month of each other. These were IPC Magazines and Reed Business Publications owned by Reed International, Haymarket Magazines owned by the top Tory politician Michael Heseltine, and Morgan-Grampian Magazines owned by United Newspapers. Reed and Haymarket took action on the same day. Preparing for that day, IPC and Haymarket managers had sacked the NUJ FoCs, respectively Peter Wrobel and Alan Mitchell. Both were highly respected senior journalists – and both were given large sums of money. There were six days of strikes at Morgan-Grampian, which, while not preserving the full agreement, did secure important concessions: the maintenance of a minimum salary and the NUJ's right to represent individual members.

A passionate letter in the *Journalist* of May 1993 expressed one member's feelings. Julie Harris wrote of her experience at IPC Magazines that

> those of us who voted to go on strike for better conditions and pay
> were always outvoted – apart from just once – by those whingeing
> about new mortgages, money problems, families etc. Funny really,
> because many of us 'militants' had all those problems too, and
> more. The reason unions are having difficulties is not a result
> of management becoming more ruthless but of those in power
> realising they can treat employees badly because there is no effective
> retaliation. If all IPC employees walked out the union would soon be
> recognised.

Moving the elephant

Saints and signers

Once in a while the actions of a single NUJ member can have far-reaching consequences. Unions are collective organisations, but they need brave leaders and members who are prepared to take a stand. Over the years a number of activists have put their jobs on the line when the union was under attack and a couple of dozen have been sacked.[1]

The NUJ had two such members in the 1990s, both lauded as heroes and made union Members of Honour. Both took legal cases all the way to the European Court of Human Rights in Strasbourg. Bill Goodwin took his stand against betraying a confidential source and established a legal precedent that has benefited the whole of journalism ever since; the other, Dave Wilson, carried on a twelve-year battle that won employment rights for every worker in Europe. He was Father of the NUJ Chapel at the *Daily Mail*, where union agreements were destroyed and personal contracts introduced in December 1989.

While the trauma of derecognition was being played out on picket lines around the country, UK national newspapers were beginning to experience it too. After another decade of chapel power in which some offices had won relatively generous salaries it looked at the end of 1989 as though the hurricane was about to hit Fleet Street. Personal contracts were introduced at the Mirror, Telegraph, News International, Express and Mail groups. One or two offices did hold ballots for action, but none took any. Instead the national paper chapels used their strength to negotiate the best terms they could. In some offices where personal contracts were foisted on to people, the union succeeded in retaining the right to represent members and agreements covering matters other than pay; this, of course, made it less disadvantageous for members to sign them – not the only dilemma the union faced in handling the problem. Among national papers, those working for the News International, Telegraph, Mail and Mirror groups and the *Independent* lost everything; the *Express* retained a modest agreement; and the *Guardian*, *Financial Times* and *Morning Star* held on to complete agreements with pay bargaining.

The *Telegraph* had come under the ownership of the Napoleonic Canadian Conrad Black, and journalists there had a hard time of it. When recognition was threatened the unions organised a ballot that revealed that 98.5 per cent of staff – union members and non-members alike –

thought that recognition should be maintained. The company ignored it. At the same time it held a ballot of its own to decide on a possible no-smoking policy for its new offices in the Canary Wharf tower in London's Docklands. The vote was 65 per cent for a smoking ban – which the company then implemented. When the NUJ FoC Glyn Roberts queried some aspects of the smoking policy he was told it was 'not a management dictate but a decision arrived at by a ballot of the staff'. But derecognition went ahead, followed by waves of redundancies, frantic pressure on the overworked staff and one of the worst plagues of RSI ever suffered in the national press.

At the *Guardian*, journalists were able to see the threat off. They were presented with the contracts but four months of tough talking retained bargaining rights, and senior journalists who had signed the contracts were brought back into the agreement. In return the chapel ceded the right for twenty-five executives to receive higher increases and gave up its formal closed shop – but still had 100 per cent NUJ membership. At the *FT* there was never even a threat.[2]

The proposals at the *Daily Mail*, and at its sister Associated Newspapers chapels at the *Mail on Sunday* and London *Evening Standard*, contained a sinister element: pay rises for those who signed contracts – 10 per cent for executives and 4 per cent for other ranks – and nothing for those that did not.

This penalising of those who preferred to stick to union-negotiated salaries was the issue in the long battle that followed. There was no doubting the *Mail*'s intentions: the paper's editor Sir David English, knighted by Margaret Thatcher, said the purpose was 'to make the union wither on the vine'. To speed that process managers started the familiar round of intimidatory tactics, calling people in for interviews and threatening them with the sack. One who had just had a baby was told that it would be a 'rotten time to lose your job wouldn't it'? Managing director Bert Hardy said to a union official: 'There is no law that makes us recognise the union. It doesn't matter if you have 10 per cent or 100 per cent or 110 per cent membership – we don't have to talk to you.'

Nonetheless, after four months of dispute, thirteen journalists on the three Associated titles did decline personal contracts, and forfeited rises of £30 a week. They were known as the 'saints' – as opposed to the 'signers' – and a lapel badge was made for them with the matchstick 'Saint' figure from the Leslie Charteris thrillers of the 1930s. Ironically it was the chapel officers' success in negotiating the best terms they could under the contracts that made it easier for the majority to sign. The *Mail* chapel had voted heavily for industrial action and started a work-to-rule, but they didn't strike – partly on the advice of the union. The NUJ had just appointed a new full-time organiser for national newspapers, John Foster. He and Dave Wilson hit it off from the start and plotted the path that got the union through the wood, and it did not involve industrial action.

The union had learned that the *Mail* had set up an emergency newsroom at its new printworks in London's Docklands. It was supposed to cover for power cuts or other emergencies but the union reckoned it was also for strikebreaking. Foster remembers Wilson telling him that the *Mail* chapel could take strike action. 'I said no: if you go on strike you will lose. Even if you win the strike it does not mean anything, you have not changed the world. What you have got to do is change the law.'

Foster regarded himself as a professional trade union official; his father had been a communist official in the engineering union, so he grew up in union circles. He had never been a journalist but came from the tightly organised world of the print unions as a former Father of Chapel with the union SLADE, which represented picture engravers, skilled workers with a strong craft tradition, and had been taken over by the NGA in the 1980s. He had worked as an official for the actors' union Equity and joined the NUJ as an official in broadcasting, a regulated environment where things were done by the rules. On his own admission he knew nothing of newspapers. But he had sound judgement and a good sense of strategy, and he was tough. At home he kept Staffordshire terriers, and if proof were needed that owners take on the characteristics of their pets, Foster the bull terrier would provide it.

Dave Wilson had no such political motivation. He described himself as 'an unlikely foot soldier in this battle – a moderate, church-going, monarchist, Eurosceptic floating voter. I had never even sought to become Father of the *Daily Mail* chapel; I was just taking my turn.' He was – is – a skilled sub-editor who had come from the *Sheffield Star*. Though proudly lacking radical ideology, he had always worked in a strongly unionised environment. That and his personal determination were more than enough for the task.

Foster brought together a group of national paper FoCs to plan the campaign around one simple objective: the right of every employee to be represented by a union. There was in English law a right to union membership, but no right to make use of that membership by having the

Dave Wilson, who fought a 12-year legal battle for NUJ members' rights, in the audience at the launch of the Press for Union Rights campaign. (Caroline Penn)

union represent you. Without that, of course, membership is pointless. But once employees have that right, the reasoning ran, the union has a right to represent *them*. 'It is not the answer to everything,' Foster commented, 'but it opens the door so we can get in and do something else.' He kept hammering away at the point: 'I cannot push the elephant over. I have just got a little pin and if I keep on pricking away at the same spot it will move.' Eventually it did, and it took an elephantine effort.

The campaign acquired a snappy title, Press for Union Rights, dreamt up during a lull in talks with union reps during a dispute at the *Telegraph*. It was launched at a meeting in February 1990, with speakers from the other media unions, and a junior Labour frontbencher, Mark Fisher MP – the party leadership was very suspicious at the time. Dave Wilson was in the audience: his part would be to bring the legal test case on which the campaign would ride. 'We knew it would have to go to Europe,' says Foster. 'I told Dave Wilson it would take ten years. I said, "It is much more difficult than a strike. You will lose your job."' Again, he was right.

The case was that Wilson had been discriminated against by the *Mail* in not receiving the pay rise awarded to others, on grounds of union membership. This contravened the 1978 Employment Protection Act, which outlawed not just dismissal but any 'action short of dismissal' against an employee for union membership. The argument was over whether his union membership was indeed the cause.

The case went first to the Employment Tribunal, which said it was. It then went to the Employment Appeals Tribunal, which said it wasn't. The next stage was the Court of Appeal, where Wilson won, and it was now that things started to get really interesting.

In an unprecedented parliamentary manoeuvre the government introduced, at the last minute, an amendment to the Trade Union Reform and Employment Rights Bill already going through Parliament – it was at the third reading in the House of Lords. The Court of Appeal had not even published its full judgement, but the amendment pre-empted it by making it lawful for an employer to penalise staff who declined to sign contracts, as long as the purpose was 'to further a change in his relationship with his employees' – which by definition, in introducing contracts, an employer would be doing. The move became known as the 'Ullswater Amendment' after its progenitor, the viscount of that name, a junior minister in the Lords who had never been heard of before and never was again, but has earned his little place in history.

'CHEATS!' splashed the *Journalist*. 'Corruption,' said John Foster, by now General Secretary. 'The *Mail* have lost in court but found it easier to nobble the government and get the law changed.' Wilson commented: 'They have tried everything against us and now they are trying time travel – going back in time to before our winning judgement.' For once, the NUJ had backers in the establishment. A prominent Tory MP and former minister, Peter Bottomley, was so incensed at the injustice that he spoke in support of the union case at an NUJ press conference. It was a shame that few reporters attended, but this story, though it concerned a fundamental change in industrial relations, and though John Major's government was under constant fire from the media at the time, was hardly reported at all outside the specialist media. Newspaper publishers are employers, after all, and had a direct interest in it.

But one influential journalist did join the cause: Hugo Young, the Olympian political commentator on the *Guardian*. In an uncharacteristically splenetic piece he wrote of a 'sheer blatant defilement of the legislative process … with the purpose of pressuring people to leave trade unions altogether … a shameful saga, showing up a politically sick society'. Perhaps Young was as frustrated as everyone else. He was on first-name terms with ministers, yet this time no one took any notice of him. And no other Tory voted with Peter Bottomley against the Ullswater amendment.

The House of Lords saw the next and last stage – in Britain – of

Wilson's case. Of course he lost, but in March 1995, five years after the case opened, the Lords dredged the barrel of judicial perversity in attempting to rationalise the judgement. Dealing with the Employment Protection Act's forbidding 'action short of dismissal' against workers for their union membership, the Lords said that penalising Dave Wilson and the others was not an action at all, but an 'omission'. They reached this conclusion 'with regret since it leaves an undesirable lacuna in the legislation protecting employees against victimisation'. It did indeed – but it was they who created it.

The Lords ruled that though the law protected the right to be a member of a union, this did not extend to a right to be represented by that union. 'Thus it cannot be said that the service of collective bargaining is an essential union service'; furthermore, to lose that right need not deter anyone from being a member. This was convoluted nonsense to anyone who had ever belonged to a union, which presumably none of their Lordships had: the NUJ and all other unions lost a lot of members when they ceased to be able to represent them in the 1980s and 90s. 'It was terrible,' says Foster. 'I was in tears.'

The *Mail* then sacked Wilson, as Foster had predicted. In his sacking letter editor Paul Dacre wrote, apparently unaware of any irony: 'You have persisted in a "them and us" policy to management which is the antithesis of the type of relationship which I promote ... This cannot be allowed to continue.' He made no attempt to find fault with Wilson's work, and gave him £100,000 compensation. By now Wilson had forfeited more than £8,000 in lost pay rises, and during those five years, he pointed out, the *Mail* had doubled the salaries of its top directors and trebled its profits. Wilson said: 'I am not the first and will not be the last FoC to be sacked. I have no regrets about pursuing fairness at work and have been happy to be able to represent staff.' Union help for members at the *Mail* over the previous year had been worth more than £100,000; the union had also secured reasonable conditions for journalists since the company had been compelled to swear to the court that it would not worsen them. Wilson had the good luck he deserved, quickly landing himself a job as a sub on *The Times*.

The case went on, to Strasbourg, where according to the right to 'freedom of association' under the European Convention of Human Rights Wilson's victory became absolute. The final, unanimous judgement came in July 2002, more than twelve years after the case was filed. The judges ruled that workers must not suffer discrimination for trying to use their union voice. It was the first time any union had won a case on union rights at the European Court of Human Rights. The UK government was humiliated; again, it was lucky for them that the case was hardly reported at all. Wilson said: 'Was it worth it? Oh yes. Our victory is the NUJ's gift to the trade union movement across Europe. In my whole life, I never thought that I would help to achieve something so important.'

Never regained

Recognition was not regained at any of the four workplaces where journalists held the big strikes against derecognition in 1998–90. Pergamon Press no longer exists; Aberdeen Journals were taken over by the anti-union outfit Northcliffe, then in 2006 by Johnston Press. The union has not been able to reassert its presence at VNU Magazines or at the *Essex Chronicle*, still a Northcliffe publication – but there was a bid for union recognition there. After the NUJ's defeat Steve Turner's British Association of Journalists began to recruit members (Turner himself was from Essex and began his union career as a local branch secretary). In 2002 the BAJ applied for recognition and a ballot was held. It failed.

The elephant moves

The Wilson case had taken so long that by now the Press for Union Rights campaign had run its course, a new employment law had been won, and NUJ chapels were reorganising and even taking industrial action: two chapels were on strike – at the Newcastle Journal and Chronicle and the *Spalding Guardian* – when the European judgement was delivered. The law, the 1999 Employment Relations Act, did not redress the Wilson wrong – personal contracts and discrimination against individuals were still permissible. But it did allow Foster a foot in the door: the rights to representation and recognition were now established – in restricted form – but they were there. To win them was something of a political battle.

Press for Union Rights had commissioned an opinion poll by MORI

Tony Blair, then Labour's opposition employment frontbencher, at an NUJ-organised Press for Union Rights press conference in 1992, with SOGAT leader Brenda Dean (left) and Ben Young of the Aberdeen Journals NUJ chapel. (Stefano Cagnoni)

in 1992 and discovered that union rights had public support: no fewer than 89 per cent of British people thought that the right to recognition should be restored.[3] Yet the Labour Party, then in opposition, seemed nervous of the campaign. When a national conference was called the party, as at the PUR launch, declined to supply an official speaker; though Foster did get a Conservative, Emma Nicholson, to speak. Labour leader Neil Kinnock did eventually agree to meet the union. Foster had already made contact with the party's employment frontbencher, a fresh-faced young lawyer called Tony Blair.

'We had a meeting with Kinnock and [Roy] Hattersley [the deputy leader],' Foster recalls. 'We asked Blair if he was going to the meeting and he said he didn't know about it. He did come along but didn't say anything.' But the contact paid off and in July 1990 Blair turned out for a PUR press conference, to announce: 'The Labour Party supports the principle of a legally enforceable right to union recognition. We support the right for people to be represented by their union and have their union's support and assistance.' He even wrote an article in the *Journalist* in 1992, spelling out Labour's plans. From then on the exercise was to keep Labour to its pledge. The next leader John Smith reaffirmed it at an NUJ rally in Sutton, Surrey.

Paradoxically, it was harder to convince the TUC. It took the NUJ eight years to do so. Foster explains: 'We tried every year to get the basic point across but it was too radical for them. The Labour Party thought it would upset Rupert Murdoch and the press. For the unions, it was threatening their turf if any other union could get members in their workplaces and represent them. They were losing members hand over fist.' But not all were losing their bargaining rights: the media, like the mining industry, had been singled out for attack by government and employers, and unions in the public sector and heavy industry were hardly affected at first. Their leaders didn't, for diverse reasons, want to know about moaning miners, printers and journalists. They preferred to look the other way.

In fact, says Foster, they were wrong.

> It was going to happen to them too. They were living in the past. They couldn't see it. They pretended it was just a problem for our industry but it wasn't. In fact the NUJ could always survive because of the nature of our membership, we could always struggle through. But they weren't having it. Every year at Congress we had the same problem. They would pick nits in the motions we put up ... and do everything they could to keep our wording out. It was always, we can't do it, we're not doing it. When I started talking they would roll their eyes and say, here's the NUJ again.

But Foster steered the union away from the left-wing campaign led by the miners for the repeal of all the 'Tory laws' passed against unions in the 1980s. 'Arthur Scargill tried to get us to come in with him,' said Foster, 'and the TUC wanted us to because we would lose. But I said, we are not doing that.'

At the 1998 TUC conference Blair, now Prime Minister, made a complacent speech in which he said the Employment Relations Act, then going through Parliament, would be the limit of New Labour's improvements to union rights. He called it a 'settlement' – effectively a deal with the trade union movement while the party was in opposition. Afterwards he bumped into Foster at a reception: 'You see, John,' he said, 'we did what we said we would.' The government was much criticised by unions, including the NUJ, for not going further in dismantling the legal barriers to effective union organisation. But to some extent it was down to the

NUJ, and to John Foster and Dave Wilson, that unions and the workers they represent got as much as they did.

Further cases

Dave Wilson was not the only NUJ member to bring legal action against personal contracts. Others were brought by union reps at United Newspapers' *Lancaster Guardian*, at the *Yorkshire Post* and at the *Times* supplements in London, an offshoot of News International, where a well organised NUJ chapel was left high and dry when all the unions at NI were derecognised by their owner, Rupert Murdoch, in 1990. They had to wait sixteen years, until most of the supplements were sold off, to get their union rights back.

Two FoCs in United Newspapers – Andy Courtney of the *Ormskirk Advertiser* and Tony Harcup at the *Harrogate Advertiser* – brought successful unfair dismissal cases after losing their jobs in the derecognition process.

Back from the brink

'Why isn't everyone doing it?'

'Since 16 January 2002 things in the NUJ will never be the same again,' NUJ organiser Miles Barter told that year's Annual Delegate Meeting. On that freezing morning journalists on the *Bradford Telegraph and Argus* took a half-day strike. It was just for the morning, but managers docked a full day's pay. They also paid up. For that short, sharp action the Bradford chapel won rises of up to 14 per cent for their grossly underpaid juniors, with a flat-rate minimum increase to benefit the lower-paid seniors too – and this after an initial offer of 2 per cent.

Managing director Tim Blott, whose father Eric had been a predecessor of Barter as NUJ organiser for the North of England thirty years before, had tried the usual tactics to stop people joining the strike. Young journalists were urged to 'think about their careers', offered bonuses to work from home, and promised police protection to cross the picket line. It didn't work, and they all came out. The deputy Mother of Chapel, Sarah

The half-day strike at the Bradford Telegraph & Argus *in January 2002 marked the revival of NUJ activity in local newspapers after a decade of union derecognition. (Stalingrad O'Neill)*

Walsh, wrote in the *Journalist*: 'Our strike won us more money, solidified the chapel, raised morale and widened the scope of our recognition deal. I honestly can't see why everyone isn't doing it.' Excitement greeted the Bradford strike because it was the first over pay on any newspaper in Britain for thirteen years. It was also a success, which could not be said of all of the stoppages over union recognition that had happened in the meantime.

The 2002 ADM delegates cheered the Bradford chapel to the rafters, and after the session Barter called together a group of activists for an informal gathering at the back of the hall to plan a campaign of action. Within months there had been half a dozen stoppages – the most spectacular being that on the Guardian group's Greater Manchester (North) weeklies in Lancashire, where the pay increases went up to 24 per cent.

These were a string of papers owned by the *Guardian*, part of the herd of highly profitable provincial cash cows milked by the group to keep the *Guardian* and *Observer* afloat in London. The young journalists on the

Young journalists on the Greater Manchester weekly group protesting against low pay during their 10-day strike in 2002. (NUJ Collection)

weeklies threw themselves into the campaign like students in rag week, careering round in old bangers with placards and balloons, getting lost on the way to remote offices, pulling on knickers proclaiming 'Our Pay Is Pants' over their clothes and retiring to pubs to think up new ideas. Barter, who as a young militant in local radio had pulled a few stunts himself in his time, beamed over them like an indulgent principal.

Their success – raising the starting rate from £10,486 to £13,060 and winning a new senior grade of £19,000, when £17,000 had been the ceiling before – was no doubt partly down to embarrassment in the group, because union officials and supporters from head office had gone down to picket the *Guardian* office one lunchtime and leafleted the journalists. The chapel had a whip-round that raised more than £1,200 for the strikers. Mother of Chapel Helen Oldfield, who knew what local papers were like from her days at the Westminster Press newspaper factory in Uxbridge, went up to Rochdale to join the picket line – not something that national paper chapel leaders do very often. The Manchester management blundered badly by announcing in mid-strike that they were dere-

The NUJ chapel at the Spalding Guardian *won increases of up to 39 per cent with a two-week strike in 2002. (Dave Roberts)*

cognising the NUJ – this in 2002, from one of the few groups that had not done so in the 1990s. There was an angry reaction: the TUC put out a statement in support of the NUJ – not something that happens very often, either. Managers beat a hasty retreat and settled.

At the *Spalding Guardian* in Lincolnshire journalists won a pay structure that gave some members rises of 39 per cent. In other centres the mere threat of action secured sizeable rises for the low-paid; on the Trinity weeklies in Merseyside the top whack was a stunning 58 per cent. It was as if the union had been reborn – and it happened in the North of England, where the NUJ began.

Just as it had been a hundred years earlier, the impulse for this union revival was the miserable treatment of journalists on local papers. The union also had a new leader – General Secretary Jeremy Dear, the former leader of the *Essex Chronicle* strikers, who set about attacking the scourge of low pay as a centrepiece of his strategy. Dear had assumed the mantle of John Foster, with his blessing, and was able to use the legal foundation laid by Foster for his new campaigns. Pay on local papers was still pitiful, in fact proportionately lower than ever before; during the bleakest years some salaries had not risen at all and most had fallen in real terms. Juniors on weeklies were still earning around £10,000 – barely above the national minimum wage, and probably below it if the long hours were taken into account. Even on a biggish evening paper like the *Telegraph and Argus* the minimum was only £12,000. Bullying was rife, as was what Barter called

> [the] generally contemptuous treatment by editors and managers. The anger and resentment in newsrooms is intense. People are totally and utterly undervalued and alienated. They go to work, they're bullied, they work long hours for low wages, they are treated as if beneath contempt. Someone needed to stand up for these people who ring us up every day, broken by the way they have been treated at work.

Barter started a sparky email news service, Northern Soul, which carried instant updates on every active chapel, encouraging members in the offices concerned and in others too. The journalists on the Merseyside weeklies, he says,

> had seen the story of the Greater Manchester weeklies' triumph on the NUJ website and they asked, Can we have a strike? There had been only one member there. I went across for a meeting, fourteen people joined on the spot and thirty more within weeks. They had a ballot in which 89 per cent voted to strike and management agreed pay rises before they even had to walk out. So in three months, starting with nothing, they won themselves in some cases more than 50 per cent rises. Not bad, eh?

The Bradford chapel had positioned itself in the front line of the union revival two years earlier, when New Labour's Employment Relations Act came into force. The ERA set a rigid procedure for unions to regain recognition: they either had to show they had a majority of staff in the 'bargaining unit' in membership, or trigger a ballot of all the staff, conducted by a government agency; in such a case those voting 'yes' for union rights – from the whole workforce, not just union members – must be more than 40 per cent of the payroll. The Act came into force on 6 June 2000 – a great start to a new century for the NUJ. A queue of chapels rapidly lined up for their ballots. First was Bradford, who won an 86 per cent 'yes' and were the first to regain recognition in the Newsquest group.

Newsquest had been a management buy-out from the Reed group when it disposed of its regional papers, and the new company had taken over the old Westminster Press chain. In 1999 it was itself taken over by the American newspaper giant Gannett Corporation. Of the former provincial groups, all but Northcliffe had now gone: Thomson had been taken over by Trinity and the others broken up and swallowed by the four big groups (Johnston Press was the fourth). After winning their rights in 2000, the next year the Bradford chapel flexed their muscles and saw off an attempt by Newsquest managers to foist detrimental changes on to journalists' contracts. More than a hundred members across the Newsquest group in the north refused to sign, and the company had to withdraw them.

But in 2003 when, a year after the strike, the Bradford pay talks came round again and the euphoria had died down, Newsquest offered an insulting 1 per cent – this from the subsidiary of a US company that counts its profits in billions of dollars. Members came out again, but this time made little progress; in all, the Bradford journalists took forty-seven strike days in the spring of that year, and ended up with 2 per cent. By now the Newsquest strategy was clear: it did not resist ballots, it let the union enjoy its big majorities; then it dragged its feet and sat on its money. There were strikes too at the Newsquest centres in Bolton and Kendal, but the rewards again were slight.

Two of the union's greatest successes at the group were achieved without industrial action. The first was a publicity coup, after the NUJ conducted a survey on pay in the West Midlands. Newsquest chief executive Jim Brown, giving evidence to a Parliamentary Committee, was challenged with the survey results, which showed trainees on his local papers were on less than £10,000 a year. He protested that none of his journalists were so badly rewarded. A few days later the trainees concerned suddenly received rises to exactly £10,000.

Then there was the triumph at the *News Shopper*, a big series of fat weeklies in south-east London. Rises averaged 6 per cent and 9 per cent for trainees, bringing their starting rate to £15,200 – a step towards making London affordable for young journalists. These rates were won by a crafty strategy of keeping managers on the hop, holding long mandatory meetings and threatening to stop, but never actually doing so. As the Mother of Chapel said, 'When we had our mandatory meetings it was the devil's job to stop them walking out of the door. I and my deputy kept saying, "Slow down, slow down! Give us another week." I told the company, "If there is a potential to settle this we really must get our socks on because the chapel is ready to go out at the drop of a hat."' That MoC was Linda Piper, former NUJ leader at the *Kentish Times* and chairperson of the Provincial Newspapers Industrial Council in the great 1978–9 strike, who had returned to union activity after nearly twenty years.

The Birmingham Post and Mail newsroom in 1999 when union recognition was being regained. The image of the computer screen with the (digitally added) slogan, 'UNIONS ARE BACK', was used by the NUJ on publicity material at the time. (John Harris)

The NUJ had been well prepared to make use of the Employment Relations Act; compared with other unions it had a lot of ground to make up. The first year of the new Act (summer 2000–1) was an astounding success. A survey for the *Journalist* showed thirty offices where recognition agreements had been reached – sixteen of them after ballots – covering 3,721 journalists. Totted up, the ballot votes came to 1,473 to 78 – an overall majority of 95 per cent. There was no doubt, if there ever had been, that journalists wanted a union. The number of journalists in Britain covered by collective agreements rose during that one year from 7,600 (predominantly in broadcasting and national papers and agencies) to 11,650. There was great joy at their return in such offices as Reed Business Information, the *Yorkshire Post*, the Birmingham Post and Mail, and the Scotsman group in Edinburgh – big, important offices whose owners had set out to eliminate the union.

In 1999 the Newspaper Society had conducted a survey of its members' reactions to NUJ claims for recognition. The report was leaked to the union and, though the companies were not named, it was not difficult to identify Northcliffe as the group that said it would 'fight them on the beaches'.

In addition to the expected intimidation, as chapels in Bristol, Stoke and Gloucester put in their applications with proof of majority membership, managers resorted to legal shenanigans to stave off the claims. They dragged the procedures out for months and rigged the 'bargaining units' by bringing in non-journalists to swing votes against the union: at the *Bristol Evening Post* one NUJ member found that his fifteen-year-old daughter, who had done ten weeks' unpaid work experience, was counted as being on the staff and was sent one of the forms asking people to declare their union membership – in the Northcliffe newsrooms' atmosphere, an act of intimidation. Staff were told there would be no wage increases for three years if the union got recognition. But thanks largely to the persistence of the FoC, Derek Brooks, the *Evening Post* had become the only Northcliffe paper by 2006 to have been made to recognise the NUJ.

Nevertheless, the NUJ's fortunes in local newspapers were transformed, not least in terms of membership. Between 2000 and 2004 the numbers in provincial papers rose by 40 per cent, from 4,008 to 5,588 – though this was still a long way short of the eight thousand-plus of twenty years earlier, and there had been many job losses. The ADM of 2004 called for an annual 'pay in the media summit', a conference of activists from every sector to develop strategies. Group chapels, the engines of action in the 1970s, were revived, bringing together all the offices of the major companies. But it was hard going. Jeremy Dear said at the 2005 event: 'We have won 150 new recognition agreements over the last four years and rebuilt our group chapels. This has meant we have won back holidays and have seen pay figures rise in double percentage figures. Trainee pay has gone up by 25 per cent.' But, he stressed, pay in many areas was 'appalling, and journalists were far from being paid a professional wage for a professional job'. A target was set of £20,000 a year for senior journalists on regional papers and that target was met first at the Yorkshire Post group in 2005. The Father of the *Evening Post* chapel was Pete Lazenby, the paper's industrial reporter, veteran of the 1978–9 Newspaper Society strike, who had kept the chapel going through the decade of derecognition – one of the band of stalwarts who had ensured there *was* an NUJ to revive.

Bitter sweethearts

There were joyous returns for the union at the *Telegraph* and the *Independent*, where staff ballots overwhelmingly opted for NUJ representation.

At the *Telegraph*, where Conrad (now Lord) Black liked to boast he had gotten rid of the union, the comeback was led in 2003 by a remarkable team that manifested a kind of dual consciousness among the journalists: upper-middle-class Tories on the one hand, exploited wage slaves on the other. Joint parents of the chapel were Charlie Methven, a roguish Old Etonian horseracing buff who came from the *Sporting Life* and edited its gossip column, and Sandra Laville, a former left-wing activist whose previous claim to NUJ fame had been in 1991 when as a trainee she was sacked by the *Northampton Chronicle and Echo* over her refusal to pay the poll tax. The paper's chapel had rallied round her and a fellow non-payer, and after three weeks in which the entire chapel, including executives, were locked out they got their jobs back.

At any rate, the combination worked at the *Telegraph*, and staff voted by a whopping 91 per cent for the NUJ. Methven said: 'We are really chuffed. If we can get in at the *Telegraph* we can do it anywhere.'

Both he and Laville left the paper before long, she to the *Guardian*, he to edit *The Sportsman*, a new betting paper. But with the upheavals that followed the ousting of Conrad Black amid charges of theft, fraud and all manner of financial shenanigans, the chapel needed to maintain its strength. In 2005 the new owners, the Barclay twins, got rid of ninety journalists, and the chapel's efforts to stem the tide were hampered by employment

The duo who led the NUJ recovery at the Telegraph group: Charlie Methven and Sandra Laville. (Janina Struk)

law. Among the most restrictive of the Thatcher laws of the 1980s are those governing ballots for strike action, which set such stringent terms – breach of which renders the action unlawful – that it can take more than a month for a chapel's decision to hold a ballot to actually result in a stoppage. At the *Telegraph* they voted heavily to strike – for the second time in a year – but by the time they could take action the ninety had all gone. These legal restrictions are serious enough in disputes over pay, because they give managements plenty of time to prepare to get round the action, but in circumstances like redundancy they are disabling.

The *Independent* journalists had an even worse time. As the paper, born in 1986, lurched from one crisis to another and staffing was forever cut back, it fell under the management of the Mirror group at the time (1992) when it too was hacking back so as to repair the damage done by Robert Maxwell. The two tottering groups were subjected to the brutal surgery of chief executive David Montgomery, the man the *Mirror* journalists called 'Rommel' because 'Monty was on our side'. The *Independent's* joint chapel (daily and Sunday) was derecognised and two successive chapel leaders – Nigel Wilmott and a former NUJ President Barbara Gunnell – were sacked.

In 1997 Gunnell was assistant editor of the Sunday paper (it had three editors in as many years):

I was determined that the union would continue at the *Independent*, so I took on the role of MoC because no one else would do it. Montgomery was furious, and told Peter Wilby [who had just become editor] that I either had to resign as assistant editor or as MoC. Montgomery decided to set up what they called an 'academy of excellence' – essentially a strategy to lose sub-editors' jobs.

The chapel held a series of meetings to discuss its response and sought negotiations, which further infuriated Montgomery, who announced that everyone who attended a meeting scheduled for the next Monday would be fired. 'On the Saturday,' Gunnell recalls, 'I wrote a column, did the leaders and subbed and edited the front page. Then they said: "We're going to make you redundant". At 6 p.m. on a Saturday evening on a Sunday paper, while the pages were going through!'

Next week was the TUC conference, where Gunnell appeared at an NUJ press conference to launch the post-1997-election revival of the NUJ's campaign against the Mirror group management. For what had been happening on the other Mirror titles was worse still.

After Robert Maxwell had run up millions of pounds' worth of unsecured debts and looted the pension fund of £420 million, something clearly had to be done. But it was the journalists above all others who bore the brunt. The union thought the banks that had so irresponsibly advanced the money should bear the losses, but instead they installed Montgomery with a remit to cut the group's costs to the bone. The first thing he did was to sack a hundred casuals on the *Mirror*, overnight – or rather, one morning, when they turned up for shifts that had been booked, only to be turned away by security. Then he turned on the union reps, sacking six chapel officers, and refused to meet the NUJ.

This was the sort of confrontation that brought out the best in General Secretary John Foster. He recalls:

> When Montgomery started getting rid of people we had meetings on the editorial floor. A group went into David Banks's [the *Daily Mirror* editor] office. Every single one who went in with me got sacked. I told Banks I wanted to see Montgomery. He said, 'He won't see you.' The next time we had a disruptive meeting on the floor Banks would not see us so we went barging in. He accused me of pushing him. I did go up and barge into him but he was about twenty-two stone and I am eleven stone.

After that Foster was barred from the building. A photo was pinned behind the reception desk so that security would recognise him.

The *Mirror* chapel now passed a motion: 'We have no confidence in David Montgomery. He has acted like a tyrant. He has destroyed the morale of staff on all titles. He is undermining the future of the *Daily Mirror*. We call on the board to sack him immediately.' Conditions were so dire that the celebrated investigative journalist Paul Foot, a one-time chairman of the NUJ Magazine branch who produced a weekly page of devastating exposés, devoted one week's page to the bullying inside the *Mirror* itself. Management, of course, wouldn't run it so the union had it printed and Foot handed it out to people outside the building; he was forced to resign. The *Mirror* put out a statement saying he was mentally disturbed.

The union at the *Mirror* had been split following the sacking of General Secretary Steve Turner, who had held the job for a year between Conroy and Foster but had fallen foul of the NEC. Turner had been FoC at the *Mirror* in the 1980s, just at the peak of Fleet Street chapel power; former

Mirror editor Roy Greenslade described him as 'arguably the most effective NUJ chapel negotiator in Fleet Street history'.[4] When he failed to get his job back at the ADM in 1992 he set up a rival union, the British Association of Journalists, whose membership was concentrated in his former power base at the *Mirror*. The NUJ chapel, for years a closed shop, lost members to the BAJ, which fatally weakened it.

Foster decided to organise a public campaign against the *Mirror*. The momentum had already been sparked at the union's 1993 ADM, held in a hall at King's Cross in central London, when as the conference was debating the sackings the great orator Foot had called on delegates to proceed to the *Mirror* building in protest – which they did. Without getting police permission to hold up the traffic, the entire two-hundred-plus contingent marched the mile and a half down Gray's Inn Road, past the NUJ HQ, behind the union banner, to the *Mirror* office in High Holborn, where an impromptu rally was held. Foster, Foot and a few others went into reception and started haranguing any managers they could get hold of.

Now in 1994 Foster began a campaign of pressuring labour movement leaders in the TUC and the Labour Party, who had traditionally close relations with the *Mirror*, to exert their influence, but he found himself in more confrontations. In 1994 the *Mirror* sponsored a conference at the TUC called Unions 94, the launch of a 'modernising' group within the union movement, at which Tony Blair was to speak. On the stage was a sign saying 'DAILY MIRROR': the NUJ questioned the TUC as to whether, given the paper's recent track record, this was really appropriate. After much haggling, Foster was allowed to speak right after Blair and treat the audience to a rehearsal of the crimes of the sponsor. A petition was circulated, asking the *Mirror* to recognise the NUJ, which virtually everybody at the conference signed.

The next thing the *Mirror* sponsored was the excruciating 'Rolling Rose' campaign, in which a bus toured Britain to drum up support for the Labour Party. In charge was Deputy Leader John Prescott, a former trade unionist whom Foster went to see, in March 1995, to ask him to put some pressure on *Mirror* managers to talk to the unions. This might have seemed reasonable enough, but it drove Prescott to fury. According to Foster:

> He was behind a big table. He started lecturing us about trade unionism. He said, 'Wait until we are in government.' I said, 'You can do it now. You can persuade the *Mirror* to recognise the NUJ.'

NUJ leader John Foster attacks the Mirror group over its treatment of staff at a conference sponsored by the company in 1994. (Andrew Wiard)

> Prescott stood up and slammed his papers on the table. Tom Sawyer [party General Secretary] was there. Prescott said to him, 'They are trying to blackmail us.' I said, 'We are not blackmailing you – for once in your life stand up for your so-called principles.' He went spare, he shouted: 'Do what you fucking like then.' I said: 'I have been in the Labour Party for twenty-five years but if it is a choice between the Labour Party and my principles I will go for my principles.'

Foster concedes that he may not have been at his best that day; he had just heard the House of Lords judgement in the Wilson case and he was, he says, very upset. Nothing came of the meeting, nor of all the petitions or the publicity, or of the strange demonstration held at Brighton races in September 1995 when the *Mirror* sponsored a race during TUC week. The NUJ hired a pantomime horse, put a sign – 'UNION RIGHTS – THE NAG THAT WAS NOBBLED' – round its neck, and paraded it round the course.

In 2000 Turner's British Association of Journalists applied for formal recognition at the *Mirror* under the Employment Relations Act. The NUJ had at least as many members there but not enough to secure recognition, and the union agonised over how to respond. There was to be a staff ballot – how should NUJ members vote? Eventually it agreed to swallow its distaste at the BAJ's activities, to follow its own principles of union recognition and recommend a yes vote.

This magnanimity was not rewarded: following its success, the BAJ not only failed to stop further job losses but proceeded to tie up a deal that extended its representation to the *Racing Post*, a branch of the Mirror group not covered by the main agreement. The NUJ had a big majority of members there – ninety-odd out of 120 – and the BAJ had none (it did have one but he resigned, understandably reluctant to be the focus of an inter-union dispute). Management gave Turner facilities to recruit *Racing Post* staff but he failed to attract a single one, sitting alone in a room one lunchtime hoping, in vain, for takers.

Legally the NUJ could do nothing about it: it was another of the flaws in the ERA that a union such as the BAJ could get a voluntary agreement with an employer without having to have a majority of members, while another union with a high membership couldn't get it overturned.

There was a more serious instance at another national group, Rupert Murdoch's News International in Wapping. The NUJ had repeatedly warned members who went to work there that Murdoch would get rid of the unions, and by 1988 he had done so; he even rebuffed Turner, who had written offering a no-strike agreement. Instead, NI set up a News International Staff Association. This body was entirely dependent on company funding; its 'members' paid no subscriptions. In 1999 NI conducted a ballot – there were no opportunities for concerned unions to campaign against – and the NISA was approved by 1,618 votes to 588. Murdoch 'recognised' it. A General Secretary was appointed on a full-time NI salary. It could have been a joke, but for the fact that again the NUJ could not challenge it. NISA was refused a certificate of independence as a trade union, because under the ERA no union can apply for recognition when another union of whatever kind is already recognised.

The union rot had set in at Wapping in 1986 with the collaboration of the electricians' union EETPU, and in 1999 the electricians were causing problems again, this time at the Western Mail and Echo in Cardiff, the major newspaper group in Wales, which Trinity had taken over when it bought up TRN.

Managing director Mark Haysom, a former NUJ member, had decided to pre-empt the Employment Relations Act, which was just over the horizon, by installing a staff forum with just one union to represent all employees. He invited several unions to make presentations. The EETPU had by now merged with the engineering union to form the Amalgamated Engineering and Electrical Union (AEEU), and its leader Sir Ken Jackson, recently knighted by Blair, came from the old electricians' school. When the NUJ, the Graphical, Paper and Media Union and the AEEU came to make their pitches Jackson, with management complicity, landed a single-union no-strike 'partnership' agreement – a 'sweetheart' deal in the Labour movement vernacular.

The AEEU had fewer than a dozen electricians in membership at the plant, while the NUJ had around a hundred. To help the AEEU get its numbers up the company had given it free use of an office and free distribution of recruiting material – which carried the company logo. The AEEU offered free membership, and although it succeeded in meeting the target of a hundred, no journalists joined – not one. Haysom dismissed the NUJ's concerns as 'a narrow point of principle', prompting more than one journalist to respond that it was better to have a narrow principle than none at all. Now, finding themselves without their union, they were outraged.

So was the NUJ. The agreement was against TUC rules and the union lodged a formal complaint with that body, but no hearing was held. The union submitted a motion to the 1999 TUC conference calling on the AEEU to withdraw from the Cardiff deal but it was blocked by TUC officials. The fact was that the TUC was petrified that inter-union disputes could destabilise the introduction of the ERA, and the government had made it clear that it would prefer single-union deals to the 'fragmentation' that might occur if different unions tried to use the new rights to represent employees in the same workplace. Instead the TUC tried to smooth things over and bring the parties together; they invited leaders of the NUJ, GPMU and AEEU to a weekend retreat to talk things over, but Foster – whose father, ironically, had been an official in the former AEU – declined, with the memorable riposte: 'I'll sit down and negotiate with anybody but I won't sit down to dinner with a scab.'

Again, under the law, with the deal in place the NUJ was barred from going for recognition itself. The NUJ reps refused to sign the agreement and withdrew from the staff forum. But if no one else would help them they would help themselves, and in July 2002 they voted to hold a ballot

Unfair ERA

Attempts by journalists to get their union back at IPC Magazines, Britain's biggest consumer magazine publisher, fell foul of a provision in the Employment Relations Act (ERA) that sets a uniquely unfair test to determine the validity of a recognition vote.

The journalists lost their union rights in 1993 at the same time as most of the other big magazine groups, and have twice in the last few years voted in favour of getting them back: first in an unofficial opinion-testing poll by the union itself, and then in a vote agreed with management under the provisions of the ERA. Like every other NUJ chapel that has balloted on the question they voted yes by a handsome margin – 178 to 93 – but the margin was not the point. The ERA requires that the yes vote constitute more than 40 per cent of the workforce, and this vote did not.

The 40 per cent threshold exists nowhere else in law; unions have repeatedly made the point that no UK government could have taken office had the same proviso applied to electoral law, since none has ever secured the support of 40 per cent of the entire voting population. The clause was reportedly included in the Bill at a late stage, at the behest of Rupert Murdoch, but the beneficiary on this occasion was not Murdoch's News International but his mightier American rival AoL Time Warner, the world's biggest media conglomerate, which bought IPC magazines in 2002.

The magazine sector of the NUJ as a whole has not fared well in recovering from derecognition, though there was a triumphant return at Reed Business Information at Sutton, Surrey, where a record 95 per cent vote in favour of recognition was recorded. The RBI chapel had kept going throughout the years of derecognition, organising social events, raising members' problems and taking part in the company's European Works Council – an EU-instituted consultative requirement for transnational companies operating in more than one country (Reed Elsevier is half Dutch-owned). Within a year they had achieved the first £20,000 a year minimum rate in magazines in Britain.

The NUJ chapel at the Western Mail *in Cardiff, where union rights were won back in 2003 after fifteen years. (Mo Wilson)*

on strike action over their pay and conditions – and the company suddenly showed interest in what they had to say. (At the same time members of the AEEU in their leadership election booted Jackson out and elected a left-winger, Derek Simpson.) Talks went ahead with management and an NUJ house agreement was signed amid joyful celebrations in June 2003, fifteen years after TRN had annulled their last one in the great derecognition plague of the late 1980s. The chapel could justly claim: 'We have remained true to the NUJ's principles.'

PART TWO

OUR WORLD

PART OF THE MOVEMENT

Where do we fit?

Some of the founders may have thought that with the formation of the NUJ journalists were joining the wider Labour movement; at its inaugural conference in Birmingham in 1907 one of the newly born union's first acts was to send greetings to another union which was meeting in the city. But such sentiments were not universally shared. Ambivalence over perceived differences between white-collar, or 'black-coat', and industrial workers was the stumbling block, and the NUJ hesitated before forging formal links with other unions.

Relations with other unions have, at times, been strained. This has been due, in part, to the tensions between journalists who see themselves as professionals, and other media unions who have thought journalists unwilling to act as industrial unionists. Such episodes as the General Strike of 1926 and the Wapping dispute sixty years later saw the NUJ divided over whether or not to support the printers' unions, and played a part in preventing the amalgamation of the NUJ and the print union the National Graphical Association in the 1980s – indeed, such divisions surfaced again in the virtual warfare between the two unions over the introduction of new technology during that decade.

Chapels: It's very old hat

NUJ office branches have always been called 'chapels'. The term was inherited from the printing unions, and many people have assumed that it has a religious origin – from eighteenth-century English Methodism, perhaps? *The Oxford English Dictionary* gives this definition:

> **chapel**: a printer's workshop, a printing office; a meeting or association of journeymen in a printing office for promoting and enforcing order among themselves, settling disputes as to the price of work etc. It is presided over by a Father of Chapel, annually elected.

NUJ chapel that meets in a chapel: journalists at the Open University in Milton Keynes use the converted chapel at Walton Hall for their meetings. (John Harris/Reportdigital)

The earliest-known reference is from 1683, in Joseph Moxon's *Mechanic Exercises on the Whole Art of Printing*, which says: 'Every printing house is termed a chapel.' Yet this was a hundred years before Methodism, practised in Wesleyan chapels, was to figure centre stage in the early stirrings of the trade union movement.

It has also been suggested that the term derives from the origins of printing, from links between William Caxton, the first British printer, and the Church. Caxton began printing in Westminster in 1475; it used to be thought that he set up his press inside the Abbey – now known not to have been so. But Nigel Roche, press historian and curator of the St Bride's Printing Museum just off Fleet Street in central London, maintains that 'chapel' has nothing to do with religion but comes from the French for hat, *chapeau*, variously derived as cap, capel or chapel. Printers made hats from folded paper, possibly to keep their hair from catching in the machines. So this union tradition may not be ritualistic, but practical, relating to health and safety in the workplace – to the essence of trade unionism, in fact.

These tensions began to emerge early. Soon after the NUJ's foundation, some of its leading figures began to argue that the union should seek closer formal links with the printing unions, and in particular with their umbrella organisation, the Printing and Kindred Trades Federation. The PKTF had been founded in the early 1890s and established as a national organisation in 1901. Its constitution sought to ally the various printing unions in pursuit of improved pay and conditions, but also called for strikes to be prevented wherever possible – disputes to be settled through negotiation.

Henry Richardson, who would become the union's second General Secretary, was an early advocate of closer links with the print unions. At the annual conference in 1913, it was agreed to approach three of them – the Typographical Association, representing provincial printers; the London Society of Compositors; and the Scottish Typographical Association – over a possible formal relationship.

Richardson's argument would be echoed by many NUJ leaders over the next seven decades: for a journalists' union to succeed in winning improved pay and conditions, it would have to enjoy the support of workers with real muscle – the printers. Put more bluntly, and in terms of industrial muscle, a printers' strike could stop a newspaper from appearing; the fledgling NUJ – at that time numbering fewer than four thousand members – did not have that kind of power. Such arguments were also apparent to the printers, and it is probably not surprising that at the 1914 ADM it was reported that the TA (16,000-strong) and the LSC (12,000) had rejected any binding agreement with the journalists.

It was not until after the First World War that external pressures led to change. Just before the Armistice in November 1918, the NUJ, the PKTF and the newspaper proprietors began to discuss setting up a Whitley council for the newspaper industry.[1] When news reached NUJ members that the Institute of Journalists was hoping to join the proposed new council, it galvanised opinion, and at the union's annual delegate meeting in 1919 it was agreed that a ballot should be held on joining the PKTF. It was duly held, in the early summer.[2] Affiliation was supported by 1,192 votes to 192, and the NUJ became a member of the Printing and Kindred Trades Federation in July 1919. It was a lasting relationship: the PKTF was eventually dissolved in 1974, after print union mergers in the 1960s and 1970s effectively removed its rationale. Instead, the TUC set up the Printing Industries Committee, which proved useful during the Wapping dispute but folded in the 1990s.[3]

Brothers and sisters – the union joins the TUC

The decision to affiliate to the PKTF removed many of the objections within the NUJ to joining the Trades Union Congress. Many NUJ members – in the Parliamentary branch, for example – had argued that as journalists it would be inappropriate for their union to affiliate to the TUC, given its links with the infant Labour Party. But such reservations had dwindled, and the 1920 ADM resolved to hold a union-wide ballot. Members decided, by 1,380 to 816, that the union should embrace TUC membership. A number of Parliamentary branch members resigned – some working for Conservative- or Liberal-supporting newspapers, others on principle.

The union's first motion to a TUC conference – that of 1920 in Portsmouth – was an attempt to stop trade union and other Labour leaders writing for newspapers (and being paid for it), rather than being interviewed by journalists. TUC feathers were ruffled, and the NUJ's motion was referred for consideration. The new-found spirit of comradeship was also strained when John Bromley, secretary of the train drivers' union ASLEF, commented:

> It is necessary for every trade unionist at this Congress to put up with the general misrepresentation, vilification and abuse of the capitalistic press. We understand it. We know, unfortunately, that the brains of the members of the Journalists' Union here are bought and paid for to be used against members of their own class.

NUJ members reporting the conference were sufficiently angered by this to protest. The *Journalist* reported 'No apology was made either then or later. More will be heard of the matter in the future.'

The *Daily Herald*

The *Daily Herald*, founded in 1912, followed one of the most astonishing trajectories of any British newspaper. It began life as radical and pro-trade union, and ended by changing its name, and ultimately its political allegiance, when it became the *Sun* and was taken over by Rupert Murdoch.

The *Herald* had a daily circulation of nearly 250,000 by the First World War, but then suffered a drop in sales not unconnected with its anti-war editorials, and briefly became a weekly. In 1922 when it was taken over by the TUC, sales began to rise, though its editor Hamilton Fyfe resigned in 1926 after rows with the TUC leadership over what he saw as their attempts to control the paper. But financial problems led to the TUC ceding its running to Odhams Press. In the early 1930s the *Herald* became the world's best-selling daily, with sales of over two million. But it failed to maintain its competitiveness in the face of challenges from Fleet Street's circulation-boosting strategies. The TUC relinquished its 51 per cent stake and Odhams was acquired by the publishers of the *Daily Mirror*.

Faced with mounting losses, in 1964, the *Herald* was transformed into an experimental daily, the *Sun*, 'a paper born of the age we live in' as its publicity proclaimed. But it still lost money, and in 1969 was sold – with the print unions agreeing to favourable manning levels – to the Australian publisher Rupert Murdoch. Its transformation into a populist down-market right-wing tabloid helped lay the fortunes not only of Murdoch's British newspaper empire but also of Margaret Thatcher, whose Tory policies it enthusiastically endorsed in the 1980s.

The *Journalist* was right. Within two years of voting to join the TUC, NUJ members voted to pull out. The volte-face came at a moment of particular embarrassment for the NUJ: the decision as to whether or not to support a struggling newspaper – the *Daily Herald*, which had strong links to Labour and the unions and was in the financial doldrums. At the 1923 ADM, the South Wales branch, which earlier had been a strong supporter of TUC membership, submitted a motion urging withdrawal: 'It is inimical to the interests of the Union, and derogatory to our professional standing that journalists collectively should be identified with the interests of any particular newspaper, and with the opinions and policy which it maintains on subjects of public controversy.'

The motion was carried, and in a subsequent ballot NUJ members voted by 943 to 802 to withdraw. It would be seventeen years before the union rejoined – a period during which the General Strike would strain relationships with other unions too. But eventually, the tide of opinion turned. In 1939 NUJ members voted in favour of rejoining the TUC – by 2,050 to 1,376 – but fell just short of the required three-fifths majority. The next year, amid general moves for national unity, the membership voted again, this time by 1,946 to 865, and the union was back in the fold. This time, it stayed.

The General Strike

The General Strike of May 1926 highlighted the differences in outlook within the union. 'The field of battle is no longer transport, but news,' Winston Churchill, then a leading figure in Stanley Baldwin's Conservative government, was soon to declare, and certainly the dispute put journalists under the pressures of contending loyalties.

The strike had its origins in the conflict within the coal industry that followed the First World War. A full-scale pit dispute was seen by many as inevitable once the wartime state subsidies ended, and the government began to plan for the maintenance of transport and supplies if other unions joined in. By April 1926, government plans were well ahead. The TUC, by contrast, was poorly prepared. Even so, by 29 April its General Council was given authority by more than 140 member unions to call a national strike if the miners were locked out for refusing to accept pay cuts.

Crucially for many NUJ members, the General Strike – when it came just a few days later – was triggered by a newspaper stoppage. Early in the morning of Monday 3 May, a TUC delegation went to Downing Street, expecting to meet ministers for talks on the coal crisis. Instead, they found only Baldwin, who told them negotiations were over. Print workers at the *Daily Mail* had refused to set an anti-union leading article, 'For King and

Country'. For Baldwin, that was 'gross interference with the freedom of the Press' and 'a challenge to the constitutional rights and freedom of the nation'. Clement Bundock, the NUJ's General Secretary during 1937–52, wrote in his 1958 history of the National Union of Printing, Bookbinding and Paper Workers: 'The [print workers'] action was unofficial. It was a spontaneous gesture by indignant men against a ridiculous distortion of the situation. But it was sufficient for the Government.'[4] For many NUJ members, however, aversion to a newspaper stoppage outweighed their sense of solidarity with other trade unionists.

Being now outside the TUC, the NUJ was not officially involved in the strike. Nor was it in any way prepared. Bundock, then the full-time national organiser, was on a train at Carlisle when the crew walked off. It took him two days to get back to London by hired car. General Secretary Richardson called an emergency meeting of those executive members able to get to London. Telegrams were sent to the branches, emphasising that the NUJ was not on strike and that members should continue to work normally. But, it added, they should not do the work of others – effectively, the printers – or work with anyone brought in to replace them. Next day Richardson elaborated this message in a circular to the branches, adding that NUJ members should not work on 'makeshift' papers.

Within days the NUJ was split. Richardson and his colleagues in London were assailed by dissenting telegrams. Frederick Mansfield, who was against the strike, wrote that a 'terrific rumpus spread among the branches, and news of conflicting decisions was sent out almost hourly by the Agencies to the Press at large. Friends of the union were dismayed: enemies rejoiced.' When the NUJ Parliamentary branch declared its intention of repudiating any call to withdraw labour, its statement was reported on the BBC – possibly the union's first mention over the airwaves – and in the government's *British Gazette*, a widely derided propaganda paper edited by Churchill.

The attitude of many journalists may have been expressed by Arthur Christiansen, at the time a freelance sub-editor but later to become a legendary editor of the *Daily Express*. In his autobiography he wrote:

> I had given my situation much thought, since I had been a
> probationary member of the National Union of Journalists at the
> age of sixteen and active in the Liverpool branch in a campaign to
> secure votes for the under-twenty-ones. But the union's attitude to
> the General Strike was confused: first-we-could-and-then-we-could-

Workers reading one of the many publications produced during the General Strike. (Hulton Getty)

not about summed up instructions from our headquarters. I was not prepared to be mucked about, so I resigned from the union – I never rejoined it – and carried on with my job.

The *Express* was a particular embarrassment to the NUJ. After the General Strike ended – with the decision by the TUC leaders to call it off after a week – the paper attacked the union in an editorial that boasted of its success in maintaining production throughout:

> What of those junior members of the editorial staff who were members of the National Union of Journalists? Supposing their union issued orders? It did – and the Union collapsed like a house of cards. Without an exception, every member of the editorial staff volunteered for any task to keep their paper on the street. There was only one loyalty: there could be only one – the *Daily Express*.

Express editorial hyperbole notwithstanding, there is no doubt that many NUJ members were opposed to their union leadership's instructions. Faced with numerous protests, then realising that many papers were appearing in 'makeshift' emergency formats – some as simple duplicated sheets – the executive issued new instructions three days into the strike, that members could work on makeshift papers where they were being produced by labour that could not permanently replace printers who were in dispute.

Some journalists, of course, strongly supported the General Strike and the union's initial instructions. Some lost their jobs as a result – in Dundee the D. C. Thomson company became a strictly non-union workplace. Some helped produce papers supporting the strike. Fenner Brockway, later an MP and a leading figure on Labour's left, edited the northern edition of the TUC's *British Worker*, recording in his diary that he got no support from local NUJ officials in Manchester. And there were many members who saw the strike as an opportunity to support the wider union movement.

At a stormy meeting of the Central London branch, Tom Foster, now the union's Treasurer, replied to the criticism that the strike was 'against the nation' by asking: 'And isn't the lock-out of a million miners against the nation?' Much criticism of other unions was due to 'snobbishness', he continued. 'Journalists had an idea that the modern newspaper industry was built up on the product of their brain alone. In reality, it would not be possible without the trade union labour of other departments. The journalist was no more than a cog in a great wheel.' Also at that meeting, Richardson took on his critics:

> Some journalists took the view that nothing would justify a stoppage of the newspapers. If the Union believed that, it is an invitation for the employers to ask for a reduction in salaries.

The compromise over producing makeshift papers – and the quick end to the General Strike – prevented further divisions. Two NEC members (both from Scotland) resigned, but at a special NUJ conference in July 1926 motions of censure upon the executive and the General Secretary were defeated amid a general mood to sink political differences.

Honouring a principle

There was no edition of the *Journalist* in July 1959. There was no edition in August, either. The reason was a nationwide strike for improved pay and conditions by ten printing unions against the Newspaper Society and the British Federation of Master Printers that stopped production of many of the country's local newspapers and periodicals. Some hundred thousand employees and nearly a thousand newspapers were affected. Jim Bradley, then the union's General Secretary, commented: 'Since the NUJ

Political independence

Although it has been embedded in the TUC since 1940, the union
is still ambivalent about its political role in the Labour movement.
While there could never be any question of affiliating to the Labour
Party, as many – though by no means all – unions do, there has been
a running debate on what else it might support. Even unions not
linked to Labour have had 'political funds' that have allowed them to
undertake 'political' activities, essentially defined by UK law as relating
to political parties (otherwise, such activities would be unlawful). There
have been running attempts by the NUJ leadership to get such a fund
established – in 1981, 1984, 1988 and 2003 – but all came to nothing.

*Anita Halpin, third of three woman Presidents, who was also the union's first
member of the TUC General Council. (John Harris/IFL)*

The first attempt was made when the ADM wanted to forge a link
with the Campaign for Nuclear Disarmament and lawyers advised that
such a step would require a political fund. A membership ballot had to
be held, and the motion was defeated by a 2:1 majority. In 1984 a move
to get the ADM to add 'political' objects to the union's aims as set out
in the rule book was thrown out. Then the 1988 conference proposed
to hold another ballot on the same issue, but it never took place – the

NEC decided it was going to lose and ignored it. In 2002 the ADM told them to have another go; this time a ballot did take place but again members turned the motion down, albeit more narrowly.

Journalists prize their union's political independence and in the main have been suspicious of the motivation behind such moves. The new General Secretary, Jeremy Dear, has personally supported linking with Labour but stated that he was neither advocating nor anticipating such an eventuality.

Within the TUC, however, the NUJ's position improved; though a small union with a reputation for rocking the boat, it won the movement's backing for a range of policies on broadcasting and the handling of official information – and most importantly, after the long struggle in the 1990s, for the reform of employment law to guarantee the right of unions to represent their members. That was the triumph of General Secretary John Foster, but he never succeeded in his repeated attempts to win a seat on the TUC General Council. NUJ Treasurer Anita Halpin (in 1999) and Dear (in 2002) did so, becoming the first journalists ever to join the highest body in the UK Labour movement. In Ireland, NUJ leaders had been on the executive of the Irish Congress of Trade Unions since the 1980s.

was founded fifty-two years ago, there has been no event in our industry comparable to the seven-week printing stoppage.'

Like the General Strike of 1926 the dispute was a test of the unity of the NUJ and in particular of its members' attitudes towards other unions when employers tried to produce papers while printers were on strike. As Bradley put it:

A fundamental point of principle arose. The union was not a party to the dispute but it could not insulate members from it. As a trade union and as a member of the PKTF since 1919 the only honourable course was to behave as a union and a member of the Federation. In short, it could only instruct members to do their normal work unless 'black' labour was introduced, at which point it had to say: 'We cannot co-operate.'

Again, as in 1926, the union had tried to engineer an agreement whereby journalists could work on duplicated papers to enable newspapers to maintain a public presence. Where managements decided to produce full strikebreaking editions and journalists were threatened with the sack if they did not cooperate, the NUJ's response was to order its members out. Most obeyed the call, but some did not. Among those papers where members were split were the *Derby Evening Telegraph*, the *Birmingham Post* and *Evening Mail*, the three dailies in Bristol, the *Yorkshire Post* and the *Evening Post* in Leeds and the *Bradford Telegraph and Argus*. In many offices there were strained relations between NUJ members who had risked their jobs to support the printers and members of the IoJ who had worked on. There were also strains within the union, with differences over the £30,000 it had cost to pay members called out on strike and freelances who withheld copy from strike-hit papers, but resignations were relatively few. There was general relief that the dispute had not done greater damage – in fact, the union's stance was largely endorsed by its members.

The print unions acknowledged the support the NUJ had given. For Bradley, this was 'the outstanding lesson of the dispute. NUJ members, when called upon to honour a fundamental trade union principle, responded.' He added: 'Proof of the existence of a large corps of dedicated trade unionists will be of the utmost importance in the history of the NUJ. It shows to other unionists that white-collar workers are not simply fair weather theorists. It has demonstrated the same truth to employers.'

The next year, on 17 October 1960 – which the *Journalist* called 'the blackest day in British newspaper history' – came a newspaper closure that brought the role of the print unions for the first time into public debate. The liberal-leaning *News Chronicle* and its sister London evening paper the *Star* were taken over by the Conservative-supporting Daily Mail group. Some 3,500 jobs – three hundred of them journalists' – were lost in London and Manchester. For years the death of the *News Chronicle* – often referred to as the 'murder' of a newspaper – was seen by many journalists as a particular blow to the diversity of the British press. James Cameron, one of the great reporters of his generation, wrote: 'For the trade of journalism, the writing is no longer in the column, but on the wall.' Most commentators were critical of the *Chronicle*'s management, but there were also voices arguing that both papers had suffered from restrictive practices insisted on by the unions. *The Murder of the News Chronicle and The Star*, a pamphlet by Edward Martell and Ewan Butler of the right-wing National Fellowship, blamed overmanning and high wage demands acceded to by weak management – a charge of which much more was to be heard.

Technology and the unions: a less than golden era

A lot of journalists in the late 1980s thought the advent of computerised setting would make them kings of the castle: when their own work went directly into a system that could be converted into print without having to be input again they would have control of production and could command their price. This was a popular view on national newspapers, where journalists had watched in awe as the printers had exercised their industrial muscle to screw colossal payments out of the owners. The compositors at least, the elite of the trade, earned a lot more than the journalists, and journalists said to themselves, 'We wouldn't mind some of that.'

The view was best articulated by Steve Turner, leader of the NUJ closed shop at the *Daily Mirror* in the 1980s, who was briefly NUJ General Secretary after winning an election in 1990 on the platform of leading journalists into a 'golden era' of industrial power. Turner regarded printers with disdain, as dinosaurs. 'We are the masters now' was the message. It was just a dream.

If there was one episode that symbolised the effect on journalists of the industrial changes then taking place, it was the traumatic NUJ chapel meeting at the *Sun* on Friday 24 January 1986, the eve of the Wapping dispute. General Secretary Harry Conroy – the man who four years later would lose his job to Turner – tried to persuade members to resist

Steve Turner, NUJ General Secretary for just under a year before being sacked in 1991. (John Gladwin)

management blandishments to make the big move. He had a rough ride. The journalists had been told by editor Kelvin MacKenzie that they now had the whip hand: the print unions, he had said, were 'screwed'. 'But once they have finished with the printers they will come for you,' Conroy told them, to which the members replied that they would have the power of the printers because they would control input. Conroy countered: 'The printers had the power not because they had their hands on the keyboard but because they were prepared to take their hands *off* the keyboard.'

The journalists, of course, ignored him, took Rupert Murdoch's money and went to Wapping – all but six of them. Far from exercising power, they had betrayed their weakness. If they were really going to behave like print unions, they wouldn't have gone. Murdoch couldn't produce his papers without them.

Conroy was shaken by the confrontation. His mission as General Secretary was to bring the unions together, right across the media, to forge a common front against the effects of technology – not just so as to smooth its arrival with the minimum disruption and loss of jobs, but to establish a united workforce for the coming convergence of disparate elements of the industry.

In Fleet Street, now near the end of the road as a centre for newspaper production, it was not a case of the owners rushing in new equipment to get rid of workers – far from it. Technically, it would have been possible ten years earlier to produce a national paper at much reduced cost, using new technology, but employers and unions had combined to prevent it. If the unions had cooperated then it would have opened up the market to competitors that would have destroyed the publishers' cartel. The apparently grasping behaviour of the print unions, much cited as the cause and even the justification of their demise, did not take place entirely in opposition to managements but often with their connivance. The newspapers presented it as extortion by the unions, but they were their employers, after all.

As John Foster, General Secretary after Turner, puts it: 'They say there was corruption in Fleet Street, with the overmanning and overpayment. But who was paying the cheques? The employers were paying the cheques because they colluded with the unions to stop others breaking into the market and keep the industry under control.' Ken Morgan, his predecessor in the 1970s, says the same was true then: 'Unions were not the only people seeking a closed shop. Employers wanted to put the pressure on other proprietors. It sounds like a myth – "it's not our fault, guv. The employers keep throwing money at us" – but there is a serious element of truth in it.'

Computers had been brought into provincial offices with much less hullabaloo, though there were disputes that were almost as bitter as the one at Wapping. All involved the NUJ, which generally gave such support to the print unions as it could, to alleviate the damage. Journalists had even been on strike in solidarity with their printers. 1980 saw a national dispute between the National Graphical Association and the Newspaper Society in which a number of NUJ chapels came out in support. Then in 1982–3 came the momentous clash at the Stockport Messenger group where Eddie Shah took on the NGA by setting and printing his weeklies without them, and NUJ members not only came out in solidarity but sacrificed their own jobs. The dispute flared up into the first violent industrial confrontations of the Thatcher period, with police charging mass pickets at Shah's Warrington plant. Shah liked to present himself as a buccaneering maverick; in fact he was used by the big groups as a stalking horse, taking the flak in the first skirmishes so as to soften the unions up. When in 1986 he launched his national paper *Today*, he found his one-time supporters on Fleet Street quickly became hostile competitors.

From the late 1970s the union was aware of what might be coming and prepared itself as well as it could. The conference of 1977 set up the ADM Committee on Technology which produced an authoritative and well received booklet, *Journalists and New Technology*, and a policy that included a crucial determination that held throughout the coming crises: NUJ members would not take over any extra work unless it had been ceded by the union concerned.

It had been NUJ policy since 1974 to aim for a single media union. Preliminary discussions had taken place with all the printers and with the two broadcasting unions as well – the Association of Broadcasting Staffs at the BBC and the Association of Cinematographic and Television Technicians (the latter, commercial; the two later merged). In 1979 the union took the plunge and embarked on negotiations with the most powerful of all, the NGA, representing the compositors who set the type, the printing machine managers and the proofreaders: a craft union with centuries of tradition and the superior attitudes derived from immense industrial clout. Whether the NUJ was going to inherit its power or not, the NGA wasn't about to surrender it without a fight.

There followed three rancorous years, as two polar opposites of the trade union movement struggled to find common ground. The NUJ in its democratic way had elected an Amalgamation Working Party for the talks: three women and three men, among them some of the most forceful radical activists such as Barbara Gunnell and Aidan White, and a representative of the Equality Council to make sure women members' interests were safeguarded. The NGA fielded a team of officials led by their abrasive Assistant General Secretary Tony Dubbins, an alpha male of the movement. There was barely an available common language, let alone a meeting of minds.

'The talks were just awful,' says Gunnell. 'I knew, we all knew I am sure, that they were going to break down. The NGA didn't understand journalists even though they had spent years working with them.' They were 'a farce', says Jake Ecclestone, the NUJ's Deputy General Secretary. 'Dubbins and co. behaved with such arrogance. They weren't interested in a marriage – rather, an abduction.' 'It was clear that for it to work journalists required a far greater commitment to change from the printers than they could give,' says White more diplomatically.

The NGA's policy was to 'follow the work'. If inputting was to move from compositors to journalists, then comps would become sub-editors and the NGA would represent them. 'They thought that typesetters could become subs overnight and that our members would accept that,' says Gunnell. 'They thought we would lie down and abandon our members in those jobs. The NGA's ideas of continuing to run the industry were grandiose and overblown.' In the discussions on the shape a joint union would take it soon became clear that the NUJ's democratic practice was incomprehensible to the printers. 'Despite a need to be civil,' says Gunnell, 'it was obvious that they thought some of us ludicrously liberal and flaky. Their strength had been in being rigid and disciplined.'

This view of the NGA is held by a union official who knew them at first hand: Barry Fitzpatrick became a full-time organiser for the NUJ in 2002 and is a former Father of Chapel in the clerical union NATSOPA at *The Times*. 'The print unions did not regard the NUJ as trade unionists,' he says, 'especially the NGA. They had no concept of anyone else's point of view. It was all about rigid obedience to the rules. They could not accept democracy, they saw it as anarchy.' The NGA couldn't accept, either, the idea of an annual conference or the right of all members to speak and vote at branch meetings, but the manifestation of NUJ democracy they found most baffling was the independent editorship of the *Journalist*. The NGA's journal was edited by the General Secretary, and that's how it would remain.

The attempt to merge the two unions finally disintegrated in a seven-hour debate at the NUJ ADM at Dundee in 1983. But the talks had already broken down in acrimony – within the NUJ as much as across the bargaining table. The NGA had had enough of the Amalgamation Working Party. It broke off the talks and announced that in future it would talk only to the NUJ executive. There were those in the NUJ leadership who would have been happy with that. General Secretary Ken Ashton led a move for the NEC take over the talks, but it failed at a fraught NEC meeting by just one vote.

So when it came to Dundee, the issue to be decided was: who should represent the NUJ in the talks? Perhaps unsurprisingly, since the ADM had appointed them in the first place, the conference overwhelmingly backed the AWP – and that was the end of the road, as Dubbins, who was invited to speak, made quite clear. 'The NUJ sought to amalgamate for the prime purpose of creating a union that would have the industrial power not possessed [at present by] the NUJ,' he said. 'It is in the NUJ's interest to ensure that in a new structure … the existing power of the NGA vis a vis employers is not diminished. We have spent many hours talking about democracy … but once democracy inhibits the ability to make decisions and act resolutely it becomes a handicap.'

His words, the *Journalist* reported, 'fell on deaf ears.' But the conference vote was not really about who should talk to whom: it was a recognition that no deal could be reached. Any agreement would have had to be approved by a vote of the full NUJ membership, and there was little chance of anything the NGA wanted being approved. 'We know what our members would say,' said White. 'They would vote against it in their thousands and their tens of thousands.' In fact, it's questionable whether any deal with any print union would have cleared a vote of NUJ members.

As White explains it:

> The difficulty was the professional edge to the NUJ's work,
> which meant we were different. It would have required a greater
> commitment to change from the printers than they could give.
> The journalists' place in the industry needed to be autonomous
> because we had to protect what we were doing – the independence

of our work. And that was something the printers could not accept.
Journalists' strength depends on their identity. Without it the
journalists' union and community would disappear. That had to be
protected.

White says he only really understood this after the talks had broken
down; but the bulk of NUJ members have known it instinctively for a
hundred years.

Conflict and resolution

In the outside world, meanwhile, employers were wheeling in the
computers, and in the wake of the merger debacle there followed a
couple of years of bloody conflict between the two unions. In 1984 a new
technology agreement was reached at the *Portsmouth News* that allowed
compositors to 'follow the job' on to the subs' desks and retain their representation by the NGA, which would have full bargaining rights in the
editorial area. The deal had actually been approved by two NUJ officials,
Mike Smith and Gary Morton, who were sympathetic to the NGA, but
the Portsmouth chapel, up in arms, affirmed (with official union support)
that their members would not sub on screen until the chapel itself had
come to an agreement on the issue. The first member ordered by management to do so refused and the chapel walked out and staff were suspended.
'It was the NUJ versus the management, abetted by the NGA,' says Ecclestone, who had been placed in charge of the dispute. 'It was an organised
attack on us.'

Management was certainly stirring divisions between the unions for
all it was worth. NGA staff, three of whom had crossed into editorial jobs,
crossed the Portsmouth NUJ picket line. NUJ members in other papers
in the group, on the *Sunderland Echo*, *Hartlepool Evening Mail* and *Croydon
Advertiser*, held mandatory chapel meetings and were suspended as well. It
took four months to get the company to come to an agreement that the
NUJ should represent all editorial staff. It looked as if Portsmouth was the
NGA's revenge, and an article in the *Journalist* from a supporter of amalgamation said that after the breakdown the NGA had 'no choice but to
gatecrash the editorial floor'.

The NUJ made a crucial decision when the ADM in 1985 agreed that
if no agreement were reached with the NGA at a newspaper, the jour-

nalists there would undertake 'direct input'. Then, while the Portsmouth dispute was still ongoing, came the bloodiest fight of all, at the *Wolverhampton Express and Star* where in 1980 NUJ members had come out in solidarity with the NGA in a national dispute. Now it was the turn of the NUJ, or some within it, to seek revenge for the NGA's present stance. The NGA were involved in a disagreement at Wolverhampton over computer input in the tele-ad department that had led to seventy-five members being sacked. At the same time, the NUJ chapel there was starting talks on a technology agreement. Taking over the negotiations, Ecclestone quickly arrived at an agreement that gave the NUJ everything it wanted, including handsome rewards for working on screen. The NGA were locked out and NUJ members began to cross the picket line.

There was outrage, not just from the NGA, whose leaders had been nurturing a profound distaste for the NUJ's number two – but from some in the NUJ chapel. 'What we did was shoddy and contemptible,' one member wrote to the *Journalist*. 'Jake let it be known at a chapel meeting that he was very anxious to reach a deal so he could show the NGA that the NUJ would fight back [after the Portsmouth affair].' Miles Barter of the Birmingham branch, who became a full-time NUJ official in Manchester, wrote of the 'suicidal macho posturing of the NUJ and NGA leaderships'. At the time there was an election under way for the NUJ's top job and Ecclestone was running for General Secretary on a 'bash the NGA' platform (it didn't work – he came third).

Ecclestone remains unrepentant about the Wolverhampton deal:

> The management invited us to a dinner at the Savoy, and we
> sketched out an agreement on new technology. We had warned
> the NGA that if they played silly buggers with us, we'd know what
> to do: unless they backed off [at Portsmouth] we would have no
> option but to defend our members. The deal at the *Express and Star*
> was a turning point in the whole business of new technology – it
> demonstrated that the NUJ was needed more than the NGA. In
> six months the whole of the relationship between the NUJ and the
> NGA had turned. It was an extraordinary turn of events, given the
> previous half-century. The little boy–big boy relationship was over
> … As a result a great many NGA members lost their jobs, which was
> pretty awful.

It was a similar story at the *Kent Messenger* in Maidstone, which engineered a dispute with the NGA, introduced computers and sacked the

Jake Ecclestone, Deputy General Secretary from 1981 to 1997. (Andrew Wiard / Report)

printers. The NGA appealed for support and the NUJ tried to give it. The NEC issued repeated instructions to members to respect the NGA picket lines, and loyal chapel members did; but most did not and the dispute was lost.

It was clear to everyone that this could not go on. Conroy, now General Secretary, immediately moved to restore good relations with the NGA. A worried TUC called an urgent meeting to sort the two unions out. Here was an old-fashioned union turf war – a novelty for the NUJ but bread and butter for the TUC, which sorted it out in short order.

> It was getting very very bad [says Conroy]. People were bellowing and shouting across the table at each other, accusing them of stealing jobs. It didn't look as if it was going to get anywhere. The talks lasted from 10 a.m. to 1.30 the next morning. Afterwards we went for a drink and it almost broke up in fisticuffs. Dubbins was telling Jake that he if didn't shut his mouth he would shut it for him.

But the outcome was positive. After a year of bloodshed the NUJ and NGA reached an 'Accord' that came near to satisfying both sides. NGA members could 'follow the job' and would become NUJ members, but carry on paying their dues to the NGA for a time. Inputting contributed material and page make-up remained with the NGA. There must be no

Gary Morton, national organiser for provincial newspapers during the recognition disputes of 1989–90. (Bob Gannon)

compulsory redundancies, and all new technology deals must be agreed by both unions. Quite a number of NGA members came across and several became Fathers of NUJ chapels, bringing experience of 'serious' trade unionism, among them Paul Holleran of the *Rutherglen Reformer* in Glasgow, who became chair of the NUJ Scottish Council and the union's national organiser for Scotland.[5]

'The Accord was the most important thing I did as General Secretary,' Conroy says. Now officials of both unions set off around Britain negotiating new technology agreements, with little difficulty; in fact the officials who handled most of them – Gary Morton, the NUJ provincial newspapers organiser, and his NGA counterpart Bob Tomlins – worked together well. In four years they notched up more than a hundred deals, winning the terms of the Accord as well as substantial pay increases. Companies were happy to pay up: to them, getting rid of the NGA would be worth it. Morton concedes: 'Yes, it was blood money. We knew that and the NGA knew that. But the members took the money.' In some cases, notably at the TRN and Northcliffe groups, new technology payments were made at the same time as payments for personal contracts.[6]

Heartened by this success, Conroy moved on to fulfil his dream of the single media union. For all that he liked to conduct himself, and be seen, as an old-fashioned union baron he had a clear vision of the tech-

Robohack, a prophetic fantasy to illustrate the multi-skilled journalist of the future, was created for the Journalist *by photographer/montage artist John Harris in 1993.*

nological future. Under the headline 'All Our Tomorrows' the *Journalist* in December 1988 front-paged a Conroy prophecy: 'The journalist of the future will carry a still camera in one hand, a video camera in the other, a tape recorder in the pocket and a notebook somewhere else.' It was not appreciated then that one device might perform all these functions, but the point that multiskilled work would blur traditional craft distinctions was spot on. The single union was Conroy's solution.

The first step in his plan was to merge not with a British union but with the Irish Print Union, a small but strong – and wealthy – organisation representing printworkers on Dublin daily papers, which looked across the sea and saw its future as uncertain. 'The plan was to merge with the IPU,' Conroy explains, 'that BETA and ACTT [the broadcast unions] would merge, the NUJ would join with them, the NGA and SOGAT would merge and then we would all join up.'

Conroy himself was, he says, 'the linchpin of the whole thing. At that time there were quarterly meetings of all the five UK unions, which had never happened before, to discuss common policy. I chaired all the meetings. When I left the room to go to the lavvy the meetings stopped because no one trusted anyone else.'

Everything was mapped out like a military campaign; but as soldiers like to say, no battle plan survives contact with the enemy, and this one went wrong from the first shot. An agreement was reached to merge with the IPU – crucially, without an NUJ membership ballot, which would have been unlikely to produce a positive vote; it was called a 'transfer of undertakings'. But the Irish government stepped in and said it was illegal to transfer the assets of an Irish union to a British organisation. The IPU appealed and won at the Irish Supreme Court, but by then Conroy had been voted out of office, Turner had taken over on his 'stop the mergers' platform, the IPU had become disenchanted and reversed their decision and so the whole edifice collapsed. The NUJ, though, maintained its regular contacts with the broadcasting unions – who merged to form BECTU in 1991 – through the Federation of Entertainment Unions.

The NEC sacked Turner over a calamitous intervention in the merger process. His election had been so contentious that it had taken six months of fraught negotiating to get him into the job. The executive, anxious to stop him derailing the plan, won his agreement that he would confine his campaigning within the union. Turner promptly wrote to the IPU in Dublin to tell them there would be no merger because he was going to get the issue put to a vote of NUJ members and it would be defeated; small wonder the IPU lost interest. But the NEC wouldn't tolerate any more of this internal disruption, and kicked him out after less than a year in office. He sued the union, accepting a settlement of £66,500. He also bid for reinstatement to the job at the 1992 ADM – and failed – despite offering to return the compensation.[7]

It may seem ironic that in 1985, when it really mattered, NUJ members voted for Conroy, with his vision of a single media union, above Turner and Ecclestone; then five years later for Turner, known for his hostility to mergers and his vision of a 'golden era', above Conroy. Neither dream stood any chance of becoming reality, but by 1990 it was all over anyway. The print unions were broken. To try and pool their strength, in 1991 the NGA and SOGAT merged to form the Graphical, Paper and Media Union, and in 2004 the GPMU, with membership dwindling, was swallowed up by the giant union Amicus. For the first time in hundreds of years there was no dedicated guild or union for printers in Britain.

It's hard to see what more the NUJ could have done to help their print colleagues get through the calamity of direct input. Nothing could have stopped it happening and, Wolverhampton apart, the NUJ has reason to believe it conducted itself well. But as Barry Fitzpatrick sums up: 'The print unions squandered the solidarity of the NUJ.'

RSI: a plague in our houses

The union prepared carefully for the introduction of computers into newsrooms in the 1980s. All aspects of workplace agreements and working practices were covered. But one thing took it by surprise: a plague of cases of repetitive strain injury (RSI) that swept through some offices leaving hundreds of journalists in constant pain, many for life; for some their careers were ruined. The union sought to bring legal cases on behalf of some of them against their employers for personal injury, a strategy that led to catastrophe.

Reuters sub-editor Rafiq Mughal brought the union's first losing case for compensation for his repetitive strain injury in 1993. (Jez Coulson)

Two major test cases were mounted: the first, for Rafiq Mughal, a sub at Reuters. After twenty-three years working in national newsrooms he was suffering so badly that his wrists were permanently in splints and he could barely move his arms. After a ten-day trial at the High Court in 1993 the case crashed, with Judge John Prosser saying: 'Psychological factors lie at the root of his problems, nothing to do with an injury caused by his employment.' The judge earned a certain notoriety for his remark that RSI sufferers were 'eggshell personalities' whose suffering was imaginary. One union journal ran a competition for limericks beginning 'There once was a judge called Prosser'. Most of the entries were unprintable.

The union then had seventy legal cases in the queue, which it pledged to bring on. Behind the scenes the lawyers were worried, and the cases were whittled down to a handful on the *Financial Times*. Many others were settled out of court – in particular a number with the BBC. The *FT*, though, was a different matter. As with other employers its response was guided by its insurance company. It was likely to be a costly matter: the paper had more than a hundred cases of RSI among its staff. The *Journalist* splashed in December 1988 on 'The Most Dangerous Newsroom in Britain'.

The outbreak took the chapel by surprise, says its then Father Alan Pike: 'We had negotiated for over a year for very stringent health and safety standards.' He attributes the problem to a complex computer system and the fact that the *FT* was a 'decimal-point-accuracy paper – a lot of people were dealing every day with very precise factual information'. At the same time the office was 'decasualised', with freelance sub-editors being cleared out in favour of staff replacements that didn't actually materialise, so there were fewer subs to do more work.

The chapel negotiated 'a very good deal' for thirty-five people whose incapacity had forced them to leave the paper, with full pensions and guarantees of a return to work if they recovered. These 'yellow book terms', held up by the union as a model settlement for others to aim for, were achieved after it came close to strike action to win them – the nearest the NUJ ever came to a dispute over health and safety.

Twenty-three *FT* members were lined up for a major trial. The insurers offered a deal: £5,000 for each claimant plus the union's costs. The snag was that all twenty-three must accept it – all grudgingly agreed to do so, except one. That member was eventually persuaded to change his mind, but the deadline had passed and the insurance company would not relent. After stringent medical and legal examinations the remaining twenty-two were whittled down to five; another was dropped on the first day of the trial, in 1998. The four remaining – Akwe Amosu, Paul Hannan, Pip Little and Patrick Stiles – were dragged through a three-week ordeal. Their case wasn't helped when the company doctor, a GP on retainer from the *FT* who had diagnosed 'RSI' in all the cases, withdrew his evidence just before the trial and could not be called; an expert witness in the Rafiq Mughal case had done the same.

As well as the claimants' states of health, the ergonomic evidence should have been compelling. A major difficulty had been a chronic shortage of suitable office chairs. The *FT* spent millions on computers

▶

but wouldn't buy decent furniture. But Mr Justice Ian Kennedy concluded: 'I remain unpersuaded that the plaintiffs have on balance suffered from the physical problems they variously set out to establish.' The case cost the NUJ £700,000. In addition, the Reuters case had cost £300,000. A halt was called before the union could risk another. Another approach to the problem had to be found.

Health and safety (H&S) is a mainstream activity in most unions, but for journalists it had always been a matter for workers with ink on their hands and the NUJ had never really bothered with it. In the 1990s, propelled by the RSI epidemic, it was taken up seriously. An RSI Committee was set up on which sufferers worked with H&S activists. This became the Health and Safety Committee and *Journalist* editor Tim Gopsill became the NUJ's first national H&S officer. He had more than 450 RSI sufferers on his books. There was an annual RSI Day giving advice and demonstrations of equipment that could help them, and training for health and safety reps as chapels around the country took up the issue.

In some offices where the union was derecognised, health and safety activity, which enjoyed statutory protection, was a useful avenue for keeping the NUJ in business. At the Newcastle Journal and Chronicle the chapel was able to negotiate agreements not only on RSI and H&S but also on fair treatment for members who were HIV-positive. The FoC was George Macintyre, one of the stalwarts who kept the NUJ going through the dark years. When union recognition returned, the Newcastle office was one of the first to win it back.

Crisis: Wapping 1986

The Wapping dispute was the NUJ's biggest confrontation with a single employer – at least, in the newspaper industry – and one of the most significant events in British industrial relations in the second half of the twentieth century. It caused significant tensions within the union, and would have repercussions throughout journalism and beyond.

On Friday 24 January 1986, members of the print unions at Rupert Murdoch's News International – employed at the *Sun*, the *News of the World*, *The Times* and the *Sunday Times* – began a strike over a dispute that had been rumbling on for several years. In response, NI sacked more than five thousand printing and clerical staff and moved the production of its newspapers to a new and secretly prepared factory in Tower Hamlets, east London – 'Fortress Wapping', as it became known.

For wider British society the dispute summed up, as much as the long-running miners' strike that had ended the year before, the transformation of industrial relations begun by Margaret Thatcher's Conservative government in the early 1980s. For journalists, and for the NUJ, Wapping was equally momentous. Unlike in most previous disputes in a Fleet Street then plagued by poor industrial relations, journalists and their union found themselves playing an unaccustomed central role. Within moments of the dispute beginning, NUJ members were being forced to take sides; their jobs, their union principles and organisation were all at issue.

The Conservative government's tough new laws curbed 'secondary action', the practice of a union picketing not just the workplace where a strike was in progress, but other plants where the employer might attempt to transfer work. Unions could be fined, or have their funds sequestered, for breaking these laws. This encouraged some employers to set up new, in some cases 'dummy' companies, beyond a union's reach in disputes.

Murdoch was among these. He had owned the Wapping site since the late 1970s, and had originally planned to print the *Sun* and *News of the World* there, lacking further capacity at the papers' Fleet Street home. But when lengthy negotiations with the print unions failed, a new plan was devised. Under cover of launching a new paper, the *London Post*, at Wapping, Murdoch confronted the print unions with new, stringent, legally binding contracts curbing their rights to organise or strike. Wapping had been secretly equipped with new computer technology which would allow all NI's newspapers to be produced there, and a whole new workforce recruited – apart from the journalists – many with the cooperation of senior officials of the electricians' union, EETPU. News International then turned the screw, insisting that the new contracts be introduced on its existing titles too. To counter the legislation that would prevent them taking action against new Murdoch companies, the print unions retaliated by demanding security of employment – effectively jobs for life – and voted to strike if this was not acceded to.

The NUJ had been put on the spot. As the dispute loomed, the new General Secretary, Harry Conroy, sought to support the printers, not just to show solidarity but also to protect NUJ chapels from similarly restrictive contracts. Conroy's plan was that NUJ members – not involved in the dispute – should continue to work at their existing offices and resist any attempt to force them to Wapping. But the speed with which the dispute escalated overtook such contingencies. Within minutes of the strike beginning, journalists were receiving an ultimatum from their editors: move to Wapping and work the new technology that would help replace the printers, in exchange for a £2,000 pay rise and free health insurance. Refuse, and they would be regarded as having 'dismissed themselves'.

The *Sun* and *News of the World* chapels voted by large majorities to accept the ultimatum – at the *Sun*, relations with the print unions had been strained after printers had produced the paper during an earlier NUJ strike. The chapels at *The Times* and *Sunday Times* agonised over their decision for days. And although both chapels finally voted to accept the ultimatum – the *Sunday Times* by a whisker – a number of journalists on both papers, together with a smaller number from the *Sun* and the *News of the World*, decided not to go to Wapping, earning themselves the epithet of the 'refuseniks'. Over the months of the dispute, others would join them, and with the launch of the *Independent* in September 1986 many others gladly left Wapping.

For the NUJ, however, the dispute presented a dilemma. Support within the union for the line taken by Conroy and the NEC and for the stance of the refuseniks was high – indicated by numerous messages and gestures of solidarity on the part of branches and chapels. Most freelances accepted instructions not to file copy to Wapping, thereby losing income. There were also odd spin-offs elsewhere – at Bristol University, students demonstrated against a don, John Vincent, who wrote for *The Times*; at the *Observer*, print unions refused to work with *Times* journalists who did weekend casual shifts there and were working at Wapping; legal action was taken against local libraries whose Labour councillors refused to take

News International titles; and there were spin-off disputes at the *Irish Times* and elsewhere over the syndicated use of *Sunday Times* columnist Peter Jenkins.

Refuseniks

The Wapping 'refuseniks' included some top journalists. Among them was the entire labour team of *The Times*: Barrie Clement, David Felton and Donald MacIntyre, and a former labour editor turned foreign correspondent, Paul Routledge. Others from *The Times* included reporters Greg Neale and Pat Healy; Martin Huckerby, a foreign editor sacked for writing in the *UK Press Gazette* about his stance, and sub-editors Cyril McDermott and Mike Sumner. *Sunday Times* journalists who refused to work at Wapping included Lew Chester, Paul Webster, Brian Whittaker, Colin Clifford, Peter Murtagh and Literary Editor Claire Tomalin. Mike Topp, Eric Butler, Olly Duke, Peter Court and Ian Blunt were among the refuseniks from the *Sun* and *News of the World*.

Routledge had been exiled to Singapore as the *The Times*'s Far East correspondent after a supposed indiscretion following a conversation with the Queen. He now adopted an 'electronic picket line', refusing to telephone copy to Wapping. Harry Coen, a sub-editor on the *Sunday Times*, had reason to spurn the sacked printers: when the paper's compositors had earlier learned of his alleged homosexuality, they had threatened to refuse to work with him. Instead, he was among the first from his chapel to refuse to work at Wapping.

Twenty years later, Greg Neale, former FoC of *The Times* whom the refuseniks elected as their spokesman, said:

Sometimes I think the term 'refusenik' suggested that people were simply resisting change – that's simply not true. If you asked them why they took the decision they did, you'd get differing responses – including a sense of fairness, or loyalty to sacked colleagues and a determination not to be bullied, as much as trade union principles. And though the industrial dispute was lost, I think those human principles triumphed.

But there was also, both within the union and among sections of the public – including those disenchanted with what they had read of printers'

The truth?
He couldn't give
a XXXX
(If you care, don't buy Murdoch's papers: The Sun,
News of the World, Times & Sunday Times)

Poster of Rupert Murdoch produced by the unions in the Wapping dispute aping a TV advert of the time for Castlemaine XXXX beer. (NUJ Collection)

practices – some sympathy for those journalists who had been placed under pressure to move to Wapping, reflected by razor-thin votes on the NEC over moves to order them out on strike and take disciplinary action against them. Conroy's concern was how to square solidarity with the print unions and support for the NUJ refuseniks, with keeping the hundreds of journalists who had gone to Wapping within the union. Inevitably, attitudes hardened as the refuseniks were sacked. They were supported financially by the union, which helped them find casual work; such figures as Eric Butler, a sacked sixty-three-year-old *Sun* sports sub-editor, carved out roles speaking at branch meetings around the country.

Murdoch had used a private haulage company, TNT, to prevent rail unions blocking distribution. In the provinces, some SOGAT members were prepared to stop handling the News International titles, while others balked at the order. Murdoch attempted a PR coup by offering the unions a share of the now redundant *Sunday Times* building and presses to publish their own paper, but the unions declined such a poisoned chalice. Many Labour MPs – including a newly elected Tony Blair – signed anti-Murdoch motions. Thatcher saw it as essential that Murdoch should win the dispute, though, and a heavy police presence at Wapping ensured that the papers were distributed (other editions were printed at Kinning Park,

Police charge demonstrators outside the Wapping plant in east London during the year-long dispute. (Stefano Cagnoni)

in Glasgow), despite heavy picketing, occasionally accompanied by violent scenes. Two Murdoch offers of compensation, but no jobs, were rejected by the printers, whose leaders realised that the consequences of defeat would resound across Fleet Street and elsewhere.

The arguments within the NUJ came to a head at the 1986 ADM in Sheffield. A motion instructing the union executive to discipline those members still working at Wapping found most of the refuseniks speaking against – the desire not to make the split permanent was still strong. A narrow majority voted for disciplinary action; the NEC deferred action. Saturday night demonstrations at Wapping saw clashes between police, the printers and their supporters. Casualties mounted. A speeding newspaper lorry struck and killed a local resident, Michael Delaney. Several print workers were reported to have subsequently committed suicide, having failed to find work. A working *Times* journalist was badly injured in an encounter with a striking printer. Clifford Longley, who took over as FoC at *The Times* while his predecessor, Greg Neale, headed the paper's refuseniks, received abusive late-night phone calls and, on one occasion, an unwanted delivery of a lorryload of sand. 'In the end, I think that Harry Conroy had a word with Brenda Dean, who told her activists to lay off the NUJ,' Longley said later.

Wapping 'refuseniks' – News International (NI) journalists who refused to work at Murdoch's new plant – queue up at ADM 1986 to speak against an all-out strike. Left to right: Greg Neale and Pat Healy of The Times, *Tom Lynch of the* Financial Times *(not from NI), Don MacIntyre of* The Times, *Ian Blunt of the* Sun, *Kim Fletcher of the* Sunday Times *and Mike Topp of the* Sun. *(Martin Jenkinson)*

Wapping refuseniks at a reunion in January 2006, 20 years after the start of the dispute. Left to right: Cyril McDermott (formerly of The Times*), Lew Chester (formerly* Sunday Times*), David Felton and Barrie Clement (formerly* The Times*), Pat Healy, Greg Neale, Mike Sumner and Paul Routledge (formerly* The Times*). (Stefano Cagnoni)*

The dispute ended in February 1987. The print unions, having failed to stop the Murdoch papers, and with their funds drained in a continual legal fight, were forced to accept limited compensation. The NUJ followed. It had fought for the sacked journalists to be reinstated: none was, though most found new jobs with editors keen to pick up talent from the Murdoch titles. Disciplinary action was eventually taken against ninety-seven of the many hundreds of NUJ members who had worked at Wapping, but was later dropped. At Wapping, Murdoch's management would eventually derecognise the NUJ – as the union had warned it would.

5

AN INTERNATIONAL UNION

Two nations, one union

British journalists often forget that the NUJ is an international union that covers two nations. Ireland was part of Britain when the union was founded and its journalists stayed in the NUJ when the island was partitioned; and they have stayed in it ever since – despite the attractions, at different times, of three other unions. Now and then Irish members may have grumbled at a perceived lack of interest on the part of London, but they have retained the link and have always played a full part in the union.[1]

The semi-autonomous status and structure that Irish journalists have attained within the union covers north and south, and those in Northern Ireland are 'serviced', to use union officials' terminology, from the Irish office in Dublin. Foreign journalists are often amazed to hear that in the 'six counties' of the north, where there was a virtual civil war for twenty-five years, all the journalists, including those on papers pretty closely identified with the warring communities, have been able to work together in the same union and that none challenged that state of affairs. A professional sense of community prevailed.

But it was still not in the best political taste when Frederick Mansfield, the NUJ's first historian, described the first visit of NUJ officials in 1909 as 'the invasion of Ireland'. Three of the union's founders led by General Secretary William Watts had sailed to Dublin, and there a branch was formed with twenty members; and via meetings in Waterford, Derry and Newry they rounded up around a hundred more. Dublin sent delegates to the 1910 ADM, but then things began to slide. The issue was competition for journalists' loyalty. The Institute of Journalists was already established in Ireland, and was to hold the allegiance of journalists on the *Cork Examiner*, the only daily in the republic outside Dublin, until the 1960s. Then, no sooner had the NUJ missionaries departed than moves were made to start another, nationalist union: the Irish Journalists' Association (IJA) was launched in December 1909.

Irish journalists had been, if anything, even more wretchedly treated than the British. The IJA set out to improve working conditions, which the NUJ was hardly in a position even to contemplate, and like the NUJ it had no confidence in the ability of the Institute to do so either. From 1914 it published a newsletter, *The Irish Journalist*, which reported in its first issue: 'The death-rate of journalists, in Dublin, is perfectly appalling … it is largely because their business duties are flung at them in such an unintelligent fashion that all methodical life is impossible; they cannot have fixed regular hours for meals; their day may just as readily end at two o'clock in the morning as at six o'clock in the evening.' It set the six-day week as an immediate target.

In 1915 the IJA was claiming more members than either of the other unions, and delegates from the NUJ made a second foray to Ireland to discuss a working arrangement between itself and the IJA. Some IJA members, however, resisted the idea of trade unionism. Union members, according to *The Irish Journalist*, were seen as 'slackers' and 'shirkers'. The IJA did vote at its AGM in January 1916 to register as a trade union, but this was never implemented. In fact nothing more was done at all. The IJA disappeared from the records after March 1916; it has been speculated that 'nationalist' activity was difficult or suppressed after the defeat of the Easter Rising. There was an attempt to revive it in 1935, but it soon foundered.

In 1926 the NUJ embarked on its third Irish crusade. The national organiser, Clem Bundock, visited Dublin and Belfast, where the old branches were revived. A year later the union attempted to open negotiations with the national newspaper proprietors, but without success. The great boost to NUJ organisation in Ireland, ironically, came with the launch of the *Irish Press* in 1931. This was the first 'nationalist' paper, the mouthpiece of the dominant party of the republic Fianna Fáil, owned and wholly controlled throughout its sixty-four-year existence by the family of President Eamonn de Valera, yet virtually all the staff joined the English-based union from the start. By 1934 the NUJ had acquired formal recognition from the Dublin managements; then the journalists confirmed their commitment to it in 1941, when they had the opportunity to go their own way and emphatically rejected it.

This episode was the first great Irish-inspired ruction to rock the union. The Irish government had adopted a Trade Union Act that required unions to obtain a negotiating licence and pay a deposit of £1,000. The NUJ's NEC felt this was a 'fascist' measure – not an idle description in 1941 – aimed at putting trade unions under state control, and decided against registration. Instead it proposed to let the Irish establish their own union and to give them the £1,000 to acquire a licence and a further £600 to help them get going. But the Dublin branch would have none of it. At the 1942 ADM a Dublin delegate, R. M. Fox of the *Evening Mail*, spoke strongly against the executive decision, claiming it was 'abandoning' the Dublin branch, 'spending £1,600 to smash the branch but was not prepared to keep it alive at no cost at all'. He persuaded the conference to leave the matter open, and later in the year the executive turned on its head and paid the money to register with a face-saving statement that it was nonetheless 'strongly opposed to the legislation ... and would resist by every means in its power these dangerous principles'.

It was what the members wanted, but it was not the end of the matter. The affair pitched the union into one of its constitutional crises.

During that year's ADM debate, five members of the executive had spoken against the official line and now, no doubt looking for scape-goats for its embarrassment, the NEC passed a motion that no member should be allowed to speak against its decisions, except at their own local meetings. The President at the time, D. M. Elliott, from Scotland, resigned in protest, as did four others with him. Elliott wrote in the *Journalist*: 'When the day dawns on which I cannot speak freely on union affairs my usefulness on the NEC will have passed. To muzzle [members] as the executive has now decided is at once to stultify their rights and rob the membership of their independent judgement and guidance.' The issue was fought out at the next ADM, where a convoluted compromise was reached, described by one delegate as 'reading like a *Times* leader in the days of appeasement'. No one wanted to prolong the row, but it had achieved one thing: the subsequent custom of the union that allows the

ADM to invite representatives of a minority view on the NEC to speak against the executive line.

The Irish members' choice was soon vindicated: the NUJ, as part of Dublin's Printing Trades Group, achieved two pay rises in 1943 alone, and in 1947 secured full-scale agreements covering all terms and conditions and bringing huge pay rises. The basic rate for seniors went up from £4.20 to £9.45 a week. On the back of this success the union pursued an intensive membership campaign, opening new branches around the country.

But with the principle of trade unionism now established, there was another attempt to set up an indigenous union, and the Guild of Irish Journalists was founded in March 1949. The Guild adopted a strident nationalist tone, proclaiming itself 'a National Trade Union, founded and controlled by Irishmen, with a place in its ranks for each and every Irish journalist', and calling on them to work 'for the implementation of a progressive Social policy, based on Christian principles'. But it was more than that. Research by Ireland's premier media historian John Horgan has shown that it grew out of an anti-communist campaign run by government and the Church.[2]

Horgan describes the Guild as 'one of the legacies of the Cold War to Irish journalism'. A witch-hunt was being carried out against perceived communist influence in the press, targeting the NUJ, which involved regular exchanges of information between the government and the US embassy in Dublin. De Valera had complained that there were communists on his own paper, the *Irish Press*, who had not been reporting his speeches to his liking. When the NUJ sent a deputation to see the Irish police, the Garda Siochana, in 1948, to seek better working relationships, the Garda were warned of the 'possible dangers of taking journalists into police confidence'. The former Fianna Fail Prime Minister Sean Lemass, invited to the NUJ's Irish district council annual meeting in 1949, told them that it was particularly important that Irish workers should be enrolled in Irish unions.

But the NUJ was too well grounded in Ireland by now and the Guild made little headway. In 1953 it resorted to presenting joint claims, with the Institute, to the newspaper owners, the NUJ having rebuffed its approach for a three-way alliance. Its newsletter, *An Glór*, raged at 'the fact that Irish journalists ... had, in effect, to accept an Agreement regarding salaries etc., negotiated by men "from across the water"'. By 1960 the Guild too had disappeared.

Jim Eadie, the union's first full-time official in Ireland. (Kevin Cooper)

These men from across the sea, of course, were professional NUJ nego-tiators who flew in every two years for the biennial agreement covering Dublin newspapers. They were not beholden to the Irish proprietors and could be uninhibited in their approach, winning the best deal they could and returning home without fear of reprisals. There were no agreements in the Irish provinces then, but journalists there had noticed what was going on, among them an eighteen-year-old probationary trainee on the *Roscommon Herald* who was 'mad on dancing, girls and Gaelic football' called Jim Eadie. Being a probationer then, he recalls, involved touting for sales and advertising as well as reporting. He read about the great 1947 pay rises in the press and decided to join the NUJ. The nearest branch (Athlone) wouldn't have him at first: they wouldn't take probationers for fear of having to defend them if they weren't taken on permanently. When Eadie became head of the union in Ireland in 1965 he would go out of his way to fight for trainees who weren't taken on.

But the provincial members were getting themselves organised and in 1949 concluded another landmark deal with the Irish Master Printers' Association, representing the local publishers. The *Journalist* presented it as 'a charter for Ireland's forgotten men', introducing a minimum rate of £7 for a forty-four-hour week for journalists who had hitherto worked all hours for £3 or less.

Ivan Peebles defied his newspaper owner father to win the union's first agreement in the west of Ireland. (Andrew Wiard)

Now the union expanded rapidly. On the *Sligo Independent* the first pay deal in the west was won by a twenty-five-year-old reporter, Ivan Peebles – from his own father. William D. Peebles was owner and editor of the *Independent*, a unionist weekly, and when Ivan threatened to leave his father paid up. He went on to work on the *Belfast Telegraph* and became President of the NUJ in 1974. He commented: 'It does sound difficult but I was absolutely determined. I always have been as far as the union is concerned.'

Irish members may have been content with the flying squad's work but there is more to a union than formal pay talks, and in the early 1960s they began agitating for their own full-time organiser. The NEC, as is its way, resisted on grounds of cost, but the ADM in 1964 moved against the executive and decided on the appointment. The job was offered to the NEC member for Ireland, Pat Nolan of the *Irish Times*, who accepted subject to a strange condition: that the Irish members would pay a levy to cover his salary – he did not want the Irish membership to be 'beholden' to London, he said. Nolan was a man of firm principles. He was a devout Catholic, yet in the Cold War days when the NUJ was denounced by the Church as being dominated by communists – and some members did resign to join the Guild – he stuck with it. He did say his conscience bothered him when he found himself voting with the communists on the

NEC, but he consoled himself with the thought that they were invariably outvoted. Now, despite having earlier objected to the cost, the NEC
rejected his condition. The post was re-advertised and Eadie, who by now
was Father of the Chapel at the Irish *Independent*, was appointed. His
starting the job coincided with the entire Dublin newspaper membership being laid off by a print dispute and becoming dependent on union
benefit for twelve weeks.

At the same time the union opened a new office in Liberty Hall,
the tower block HQ of Ireland's biggest union, the Irish Transport and
General Workers'. Eadie's administrative assistant, Patsi Dunne, was to
mark a milestone in union history when in 1982, as the office expanded,
she became the first and only member of the clerical staff to be promoted
to a full organiser's job.

Now, in 1966, Eadie set about organising the provincial sector he had
come from. The Dublin chapels by now could pretty much look after
themselves; all established virtual closed shops and by the 1980s could
claim to be the highest-paid, in comparative terms, in the whole union.
So could journalists at the state broadcaster Radio Eireann (later Radio
Telefis Eireann). The NUJ had no recognition and few members there
before the broadcaster was established as an independent entity, modelled
on the BBC, in 1960, but it quickly thrived. In 1963 members ran a nine-
week strike that won increases of over 10 per cent. RTE also became
a closed shop and the union staged half a dozen strikes over the years.
It was the success of one in 1992 that propelled the Father of Chapel
Eoin (pronounced 'Owen') Ronayne into the Irish Secretary's job when
Eadie retired two years later. That was a difficult strike, not about money
but technology and jobs – RTE was cutting camera crew numbers and
journalists refused to work with the reduced crews – but it was another
success. There was an unpleasant aftermath, though, as ten members in
senior posts sued the union after being disciplined for breaking the strike.
The case was settled, with RTE repaying the union's costs.

The border? What border?

While the Dublin office covered the whole island there were constant
debates over the relations between north and south and between both
and Britain. In the north – where in 1951 the Belfast dailies had become
the last in the union to secure pay agreements – members wanted their

own structure, and in 1972 proposed a Northern Ireland area council: Area Councils were an intermediate level in the NUJ's structure, between local branches and the national executive, and until then Ireland had had just the one, from which the north now proposed to secede. A committee was set up that forestalled the potential crisis in masterly fashion: the Irish Area Council (IAC) acquired two subcommittees. 'There will be no partition of the NUJ in Ireland,' the IAC announced.

Four years later, the NUJ overhauled its whole structure, replacing the area councils with 'industrial' ones covering sectors of the media – national and provincial newspapers, broadcasting, magazine and book, freelance and PR – rather than geographical areas, and again for Ireland a sensible compromise was reached. The Republic of Ireland Industrial Council was in effect an area council because it covered all the industrial sectors, but the IAC continued in being, to include the north. The two were finally amalgamated into the Irish Council in 1986. Its powers steadily increased until in 1993 it became the Irish Executive Council with full powers in Ireland, subject only to the NEC on all-union matters, and, of course, to the ADM.

At each stage voices warned that the union was about to break in half, but it never came to pass. Irish members have proved adept at securing maximum autonomy while retaining the advantages of the British link, principally in the access to greater resources – and all without having to threaten to secede. The union has survived major ructions, the worst of which was a five-year row over abortion. In 1975 the NUJ Equality Working Party, set up by the ADM to work for the fairer treatment of women in the industry, decided to support abortion on demand and the 1976 ADM endorsed it as union policy. The right of women to choose not to have a child was essential for them as workers, the conference agreed; it was therefore a proper matter for the union to discuss. In the Republic of Ireland there was uproar. The *Journalist* published masses of letters. 'I regard it as murder,' wrote Sean Ryan from Dublin. 'I am a Catholic first and a member of the union second. Sorry about that!' There were protests in England too. Gillian James from Surrey wrote: 'I thought the NUJ stood for decency and personal freedom, but when it backs wholesale killing who can think that?'

In 1980 the IAC held a special conference on abortion in Dublin, where members voted emphatically to oppose the policy and to seek to get it overturned. A move by Eadie to allow it to apply in the UK but not in Ireland was defeated. Instead, branch delegates heeded the call to revolt from Cian OhEigeartaigh ('O'Hegarty') of RTE, who said he supported abortion on demand but that it was 'a personal decision and no business of the NUJ. It is time to get the union out of a difficulty it has got itself into.'

But there were pro-abortion voices too. Mary Maher of the *Irish Times* said control of fertility *was* a trade union issue, and Mairin de Burca of the Dublin Publications branch said she could never say to a woman, 'You must bear a child whether or not you want it.' Those who opposed abortion were concerned with the unborn; she was concerned with those already born. All speakers at the conference urged members not to quit the union but to fight for policy changes within it. A dozen or so had resigned and been welcomed with great fanfares into the IoJ, but yet again most Irish journalists, presented with a pretext to leave, maintained their loyalty to the international union.

Following the conference the NEC in London fell back on its talent for compromise, affirming that while the policy should stand, there would be no attempt to enforce it in Ireland. The statement was a triumph for the sophistry of Vincent Hanna, the legally trained BBC political journalist who led the NUJ broadcasting sector. The policy was 'not pro-abortion but pro the right to choose', he said, as if there was a difference. Like most compromises it enraged both sides, but like all the best ones, it worked. The EWP were angry that a woman delegate who had asked to address the all-male meeting had been rebuffed, and that the NEC had under-mined 'a democratically agreed policy by manipulating words to create a convenient interpretation'. The Irish responded by tabling motions to overturn the policy and hold a referendum of all union members on the issue. Both were lost, the next ADM reaffirmed the policy, and no more was heard, at least in union forums. The UK never sought to force it down Irish throats, and individuals in Ireland have been able to support the movement to liberalise the abortion laws.

There were two further Irish-connected rows that shook the union. The first was in 1991 when General Secretary Steve Turner was sacked over his attempts to derail the NEC's policy of taking over the Irish Print Union (IPU), which represented print workers in Dublin, as a step towards the NUJ policy of working towards a single media union. The second was six years later when Deputy General Secretary Jake Ecclestone was sacked by the NEC for challenging a plan to extend Irish autonomy within the union to cover its finances. In both cases the central issue was not Ireland, but the nature of working relationships at the top of the union. And though both could have threatened the link between London and Dublin, neither did. The IPU merger fell through for other reasons, and Ireland's increased financial independence, like its political authority, in fact strengthened the union, rather than weakened it.

Two brave reporters – too brave

Ireland can be a dangerous place for journalists to work, especially for the brave and challenging type of reporter. In the Northern Ireland conflict both sides were prone to attack the media, kidnapping and threatening journalists and bombing their offices. The *Belfast Telegraph* was bombed in 1974 and again in 1976 – it was presumed, by the IRA; amazingly, no one was killed, though people were injured in a shoot-out between the bombers and British troops after the second attack. After the first bombing the NUJ arranged with the owners, Thomson Regional Newspapers, to transfer a photographer who appeared to be under particular threat to work in England.

The Belfast bureau of the Dublin-based *Sunday World*, an outspoken

The Belfast Telegraph building after an IRA bomb blast in 1974. (Belfast Telegraph)

and often outrageous tabloid, has an impressive record of producing uninhibited investigative stories that have angered the 'paramilitaries' on both
sides of the conflict. In 1984 Jim Campbell, its northern editor, was shot
at the door of his home by two loyalist gunmen. He barely survived,
condemned to carry a bullet in his spine for the rest of his days. He
returned to work as a political columnist, working from home. In 1992
the *Sunday World* office was bombed by the Ulster Volunteer Force, and
death threats were made against a reporter, Martin O'Hagan, a dogged
investigator who had served time in jail as an IRA volunteer in his youth
but had renounced violence. This was where the all-Ireland connection
proved vital. The Belfast NUJ, with contacts in both loyalist and republican
communities, was able to negotiate his safety, first to allay the threat and
second to get the *Sunday World*, owned by Tony O'Reilly's Irish Independent group that later bought the *Independent* in London, to transfer him out
of Belfast to work in Cork. The NUJ used to say that its special position
in Northern Ireland had prevented any journalists being killed, uniquely
in any recent conflict. It was luck in the case of Campbell; but it still held
true, up to a point.

O'Hagan was unhappy in Cork. He had a family with three young
children, and decided to go home. On 28 September 2001 he was shot
dead at his front gate in Lurgan, returning home from an evening in
the local pub with his wife Marie. It was a terrible irony that the first
journalist was murdered in Northern Ireland after the ceasefires and the
Good Friday Agreement. Suspicions immediately centred on the Loyalist
Volunteer Force (LVF), a breakaway from the Ulster Volunteer Force that
was heavily infiltrated by police informers and whose activities O'Hagan
had exposed many times. At the union's biennial Irish conference a month
later Campbell paid tribute to his friend: 'When he got involved in a story
he was like a terrier and kept worrying at it until the truth dropped out.'
He revealed that the assassination attempt on himself in 1984 had followed
a story he and O'Hagan had worked on together. 'Marty was racked with
guilt and said he himself should have been the target. Little did he know
that one day he would be.'

The identities of O'Hagan's alleged assassins were widely circulated
and a number of men were questioned – the *Journalist* ran a feature on
them headlined 'We name the innocent men' – but no charges were
brought. Led by the new NUJ Irish Secretary Seamus Dooley, who had
taken over from Eoin Ronayne in 1999, the union had meetings with the

Jim Campbell, former Belfast editor of the Sunday World, who was shot by loyalist paramilitaries in 1984 but survived, pays tribute to his friend and colleague Martin O'Hagan, shot and killed by loyalist paramilitaries in 2001, at the union's Irish conference that year. (John Power)

Martin O'Hagan, reporter gunned down in Lurgan in 2001. (Alwyn James)

Chief Constable of Northern Ireland and government security ministers, at which pious assurances were given. There was much speculation that the police were deeply involved in the LVF and were protecting the killers, and there was growing frustration in the union, but five years on there was no sign of anyone being brought to justice.

O'Hagan was not, however, the first Irish journalist to be shot dead. On 29 June 1996 the crime reporter of the *Sunday Independent* in Dublin, Veronica Guerin, was killed as she sat in her car. This time the killer was acting for a gang of criminals, for Guerin, an astonishingly tenacious and fearless – some did say foolhardy – reporter, had probed deep into Dublin's criminal underworld and even confronted some of its most ruthless godfathers. 'She did not rely on Garda contacts but met the criminals face to face,' said Dooley, who was then a colleague at the *Independent*. 'It was a dangerous game, but she got stories that no one else got near to.' Guerin too had been warned often enough: shots had been fired at her house on

Veronica Guerin, reporter shot dead in Dublin in 1996. (Derek Speirs/ Report)

two occasions and then, eighteen months before she died, she had been shot, but survived. A gunman came to her front door and shot her in the thigh. 'The shots were a warning,' she told the *Journalist*, 'but it did not deter me from my work and nor will this.'

The killing was greeted with national grief and outrage. At the union's suggestion the republic held a nationwide minute's silence. Again fingers were pointed, and the speculation centred on drug crime boss John Gilligan, with whom Guerin had clashed several times. He was eventually tried for the crime in 2002 but sensationally acquitted by the Special Criminal Court in Dublin. However, he was jailed for twenty-eight years on drug trafficking; the judge said the court had 'grave suspicions of Gilligan's involvement in the murder of the journalist but was not convinced beyond reasonable doubt of his guilt because of the uncorroborated evidence of the chief State witnesses'. During the trial there was chilling evidence of a threat Gilligan had made to the reporter. The court heard a recording of a phone call in which he said: 'If you do one thing on me or if you write about me I will kidnap your son and ride him. Do you understand what I am saying? I will kidnap your fucking son and ride him. I will fucking shoot him. I will kill you.' The unreliability of witnesses was also the reason given for the acquittal on appeal of another man, Paul Ward, who had been convicted of the murder in 1998.

Veronica Guerin became an iconic figure. A Hollywood movie was made with Cate Blanchett in the lead role. Editors pledged to provide better protection for staff engaged in hazardous work, and the NUJ drew up a manifesto for challenging but safe journalism under the title 'The Guerin Principles'. They were too late for her, and they didn't help Martin O'Hagan either.

Celts far from the fringe

The Celtic contribution to the NUJ has been a strong one, embracing rather more than the traditional Scots evening at the union's annual conference. Chapel and branch organisation in Scotland and Wales began soon after the union's foundation in 1907, and both countries have supplied leading figures – and important moments – in the NUJ's history.

The first Scottish delegates to attend ADMs did so in 1910, by which time recruitment and organisation had been proceeding apace. The first Scottish members joined in 1909 when Jimmy Aitken, a young reporter, and two fellow juniors (Frank Dodson and John Gordon, who later became editor of the *Sunday Express*) at the *Dundee Advertiser* decided to join the fledgling organisation and form a branch. At the same time, and unknown to them, a handful of journalists in Glasgow were doing the same thing.

'Frequently we discussed, with the earnestness possible only to extreme youth, what could be done to improve matters,' Aitken wrote later. 'After long cogitation, and much wordy discussion, we solemnly came to the conclusion that the only way in which journalism could be made fit for journalists was to organise on a trade union basis.' Aitken contacted George Lethem, a Scot who had been responsible for founding the Leeds union branch, who agreed to travel to Dundee – stipulating only that their meeting should take place in the afternoon, allowing him to go on to Glasgow for the evening meeting that would result in a branch being founded there. Dundee has a doubly special place in NUJ history – after the General Strike of 1926, both daily newspapers in the city banned trade unionism among their employees. D. C. Thomson – also publishers of a series of children's comics – thereafter remained resolutely anti-union, and the focus of many NUJ campaigns.

▶

Scots journalists had long made the journey to Fleet Street and to senior jobs on the English national papers, but more chose to remain and build careers, and the union, north of the border. Glasgow in particular had a strong history of trade unionism, and close links were forged between the NUJ and the print unions. Harry Conroy, NUJ General Secretary during 1985–90, honed his skills at the *Daily Record* in Glasgow – the paper that Jimmy Aitken joined in 1911 – and became Imperial Father of the *Daily Record* and *Sunday Mail* federated chapel, which united seven unions and twenty-seven chapels. The experience of working closely with other unions coloured his attitude when he took the top job.

The union set up a Scottish Council in 1989, upgraded to an Executive Council ten years later in partial recognition of the enhanced status of the nation after the establishment of the Scottish Parliament. The union immediately began taking advantage of the opportunities presented, both in lobbying MSPs on media and employment questions and in recruiting research and PR staff working at the Parliament.

Welsh involvement in the NUJ began even earlier than in Scotland, two delegates from South Wales and Monmouthshire being among those who founded the union at Birmingham in 1907. Branches were formed in many Welsh towns, and NUJ members in the principality soon developed a reputation for militancy. In his history of the union, published in 1957, Clem Bundock wrote: 'The South Wales branch was certainly full of life and vigour.' That may well have been the case, but its leaders were said to be Conservative – with one Liberal – in their private politics. One of the early women activists in the NUJ, the reporter Dolly Dungworth, was also an active figure in the branch later in the century.

The South Wales reputation for militancy was compounded in 1918 when Henry Richardson, the union's newly elected General Secretary, was invited to a mass meeting in Cardiff. Richardson, who was widely seen as a left-winger, found himself addressing a branch considering strike action in support of a pay claim. Halfway through the meeting a telegram arrived for him from the union's President, Frederick Mansfield, informing him that the national executive would not support a South Wales strike, as it would jeopardise a national pay claim. Richardson, embarrassed, had to read out the telegram and do a quick about-face. This is the sort of thing that union leaders sometimes have to do, but the branch activists were not deterred, and decided to call another meeting, which resolved to press on with their local claim.

It succeeded – and without national support the South Wales branch won an extra £1 a week for experienced journalists.

Welsh journalists have given strong support to NUJ campaigns, notably in the BBC, where John O'Sullivan, a prominent figure in the union in Wales, was a long-time FoC. He recalls a 'golden generation' of journalists in the 1960s, including the broadcasters Sue Lawley, Michael Buerk and John Humphrys, as well as Alun Michael, a future Secretary of State for Wales, and Donald Woods, the South African journalist who had helped lead the fight against apartheid. Welsh members honoured several of their traditions when they joined NUJ-supported protests against what in ordinary circumstances would have been a high point of the year: when the South African rugby team toured in 1970, NUJ members were among those who joined the anti-apartheid protests.

Journalists in the wider world

The British press, though often parochial, has never been completely insular. Among the early newssheets 'foreign intelligence' was a frequent ingredient – it was less liable than domestic political news to attract official suspicion – while the spread of the British Empire and such nineteenth-century innovations as the telegraph all helped create an interest in foreign affairs. The NUJ had an early awareness of the international dimension to its work, and saw itself as part of a community of journalistic organisations. With sizeable numbers of British journalists working in Europe it organised branches in Paris, Brussels, Geneva and the Netherlands – then spreading further afield in the 1950s, to East Africa. Early issues of the *Journalist* show an interest in developments in journalism overseas, and this was followed by official links with other journalist unions.

In 1926, the union played a part in the formation of the International Federation of Journalists (IFJ). It was a time when ideas of internationalism were being mooted as a way of avoiding another war as horrendous as the one that had ended in 1918. The young League of Nations soon recognised the Federation, and at the inaugural conference in Geneva where thirteen nations were represented, the NUJ was the largest national organisation, with 4,800 members to Germany's 4,300.

An early initiative of the IFJ was to attempt to discourage 'irresponsible' reporting of international matters, which it was thought could lead to war. Henry Richardson apparently found little support on the continent for his advocacy of closer links between journalists and printers' unions, but won approval for his belief that journalists had a role to play in the preservation of peace. This eventually produced a decision at the IFJ's congress in Berlin in 1930 – when Richardson was elected IFJ President – to establish an international 'Court of Honour' at the Palace of Peace in The Hague. At the inauguration of this Court – later renamed the International Tribune of Honour for Journalists – in 1931, Richardson declared the IFJ's intention to 'drive out of journalism men who would create ill-will between peoples by stating as truth mischievous things which they knew to be false'. Back home, the NUJ agreed to this potential challenge to its own autonomy, inserting a new rule to the effect that any member 'found by the International Tribune of Honour to be unfit to be a journalist shall, failing a successful appeal to the executive of the IFJ by the Union, forthwith cease to be a member of the Union'.

Such a scheme would surely have proved unworkable, and the Court of Honour never got going. But in any case the IFJ was already under strain. The rise of Hitler led to the Nazification of the German press, with Jews, communists and others being driven out of the profession. The German journalists' union withdrew from the IFJ in 1934, at the same time as the eight-thousand-strong American Newspaper Guild was welcomed into membership. As Europe drifted to war in the late 1930s, the IFJ tried to help the growing number of journalist refugees from Germany and those countries suffering from Nazi expansionism, as well as those from Spain and the Soviet Union. It also adopted a 'Code of Professional Honour' based on the NUJ's new Code of Conduct.[3]

With the start of the Second World War the IFJ's existence was effectively ended, as the German army occupied Paris where its headquarters were. The NUJ helped to set up a wartime organisation, the International Federation of Journalists of Allied or Free Countries. The first meeting was held at the Café Royal in London in December 1941, with journalist union representatives from the Nazi-occupied states of Czechoslovakia, France, Greece, Holland, Norway and Poland, in addition to Britain and the Soviet Union. Archie Kenyon of the NUJ was elected President, and gave a speech praising those journalists who were still working to produce underground newspapers despite Nazi oppression. The BBC broadcast the conference speeches.

In 1946, there was a brief attempt to revive the ideals of the IFJ when an International Organisation of Journalists (the IOJ – not to be confused with the IoJ, the Institute of Journalists, in Britain and Ireland) was set up at a world congress in Copenhagen. As it was a successor to the IFJ, Kenyon was elected the first President. The IOJ was intended to bring together, as its draft constitution put it, 'national organisations of working journalists who subscribe to trade union principles and who accept the primary principle of the freedom of the Press'. But it soon fell victim to the increasing chill of the Cold War. As East and West manoeuvred for position, journalism became even more a battleground of ideologies. Within a year, the divisions within the IOJ became apparent at an acrimonious congress in Prague, then at a deadlocked meeting in Budapest in 1948 at which the United States delegates withdrew. The NUJ soon followed, though not without some anguish. The union's executive voted to recommend the NUJ withdraw from the IOJ as a supposed 'communist front'. The subsequent ballot supported withdrawal by 3,375 votes to 769.

International organisation was now frozen in the Cold War pattern. In 1952 a new International Federation of Journalists was formed, in Brussels, with thirteen Western nations initially involved. Its constitution proclaimed that it would comprise 'national trade unions of professional journalists which are dedicated to the freedom of the Press'. Clement Bundock, the outgoing NUJ General Secretary, was elected the first President. The IFJ slowly attracted international support but for the next four decades the east–west division remained icebound. The NUJ maintained a leading role, with General Secretary Jim Bradley elected President three times, and other leading union members holding senior posts.

A more enduring British influence was the appointment in 1987 of Aidan White, former NUJ Treasurer, as the IFJ's General Secretary. Under White's direction, the organisation began to adopt a more pro-active, interventionist stance, and to embrace new members; in 2006, White was still in the job. It took time, but after the Cold War ended and more unions left the declining IOJ's communist embrace, by 2006 the IFJ comprised 164 affiliated unions from 117 countries – a total that had trebled in twenty years. In 2001 Jim Boumelha, the leader of the three-year NUJ strike at Pergamon Press back in the early nineties who became chairman of the union's Policy Committee (handling international matters), was elected Treasurer of the IFJ.

The IFJ joined the International Freedom of Expression Exchange, a burgeoning group of NGOs in what the NUJ called the 'press freedom

NUJ members to the fore at a press freedom rally at the IFJ World Congress in Seoul in 2001. Front, from right: NUJ delegates Rory MacLeod, Michael Foley, Mindy Ran and Jim Boumelha. (IFJ)

industry'. The IFJ's interests differed from most of the other organisations' in that it was concerned with journalists themselves, rather than press freedom in the abstract. It became particularly concerned to defend journalists from attack and to protect those working in war zones. The number killed reporting wars was rising rapidly – on occasion, more than a hundred a year – and in 2001 the IFJ, together with press freedom NGOs and media employers' associations, set up the International News Safety Institute (INSI). NUJ General Secretary Jeremy Dear became a director.

International activity has involved a lot more than taking part in international gatherings. For instance, the NUJ's experience has made it useful to colleagues in countries where free unions were being developed for the first time. In the early 1990s there was a huge expansion of training programmes for journalists in Eastern Europe and sub-Saharan Africa, in which NUJ activists – sometimes known as the 'missionaries' – took part, either as members of a programme or as individuals. Many 'missions' were organised through the IFJ, which became a conduit for funds from the aid programmes of the European Community (EC) and of member governments. NUJ members led a seminar programme in Russia as part of the EC's wide-ranging Phare Programme to develop human rights in the former socialist states, and by the end of the century there was probably not a country in Eastern Europe whose journalists had not heard the NUJ message.

They gave their lives

The establishment of the INSI followed an alarming rise in the killing of journalists. They had always been killed in wars, and in some parts of the world, notably Latin America, some had become political targets too, murdered by criminal or paramilitary gangs, often backed by military regimes. In the 1990s this changed. Now journalists in more countries were targeted, including in war zones. The annual total of killings worldwide rose inexorably, from 83 in 1991 to 150 in 2005. More than 100 journalists and their colleagues – producers, camera operators, drivers, translators and fixers, who are just as much at risk – were killed in the first three years of the war in Iraq that began with the US–UK invasion in March 2003.

One of the first killed in that war was an NUJ member: ITN's longest-serving international reporter, Terry Lloyd. He died in a firefight between US troops and fleeing Iraqis; the bodies of his camera operator and translator were never found. For more than three years the NUJ demanded a thorough investigation; its leaders met ministers who wrung their hands and said they were doing all they could. NUJ members were not the only people who held suspicions that he might have been targeted by the Americans 'to encourage the others', for Lloyd was a 'unilateral' reporter, making his own way round the battlefield while the majority had become 'embedded' into advancing military units. Political and military leaders on both sides of the Atlantic had made it chillingly clear that the 'embeds' were expected to give favourable coverage in return for protection, and the 'unilaterals' could be at greater risk.

It took three and a half years of pressure even to get an inquest held; when it did take place, evidence came out that Lloyd had been shot by American troops, which the government had known all along. The coroner returned a verdict of unlawful killing – a breakthrough in the campaign for justice for fallen journalists. The union was working closely with ITN, and they jointly set up a bursary in Lloyd's memory to help each year a young newspaper or radio journalist get into TV.

Two BBC reporters have been shot dead in recent wars: John Schofield from Radio 4 in Croatia in 1995 and Kate Peyton from World Service TV in Somalia ten years later. But the killing that caused the greatest anger in the union was that of Farzad Bazoft, a reporter with the *Observer*, who was hanged in Baghdad in 1993. Bazoft was an Iranian – not really a wise choice to despatch to Iraq on a highly sensitive search for biological weapons just after the ten-year war between the two countries, and the first US-led invasion of 1991. But he was a freelance, anxious to establish himself on the paper, and there was much criticism of management for exploiting his eagerness – and for doing little to help after his arrest: Bazoft was caught with soil samples outside a chemical lab and accused by the Saddam Hussein regime of being an Israeli spy – on misinformation reportedly supplied by a British source.

In these circumstances there was probably little anybody could have done, but the union – though late on the case – kept up frantic protests to the Iraqi and British governments as the wretched Bazoft went through a perfunctory trial and was summarily hanged.

One particular project was run by NUJ members on a voluntary basis: in 2001 they made contact with journalists in Ukraine in order to support a campaign over the murder of a website editor, Georgy Gongadze. The Ukrainians began to campaign against censorship and launched a new independent journalists' union. More than a dozen NUJ members, acting

An NUJ delegation outside the Ukrainian embassy in London in 2002 protesting at the murder of journalist Georgy Gongadze: the protest was the origin of the union's joint programme with Ukrainian colleagues. (Molly Cooper)

independently of the union, got involved in a programme of training courses around Ukraine which boosted the development of independent journalism as well as the new union.

70 years helping refugees find asylum

After Hitler came to power in Germany in the early 1930s, a trickle of refugee journalists began: a trickle that would become a flood. The IFJ became concerned about the issue, but it was the Munich crisis of September 1938 that propelled the NUJ to concentrate on the needs of the refugees.

After the Nazi invasion of Czechoslovakia many Czech journalists fled to London and several union branches took them under their wing. The October meeting of the Trade and Periodical branch – precursor of the later Magazine and Book branch – heard an urgent plea for funds to help the Czech union. A whip-round was held on the spot, and raised ten guineas. A Czecho-Slovak Journalists' Relief Fund was launched, and the union sent national organiser Len Berry to Prague on a four-day fact-finding mission. He reported to the next branch meeting that 'every day brings pitiful letters asking if we can help them get to England'.

NUJ members responded. Those on the *Manchester Guardian* chipped in to rent a house for Czech refugees in the city. The branch reported in May 1939 that 'already three male refugees and the wives of two of them were living there, and more will be coming when rooms have been made ready for them'. Another branch report said: 'When the Germans marched into Prague the first people they searched out and arrested were journalists. Among the millions of people in Europe whose lives are being made unbearable these hundreds of journalists deserve especial attention, and we, as journalists, might make it our task to look after them.' It was the same story after the war, when the democratic Czech government that followed liberation was overthrown by the communists: again the union welcomed those who could get out and even found jobs for some.

During the struggles for the independence of British Commonwealth territories there were always exiled journalists in Britain, and a large number from South Africa.[4] Many were able to find work. But by the end of the last century refugees fleeing wars around the world and

▶

seeking asylum in Britain were finding life increasingly difficult. Amid political pressures to take a harder line on asylum seekers, the threat of deportation increased for many, and the NUJ found itself helping dozens of people often in quite desperate circumstances.

Protest at the imprisonment and threatened deportation of NUJ member Raghbir Singh, editor of a Sikh nationalist weekly paper, in Birmingham in 1995. (Tim Biller)

Local branches mounted lively campaigns to protect those facing deportation. Midlands branches can claim credit for saving two of them: Indian photographer Som Raj in Wolverhampton in 1990, and editor Raghbir Singh in Birmingham in 1995. The campaign for Raghbir, editor of a Punjabi-language Sikh nationalist weekly, took place while he was in prison awaiting deportation. The prime movers were branch officers Jeremy Dear and Miles Barter, later the union's organiser for the North of England and Wales. The union gave others legal support, and was heartened to find that those who would have been in real danger had they been returned to their homelands but had been refused leave to remain in the UK by the Home Office were invariably reprieved when the NUJ submitted statements on their behalf.

A Refugees, Asylum and Media project was founded by the PressWise Trust in Bristol in 2001 to help exiled journalists, and with the RAM project's and the NUJ's support a group of more than forty refugees from dozens of countries formed an Exiled Journalists Network in 2005, offering mutual support and help to find money and work.

The Friends of John McCarthy

In 1986 John McCarthy was a producer with the London-based Worldwide Television News in Lebanon, then in the throes of civil war. The Hizbollah guerrilla group had been kidnapping journalists and, after the bombing of the Libyan capital Tripoli by the United States in spring 1986, WTN decided he should leave. While in a taxi on the way to Beirut airport McCarthy was kidnapped: along with the Church of England emissary Terry Waite and the Irishman Brian Keenan, he would be held in atrocious conditions for five years. The campaign for his release was one of the most vigorous and rewarding that the NUJ had ever been involved in.

Jill Morrell, girlfriend of hostage NUJ member John McCarthy, releases a white dove to mark remembrance of his kidnapping outside St Bride's, the journalists' church in Fleet Street, in 1988. (Andrew Wiard)

A group of supporters set up the Friends of John McCarthy in 1987 and the union gave them free space in Acorn House. NUJ branches organised local fund-raising events using the copious literature produced by the campaign; the Paris branch was particularly active. There were postcards, T-shirts and posters – CLOSE YOUR EYES AND THINK OF ENGLAND was one slogan. There were publicity stunts: candlelit vigils, people sitting in mocked-up cages or chaining

▶

themselves to railings, releasing black balloons or flocks of doves, sponsored bike rides and the like. The *Journalist* ran a front-page panel each issue recording how many days McCarthy had been in captivity.

Unable to put much pressure on the kidnappers, the campaign worked on governments and international bodies to put the same kind of energy into political and diplomatic moves – often to apparently little avail. NUJ delegations went to the Foreign Office in London, the UN in New York and to Palestine Liberation Organisation chief Yasser Arafat in Tunis. The NUJ even gave the Iranian ambassador in London a platform at the 1991 ADM in a bid to put pressure on Hizbollah.

John McCarthy was released in September 1991 and landed at RAF Brize Norton. (Julian Simmonds / Select)

At the heart of the campaign was McCarthy's girlfriend Jill Morrell, who was Mother of the NUJ chapel at WTN. She was a photogenic woman on whom the media were pleased to focus, and though she hated the attention she stuck to the task. When McCarthy was eventually released he thanked the union, but left it and declined to be interviewed for the *Journalist*.

McCarthy's kidnap was initially overshadowed within the union by an episode that drew widespread and largely unfavourable publicity – the so-called 'Gaddafi telegram' affair. McCarthy was seized during the 1986 NUJ ADM, a day after American war planes based in Britain had bombed Libya in an apparent attempt to kill the country's leader Muammar Gaddafi, in reprisal for a terrorist bombing. On their last day of meeting, ADM delegates reacted by voting to send a 'telegram of condolence to the government of Libya'. It was a short debate; the consequences would be a little more enduring. Delegates returning to London later that day were greeted by evening-paper headlines condemning the move. Some union members reacted by calling it a 'cheap stunt'; the union was 'absurd and discredited' (to quote letters in the next *Journalist*). There was a barrage of hostile press reaction. Some branches and chapels dissociated themselves from the NUJ, and when the dust had cleared it was calculated that ninety-six members – some of long-standing – had resigned.

It was certainly one of the ADM's more overexcited reactions in the heat of a dramatic moment; and it had the disastrous effect of obliterating the seizure of McCarthy. One delegate from McCarthy's branch, London Television, did speak of the kidnap at the meeting, and the union was quickly on to the case, but it got little immediate attention. To complicate matters yet further, the mover of the 'telegram' motion at the ADM, Sabah Jawad, was Father of the NUJ chapel at the London bureau of the Libyan news agency JANA. To some this was evidence of collaboration with terrorism on the union's part; they overlooked that Sabah and his chapel were on strike against JANA, objecting to the way staff were being treated and the agency's refusal to negotiate with the union.

PART THREE

OUR WORK

6

WHOSE PRESS FREEDOM?

The unregulated press

There are two kinds of journalism in Britain, as different from each other as soccer is from rugby football. They work to different codes and regulations, yet they cross-fertilise, they work together, they mesh. Perhaps this is why British journalism is as good as any in the world, while football is not.

Journalists are hardly aware of the distinctions, though the public are. The two codes are not, as some might at first think, tabloid and broadsheet, but print and broadcast. Newspapers have for three hundred years been fiercely independent of the state, and even when in decline are so strong that no government can touch them. They can be outspoken, outrageous, irresponsible and generally over-the-top. They operate in a free market, unrestrained except by their own restrictive practices. Broadcasting, on the other hand, operates in a controlled market; it has been licensed and regulated by the state since its inception and can be more susceptible to government pressure.

Journalists working under the two codes approach their work in different ways, with different aspirations. Newspaper journalists are competitive not just for the individual story but to promote their papers. They have a free hand in the methodology they use, and push at the boundaries of law, custom and taste to produce the most spectacular results they can. Broadcast journalists, by contrast, are conscious of offering a public service providing reliable and authoritative information. Their labours are circumscribed by mountains of regulations and subject to scrutiny by statutory bodies.

Of course, newspaper journalists work hard to get their stories right, and broadcasters to make them lively and entertaining – and this is why British journalism, and Irish journalism, which has followed the British pattern, are so strong: the secret is in the mix. Both are highly professional and can withstand most attempts to influence the news; though their susceptibility to self-censorship is another matter. Unlike in football/rugby, journalists can move from print to broadcast and back with hardly a pause for thought. There is a unifying thread to their work. As individuals they work to the same set of professional standards, and this is where the NUJ comes in. Since 1936 it has had a Code of Professional Conduct that guides the way they work. And even if they are not conscious of the code, they will have absorbed its principles from their peers. Of course, there has always been a tussle between the code and the principles of journalism that all understand, on the one hand, and the demands of employers on the other. The union comes in here as well.

When the code was introduced journalists were concerned about their position when called upon to do work against their conscience. Supporting members who refused to carry out unethical work was, wrote General Secretary Harry Richardson in 1934, 'our contribution to the task of cleansing the Press of that sort of sensationalism which entails harassing and paining innocent and sensitive people by pestering them for information'. This support consisted of paying them benefit if they quit their jobs on principle. President Fred Humphrey spoke of the 'get-news-at-any-price business in which the sanctities of the home are invaded, private grief treated without respect, the most secret intimacies bared, and members of our profession called upon to do things which are degrading to them as citizens, let alone journalists. For the good name of journalism we must call a halt.' But there was no written definition of the disreputable work that members should be supported in refusing. The code, it was explained at the ADM of 1936, was therefore a 'tentative definition of the kind of things which a journalist should not be asked to do'.

Fleet Street veteran Tom Foster, who drafted the code, told that ADM that it was a matter of 'keeping control in the hands of our democratic organisation. If we allow things to drift the proprietors would get control of the craft. Or, again, Parliament might intervene.' The union was troubled

at the time by a bill going though Parliament to enact the state registration of journalists. Promoted by the Institute of Journalists, it would have
established a statutory council with the power to withdraw a journalist's
licence to work. Humphrey criticised the registration proposal at a Central
London branch meeting: 'Suppose you struck a man off, are you getting
at the man who sent him out on the job or the proprietor of the paper?
Very definitely you are not. You are merely carrying out that historic old
function of finding the scapegoat.' The Institute's bill got nowhere, and
though the threat of restrictive legislation was raised from time to time
during the twentieth century it never materialised, and in truth the press
never seriously worried that it would.

The code had another function: that of regulating relations between
journalists. As adopted in 1936 it was quite different from the one that
formed the basis for the union's work on journalistic ethics sixty-odd
years later: barely a phrase remained. Most of the 1936 version governed
relations between journalists, covering such matters as obligation to 'treat
subordinates as considerately as [a journalist] would desire to be treated by
his superiors'; the 'special obligation to help an unemployed member to
obtain work'; and the need to 'keep in mind the dangers of the laws of libel,
contempt of court and copyright'. The 'ethical' elements were compressed
into three clauses at the end, beginning: 'A journalist should fully realise
his responsibility for everything he sends to his paper or agency', a simple
sentiment lost from later versions.[1]

Concern at rampant sensationalism resurfaced after the Second World
War, and the 1946 ADM agreed to call for a Royal Commission to look
into the ownership and control of the press, with special reference to the
tendency to monopoly and, among other things, to 'the distortion and
suppression of essential facts in home and foreign news'. An NUJ MP,
Haydn Davies, raised the matter in the Commons and his proposal was
agreed on a free vote. The employers' reaction was described by General
Secretary Clem Bundock as a 'chorus of indignant protest against anything
in the nature of criticism or even impartial enquiry – particularly hysterical in some organs'.

When the Commission's report came out in June 1949 employers
continued in the same vein, and some turned on the NUJ. 'Newspapers Vindicated' was the *Daily Mail* splash, and in a front-page leader it
crowed that the report 'answered the abysmally false charges made against
their own industry by "Left-Wing journalists" who have used their own

ignorance to play upon the ignorance of others ... This agitation was political in origin. The NUJ is composed of members of all shades of political opinion but a very active and left Left-Wing steers this body.'

The Commission had in fact pulled back from radical recommendations, except in one respect, and that was in agreeing to the call for a General Council of the Press. But its report's attitude to the NUJ, which had put up the proposal, was strange. The union had gone to some trouble to gather evidence, asking every branch to set up a press inquiry subcommittee to collect instances of bad practice – not so much by journalists themselves as by editors and proprietors distorting copy, by advertisers wielding influence, by public authorities obstructing the press and so on. The Commission said the NUJ evidence had been 'a selective document [with] no coherent and comprehensive picture and no means of reaching general conclusions about the extent and character of the abuses which had been said to exist'. The NUJ responded with a pamphlet explaining that it had not set out to analyse the findings: it had merely collated the evidence sent in by the branches.

Royal Commissions do not customarily remark in this way on evidence they receive: it was as if this one had concocted the note of disparagement so as to hide the fact that it might have been influenced by the union – for several other of the NUJ's suggestions had been taken up, on training and pensions for instance.

But the Commission's strictures were mild compared with those already levelled by journalists in some of the offices where fault had been alleged. Union officials found themselves under attack as Fleet Street chapels, affronted that the union should connive in criticism of their work, joined in the chorus. 'The evidence contains unwarranted imputations of bad faith and of professional misconduct against fellow-members,' said the *Daily Express* chapel. The *Scottish Daily Express* (then a separate paper) called it 'an unjustifiable attack on the professional integrity of NUJ members'. 'It makes unwarrantable imputations of bad faith and professional misconduct,' thundered the chapel at the London *Evening News*; 'the authors show themselves to be out of touch with these aspects of journalism ... statements should not be accepted as representing the views of NUJ members'. The London Evening Papers branch passed a motion dissociating itself from the evidence as 'inaccurate, misleading and unfair', and the Parliamentary branch 'deplored that the NEC should have embarrassed and damaged its members'.

The 1948 ADM considered these denunciations and expressed support for the evidence by an emphatic 151 votes to 4. In fact, the NUJ evidence was critical not of members but of sensationalist tendencies in reporting and the inaccuracies that could be caused by the speed and pressure of work. The examples it cited – casualty figures being exaggerated in disasters and unfavourable theatre reviews suppressed to pacify advertisers – could appear tame in the light of later newspaper practice, but it was not the last time that national paper chapels and the rest of the union would find themselves at odds.

It took six years for the proposed General Council of the Press to come into being. The employers, who did not like the idea of discussing their work with their employees, dragged their feet, and it took another resolution of the House of Commons – that 'would welcome all possible action on the part of the Press' – to budge them. In 1951 the Newspaper Proprietors' Association, which changed its name to the Newspaper Publishers' Association in 1962, and the Newspaper Society, representing provincial papers, finally produced a plan for a twenty-five-member body, of whom twelve would be managerial and twelve editorial; of these last, seven were to be nominated by the NPA and NS, one by the Guild of Editors, two by the NUJ and two by the IoJ. The twenty-fifth, the chairperson, would be alternately an NPA and an NS representative. It was a simple sum to work out that the owners had given themselves 80 per cent of the places.

In the final line-up, which took another two years to negotiate, the union got four seats. The NPA and NS had ten between them and there were eight editors. The Council did not set itself a code, but accumulated case law like a civil court. Its remit included preserving the freedom of the press, promoting recruitment and training, conducting research and the study of the press, and considering complaints. It started life with the blessing of the NUJ – a 172:7 vote at the 1953 ADM – and relations were initially close. In 1968 Roper Mead, former NUJ President and chief sub of the *Middlesex Chronicle*, became assistant secretary of the Council; and then in 1977 General Secretary Ken Morgan became its joint secretary on resigning from union office, to be promoted to the top job of director two years later, when he brought in former NUJ NEC member Ray Swingler as his own deputy.

By this time, though, relations between the Council and the NUJ were becoming strained, not so much because of the view outside journalism that the Council was ineffectual as because it was seen as relentlessly anti-

union – perhaps not a surprise in view of its composition. Its chairman
Lord Shawcross, a rigid establishment figure who had been Attorney
General in the postwar Labour government, had attacked the NUJ in his
annual report for 1976, and the ADM had demanded his resignation. Later
that year the Council censured two Birmingham city councillors who had
refused to talk to a non-union reporter for 'acting against press freedom'
– a gratuitous departure from its proper role.

Morgan's appointment did not seem to halt these interventions. In
1979 the Council reprimanded the press office of a London borough for
withholding cooperation from a local paper during an NUJ strike, calling
the action 'a particularly serious threat to the public interest'. The Mother
of Chapel at the paper, Jenny Brown, said: 'Once again it has proved
itself to be the waddling dachshund of the press barons. We regard its
ruling as totally irrelevant.' The union's disdain for the Press Council was
voiced by *Journalist* editor Ron Knowles when he refused to cooperate
over a complaint from a National Front journalist who had been denied
admission to the union. Knowles said he was not worried about any ruling
against him because he had no respect for the Council.

One of the union's four representatives on the Council, Jake Ecclestone,
then Father of the NUJ chapel at *The Times*, wrote that it wasn't only the
union that held the Council in contempt; editors and journalists did as
well. 'I have never in twenty years heard of journalists giving the council a
second thought. What it is really doing is to shield from criticism the worst
features of British journalism – political bias and distortion, racial intoler-
ance and prejudice, and the ability to trivialise sex and glamorise crime.'

The union had had enough, and the 1980 ADM voted to pull out.
Aidan White, another of the union's delegates, supported the move; experience had convinced him, he said, that 'the only way to curb the crude
excesses of the press was to ensure that the NUJ Code of Conduct was
enforced' – and the Press Council did not even recognise it. That was the
course the union then decided to follow: to beef up its own mechanisms
for maintaining professional standards.

Standards and skills

Young journalists traditionally learned their trade on the job. Right up to the 1990s they started on local papers, working for a pittance under what were called 'indentures' – a kind of apprenticeship – with the old hands showing them the ropes. They went to classes and sat exams in writing, interviewing, law, government and shorthand. The union always maintained that training was a matter for employers, but it also kept on at them over the standard of training – and over the exploitation of trainees on low wages being used for senior work.

The NUJ's professional training programme was established in a custom-built training suite at head office in 2002. Photographer Martin Jenkinson teaches a Photoshop course. (Kerstin Hacker)

Only from the 1950s was there a single formal qualification, and that had pretty much disappeared by the end of the 1990s. In 1953 the National Council for the Training of Journalists began setting its Proficiency Certificate exams, which lifted 'juniors' on local papers into 'seniors' and brought them the full negotiated minimum senior salary (for what it was worth). It wasn't permitted for new journalists to start on the national papers because of the 'three-year rule', agreed with the Newspaper Proprietors' Association, which stipulated that everyone must serve their time in the provinces. It was not a popular rule among ambitious young journalists but it had a purpose, and the old hacks liked to rage at the basic errors that began appearing in national papers when the rule fell into disuse in the 1990s. When TV and radio began broadcasting news they poached the cream of the journalists from the press, in the manner of top-division football clubs, but in the 1970s they began their own training schemes.

The NCTJ had a long and difficult birth: it took nine years of negotiating with the Newspaper Society and the Guild of British Newspaper Editors, who wanted, first, complete control of who should receive training and, second, the involvement of the IoJ. Eventually the IoJ did get to sit on the Council along with the NUJ and the employers, and the NCTJ worked well. Long-serving NUJ official Bob Norris was a council member for 25 years, serving as chairman in the 1990s. But in the 1980s things began to fall apart.

Some of the big employers – Westminster Press and Thomson Regional Newspapers among them – started their own in-house schemes with their own qualifications. But the biggest blow to the old regime came from outside the media – from higher education. Local authority grants for study dried up and, in response to demand, universities began introducing courses. It quickly transpired that journalism and media studies were much sought after, and so on-the-job training rapidly gave way to the classroom. Unusually in Western countries, there was no undergraduate journalism education in the UK until 1991, when four universities unveiled the first courses. Fifteen years later there are nearly a hundred.

Employers were not slow to spot a way of saving money: why devote resources to bringing on young journalists when the education system would churn them out for nothing? At the same time the NUJ was losing its authority to enforce standards, the three-year rule collapsed and in some areas – not all – it was a free-for-all. The NCTJ lost its formal 'lead body' status as the setter of standards and turned itself into a commercial training provider – an increasingly crowded business. Its chairman in 2006 was Kim Fletcher, a Wapping refusenik as a former Father of the Chapel at the *Sunday Times*, and later editor of the *Independent on Sunday*.

But it still took time for university training to become accepted by industry leaders. Among old-school journalists – educated at the 'university of life' – there was a residual prejudice, not so much against graduates, who had been entering journalism in rising numbers since the 1960s, but against academic journalism. But this wasn't the students' fault, and the NUJ geared itself up to help them. From 1996 it gave free membership to students – a £10 fee to obtain a student press card was introduced in 2002 – in the hope they would remain in membership when they moved into work. The decision, made at the 1996 ADM, was proposed by NEC member Jeremy Dear, who six years later at the age of thirty-five became the first graduate to lead the union.

There were still gaps in journalists' training, however, which the union moved to fill. Freelances, in particular, had always lacked training, and in 1981 the London Freelance branch launched the first courses in sub-editing – to help freelances get casual shifts.

Members already in work were worried about falling behind in technology; updated production systems were constantly being introduced, and they were expected to be able to use them. The big lift-off came in 1998 when the NUJ won a grant from the government's Union Learning Fund to provide short courses in the use of word-processing and design software. These were promoted in a one-page advertisement in the *Journalist*, and the union was bowled over by the response. More than three thousand members applied. Within a few years the training department, funded with two further and bigger ULF grants, had expanded to employ four people and lay on more than fifty courses a year, covering a wide range of journalistic as well as technological skills.

Michael Foot

Michael Foot (1913–) first stood for Parliament as an unsuccessful
Labour candidate in 1935, and joined the NUJ two years later when
he became a full time journalist, working for the Labour-supporting
Daily Herald and the left-wing weekly *Tribune*. He was active in the
formation of the Socialist League, a left-wing pressure group led by
Stafford Cripps, and was one of the founders of *Tribune*, working as
assistant editor in 1937, editor 1948–52 and 1956–9, and managing
director 1945–1974. During the Second World War he became editor
of the London *Evening Standard*, but resigned in 1943 because of sharp

*Former editor and government
minister Michael Foot was made
an NUJ Member of Honour at
the 1985 ADM. (IFL)*

political differences between him and his proprietor, Lord Beaverbrook.
He entered Parliament as MP for Devonport in the Labour landslide of
1945, losing Devonport ten years later, but returning in 1965 after the
death of his friend and mentor Aneurin Bevan, as MP for Bevan's old
seat of Ebbw Vale. A left-wing backbencher throughout Harold Wilson's
first governments in 1964–70, he was made Secretary for Employment after Wilson's narrow victory in 1974 and improved workers'
rights with the Employment Protection Act, 1975. After Wilson's unex-
pected resignation in 1976, Foot narrowly lost the leadership to James
Callaghan, but won it when Callaghan retired in 1980. He resigned
after the election defeat of 1983. He has produced a constant stream of
books and articles, including studies of H. G. Wells and Jonathan Swift.
An NUJ member throughout his life, he is now a Member of Honour.

Raising the standard

When employers were blind to reason

In the mid-1970s a strange compulsion gripped the newspaper industry. The NUJ was strongly established, with effective closed shops at most of the nationals. It was publicly declaring that standards of journalism should be improved and becoming frustrated at the inability of the Press Council to ensure this. The employers considered these things and concluded that the NUJ was determined to control the press, and that there should be a law against it! – an Act of Parliament to outlaw the NUJ closed shop.

The notion that the union was seeking to usurp the authority of editors was a preposterous fantasy: the NUJ could not control its own members' work – even if it had wanted to – let alone that of a newspaper. But for a few difficult years the fantasy persisted.

In 1974, to reverse much of the anti-union legislation brought in by the Conservative government of the past four years, the new Labour government put forward a Trade Unions and Labour Relations (Amendment) Act. The Tories had outlawed closed shops. Labour was going to permit them again. The minister responsible, the Secretary of State for Employment, was NUJ member, former editor, left-wing orator and illustrious writer Michael Foot. There was to be no special favour for his union; all Labour was doing was to restore the pre-1971 state of affairs, when the NUJ had closed shops and no one bothered – publicly at least – about any threat to press freedom.

Norman Fowler

Norman Fowler (1938–) worked for *The Times* from 1961 until elected to Parliament in 1970, becoming home affairs correspondent. He held government posts at transport, social services, and employment. Despite running into NUJ opposition as Margaret Thatcher's Employment Secretary, he remained a member of the union he joined soon after joining *The Times*, and is now a life member. He was chairman of Midland Independent Newspapers from 1991 to 1998 and of Regional Independent Media from 1998 to 2002. He became Lord Fowler in 2001.

The Newspaper Society and the Newspaper Publishers' Association, however, naturally backed by the IoJ and the Tory opposition, now
declared otherwise. There were letters to *The Times* and debates in Parliament. Norman Fowler, a former journalist on *The Times* and NUJ member
who became a minister under Margaret Thatcher, spoke against his union:
'A single union which had control of journalists would be a serious threat
to the freedom of editorial expression, which is essential in a democracy.'

Foot proposed a statutorily backed Charter of Press Freedom, to
protect editorial freedom from any undue influence: from government, proprietors, political interests or advertisers, for instance. The NUJ
national executive supported the idea. But the issue was complicated by
the position of editors: the NUJ had a category of Associate Membership,
exempting editors from the instruction to join industrial action but in
return depriving them of some rights – taking part in chapel meetings,
for instance, if they had 'hire and fire' powers. In 1974 this category of
membership was abolished: editors must now be full members or not at
all. To the union's critics this meant that, if editors chose to belong, they
would be ordered out on strike. But it wasn't the case, for the NEC had
declared already that in a strike editors could do their normal work.

This was what the commotion was really all about: the effectiveness of
industrial action by NUJ chapels. In strike after strike – and there were
a lot in the early 1970s – journalists would stand on their picket lines
and see their papers coming out with copy from Press Association, IoJ
strikebreakers and whoever, shovelled through to the comps by editors
who claimed it was their 'normal work'. That is why the union ended the
special membership category, and why the chapels wanted closed shops;
it had nothing to do with wielding editorial power. And it's also why the
owners didn't – nothing to do with press freedom, either.

The frustrated local activists were now dominating decision-making
at NUJ conferences, and in 1975, in what the *Journalist* called 'one of the
best-argued and most exciting debates for several years', they overturned
the NEC's policy and rejected the charter, insisting that all chapels should
go for closed-shop agreements and that editors obey instructions, and
spurning 'any charter on press freedom agreed with proprietors, whose
policies of monopolisation, retraction and closure have made a mockery
of the free press'.

It wasn't just the young militants voicing these opinions: delegates
cheered a speech from veteran Yorkshire freelance Stan Crowther, who

The closed shop

The NUJ had pursued the closed shop since an ADM decision of 1920. There are three varieties:

● the 'pre-entry' closed shop defines an office where any journalist taken on must already be a union member; there have been only a couple in NUJ history

● the 'post-entry' closed shop, or '100 per cent shop', exists where non-members can be taken on but must then join; this requires the agreement of management

● the 'declared closed shop' exists where a chapel announces its policy and takes action to secure it by refusing to work with non-members and taking strike action if necessary. Up to the 1980s there were a lot of these, and there were half a dozen prolonged disputes over them too.

In many newsrooms it was simply assumed that everyone was in the NUJ. Alan Knowles, an activist in the BBC in Manchester for years, was Father of the Chapel in the closed shop at the *Bolton Evening News* during the 1950s. He recalls:

> On one occasion a colleague deliberately allowed his membership to lapse. A chapel meeting was called to discuss what to do. I was told that the editor would like to see me in his office. When I went in, he showed me a letter he was intending to send to the journalist in question. It read, 'I expect all journalists working here to be members of the National Union of Journalists.' He asked me, 'Will that do?' The erring member paid up his subs – together with a small fine – and the whole affair was settled without any resort to a strike or other form of industrial action.

In Fleet Street closed shops were established without any disputes; the same was true of the post-entry closed shop at IPC, the biggest magazine group, and of a few smaller magazine publishers like that of *Time Out*. In fact, the IPC chapel had surrendered a pre-entry shop, which it inherited when IPC absorbed Odhams Press magazines in 1961. The NUJ at Odhams, which also owned the pro-Labour *Daily Herald*, had enjoyed a closed shop since the early 1930s.

three years earlier had been the Mayor of Rotherham, riding in triumph to the 1972 ADM in the mayoral Daimler, and was from 1979 its Member of Parliament. 'The real freedom of the press barely exists at all,' he said. 'Have we done this? Have we introduced monopoly and censorship? Why should we be so defensive? Our hands are clean. Ours are the only clean hands in the industry.' Even Ken Morgan, the highly diplomatic General Secretary, described the employers' stance as 'five per cent concern and 95 per cent cant.'

But in overturning the NEC's carefully drawn up policy the conference had left Morgan and the NEC in a spot, which they resolved by arranging a Special Delegate Meeting and fixing its agenda so that it could discuss only one motion: to put the ADM decisions out to a vote of the whole membership. The members dutifully overturned the crucial parts of the ADM decision and the union was back in the charter business.

Meanwhile in Parliament the Trade Unions and Labour Relations (Amendment) bill was ping-ponging between the Commons and the Lords. Each time the Lords put in the amendment to outlaw the NUJ closed shop – moved by Lord Goodman, a prominent solicitor and Downing Street confidant of Prime Minister Harold Wilson, and chairman of the Newspaper Publishers' Association – the Commons took it out. There was talk of invoking the Parliament Act to overrule the Lords, but eventually they backed down and it went through, including the Charter on Press Freedom, which was to be drawn up within a year under the supervision of the Secretary of State Albert Booth, Foot having moved on. In gratitude for his steadfastness in holding off the union's enemies Michael Foot was awarded NUJ Membership of Honour in 1985.

The union was one of the bodies listed for consultation on the charter. It sent representatives to the meetings, where the NPA and the Newspaper Society obstructed every proposal. Clearly they were not about to sit down and seriously discuss their work with their employees. The talks got nowhere, and the matter simply died. After all the hullabaloo everything ended up as before. The NUJ still had its closed shops – though they were not to last long – but it did have to work out new ways to make the Code of Conduct and its policies on press standards work. The NEC set up a Media Freedom Working Party, which in 1980 took a big step forward with a plan to do just that.

Enforcing the code

How to enforce the Code of Conduct is a riddle that has bothered the NUJ for seventy years. The union believed in press freedom and had no will to enforce any line on anyone; on the other hand, it also believed in responsible journalism and wanted to stop unfair, dishonest and biased reporting. On the one hand it possessed a mechanism to discipline its members, but on the other it didn't want to force anyone out of the trade.

The causes of bad journalism, the union agreed, stemmed from the employers – whether it was pressure to distort the facts so as to make a story, a policy of stigmatising a specific group, a commercial or political interest in advancing some cause, or simply a case of understaffing and overwork leading to inadequate checking and sloppy standards generally. The way to uphold standards, therefore, was to use the union's strength against employers. As the chairperson of the NUJ Media Freedom Working Party, the broadcaster Vincent Hanna, told the ADM in 1981, the Code of Conduct should be backed by industrial action. 'Our union abounds with journalists who will beat their breasts and tell you of their trade unionism when it comes to getting high wages for their work,' he said, 'but who regard it as effete, or even worse, left-wing, when you ask them to think about their work and the use that is made of it.'

The union had agreed in the abortive charter talks not to put 'improper pressure' on editors. When the 1976 ADM had discussed the charter process it had agreed to this, with a proviso that 'action taken to enforce the NUJ Code of Conduct shall not be deemed to be improper pressure'. The NEC had accepted it, apparently on the understanding that 'action' meant disciplinary action under union rules over breaches of the code.

But now the conference agreed it could mean industrial action, and over the next few years there were half a dozen instances, the first in NUJ history. In 1981 'bold and prompt' action by the *Wimbledon News* chapel in south-west London saved the job of a sub who was sacked for refusing an editor's instruction to handle a National Front press release on the grounds that it was against the code. The NF release said that 'white British people' should be given preference over 'racial aliens'. The chapel went into mandatory session for a day and a half – effectively a strike – and the sub, Brian Hanney, was reinstated. Then journalists at *Lloyds List*, the daily shipping and insurance business paper, fought off an attempt at censorship by the owners, embarrassed at a story on insurance corruption.

Here they were supporting a principled editor, Roy Farndon, ordered by managers to kill the story. A day's run was lost before the managers backed down and the story went ahead.

The most spectacular actions were in broadcasting (see p. 264), but a twenty-four-hour strike at the *Oxford Mail* in 1987 was a shining example of a principle upheld. A staff photographer, Tony Moore, was disciplined for defying an editor's instruction to photograph a disabled five-year-old on his first day at school. The mother had asked journalists to leave them alone, but editor Eddie Duller told Moore to snatch a picture. The chapel voted to stop work and leafleted the city, winning public sympathy. Generous thanks received were from the local council and the teachers' unions.

At the same time there was a surge in attempts to enforce the code through complaints brought against members for alleged breaches. Many were about allegedly racist reporting, and most of these were on national papers – whose chapels responded with irritation. In 1981 four reporters on the *Sun* were subject to complaints over a joint-bylined account of a march of mostly but not exclusively black people from south London protesting at the deaths of some young blacks in a house fire in which arson was suspected – though never proved. The march passed peacefully near the *Sun*'s office, which must have been a terrible culture shock for staff since the paper wrote of a 'black mob running riot ... frightened mothers and their children leaping to safety as the mob surged along Fleet Street'. Three of the four reporters failed to turn up at the hearing, but the one who did explained he had no part in the racist element of the story, made clear his distaste for it and was acquitted.

The *Sun*'s editor was Kelvin MacKenzie, the swaggering embodiment of tabloid journalism in the era of Margaret Thatcher. To many journalists, and not just right-wingers, he was a hero: fearless, outspoken and dynamic. To others he was a crude and bullying lout. He was generally popular with staff, however – until in 1983 the NUJ chapel, embarrassed at a string of cooked-up stories that led even the Press Council to object, called a mandatory meeting and passed a pointedly simple motion: 'This chapel reminds all journalists that the Code of Conduct is important to each and every one.' The vote was 44:2; the arguments of the two were not reported.

The FoC, Malcolm Withers, went much further when four months later the *Sun* was caught out faking an interview with the widow of a Falklands War hero. The Press Council condemned it as a 'deplorable, insensitive deception'. Withers condemned the editor 'for publishing this deception, and also for a string of similar incidents. There has got to be a return to standards. The chapel is very angry because the Press Council's condemnation has reflected on everyone. It subjects journalists to hefty ridicule from colleagues in Fleet Street.'

At that time the *Sun* was the battleground for the most contentious professional dispute in the union's history, the Ronald Spark case. In the years since the NUJ adopted its Code of Conduct and required members to follow it, not one has been expelled for its breach, but Spark came perilously close. He was the leader-writer who in May 1982, when the *Sun* was banging the drum for 'our boys' in the Falklands War, wrote a leader headed 'Dare Call It Treason'. It began portentously, 'There are traitors in our midst', and went on to attack journalists who were raising questions about the waging of war against Argentina, citing two individuals: BBC *Newsnight* presenter Peter Snow and a *Guardian* cartoonist (unnamed), who was Leslie Gibbard.

A complaint was laid against Spark by the union's Deputy General Secretary Jake Ecclestone. Spark did not turn up at the disciplinary hearing so missed a fantastic diatribe in which Ecclestone called him 'an unscrupulous and ethically degenerate coward for whom, apparently, no depths are too great for him to sink. Since Mr Spark enjoys the moral and political cesspit, let him stay in it ... I cannot conceive of a more grievous breach of our Code of Conduct. Unless we take action we may as well toss the code out of the window.' The NEC was recommended to expel Spark from the union and, despite the pleas of officials and Fleet Street representatives, agreed to do so by 10 votes to 8.

There was an outcry from journalists as diverse as the right-wing Bernard Levin in *The Times* to the left-wing Paul Foot in the *Journalist*, which carried a leader against the sentence. The *Sun* chapel, which had urged Spark not to cooperate with the procedure – he had told the disciplinary committee to 'get stuffed' – deplored the expulsion and pledged to defend him, and to defend their closed shop.

This, of course, was the issue: management had made it clear that they would not fire the man, so his expulsion from the union would have broken the closed shop. Spark appealed to the NUJ Appeals Tribunal, an independent body of experienced union activists, which hastily reduced the penalty to a reprimand. Their reasons were several: for one thing, the

leader was an expression of opinion that the tribunal was loath to interfere
with, and its language was purely rhetorical: no one was going to be
thrown into the Tower of London and beheaded for treason. The jobs of
Snow and Gibbard were not threatened. No one should have worried too
much about being called a traitor by the *Sun*; some may even have regarded
it as a compliment. More seriously, the tribunal heeded the warnings of
Withers, who represented his member at the hearing. The reasoning was
industrial as well as ethical – perfectly reasonable for a trade union.

This clash between the national union and a Fleet Street chapel was
soon followed by another. A rule adopted in 1982 obliged chapel leaders,
if a complaint had been brought against their publications over material
that carried no byline, to find out which member was responsible and
inform the union. 'Inform' was the word: chapel leaders regarded it as an
instruction to grass their members, and Ted Simpson, for many years FoC
at the London *Evening Standard*, pursued a running battle with the NEC
that saw him first censured for refusing to do so, then exonerated with
an apology.

Simpson was a donnish, cultured man with a taste for bow-ties, a former
NEC member and for a year editor of the *Journalist*; for nearly twenty years
before that he had been assistant to the long-serving editor Allen Hutt. In
1984 the union received two complaints against the *Standard*, both over
stories that were inaccurate and unfair, and both acknowledged as such by
the paper; the Press Council had censured it over one of them. The chapel
was asked to identify the culprits, but Simpson failed to do so and so the
complaint was switched to him. His stand was not an individual one: the
Standard chapel had voted not to cooperate, and Simpson's defence was
that he was complying with a democratic decision.

The NEC was in a tricky position, since it had attempted without
success to persuade the ADM to scrap the rule. But it adopted a strict
interpretation of it, found Simpson guilty, censured him and warned him
as to his future conduct – which drove him to even greater fury since
he had by now retired. It was 'a squalid episode', he said. 'It would get
up my nose to be asked to be a common informer and I refuse to do it.'
Matters were not advanced when he led a three-strong deputation from
the *Standard* chapel to make their case at an NEC meeting. The team
included an aggressive young reporter called Richard Littlejohn, who
raised the temperature in the pub over the road afterwards by threatening
mayhem against left-wing union types 'because I am horrendously right-

David Ross, Father of the Chapel at the Daily Express, *personified Fleet Street trade unionism. (Alan Wylie)*

wing' – a trait that proved bankable in his later career as a 'you couldn't make it up' columnist on the *Sun* and the *Daily Mail*.

'I believe there were influential groupings determined on confrontation, with me a particular target,' Simpson wrote. 'Nothing else will explain the bitter persistence and vindictiveness with which this affair has been pursued.' Others believed that the NEC did so deliberately to discredit the rule. Certainly it was never used again, and was abolished. And eventually Simpson got his reprieve and his apology.

The affair had the effect of convincing more national paper chapels that the provincial-dominated NEC was out to get them. Another Fleet Street institution, David Ross, wrote in the *Journalist* that the Code of Conduct should be scrapped. 'Its use has nearly wrecked the union,' he wrote, referring to the Spark case. If Spark had been expelled, 'some of the biggest chapels would have collapsed'. The code, he said, was 'an assembly of fashionable taboos, forbidding advocacy of sexual, sexist or racial discrimination. It does not, however, prevent us from advocating ... arson, rape and bloody murder ... torture, war and nuclear extermination.'

The answer: an Ethics Council

The union was set on the course of intensifying its activity on media standards, and in 1985 it set up the Ethics Council to take over all its professional work in the field, including the handling of complaints under the code, from the NEC. It was not a new idea: the first call for such a committee had been heard at the 1950 ADM in Bath. 'There is a keen desire among members that we have a clean press,' declared Harry Cousins of the Central London branch, 'and it is not fair to expect individual members to bear the full burden.' The NEC opposed the call on the grounds that the Press Council was the chosen route to follow, and the vote was tied. On a recount it was lost by one vote.

The Ethics Council, when it arrived, had an educational remit – to promote the code. Vincent Hanna presented it to the ADM in 1985 as a 'prestige body whose primary role was to take the Code of Conduct to the members' and encourage a collective responsibility for union policy. The aim had been to avoid 'a heavy Policeman Plod-type body'. Union leaders and the Council itself have reiterated this ever since, but the disciplinary machinery was there and people were going to use it. In the first couple of years it had to deal with more than two hundred complaints, and though the level fell off, the impression was given to those who wanted to see it that the union was trying to police its members' work.

David Ross's contention that the code was a mechanism for the imposition of censorship was surely overblown, but he had a point as far as the selectivity of the union's activity on ethics was concerned. By far the most widely cited clause in the code was the one outlawing discrimination against social groups. In the 1980s it seemed that almost every year new groups were added to the list of people about whom discriminatory material must not be handled. The Ethics Council's first judgement was over a racist cartoon – in the *Sun*. It followed a Press Council ruling that a *Sun* story, 'Arab Pig Sneaks Back In', was not racist and showed pigs protesting outside the *Sun*'s Wapping office with the caption: 'Now the pigs object to being called Arabs.' It no doubt disgusted a lot of people, but the cartoonist Stanley Franklin wrote to the Council affirming that he detested racism and apologised for causing offence. His penalty was reduced from a £500 fine to a reprimand.

The portrayal of women, ethnic groups and homosexuals was the issue in virtually all the complaints; there were hardly any to do with accuracy, bribery, the correction of errors or the use of surreptitious means to get

*In 1978 the union produced a series
of recruitment posters based on
movie stills, designed by Dave King,
including this promotion for the
Code of Conduct using an image
of Humphrey Bogart as an editor
defying the mob in Richard Brooks's*
Deadline USA *(1952). (NUJ
Collection)*

**SORRY FRIENDS,
I'M STICKING TO THE CODE OF CONDUCT!
JOIN THE NUJ!**

stories. Ethics Council member Alan Mitchell wrote: 'The issue of professional ethics has been hijacked by the equality lobby.' The system allowed
members of the public to make complaints, and it seemed to some that
complainants were less interested in journalism than in social justice for
the groups concerned. There was nothing disreputable about this; many
would see no distinction, and correcting prejudicial journalism is a worthwhile activity; but it supplied an argument to critics of the Ethics Council
that the union was being used.

The late 1980s were a difficult time for any union-based campaign.
Many unions were reeling from the attacks of the Thatcher government,
and those in the media particularly. It was as if the transformation of
society that Thatcher was inspiring required the collaboration of the media
so urgently that a tighter discipline had to be imposed. Journalists could
not be permitted a collective voice that might challenge the new order,
especially in the name of good professional practice. This was a period
of shame for the British press: rarely before or since – even in wartime
– had they been so close to government. Most papers were besotted
with Margaret Thatcher. A clutch of national paper editors accepted
knighthoods – which was hitherto almost unknown; among journalists

there had been some disdain for honours, but it was apparently no disgrace in Thatcher's time.[2]

It was not just the NUJ that was suffering; the Press Council was being assailed for its failures from all sides: by politicians and celebrities over the persistence of revelations about their private lives, and by press-freedom campaigners like the NUJ over its failure to deal with falling standards. The former were perhaps the stronger faction and it became clear, as the spectre of statutory control reared its head again, that the Council would need all the friends it could get, even one as long-forsaking as the NUJ. Council director Ken Morgan had always wanted the union back in – 'It was a gross blunder to leave,' he says – and the union executive was sympathetic, but the ADM took some persuading and the decision in 1989 to reopen conditional contact with the Council was distinctly grudging. 'We should give it a chance to come up to our standards,' said former *Journalist* editor Bernie Corbett. 'The Press Council has become a byword for uselessness. The term "toothless watchdog" was invented for it.' The adoption of the NUJ Code was one of the conditions for the union's return, but in truth this proviso was just a face-saving gesture. A year later the decision to rejoin, without any conditions being met, went through almost on the nod.

Legislation was once again threatened after a government inquiry into the state of the press led by Sir David Calcutt. It was not a full Royal Commission but a quick-fix hatchet job, which recommended a tribunal with statutory powers to impose restrictions on investigatory activities, to subject newspapers that broke them to fines and to enable individuals to prevent the publication of embarrassing revelations. Everyone – publishers, journalists and the union alike – was horrified, but moves were afoot behind the scenes: in effect, the proprietors staged an internal coup to seize total control. They changed the Council's name to the Press Complaints Commission, they adopted their own Code of Practice – much weaker than the union's. They dumped all the Council's positive responsibilities – for safeguarding press freedom, supervising training and so on – and kicked out everyone except editors and a group of 'lay' members drawn from the Great and the Good. In effect the PCC became no more than a machinery for handling complaints.

The NPA hadn't even told Morgan:

I only knew about it the same time as everybody else. The NPA

Chris Frost, a former local paper activist who became a professor of journalism and has been head of the NUJ's Ethics Council since 1993. (John Gladwin)

was pulling a lot of strings in an attempt to head off anything worse than the PCC. Calcutt was full of menaces – a tribunal and criminal sanctions. Those things were being said to push the industry into doing something. So they rushed through a proposal to assuage any government desire for action.

The Calcutt proposals disappeared as mysteriously as the PCC had appeared. 'The PCC was essentially the owners,' says Morgan, 'and the professional representatives proved all to be editors.'

After a barely decent interval Morgan was forced out by the new chairman, Lord MacGregor, who came from the Advertising Standards Authority (ASA) and brought with him a new director, Mark Bolland. The ASA, a self-regulatory body, was regarded as a model; nobody – not even the NUJ – asked whether the criteria for editorial might not be rather different from those appropriate to advertising. But the PCC, too, came to be considered a success. It had seen off the Calcutt menace and would tell the world, continually, that press standards were improving. Few believed it, but few were prepared to challenge it, either.

The Ethics Council's work began to fall off. Chris Frost, a journalist turned academic who chaired it from 1993, wrote in 2000: 'The anti-union stance of the government during the 1980s and 1990s led to a general weakening of union power and this played a part in reducing the role of the Ethics Council. The union was less inclined to deal harshly with members as workers became less confident of the benefits of belonging to a union.'[3]

When journalists at the Express group in London objected to the constant pressure from proprietor Richard Desmond to produce brutally racist headlines about immigration in 2001, it was the PCC they turned to. When, for six days in a row, Desmond had pressured executives into leading the front page with such splash headlines, the chapel voted to declare that 'the media should not distort or whip up confrontational racist hatred, in pursuit of increased circulation'. But the action the chapel sought was to ask the NUJ to complain to the PCC. Unsurprisingly, the complaint was rejected – though on the hardly relevant grounds that no individuals had been named in the copy.

Three years later, in a similar episode, the *Express* cranked up a campaign over a supposed 1.6 million Gypsies who, according to the paper, were about to flood Britain with the enlargement of the European Union. Journalists were receiving calls from racists saying, 'Well done, keep it up.' The Mother of the *Express* chapel, Michelle Stanistreet, says: 'It was very upsetting, there was a great deal of anguish.' Again a crowded and angry chapel meeting of *Express* journalists decided to write to the PCC, this time to raise the need to protect journalists unwilling to work against the NUJ Code of Conduct – effectively calling for a 'conscience clause' to allow them to refuse to do such work without jeopardising their jobs. This submission, too, was rejected by the PCC, which said it was a matter between the employer and the employee. Michelle Stanistreet says the issue summed up the union's workplace role:

> It was about sticking up for someone at work; it would be harder for them to pick on us all than to pick on one. Where does it get us if all the decent people resign? If people leave, who will staff the paper then? People just out of college who will be desperate to do anything to impress? In any case, most people can't just walk out on their jobs, and we can't all work for employers we agree with.

NUJ members at the Express group took an even stronger stand in 2006 when they refused to work on a feature in the *Daily Star* mocking Britain's Muslim community. A meeting of the *Daily Star* chapel was hurriedly called, which voted with only one against to express 'deep concern at the [page] which we consider to be deliberately offensive to Muslims'. The feature had been cleared by executives but they quickly agreed to drop it. 'They were aware it was not liked because there had been objections at earlier stages,' said Chapel Father Steve Usher. 'But it was as if a light had suddenly come on and they saw what they were doing.' The journalists' action, which was without precedent in recent times, won wide applause within and outside the union.

The NUJ has a specific role to act 'as a kind of internal counter-weight to arbitrary executive power', the crusading journalist and union activist Paul Foot wrote in 1995. He wrote in the *Journalist's Handbook*: 'The effect of the destruction of unions inside the newspaper offices has been devastating. Every single journalist I know reports that free discussion and argument [have been] replaced by a sullen discipline, ruinous of independent thought and judgement.' He added: 'I can't think of a single reform which would at a stroke improve our newspapers more quickly than the revival of the NUJ as a real force in newspaper offices.'

The chapel's 'conscience clause' proposal echoed concerns the union had been raising since the 1930s. In 2005 the NEC formally adopted the text for such a clause, to be added to the Code of Conduct. It read: 'A journalist has the right to refuse assignments or be identified as the author of editorial which would break the letter and spirit of the code. No journalist can be disciplined or suffer detriment to their career for asserting his/her rights to act according to the code.' Now, as the President at the time, Tim Lezard, wrote in the *Journalist*, came the hard bit: getting employers to agree. The Society of Editors had turned the idea down, but Lezard was adamant: 'It's vital for us to have a say in our work. The conscience clause isn't about muzzling the media, it's about empowering our members and improving industry standards.'

Broadcasting finds its voice

Radio journalism came to stay

The advent of radio broadcasting in the early 1920s was seen by the press
as a threat. When the British Broadcasting Company, as it was first called,
began transmissions in 1922, the newspaper proprietors and news agencies
were anxious that the new medium should not threaten their monopolies.
The result was an agreement, overseen by the Postmaster-General, that the
BBC would not broadcast news before seven o'clock in the evening, would
not collect news itself, and would pay for and credit the news agencies
whose dispatches it used. The NUJ, failing to appreciate that the BBC
would become the largest employer of journalists, acquiesced in the deal.

By 1926, the potential importance of broadcasting was becoming
clear. During the General Strike,[4] while newspapers were reduced to
truncated emergency editions the BBC increased its news broadcasts. The
BBC's director, John Reith, attempted to prevent the government from
commandeering the airwaves by determining that the national interest
coincided with that of the government, and by denying Labour leaders
access to the new medium. Some trade unionists complained about the
coverage. The General Strike had focused attention on radio's potential:
crowds would gather round wireless sets to listen to the news. After 1926
– the BBC became a publicly owned corporation in 1927 – broadcast
news coverage was still limited. But, together with a panoply of outside
broadcasts, talks on current affairs and other strands of programming, it
continued to increase throughout the 1930s. And such was the growth in
the numbers of journalists employed that, while it did not recognise trade
unions for bargaining, in 1937 the BBC agreed to match the union-negotiated rates with the Newspaper Proprietors' Association's.

The 1943 NUJ Annual Delegate Meeting accepted that 'radio journalism has come to stay, and will almost certainly extend its field of activities after the war'. A committee was set up to examine pay, conditions
and the possibility of representing journalists at the Corporation. The
committee report accepted that the two journalisms, radio and newspaper,
were complementary. 'One of the most impressive facts brought to our
attention is the high standard demanded by BBC radio journalism,' the
report conceded. It was an early demonstration of the NUJ's admiration for public service editorial standards, and it reflected concerns about
newspaper sensationalism – concerns that found expression after the war

when the union led the call for a Royal Commission on the press. The report estimated that around one hundred members were already working for the Corporation, and that they 'generally enjoy a condition of security ... as admirable as it is unique'. Such conditions, thanks to the membership the union was able to build within the BBC, would generally remain.

The year 1946 saw the founding of the NUJ London Radio branch and the first BBC chapel, in the European News Service. But the BBC did not hurry to recognise unions. A Staff Association had existed since the war, and there was also an Association of BBC Engineers. These would merge to form the Association of Broadcasting Staffs in 1956. In the early 1950s, the NUJ began negotiations for formal recognition. It was finally agreed on 31 December 1954, making the NUJ the first independent union to be recognised. The union also made an agreement with the Staff Association to prevent the 'poaching' of members, and a committee was set up to facilitate cooperation between the two.

The introduction of commercial television in 1955 was opposed by the union, which feared that not only would it bring about a decline in standards but that it would also threaten newspaper revenues, putting print journalists' jobs at risk.

But the members working for the new commercial services were soon active. In October that year the London Radio branch welcomed news of plans to set up a chapel at Independent Television News, which secured 75 per cent penetration by the time ITN went on air. A London Television branch was formed in 1972 – launched at a champagne reception at the London Hilton hotel. The next year, despite the opposition of the NUJ, worried again that it would bleed advertising revenue from the newspapers, independent local radio joined the broadcasting mix. And the union appointed its first full-time broadcast organiser, Paddy Leech. He was also the first NUJ full-time official not to have been a journalist himself.

Back at the BBC in the 1950s, the NUJ opened negotiations with management at the Alexandra Palace site in north London. Journalists at the Lime Grove current affairs studios organised a chapel of their own. But though in successive reorganisations of its structure the union would establish a Radio Council, a Radio and Television Council and ultimately a Broadcasting Industrial Council, the broadcasting journalists often felt that their concerns were remote from the rest of the union, where the print traditions were still dominant.

Invasion of the greengrocers

Early on, the BBC developed live sports reporting, lugging equipment into the crowded press boxes at cricket and football grounds. 'Alas for reporters who use the Press Box at St James's Park, Newcastle,' complained a *Journalist* branch correspondent in 1956. 'Not only do they have to watch the weekly bumbling of Newcastle United but their refreshments are cut off, they must scramble like schoolboys for a cup of tea, and – worst of all – they are crowded out of their seats by radio engineers genuine, radio engineers phoney, and the wives, uncles and aunts of radio engineers …'

NUJ members from BBC Radio Sheffield set up a fruit and veg stall to make their point in their 1976 strike against the use of a greengrocer to broadcast sports reports on their station. (NUJ Collection)

There was another vexing question: who should do the reporting? The use of non-journalists to file sports reports – in newspapers as well – was the source of regular union complaints. A speaker at the 1953 ADM, held on the Isle of Man, complained: 'In Preston, they had a cotton mill secretary who at weekends blossomed out as a radio reporter of football matches, and there was a local government PRO who gave commentaries on rugby matches. Where is it going to end? We might well get Civil Servants doing radio sports reports in triplicate.'

In 1976 journalists at BBC Radio Sheffield pushed the issue to industrial action, striking over the use of a local vegetable wholesaler to report football. The chapel conducted a lively dispute, setting up a stall outside their studios to sell cut-price fruit and veg to make their point, but the gesture was a failure.

The union executive had decided to step up the pressure by instructing other BBC chapels to strike in support, but a number of leading BBC members in London revolted, making it clear that they would not support the action. Press coverage was hostile; the NEC lost its nerve, called off the stoppages and ordered the Sheffield members back to work. 'Greengrocers all over the country heaved a sigh of relief,' reported the *Journalist*. One of the leaders of the revolt, Chris Underwood, left the union shortly after to join the IoJ and later became its General Secretary. There was a lot of anger at the NEC's volte-face: the Sheffield branch sent it a white feather in protest at its 'scandalous behaviour'.

Alan Knowles, a leading union figure at the BBC in Manchester during the 1960s–80s, recalls that hardly any other broadcasters took part in the local union branch activities. 'I think people in broadcasting have always had a sense of loyalty to broadcasting rather than [to] the newspaper side,' he says. The public service ethos at the BBC reinforced a tendency among members to regard their programmes with pride, and to regard any industrial action that would impede them with reluctance, Knowles adds. Yet they were concerned at anything they regarded as government interference. 'The NUJ members at the BBC were not overly fond of strike action – they were concerned about getting the programmes out – but I vividly recall the indignation over what was seen as an attempt to censor coverage of Northern Ireland. I got the impression that the management was rather sympathetic to us.'

Denis MacShane

Denis MacShane (1948–) has been a professional broadcaster, an international trade union official, an author, president of the NUJ, Minister for Europe and marathon runner. After Oxford University he joined the NUJ in 1970 when working for BBC Radio Birmingham and was elected to the national executive. He rose to be NUJ president in 1978, but by then he had been sacked by the BBC for – at a colleague's request – telephoning a local radio phone-in programme that was running short of calls and (unprompted) rashly referring to Conservative politician Reginald Maudling as a crook. As NUJ president, he attracted libel suits from the then chairman of the Press Council and the managing director of a publishing company. After his presidency he became head of communications at the Geneva-based International Metalworkers Federation, and while working there he took a PhD and wrote biographies and books about the steel industry, before becoming Labour MP for the steel town of Rotherham in May 1994. He became a Minister at the Foreign Office in 2001, was deputy to the Foreign Secretary, Jack Straw, and Minister for Europe from 2002 to 2005.

Knowles observed how social changes in the 1960s and 70s were altering the makeup of the BBC's staff, as it was in newspapers and magazines. 'The days when nine out of ten broadcasters had a newspaper background gave way to bright young university graduates. When I'd started in journalism at the end of the Second World War, it was thought natural to join a trade union. Now, I was meeting new entrants to broadcasting who had no ideas about joining a union,' he remembers. Some new broadcasters were radical, however – notably Denis MacShane, whose career would take him to the union presidency and then into politics, where after 1997 he served as a Foreign Office minister.

MacShane's involvement in national NUJ affairs was unusual for a broadcast member. Long-serving radio journalist Trevor Goodchild recalls that for much of the 1980s and 90s BBC activists dealt mainly with the broadcasting organiser and kept at arm's length from head office. 'When it came to broadcasting issues,' he says, 'we usually wielded more power than the NEC.'

BBC national radio chapel leader Trevor Goodchild speaks out during a chapel reps'
meeting to plan the programme of action in a pay dispute in 1994. (Jez Coulson/Insight)

But broadcast members were impressively represented on the national executive by the remarkable double act of Vincent Hanna and Giles Smith, both well known national journalists. Hanna was a big man, a BBC political correspondent, a lawyer by training and an industrial reporter by background. He boasted that Margaret Thatcher had apparently once said he was the most intelligent man in Britain. Hanna, who by the age of fifty-nine had worked himself to death, merits a place in political history as the self-proclaimed inventor of the election exit poll, first hiring students to quiz voters for the BBC at a by-election in Darlington in 1983. John Foster, who was the union's broadcasting organiser from 1979 to 1989, recalls his first day in the job, when Hanna had the chutzpah to simply walk into Director-General Ian Trethowan's office to introduce him.

Giles Smith was a fellow industrial correspondent, for ITN in London, and another well known face; he became ITN's sport correspondent and his redundancy in the 1990s made the front of the *Daily Mirror*. Smith was tall, cool and urbane. The pair affected not to get on and each encouraged colleagues to make fun of the other, but they made a formidable combination.

While at the end of the 1980s unions were losing their strength in newspapers and magazines, they generally held their position well in

ITN reporter Giles Smith, leading union broadcasting activist of the 1980s. (Ramesh Sharma)

Broadcasting leader Vincent Hanna pictured at the 1986 ADM with one of the first mobile phones most NUJ members had ever seen. (Martin Jenkinson)

broadcasting – with the awful exception of the breakfast channel TVam. Like many new broadcast ventures the new channel quickly ran into a desperate financial crisis, and after a series of boardroom manoeuvres the company decided to take on the technicians, who were demanding full crewing and overtime payments that the company said it could not afford. It was like a mini-Wapping, with the skilled Association of Cinematograph, Television and Allied Technicians in the role of the NGA; its members were locked out and the journalists were again caught in the middle. Managers put out the programmes, secretaries operating the cameras. Foster urged the journalists to back the technicians but, as at Wapping, to little avail. The NUJ was, however, able to play the role of broker between managers and union leaders – who could not communicate directly – and a solution was eventually reached that left the ACTT much weaker but still intact.

In 1989 there was a guerrilla campaign of lightning strikes at the BBC – eleven days in all – which eventually won an 8.8 per cent pay rise. John Foster recalls:

We had a series of stoppages over pay, giving no advance notice of
them. The law about notice of strike action hadn't come in then. We
had strikes on Saturdays because a lot of light entertainment shows
were recorded on Saturdays. Our members were saying, we are not
stopping enough news, but the joint strategy with the other unions
was to stop programmes.

The BBC governors had a meeting in Cardiff so we went to
picket their meeting. They arrived in a coach and we all cheered as
we saw it go round a traffic roundabout three times when they saw
the picket line.

The governors summoned the courage to go in but John O'Sullivan, the
23-stone FoC at BBC Wales, stepped forward and insisted on reading out a
letter. The Cardiff chapel had been making itself something of a nuisance:
'We used to hold hour-long strikes at short notice,' says O'Sullivan. 'Alarm
buttons [pagers] were issued to chapel officers throughout Britain. When
they rang they signalled that a stoppage would be held that day. I was fed
up with the management and arranged for the alarm to go off during the
morning conference one day. It was good to see them sweat.'

There were more strikes at the BBC in 1994, in successful opposition
to an attempt to introduce performance-related pay; and in 1991 and 1996
there were campaign rallies to save the World Service from the threatened closure of language services and other programmes. Being separately
financed, via a direct grant from the Foreign and Commonwealth Office,
management of the World Service is more susceptible to political pressure,
and both times the support of MPs and internationally known writers and
broadcasters saved it. In 2006, though, ten language services were closed
down.

But campaigning for 'public service broadcasting' was a wider issue than
that, since legislation was introduced from 1990 onwards that progressively
weakened the public service remit of ITV companies and threatened the
commercial viability of the BBC. The 1990 and 1996 Broadcasting Acts
dismantled the regional ITV structure and led by 2004 to a single ITV
company that began hacking away at the levels of regional news and
programme production. The union joined in with the Campaign for Press
and Broadcasting Freedom, the pressure group it had been involved in
setting up twenty years earlier to agitate for higher standards in the press,
with a view to putting up last-ditch resistance to the commercialisation
of public service broadcasting.

These campaigns had their successes, and by 2006 had helped preserve the BBC as an independent publicly owned corporation funded by the licence fee – a task that becomes progressively more difficult each decade as the renewal by Parliament of the BBC Charter comes around. But the NUJ benefited from an active parliamentary group of union-friendly MPs to help the campaign. For all that the BBC had become more commercial and competitive and had hived off whole chunks of its operation to outside companies, the number of journalists continued to rise and by the end of the 90s it employed over three thousand – more than any other employer in its field, with an increasing number working in the new media.

Commercial TV, meanwhile, was contracting. The consolidation of all the regional franchises in England and Wales into one company in 2001 led to the closure of studios and the downplaying of regional input to the network. Job cuts and security were now the issues that occupied the union.

At the heart of the union

The NUJ might well declare 7 August 'Journalists' Pride' day. On that date in 1985 NUJ members made the strongest single affirmation of principled, independent journalism in the union's history. Four thousand people – virtually the whole membership in broadcasting – went on strike against censorship. It was over a BBC programme the government was trying to stop. The action was a triumph and the programme was shown.

At the Edge of the Union was a TV documentary, part of the pioneering *Real Lives* series that was a broadcasting milestone in itself. It used 'fly on the wall' filming and extended informal at-home interviewing to portray a subject's 'real life'. *At the Edge of the Union* covered the family lives of two men in Derry at the extremes of the conflict in Northern Ireland: the unionist Gregory Campbell and the republican Martin McGuinness. At a time when coverage of Northern Ireland was mostly about bombing and terrorism it was a piercing insight into the thinking of two prominent participants in the conflict. It was brilliant television, and it was fair and balanced too – in fact, much too brilliant, much too balanced, for the government to stomach.

Prime Minister Thatcher, who had narrowly survived an assassination attempt by the IRA in Brighton the previous September, had said that broadcasters must 'starve terrorists of the oxygen of publicity'. Now Home

Secretary Leon Brittan wrote to the BBC, before transmission, demanding that the programme be pulled (no one has ever explained how he knew of it). Brittan claimed it would 'materially assist the terrorist cause'.

The BBC board of governors, all government appointees, called a special meeting and decided to comply. Minutes of that meeting, discovered through a Freedom of Information Act request by the *Guardian* in 2005, showed just what establishment figures some of the governors were: Daphne Park, a senior officer in MI6, described the documentary as 'the domestication of the IRA'; Sir William Rees-Mogg, deputy chairman and a high Tory former editor of *The Times*, found it 'totally unacceptable'; Lady Faulkner, widow of a former Ulster Unionist leader, said its contents were 'utterly horrifying'. Lord Harewood, a cousin of the Queen, branded the programme 'odious and hateful'. It was the involvement of McGuinness they objected to, despite – or perhaps because of – the fact that he came across as quite a likeable family man, while Campbell appeared much less sympathetic.

BBC management and journalists were left in an impossible position. Director-General Alasdair Milne wanted to show the programme but was told by the governors he would be fired if he did, and backed off.

It was time for the NUJ to act. Mass meetings were called at the London studios, which demanded a twenty-four-hour strike, and the call spread like fire, spontaneously, throughout broadcasting – commercial as well as BBC. The NUJ broadcasters' leadership was impressive, with Hanna and Smith on the NEC and Peter Dodson chairing the Broadcasting Industrial Council. Dodson was a wise and experienced activist from provincial newspapers in the 1970s, who had left the *Middlesbrough Evening Gazette* to work as news editor in BBC local radio; he left there to go into PR shortly after, in frustration at the failure of BBC management to stand up to political pressure, this time at the local level. A Conservative MP had been attacking the station and managers wouldn't let the journalists respond. 'There I was defending *Real Lives* nationally,' he recalls, 'while back in Cleveland they wouldn't say boo to a Tory MP.'

Backing up the voluntary officers was the full-time official for broadcasting, the gritty and determined John Foster, later to become NUJ General Secretary. It was as impressive a team as the union had ever fielded. Every one of the BBC's sixty-four chapels voted to strike for *Real Lives*, and the union then turned to ITV to see what support they might expect.

The 1985 Real Lives *strike: picket line at the BBC TV Centre with (left to right) Claire Rayner, Valerie Singleton, Sue Cook, Mike Smith and Jeremy Paxman. (Stefano Cagnoni)*

To their amazement the ITN chapel voted, with only one against, to join the strike. 'We didn't think ITN would come out,' Foster recalls. 'We didn't ask them to. We were just going to ask them to make some gesture but the members wanted to come out.' So then did ten of the sixteen regional ITV stations and all but two of the forty-eight independent local radio stations. Every second of national broadcast news and current affairs was off air on 7 August; the BBC World Service stopped for the whole twenty-four hours, for the first time in fifty-three years. In London the BBC unions – the action was joined by the technicians' and general unions ACTT and BETA (the Broadcasting and Entertainment Trades Alliance) – hired a cinema to show a video of the programme, and chapels around the country organised their own showings: at BBC Belfast the journalists plugged in a TV on the footpath outside the studios to play it for passing citizens.

Under public pressure the BBC governors backed down and *At the Edge of the Union* was transmitted. The NUJ had beaten not just the BBC governors, but the government. 'We were not saying the programme should be shown,' Foster explains. 'We said that BBC managers and the

ITN journalists came out in support of the BBC Real Lives *strikers. (NUJ Collection)*

Director-General Milne should decide – not the government. We were trying to back the management. This strike was not about members' self-interest, it was about journalism, because journalists in broadcasting have standards to aim for, which are set by the regulations.'

This, again, is the difference between broadcast and print: while newspaper journalists exploit their independence and the challenge for the NUJ has been to ensure it is used responsibly, for those in broadcasting it is the other way round: their responsibility is prescribed and the battle is for independence. It is a battle the union has had to fight constantly as the regulations have been progressively weakened, and pressure stepped up on BBC managers, by successive governments. Indeed, the political establishment got its revenge for *Real Lives*: the chairman of the governors, Stuart Young, died shortly afterwards and his successor, Marmaduke Hussey, fired Alasdair Milne.

Hussey, whose wife was a lady-in-waiting to the Queen, annoyed BBC journalists by telling the Institute of Directors that he wanted to 'recapture the BBC's reputation in journalism' – a reputation the journalists weren't aware they had lost. As a former managing director of Times Newspapers, Hussey's behaviour had precipitated numerous disputes with staff; Barry Fitzpatrick, an NUJ official who worked there for the NATSOPA print union and knew Hussey well, says he had 'never met a man who was so hated by the people he worked with'. Greg Dyke, the BBC Director-General who lost his job in another government-inspired coup in 2004, mused in his memoirs: 'I often wondered whether Hussey thought that he himself might have been the problem.'

Make it public

The idea of showing a banned programme was taken up again eighteen months later in February 1987 when Special Branch police raided the BBC's Glasgow studios to seize material relating to another documentary: *Twinkle Twinkle Little Star* was one of the *Secret Society* series made by the investigative journalist Duncan Campbell. It told the story of a hitherto unknown British spy satellite programme called Project Zircon and was a great embarrassment to government. Campbell was a leading investigator of electronic and security stories and had been one of the defendants in the ABC official secrecy trial of 1978. It was announced that he would be prosecuted again for this programme, but he never was.

The NUJ staged another national day of action, in which five thousand members took part in a two-hour stoppage in protest at the raid. It also organised a showing of the film which the BBC, despite having commissioned and made it, never summoned the courage to broadcast. The *Journalist* printed the complete script.

John Foster, who was full-time organiser for broadcasting at the time, recalls the showing: 'I thought we would have trouble filling the hall but when I arrived there was a huge crowd and we had to have two showings and clear the hall between them.'

Two weeks after the *Real Lives* strike the extent of government security influence over the BBC became suddenly evident when the *Observer* unearthed the presence of an MI5 office in Broadcasting House – Room 105 on the first floor – where a Brigadier Ronnie Stonham vetted appointments and maintained records on senior staff. That corridor, curiously, was said to be the one on which George Orwell, who broadcast from the building during the Second World War, based his description of the Ministry of Truth in *1984*. The 'Christmas tree' files – personnel folders with a green symbol stamped on the front to indicate there was an extra secret file on the individual concerned – became notorious, and even a source of pride for some. Various notable journalists who had been 'blacklisted' as 'security risks' by the system were publicly outraged. The union took up the issue with Milne and the practice was formally ended, though suspicions lingered that some kind of security vetting continued at the World Service.

The *Real Lives* episode was far from the only time the union intervened to protect the independence of broadcasters from government. It had taken a long time for the NUJ to get organised at the BBC and it was not until the 1970s that chapels started to use their muscle.

The first strike came in 1976 when journalists began a campaign of action – it would last nearly two years – to win an allowance for working unsocial and unpredictable hours. Then, in 1979, came the first major conflict with government over union members' reporting. It was over footage that was never broadcast, and, like *Real Lives*, the issue was Northern Ireland. Foster recalls: 'The Mother of Chapel at BBC current affairs called and said, "You must come here but first read the *Evening Standard*." The story was that the BBC had colluded with the IRA. Thatcher was going spare in Parliament. I didn't even know about it. The footage had not been shown and never was.'

A *Panorama* team had been filming in Belfast when the reporter, Jeremy Paxman, received a call from the Provisional IRA, inviting the crew to come next day to a village called Carrickmore. There they found, says Foster, 'a few blokes with Armalites and balaclavas on' performing clandestine exercises. 'Newspapers often had pictures like that, but the politicians were making a fuss and the BBC wanted to discipline people.' Eventually the editor, Roger Bolton, and the head of current affairs John Gau were disciplined; but Paxman and his producer were not, Foster says, 'after we made it clear there would be a big fuss'. Members would without doubt have taken action.

Foster says: 'These were brave people but there is often bravery in broadcasting. There is an ethos that is to do with tradition and the way broadcasting is structured. That is why people trust TV much more than newspapers, and that is why the government is always attacking broadcasters.'

There was another instance in 1981, when Director-General Ian

Trethowan, another BBC establishment figure, tried to chop great chunks out of a *Panorama* programme on the security services. Trethowan demanded to see the film – which had been approved by all the requisite levels of BBC management – and then to have nineteen sections cut from it. Editor Bolton said the cuts would render the programme untransmittable. Vincent Hanna said: 'We either protest or take it lying down.' General Secretary Ken Ashton led a delegation to see Trethowan and he backed down. Again, the programme was shown.

In 1988 came another threat of industrial action when the government introduced its ban on broadcasting the voices of representatives of banned paramilitary organisations in Northern Ireland.[5] As with *Real Lives*, members in both the BBC and commercial stations voted to strike but action was called off by General Secretary Harry Conroy as part of an agreement to campaign jointly with broadcast managements against the ban. Conroy was heavily criticised at the NUJ's 1989 ADM for the decision – delegate Rita O'Reilly called him 'a coward or a fool' – and though broadcasting companies did maintain a formal opposition throughout the six years the ban remained in force, none would join the union's public campaigns nor contribute to the costly cases the NUJ took to the European Court.

When the ban was announced the *Journalist* front-paged a picture of a Belfast journalist, Mairtin O'Mueilloir of the *Andersonstown News*, a West Belfast weekly, wearing a gag. As a Sinn Fein city councillor in Belfast, he was banned from being broadcast. He was invited by the NUJ Left to the 1989 ADM, but delegates voted not to hear him; his speech was printed in the *Journalist*. O'Mueilloir later prospered as an unlikely entrepreneur, becoming a local media magnate in Northern Ireland, expanding the *Andersonstown News* into a big and profitable biweekly and launching in 2004 an all-Ireland daily.

Given that for twenty-five years there was conflict in Northern Ireland, it was bound to be the source of conflict between broadcasters and the state, and one of the bitterest was over an ITV programme, *Death on the Rock*, made by the London broadcaster Thames TV in 1988. The programme analysed the shooting dead of three unarmed IRA 'volunteers' in Gibraltar and, as with *Real Lives*, its fault was in being too thorough. Margaret Thatcher reacted with absolute fury, since *Death on the Rock* showed that official accounts of the incident were far from the truth. The attack was taken up by the Murdoch press, notably the *Sun* and the *Sunday*

Times, whose stories were so biased that two reporters who had worked on them quit in disgust, a highly unusual occurrence. The editor of *Death on the Rock*, a programme in the *This Week* strand, was Roger Bolton, by now an exile from the BBC, who found himself in the thick of it yet again. And again the NUJ was called on to defend his team, this time not to get a programme shown but to save their jobs.

Thames was forced to set up an inquiry into the making of the programme, and Conroy worked hard with the chapel and management to ensure it would not be stacked against the members. The inquiry report entirely vindicated the programme. The reporter on *Death on the Rock*, Julian Manyon, won an ovation at the 1989 ADM, where he praised the union's 'courageous stand'. The 'nature and the enormity of the attack against *Death on the Rock*,' he said, 'was a threat to the very right of journalists to do their job.' Privately he told Conroy that he had considered himself pretty anti-union and had voted for the Tories, but would not do so again. Conroy himself recalls with satisfaction that the affair was 'the only time Thatcher was beaten by a trade union'.

An even graver threat to the critical reporting of government came in 2004, and this time there was little the NUJ could do. At issue was the

Julian Manyon, reporter on the controversial This Week *programme* Death on the Rock, *receives the union's congratulations from joint President Scarlett MccGwire at the 1989 SDM. (Alan Wylie)*

reporting of the government case for the invasion of Iraq the year before, and the clash was cataclysmic. Andrew Gilligan, an award-winning BBC defence correspondent, had interviewed a conscientious arms control scientist, David Kelly, who was disturbed by the dishonesty of the rationale put forward by Tony Blair's New Labour government.

Gilligan's report on the Radio 4 *Today* programme led to an onslaught of quite unprecedented savagery from the government's PR machine, headed by a former political correspondent, an NUJ member called Alastair Campbell. The BBC, now with a populist and hitherto pro-Labour Party Director-General, Greg Dyke, resisted stoutly. Gilligan had not named his source, but Campbell's camp learned of the name and it was fed to journalists. Kelly had meanwhile been summoned for pitiless questioning by a Parliamentary Committee. A few days later he was found dead near his Oxfordshire home; suicide was presumed. The government set up an inquiry into his death under Lord Hutton, a judge from Northern Ireland with a record of representing the armed forces as a barrister. Hutton produced a report that wholly backed the government and condemned Gilligan and the BBC.

The BBC governors – still establishment appointees and still including

Andrew Gilligan, whose report for the Radio 4 Today *programme led to the Hutton Report in 2004, arrives at the BBC as the resulting storm broke out, accompanied by NUJ broadcasting organiser Paul McLaughlin (centre). (Michael Crabtree/Troika)*

a member from the intelligence services – forced the resignation of Dyke and accepted that of the chairman of the board, the Labour-supporting Gavyn Davies, and made a humiliating apology to the government. The NUJ defended Gilligan's position but after a couple of days of mayhem it was clearly untenable, and he had to go as well; there can't have been many stories that had such awesome consequences for the journalists concerned, but the professional consensus was that Gilligan's story was essentially correct. The board of governors was to be replaced by a new BBC Trust in 2007.

The Hutton affair was worse, much worse, than *Real Lives*. The betrayal by the BBC governors was one of the bleakest moments in British broadcasting history. The reaction of BBC staff was astonishing. On the afternoon Dyke was effectively forced out, they poured out of BBC offices on to the streets in protest. It was a spontaneous demonstration of support not just for Dyke, a rare boss who inspired real affection, but for the independence of the BBC. It was not coordinated by the NUJ or any other union, though the NUJ General Secretary, Jeremy Dear, was at the TV Centre in west London that afternoon and joined the throng. The unions did, however, make an issue of it, and organised a nationwide protest a week

Journalists throughout the BBC – here outside the World Service in central London – demonstrated against government attacks that followed the Hutton Report. (Stefano Cagnoni)

later – the most quickly it could be organised – with the slogan 'Hands off the BBC'. Members from Shetland to Derry, from Norwich to Truro, came out for two hours at lunchtime to make their point. Radio Oxford broadcast from the pavement outside the studio, with the public taking part.

As in the past, the journalists were acting not against their bosses but in support of them, trying to inspire in them some courage – 'saving the BBC from itself' has been a common NUJ maxim. A packed meeting of members in the London newsrooms angrily rejected the governors' apology to the government, and voted to 'stand by the right of the journalist, the programme and the Corporation to have broadcast the remarks of Dr Kelly' and to 'urge the news management team to join us in a robust defence of the BBC's journalistic independence'.

In keeping with the giant bureaucracy that it is, the BBC's response, once the immediate crisis had passed, was to set up various committees and inquiries to examine the Corporation's journalism and news production and to produce more volumes of guidelines and regulations. Editors and executives were shuffled off into other jobs. The NUJ was persistently rebuffed when it asked to participate in the discussions. Furthermore, the guidelines when they arrived were wanting in some respects. One particular concern was over an aspect that the NUJ has stressed more than any other in the professional field: the duty of journalists to protect their sources. Following the terrible consequences of the breach of Dr Kelly's anonymity, the BBC wanted staff to inform managers of any such confidential sources in future. The union resisted this strongly. Confidentiality is a principle that NUJ members have fought and risked imprisonment for over the years. Their story follows.

The silence of the journalists

The last journalists sentenced to prison for their work in the British Isles were the two 'silent reporters' of 1963. 'It would be an absolutely very great treachery if I submitted to this direction,' said Reginald Foster of the *Daily Sketch*. 'I am not prepared to say where it was from at all,' said Brendan Mulholland of the *Daily Mail*. They were appearing at the Court of Appeal in London, before the Master of the Rolls, Lord Denning, who was about to send them to prison for refusing to identify their sources.

The standards of British journalists may sometimes be debatable, but they will never betray people who give them information in confidence. Such an action would be in breach of clause 7 of the NUJ Code of Conduct – the unqualified statement, 'a journalist shall protect confidential sources of information' – and the union reserves a special esteem for those who run legal and personal risks to uphold it by defying court orders to divulge such information.

Critics have sometimes suggested that journalists are thereby putting themselves 'above the law', but the NUJ argues that's not the case. For one thing, the couple of dozen members who have put themselves in this position have always said they were willing to suffer the consequence of being jailed or fined. And for another, it is not for themselves that they do it, but for their sources, who can be taking much bigger risks, for their livelihoods or even – as with David Kelly – their lives.

It is not entirely an altruistic stance, since journalists know well that once they start betraying informants who need to be protected, then such people will stop trusting them and the supply of stories of significant public interest will dry up. In short, once a promise is given, it has to be kept; it's as simple as that. The union has campaigned for a legal right to maintain such confidences, and indeed, largely thanks to its campaigning, a degree of protection has been won; but law or no law, most journalists will follow their consciences anyway.

Pledges of confidentiality to sources are not at all unusual – in fact, they are routine. It happens hundreds of times a day when reporters accept requests to go 'off the record', with such phrases as 'You didn't get this from me'.

But reporters can't choose which of the promises of anonymity they give will blow up in their faces, and it has not always been over particularly edifying matters. The source that Reginald Foster was protecting in 1963 was a shop assistant, whose name he didn't even know, who had told him that an admiralty clerk, John Vassall, had bought women's clothes at the shop. Just why the security of the nation hung on this information had been a matter for a tribunal chaired by Lord Radcliffe, which had inquired into Vassall's activities as a Russian spy. Important heads, accused of failing to stop him, were in danger of rolling.

Lurid allegations were made that Vassall had been blackmailed because of his homosexual transvestite lifestyle. Here was a huge Cold War scare story in which Foster, a freelance, played a tiny role as part of an investigative team from the *Sketch*, checking the stores in Oxford Street. Lord

Denning pondered whether the information was relevant, especially since Vassall had readily conceded that he did indeed buy and wear women's clothes. But this was 'not the whole point', opined the Master of the Rolls. 'The point is: did those in the Admiralty know it earlier on before he was arrested and ought they to have reported it? On that point the type of source is a relevant question. It could and should have led to further enquiries.'

Mulholland's part in the story was slightly more substantial. He was asked to divulge who had told him that Vassall was known as 'Auntie' to his workmates; that he could not have followed the lifestyle he did on his clerical salary; and that he had been spared having to go through the full rigours of the Admiralty vetting procedures. These allegations, said Denning, 'must have been based on a trustworthy source. Heaven forbid that [journalists] should invent them!' He was dismissive of the journalists' claim to the right to decline to provide the information: 'The only profession I know which is given the privilege is the legal profession' – surprise! 'It is in the public interest to enquire as to the sources of information. How is anyone to know that this story was not pure invention … [or] the gossip of some idler seeking to impress?' He sent Foster down for four months and Mulholland for six.

There was uproar among journalists, and the cause of the 'silent reporters' was widely supported. NUJ groups met MPs – twenty-eight of whom turned out to meet Central London branch leaders – and wrote to the Prime Minister demanding their release. Five hundred people took part in a London rally. When Foster came out first, from Ford Open Prison, forty colleagues were waiting to greet him. His first action was to send a telegram to Home Secretary Henry Brooke to urge Mulholland's immediate release, but government was deaf to all appeals. Foster had had to serve his time, and so did Mulholland. But after that, things changed. Although there were more cases of journalists taking the same stance, the courts were less willing to jail them.

There had been surprisingly few cases before the Silent Two. Lord Denning in his judgement surveyed the case law and could find only three in which journalists had claimed the privilege: one in 1889 in which the managing editor of *The Times* declined to identify the unnamed writer of an article and took responsibility for it himself, without penalty; one in Ireland in 1935 in which the same thing happened with an anonymous letter to a newspaper; and one in Australia in 1941 in which a journalist was fined £15 for refusing to give the name of an informant to a government inquiry.

The law was to move a long way over the next thirty years. Two other journalists were detained behind bars for brief spells, without being sentenced, and hurriedly released. The cases of BBC reporter Bernard Falk, detained for contempt in 1971 for refusing to identify an interviewee, and of Gordon Airs of the *Daily Record* for likewise protecting an informant, were brought under anti-terrorism laws (see p. 290). But the case that advanced the journalist's 'right to silence' more than any other was fought over less weighty matters. What was at stake in the Bill Goodwin case were the finances of a computer software company.

Goodwin was a twenty-three-year-old trainee reporter on *The Engineer*, a business magazine published by Morgan Grampian. In 1989 he received a leak of a financial report produced by Tetra Ltd. He phoned the company for comment and the response was an injunction preventing publication of the story, which it said would have been commercially damaging, and an order to disclose the identity of the source. Despite being harassed with what he called a 'blitzkrieg' of writ-servers, at home as well as at work, Goodwin, as he put it, 'could not give in'. He was backed by the editor, the publisher and the NUJ.

The case went from the High Court to the Court of Appeal and the House of Lords, with Goodwin losing at every stage. He was ordered to put his notes in a sealed envelope and give them to the court, to be opened if he lost, and to give the source an order not to disclose any further information. Both demands he steadfastly declined. The case went back to the High Court, where he was fined £5,000, not a high figure in comparison with other cases. The *Independent* financial journalist Jeremy Warner had in the 1980s been fined £20,000 for defying an order to divulge a source to a Department of Trade inquiry. The judges appeared to appreciate that Goodwin's stand was one of principle, but the law was the law. Or was it?

The law does grant some protection to journalists. The Contempt of Court Act 1981, brought in after lobbying by the NUJ and other groups, says they cannot be forced to divulge confidential information. But there's a catch: the privilege can be overridden in three instances – for the protection of national security, for the detection or prevention of crime, and in 'the interests of justice'. In practice, judges have sometimes allowed one or more of these exceptions to apply, on quite flimsy evidence. In the Goodwin case, Tetra was claiming the 'detection of crime': the company

Bill Goodwin (centre), whose fight to protect a confidential source took him to the European Court of Human Rights, arrives at the High Court in London for one of the innumerable hearings of the case. (Neil Turner/Insight)

said the leak was theft and they needed to identify the culprit. No evidence was produced for this. If the leak had come from someone inside the company – as in fact it did, and Goodwin made a statement to that effect which was ignored by the courts – no crime would have been committed; it might have been a case of misconduct by an employee, but that is a civil matter. The courts accepted the company's contention and found that it was in the 'interests of justice' that the name be divulged.

The union reacted angrily. Deputy General Secretary Jake Ecclestone, who led the campaign, wrote that clause 7 of the code should now be rewritten: 'A journalist shall protect confidential sources of information unless a judge decides that the commercial interests of a private company, the punishment of disgruntled employees or his own amour propre is more important.' A fund was set up to pay Goodwin's fine; it raised more than £1,000, which in fact went towards the NUJ's costs, because the fine was surreptitiously paid by the employers. The union ran up huge costs taking Goodwin's case against the UK government to the European Court of Human Rights in Strasbourg. It was the first case on the protection of sources to be heard by the court, and the judgement, in 1996, has become an overriding international ruling on journalists' rights.

Governmental gobbledegook

Jake Ecclestone's sarcastic rewrite of clause 7 of the Code of Conduct after the Bill Goodwin verdict was not entirely a joke. The UK government produced an extraordinarily convoluted variation on that theme as part of its defence when Goodwin and the NUJ took the case to the European Court of Human Rights.

Once the ECHR had accepted the case, negotiations were supposed to take place with a view to a possible 'friendly settlement', and Foreign Office lawyers, desperate to head off a defeat that could compel the UK to change the law, devised a 'general warning' that reporters were intended to deliver to their sources, designed to promise both to protect them and betray them at the same time. This was the wording:

> You may have my word that I will not under any circumstances divulge your identity unless ordered to do so by a Court, and I will resist any attempt by the Court to impose an order on me. But you and I have to recognise that there are occasions – historically they have been very few – when the court may make an order against me in the interests of national security, to prevent disorder or crime, or when the interests of justice require it. We are, of course, neither of us above the law, but the courts can be expected to lean over backwards to preserve confidentiality if at all possible.

Fortunately – for the government as much as anyone – these 112 words of duplicitous gobbledegook were quietly brushed aside and forgotten.

The victory was sealed by a remarkable gesture from his source, who had, as Goodwin said, 'seen the judgements of the English courts and been so horrified at the wild assumptions of the judges that just before the hearing he or she decided to come forward with information that proved categorically that it was not a stolen document'.

The government was humiliated. Following the judgement it should have amended the 1981 Act to strengthen the protection of sources but, despite repeated requests from the Council of Europe, which oversees the Strasbourg court, successive governments failed to do so. They argued that the judges would henceforth take the case into account – and that turned out to be fair enough. The ruling was made under Article 10 of the European Convention of Human Rights, which guarantees freedom of expression, and since the ECHR was incorporated into British law by the 1999 Human Rights Act, the precedent has indeed applied. The courts have become noticeably fairer, often rejecting applications for disclosure orders – though it hasn't stopped companies, the police or the security forces sometimes trying to get them.

Neat footwork

The case of Adrian Galvin in 1997 was an object lesson in how reporters should act, on union advice, when confronted with orders to disclose confidential information. When his paper, the *Eastern Daily Press*, faced an order to identify a police officer who had leaked a story, the paper's lawyers resisted the application but indicated they might comply if the order was made. The editor instructed Galvin to hand over his notebooks. He contacted the union, which told him not to do so, and despite considerable employer pressure he stuck to his refusal. The union took possession of his notebooks and arranged separate legal representation for him, and the court refused the order.

Bill Goodwin's legacy, in the form of a more positive attitude on the part of the judges, became apparent in a succession of cases.

In Northern Ireland the defiance of Ed Moloney, Belfast editor of the Dublin-based *Sunday Tribune*, was rewarded when an order to disclose was quashed by the High Court in Belfast in 1999. Five years later Lord Saville, leading the inquiry into the killings in Derry in 1972, dropped all proceedings against a number of journalists who had declined requests to furnish the inquiry with confidential information. Among these were NUJ members Alex Thomson and Lena Ferguson of ITN Channel 4 News, who had conducted anonymous interviews with paratroopers who took part in the massacre (see p. 328).

The most protracted instance was the case of national paper freelance Robin Ackroyd, whose steadfast resistance over six years to the demands of a health authority was vindicated when the High Court in London refused to grant an order compelling him to name his sources for a story on the treatment of Moors murderer Ian Brady in Ashworth high-security hospital on Merseyside. The story had appeared in the *Mirror* in 1999 without Ackroyd's byline, and the Mersey Care Trust launched proceedings to get the *Mirror* to identify its source. The High Court granted an order, which the Court of Appeal confirmed, and in June 2002 the *Mirror* lost its appeal to the House of Lords.

The paper was ordered to disclose its source, so now Ackroyd had to come forward. He, of course, had his own confidential sources and the Trust switched the proceedings against him; in October 2002 the High Court gave him two days to identify them. With the NUJ's support he appealed, arguing that his circumstances were very different from the *Mirror*'s and that he was entitled to a fresh trial. The Court of Appeal agreed. But Mersey Care Trust, like Tetra Ltd, said it needed to know the identity of the source to be able to take action over the leak; it appealed to the House of Lords, but the Lords threw out its application. So it was back to the start for Ackroyd at the High Court, where in February 2006 the order was refused.

The judge, Mr Justice Tugendhat, said Ackroyd was a 'responsible journalist whose purpose was to act in the public interest'. He said there must be a 'pressing social need' for a source to be disclosed, and there was no

Latest in a long series of members facing legal action to compel them to reveal their sources, Robin Ackroyd endured a seven-year High Court case. (Stefano Cagnoni)

such need in this case; Ackroyd had 'a record of investigative journalism which has been authoritatively recognised, so that it would not be in the public interest that his sources should be discouraged from speaking to him where it is appropriate that they do so'.

It was as clear a vindication as could be found, not just of Ackroyd's conduct, but of the NUJ's unshakeable policy of backing members who stand up for professional principles. It was not enough for the Mersey Care Trust, however, which decided to throw more NHS money into appealing, but lost its case at the Court of Appeal in February 2007. Even then, Ackroyd's ordeal was not definitively over, for the trust was expected to try for a third time to appeal to the House of Lords

TAKING ON THE STATES

Official information: publish and be blessed

Within its first eighteen months of existence the NUJ had helped push through Parliament one of the foundation laws of twentieth-century press freedom, guaranteeing the right of the press to report local council meetings. This was the first triumph in its campaigning to push back the barriers to open government and the publication of official information. The Local Authorities (Admission of the Press to Meetings) Act 1908 was a real coup, establishing the right for the first time.

In January 1908 there had been a judgement in the Court of Appeal in which Tenby Council in Wales established a right to exclude reporters from its meetings. The union had appointed a 'standing counsel', a senior lawyer retained to give advice, prepare cases and so on. The counsel, George Leach, drew up a short bill, which won cross-party support and became law within the year. The IoJ was very put out and promoted an amendment to nominate itself as the only representative body for journalists, but this failed to gain support. The same year a Children's Act went through Parliament and NUJ representations secured the right of the press to report juvenile courts.

Editors take the blame

In 1926 the union intervened to protect reporters in debates on the
Judicial Proceedings Bill, a puritanical measure intended to curb
the salacious reporting of trials, principally divorce cases, involving
'indecent matter or medical, surgical or physiological details, the publication of which would be calculated to injure public morals'. NUJ
lobbying secured the inclusion of a provision that 'no person other
than a proprietor, editor, master printer or publisher' should be liable
to conviction; reporters were safe.

It was the First World War that put defenders of press freedom on their
mettle, in face of a degree of media manipulation unknown since the
growth of the popular press, according to Philip Knightley, the leading
authority on wartime journalism. In his book *The First Casualty* he wrote
that 'more deliberate lies were told than in any other period of history'.
Censorship was severe and produced numerous absurdities. NUJ historian
Frederick Mansfield relates the story of a long dispatch from a correspondent in France that was sent to the censor before it was subbed; when
it came back it was discovered that the sub had struck out every word the
censor had left in, and vice versa – which did show that the censor had
a decent sense of news, at least. Another report famously lost every word
except the sentence 'I speeded up my Rolls-Royce' repeated nine times.

Much fun was poked at this sort of thing, but the union did not object
to the principle of censorship. Among journalists there was no criticism
of the war – the 1915 ADM sent a 'loyal message of greeting' to King
George V, informing His Majesty that the NUJ 'rejoices to have been able
to stimulate recruiting [for the forces] throughout the country' – except
from what Mansfield called 'a small knot of conscientious objectors'.

These characters did cause problems. Some were jailed and appealed
to the union for support. One who had been convicted four times and
spent two years in prison protested that his detention was illegal; when the
case was reported two soldiers wrote to the *Union Journal* that 'his name
[Leonard Crisp] and the names of others of that ilk should be obliterated
for all time from the roll of the NUJ'. The NEC was rather more humane,

declaring that 'a man should not be deprived, owing to his conscience, of any benefit to which he was entitled from the Union', though it noted there was nothing it could do save sympathise.

It was not the censor that made life really difficult for journalists but DORA, the 1915 Defence of the Realm Act, which empowered any 'competent naval or military authority' to initiate prosecutions against individuals whose actions they considered unreliable, and some local commanders seemed to relish doing so. An NUJ member in Harwich in Essex was 'deported' – run out of town – for informing a news agency, in response to a query, of the movements of British warships. An appeal to the War Minister, David Lloyd George, proved fruitless, and the poor reporter was now destitute and cut off from his family. The union paid him benefit. A photographer who took pictures in a munitions factory near Newcastle-on-Tyne was prosecuted and fined £5 – even though the magistrates accepted that his intent was to show positive images of dedicated workers. The prosecutor said they might fall into the hands of a spy in a lodging house – or in the newspaper office!

What the union wanted was for journalists to direct their work to the censors, through the Press Bureau established by the War Office, rather than be put on trial under the DORA regulations. The NEC appealed to the Prime Minister, Herbert Asquith, to change the regulations, and it won the point.

The case that tipped the balance was not even one the NUJ supported. It concerned a reporter in Portland in Dorset, one Charles Dyson, who was prosecuted for sending a story to London papers about a torpedo boat striking an obstruction, thought to be a German submarine. He argued that he left it to the papers to run it past the censors, that his job was just to supply the facts. This apparently reasonable point was no defence to the Dorchester magistrates, however, or to the High Court. There was quite an outcry, with NUJ branches urging the executive to back Dyson, but Leach, the union's counsel, advised them not to, because he was bound to fail. Instead they wrote to Asquith and were granted a meeting with top brass at the Press Bureau. The outcome was an Order in Council creating a new category of 'press offences' beyond the remit of DORA, which were to be assessed instead by government law officers. It was, wrote Mansfield, 'an achievement of magnitude'. The tin-pot local despots had been seen off.

It seems curious that no use was made against journalists during the war of the Official Secrets Act, which had been rushed through Parliament on the back of a scare about German spies in 1911. It was only in peacetime that this notorious law was used against journalists, and for reasons far removed from national security.

In 1932 Frederick Budgen, a *Daily Mail* crime reporter, was jailed for two months for bribing a clerk at Somerset House, the registry of births, marriages and deaths, to leak him copies of newsworthy wills before they were published. It was a similar story five years later at Stockport Magistrates when on 20 August 1937 when Ernest Lewis, a reporter in the *Daily Dispatch* Manchester office, was convicted for possessing a leaked police crime report. Having received a police document describing a man wanted for fraud, he wrote a story with the headline 'Frauds on Workers Alleged; Warrant for a Man with Scar'. It was an everyday sort of story and a shock when police demanded he tell them his source. He declined, as reporters do, and was put on trial for failing to give 'information relating to a suspected offence under Section 2 of the Official Secrets Act 1911'.

There was then no process in criminal law for serving an order on a journalist to divulge a source, but section 6 of the OSA 1920 – an amendment to the original Act – did require citizens to inform the police of any disclosure of information. Lewis's defence was partly the professional stance of the journalist to protect sources but also a claim, as his lawyer told the court, that the Act 'was never intended to apply to circumstances such as this'. Neither argument cut any ice with the magistrates, who fined him £5. The NUJ took up the case: an appeal was mounted for Lewis – it failed, but reform of the OSA became a major campaign. A parliamentary bill was promoted by the Liberal MP Dingle Foot (father of Michael Foot, who became leader of the Labour Party in the 1980s, and grandfather of the investigative journalist Paul Foot). The fight was joined by the National Council for Civil Liberties, to which NUJ members had just voted to affiliate.

The run-up to the Second World War was a time of national jitters. Everyone knew, despite the efforts of government to appease Nazi Germany, that war was just around the corner, yet even so there were people prepared to mount a political challenge to official secrecy. The writer J. B. Priestley, vice-president of the NCCL, said: 'There is coming into existence a vast and complicated machinery of restriction. Liberties of the citizen that were once considered hard-won victories are liable to vanish in a night. The situation is serious.' Such comment was to be endorsed by the NUJ time and again as the century wore on.

In 1938 public meetings on the control of information were staged around the country. There was a conference in London, organised jointly by the NUJ and the NCCL, addressed by editors and MPs. Branches began to pester their MPs; the Crewe branch sent a delegation to their local MP, Sir Donald Somervell, who was Attorney-General at the time. The Manchester branch demanded a Special Delegate Meeting, and when this was turned down organised its own conference, at which reporter Lewis was given a hero's ovation. In March 1939 General Secretary Clem Bundock was able to report that the government had agreed to amend section 6 of the 1920 Act, restricting its remit to cover espionage only. It was not all the union wanted, but it was a more substantial gain than any it has managed to secure since, and in 1939, with war only six months away, it was extraordinary.

During the war the control of information was put on a much more professional footing. Again the union pledged support for the war effort, welcoming the National (coalition) Government and pledging at the 1941 ADM to give 'every possible support and co-operation until Hitlerism is defeated'. Again censorship was frequently imposed, particularly at local level, and again the union was able to mitigate the worst effects. What was new was the use of wartime regulations to close a newspaper and threaten others. The *Daily Worker* was the daily paper (renamed the *Morning Star* in 1967) of the Communist Party of Great Britain, which initially opposed the war because of the Soviet Union's pact with Germany. The paper was banned in February 1941 under regulation 2D of the 1920 Act, and a vociferous group of communists within the union, particularly in the two biggest branches, Central London and Trade and Publications, wanted the ban lifted. The union opposed the closure on press freedom grounds; instead, it wanted the paper taken to court under regulation 2C, which allowed the prosecution of newspapers accused of 'fomenting opposition'.

This was a difficult matter for the union. Communists were among the most committed and active members, but the *Daily Worker*'s diametric change of line, on direct orders from Moscow, sickened many on the left as well as the right. In the eyes of many the communists were virtually traitors, undermining the struggle against the Nazi threat.

It was particularly difficult for General Secretary Clem Bundock, who was a pacifist yet was obliged as leader of the union to take the patriotic line. So too did the NUJ President in 1941, Fleet Street veteran Tom Foster, who wrote a long piece in the *Journalist* headed 'All We Have of Freedom', arguing that in times of peril action was imperative, and that the union should accept the assurances that the measures would be removed at the end of the war. In the debate at that year's ADM Bundock said the issue was 'not freedom of the press but the abuse of the freedom of the press'. The *Daily Worker* was 'dishonest journalism, and that is what the union is protesting against'.

The conference agreed to a convoluted compromise of the kind that often results from such difficulties. It dissociated the union from the 'defeatist and subversive propaganda of the *Daily Worker*', but protested at its suppression; it upheld 'the right to criticise freely the government of the day' but then distinguished between 'legitimate criticism and that designed to weaken the national effort and spread despondency and alarm'; and it called for a fair and open trial if the government were to present evidence against the paper.

In 1942 the ban on the *Daily Worker* was lifted, following the miraculous restoration of the Communist Party's proper politics after Hitler invaded the Soviet Union. But now the government threatened to use regulation 2D against the *Daily Mirror*, over a cartoon attacking profiteering in the oil industry. The *Mirror* was the most popular paper during the war, particularly among the troops, for whom its barrack room populism struck a chord. This time the union had no compunction and reiterated its 'emphatic condemnation of this method of attack on our free institutions. Variety of opinion and expression is the lifeblood of democracy and the NUJ warns its fellow citizens of the danger to the foundations of liberty.'

The threat was never carried through. The union reflected the popular wartime spirit of intense social patriotism and irreverence towards officialdom. The *Journalist* carried dispatches from the battlefields and, from 1941, cartoons by Carl Giles – who later became a national institution for his work for the *Sunday Express* – which satirised the military mindset.

Whatever goodwill journalists felt towards the war effort, there was a need for constant vigilance. In 1940 the Minister of Information, Duff Cooper, announced a plan for compulsory censorship. The NUJ convened another national conference, which called for the repeal of 2D and other regulations. The Duff Cooper plan was abandoned, but in 1942 Home Secretary Herbert Morrison came up with another: to establish a 'representative body' of the newspaper profession so as to ensure 'the

One of the cartoons the great cartoonist Carl Giles contributed to the Journalist *during the Second World War. (* Journalist*)*

maintenance of a proper sense of responsibility in the press, and control of irresponsible newspapers and journalists'. The union rejected it as 'a most dangerous agency for the suppression of legitimate criticism [that] must inevitably lead to a still further invasion of the freedom of the press'.

Morrison met a union delegation; he understood the objections, he said, and would be happy to give way to an alternative proposal from the industry itself. No such proposal materialised and again the idea was dropped. In any case, as far as most journalists were concerned, the economic effects of war were more serious than the censorship. Shortage of newsprint was the main concern. Dozens of papers and magazines closed and others, particularly local papers, were 'telescoped' – compulsorily merged with their rivals.

The wartime regulations were dissolved in 1945, but much of the political sensitivity carried over into the Cold War, and the questioning of national security precautions was considered by some to be a communist activity. With a Labour government tightly committed to the Atlantic alliance, there was pressure on trade unions to conform. The NUJ kept its head down, resisting excessive political pressure when it could – for instance, demands for the dismissal of *Journalist* editor Allen Hutt because he was a communist, albeit a singularly non-threatening one – but holding back from outright defiance. There were calls to ban communists from union office and to cut ties with organisations considered communist fronts; among these was the NCCL, from which the union formally disaffiliated in 1951, with a crushing vote of 3,255 to 779 in a ballot of the membership.

Forbidden tales

A flowering of political and journalistic freedoms in the 1970s inspired confidence among journalists to publish challenging stories, and the union's keenness to defend those freedoms. In some ways the NUJ had little choice but to act, because in the new climate journalists were writing stories that upset the secret state, and the union had to keep them out of jail. In 1963 it had failed in this when the 'silent reporters' Reginald Foster and Brendan Mulholland served their time for protecting their sources.

In 1971 the sensational trial took place of a young freelance, Jonathan Aitken, and the editor of the *Sunday Telegraph*, Brian Roberts, under section 2 of the Official Secrets Act, for publishing a leaked military report revealing that Britain had been secretly arming one side in the civil war in Nigeria. The defendants pleaded 'public interest' and were acquitted by the jury. Aitken's gratitude to the NUJ for its support impelled him to remain a union member throughout his career as a Tory MP and for a time, ironically, as a defence minister, before his imprisonment for perjury in 1997.

Two members were imprisoned, for very short periods, in the 1970s, but since then, no one has been sentenced to jail in Britain for a journalistic 'crime'. BBC reporter Bernard Falk was locked up for four days for contempt in Belfast in 1971 for refusing to confirm that a defendant charged with IRA membership was a person he had previously interviewed, and four years later Gordon Airs of the *Daily Record* in Glasgow spent just one night in the cells for likewise protecting an informant in the Scottish nationalist 'Tartan Army'. Both cases involved police using the prevention of terrorism – then a new concern – as an argument for disclosure, and in a prescient article in the *Journalist* in October 1975 another journalist who was facing charges, David May, asked: 'Have modern political events then outmoded accepted forms of practice and codes of conduct, and can journalists really be expected to refuse to disclose their sources if the police say that such information is vital if they are to be successful in the war against terrorism?'

May, co-editor of the radical London listings magazine *Time Out*, had

Leaders of the three unions in broadcasting – Harry Conroy of the NUJ, Tony Hearn of BECTU and Alan Sapper of ACTT – don symbolic gags outside the BBC headquarters in London as they join a protest against the UK government's Northern Ireland broadcasting ban on its first anniversary in October 1989. (Andrew Moore/Reflex)

faced trial under the Theft Act charged with dishonestly handling stolen material – a document he had used for a story – and had been acquitted. He answered his own question: 'The outcome of my trial shows that, however much the political temperature has risen, a journalist honestly intent on bringing in news of the actions of others will not find himself punished.' The NUJ has always held to the view that honest journalism questioning the actions of the state is justified, and in all subsequent cases the journalists have, with the union's support, been vindicated.

The most dramatic were the official secrecy cases of 1977–8, the so-called 'ABC' and 'Colonel B' cases. The saga began in November 1976 when Home Secretary Merlyn Rees ordered the deportation of two NUJ members, Philip Agee and Mark Hosenball, both American citizens working in Britain. Agee was a former Central Intelligence Agency officer who had blown the whistle on the agency's activities, notably in Latin America, in a best-selling book. Hosenball was a dogged young investigative journalist in the American tradition, for whom all that mattered was the story. He had collaborated with a British freelance colleague, Duncan Campbell, on an article in *Time Out* headlined 'The Eavesdroppers', which exposed the activities of the Government Communications Headquarters, the UK electronic spying centre that forms a worldwide surveillance network with the National Security Agency of the USA.

This article was a small milestone in British journalism. As far as anyone knew it was the first time GCHQ had been the subject of any kind of story; but, further, it represented a new kind of reporting, with its disregard for official secrecy and its total lack of deference towards the security establishment.

The campaign against the deportations followed the same style: for instance, supporters leafleted the London streets where CIA agents lived, identifying them to their neighbours. The NUJ was drawn deeper into the affair with the arrest in February 1977 of two further members, the freelance Campbell and another *Time Out* reporter, Crispin Aubrey. Campbell was a scientifically trained investigator, with something of the anorak about him, but he was a brilliant and fearless journalist. Aubrey was less abrasive – a cool, easy-going character with a wry wit. They had arranged to interview John Berry, a former soldier in signals intelligence who came forward to give a statement in support of Agee and Hosenball. The three were detained by Special Branch police who (naturally) had known of their meeting through electronic surveillance – tapping their phones – and charged under sections 1 and 7 of the Official Secrets Act of 1911, with spying.

There was uproar at the arrests and the charges, and the ABC (Aubrey/Berry/Campbell) Defence Campaign was launched. When the three appeared for committal at Tottenham Magistrates Court in north London the crown called a secret witness, one 'Colonel B', to testify as to the supposed damage to national security. It didn't take long for investigative journalists on two radical magazines, *The Leveller* and *Peace News*, to find out his name, which was Hugh Johnstone, the commanding officer of 9 Signals Regiment, and publish it. The magazines' journalists were threatened with summonses for contempt for defying the magistrates' order to keep the name secret. Tim Gopsill of *The Leveller*, who was organiser of the Agee–Hosenball Defence Committee, wrote the story, with Johnstone's name included, for the *Journalist* in March 1978.

Journalist editor Ron Knowles declared that it was 'up to us to make Johnstone the most celebrated British soldier since Montgomery'. The object, he said, was to 'underline the furtive nature of the evidence against ABC and the prosecution's attempt to whip up a prejudicial hysteria of secrecy around the trial'.[1]

By now NUJ branches were tabling motions for the 1978 ADM in Whitley Bay, Northumberland, three of them naming the colonel in their texts. The story got into the papers – though none summoned the courage to 'Johnstone', to use the newly coined verb – and there was a stern warning from the Director of Public Prosecutions that to do so would entail prosecution.

The scene at Whitley Bay bordered on farce. The name JOHNSTONE appeared in huge letters on the beach for all the town to see, carved in the sand with the wheels of the pram of Christian Knowles, the editor's three-month-old son. The conference venue, the Rex Hotel, was plastered with Johnstoniana – posters, leaflets, badges, graffiti ... and in the midst of it all, the foyer, stood two nervous Special Branch policemen, DS Peter Fickling and DS Anthony Shaw, clutching an injunction ready to serve on General Secretary Ken Ashton.

Helpful delegates gathered round and told them that Ashton was on the conference platform and they could go inside and serve their papers there and then. The officers felt this would be 'not politically wise' and said they would wait. At lunchtime Ashton was smuggled out, then back in, through the hotel kitchen. The General Secretary was not available, an official told the officers.

'Who are you, anyway?' one of them asked.

'I'm Charles Harkness, the Deputy General Secretary.'

'You'll do,' they said, and thrust the writ into his hands.

In the kitchen, Harkness steamed open the envelope to examine the injunction against naming the colonel, then sealed it up again and gave it back to the police, saying he still couldn't find his boss, and the Special Branch men returned to London full-handed.

Inside the hall, meanwhile, there was procedural mayhem as the President, John Devine, tried to stop delegates naming the name. Just as the debate was about to start, on a 'Johnstone' motion from the London Freelance branch, *Times* columnist Bernard Levin, himself an LFB delegate, leapt to the microphone and called on the conference not to debate it. It would cost the union £100,000 in fines, he said, 'and those who seek spurious martyrdom should not have their halo paid for by our subscriptions'. A compromise was reached under which another motion was taken which did not name Johnstone; but three delegates still did so during the debate, among them Phil Kelly of *The Leveller*, whose research had uncovered the colonel's identity. ABC defendant Crispin Aubrey, who spoke to rapturous applause, said: 'It is only by naming his name time and again that the mystique around him can be broken.'

Suddenly a whisper began to spread through the conference: word had been received that four Labour MPs had stood up and named Johnstone in the Commons under the cloak of parliamentary privilege. They were Chris Price, Jo Richardson, Ron Thomas and Robert Kilroy Silk. This changed the rules: now the press could name him, and poor Johnstone was in every national paper the next day. For one day it appeared the authorities might have lost control and the case would collapse. But the Director of Public Prosecutions announced that any paper that repeated the name after the initial report would be in contempt, and not one of them did. The case against the *Journalist* and the magazines that had named Johnstone went ahead, but no charges were brought against the national papers that had done so.

The case came up in the High Court before Lord Chief Justice Widgery. Ten of the defendants were union members.[2] It transpired during the trial that the magistrates had not even made the order that the name should not be published. The government's advocate, Treasury counsel Harry Woolf, demonstrated the legal virtuosity that was to lead to him later becoming Chief Justice himself. The fact that a court had not made an order, and was not even aware that an order should or could have been made, didn't matter, he argued: the order was implicit. This was enough to convince Lord Widgery, who found all parties guilty, but imposed fines of only £500 against the magazines and £200 against the union (lower because Ashton apologised to the court), which was taken as an admission that there was not much of a case. An appeal was made to the House of Lords, where in January 1979 Widgery's judgement was quickly thrown out on the unanimous verdict of the Law Lords.

It was a let-off for the union. The Colonel B case had been highly entertaining for everyone involved, except the hapless colonel, but really it was a sideshow. The ABC trial, on the other hand, was a serious matter. Here were two journalists and a source, to recall David May, 'honestly intent on bringing in news of the actions of others' who found themselves being punished – and facing seven-year sentences. The 1978 ADM acknowledged this when the entire conference, at the end of one session, marched through the streets of Whitley Bay to accompany Crispin Aubrey as he went to sign in at the police station – a condition of his bail.

The trial began in September 1978 with the offer of a plea bargain:

Berry and Campbell were told that if they pleaded guilty to lesser (section 2) charges, of disclosing and receiving classified information, those under section 1 of the OSA (spying) would be dropped. They rejected the offer. Berry told the Crown lawyers to 'stick it up their legal rectums'.

After ten days of the prosecution case the trial was dramatically halted by the judge, because it had become public knowledge that the foreman of the jury was an ex-SAS soldier. This – and the fact that three of the heavily vetted jury had signed the OSA – had been known to those in the courtroom for days, since the defence had applied for these jurors to be discharged. Judge Willis – who had been appointed to hear the case at the last minute and was by an astounding coincidence a former officer in the Royal Corps of Signals – had refused the request and ordered it not to be reported, but journalist Christopher Hitchens of the *New Statesman* blew the gaffe on a TV chat show, and a new trial had to be ordered with a new judge and jury. It turned out there had been a serious attempt to rig the jury: MI5 had been given the panel list two months in advance and had questioned everyone on it.

One feature of the new trial was that Colonel Johnstone, whose identity was so sensitive that journalists had to be brought before the Lord Chief Justice of England to protect it, gave evidence under his real name. His ordeal in the witness box, manifesting a miserable incomprehension of public accountability, was painful even for ABC supporters. The new judge, Mr Justice William Mars-Jones, announced that the spying charges were dropped, lifting the threat of seven-year sentences. Later he said, in the absence of the jury, that he would not be imposing custodial sentences, whatever the verdicts. Not knowing this, the jury agonised for sixty-eight hours before bringing in three guilty and five not guilty verdicts on the various remaining charges, and Mars-Jones handed down a suspended sentence to Berry and conditional discharges to the journalists.

The jury, almost delirious with relief, came to the post-trial party and joined the celebrations with gusto. A subsequent downside of the outcome was the ban on any communication with jurors during or after a trial, enacted in the Contempt of Court Act 1981. This was promoted as a protection against bribery or harassment, but the embarrassment caused to the Crown by the jury's conduct after the ABC case was considered by some to have been a factor.

The issue of conditional discharges for breach of the Official Secrets Act only emphasised the ludicrous nature of the proceedings. It did look as if the NUJ's campaigning had had its effect. The state legal and prosecuting machinery, the careers of two Labour ministers – Home Secretary Merlyn Rees and Attorney-General Sam Silkin – and the OSA itself had been severely damaged. As Campbell's lawyer Jeremy Hutchinson QC said of the Act at the end of the trial: 'Perhaps this will be the last performance on the public stage of that raddled and discredited prima donna, and we must hope that no government impresario will call upon her seductive services again.'

'I bet you got a note of that,' Mars-Jones remarked to the press bench.

There were hopes that section 2 of the 1911 Act (outlawing all disclosure of any government information) would be swept away. A Private Members Bill promoted by the Liberal MP Clement Freud and supported by the union made considerable parliamentary headway. The Official Information Bill would have scrapped section 2 and introduced freedom of information provisions. It was unopposed by the Labour government and would have become law, but sadly fell with it in March 1979. Nothing more was heard on the subject for two decades. Labour promised a Freedom of Information Act, and though it did manage a weak and much criticised measure in 2000, it never dared relax the Official Secrets Act.

In 1985 came an even more spectacular defeat for official secrecy, with the acquittal of Clive Ponting, a senior civil servant at the Ministry of Defence, who leaked to Tam Dalyell MP a document showing that the government had misled Parliament about the sinking of the Argentinian cruiser *General Belgrano* in the Falklands War, when 323 sailors died. Despite overwhelming evidence the jury acknowledged the 'public interest' defence and Ponting was freed, just as Aitken had been fourteen years before.

In 1989 the government made a response to this case: it amended the OSA to remove the public interest defence. The NUJ managed to mobilise a dozen Tory MPs to defy a three-line whip and join the Labour opposition in voting for a public interest amendment. Among them was Jonathan Aitken, who even voted, alone of the Tories, against the final bill after the amendment was defeated.

Unprotected disclosure

In 1983 one whistleblower did go to prison. The journalists in the case did not; in fact, it was the journalists who effectively condemned her. Sarah Tisdall, a junior official in the Foreign Office, was outraged that Defence Secretary Michael Heseltine had lied to Parliament about the deployment of Cruise missiles at the US air base at Greenham Common in Berkshire; again American security was the issue. She leaked a couple of documents anonymously to the *Guardian* in London. The Crown secured an order for the return of the documents, and editor Peter Preston reluctantly complied, after which Tisdall was quickly traced, confessed and sentenced to six months' imprisonment under the Official Secrets Act.

While Preston, a union member, was agonising over whether to return the documents, the father of the NUJ Chapel at the *Guardian*, Aidan White, went to see him. According to White,

> the first thing [Preston] said to me was, 'I hope you are not telling me to go to jail.' He wanted the staff to support him and I said they would. I raised the question of the Code of Conduct. But no one could get in the way of Peter Preston's thought processes, which were, 'I don't want to go to jail and I don't want the *Guardian* to be subjected to fines.'

At an urgent meeting of senior staff – most of them NUJ members – to decide what to do, White says he was the only voice arguing against compliance with the order.

Preston was widely condemned – though by deciding earlier not to destroy the documents he had put himself in a difficult position – but the affair was far from glorious for the NUJ chapel, which affirmed its support for the editor and reacted angrily when others in the union attacked him. The national executive came within one vote of instigating disciplinary action against Preston. As for Tisdall, she turned down contemptuously his offer to help her when she came out of jail.

Informing the people

In 1989 the International Federation of Journalists sent a delegation to examine the state of press freedom in Britain. It was the sort of exercise customarily directed at countries with less developed media and fewer pretensions to a free press, but the NUJ did not take offence. Indeed, the occasion for the mission was the introduction of the Northern Ireland broadcasting ban, and the union cooperated happily. The IFJ team produced quite a damning report that summarised its conclusion in two memorable sentences: 'In Britain there is freedom of expression. Everybody is free to express a badly informed opinion.'

To make people better informed there was already an active campaign for freedom of information, which the NUJ strongly supported. So did the TUC, at the urging of the union, as well as the Labour Party, which had been committed to introducing a law since the 1970s. When Labour came to power in 1997 it did publish a positive White Paper, but its proposals, welcomed by campaigners, were dropped, reportedly on the orders of the Prime Minister, Tony Blair. A much inferior alternative bill materialised, and the union joined the campaign to beef it up.

In Ireland by now the NUJ-led 'Let in the Light' campaign had triumphed (see p. 327) and a strong Freedom of Information Act (FoIA) had been introduced. The union flew over the Irish Information Commissioner, Kevin Murphy, to tell the Brits how it might be done. As the bill went through Parliament the efforts of a small number of committed

Irish Information Commissioner Kevin Murphy speaking at Parliament in London after the NUJ invited him to address British MPs on freedom of information. (Stefano Cagnoni)

NUJ MPs won some concessions, and though implementation of the 2000 FoIA was delayed as long as the government could manage, it did come into force in 2005. There were worries that journalists had become so unused to digging for official information that they wouldn't know how to take advantage of it, so the NUJ added a course in using the Act to its professional training programme.

MPs at the meeting in Parliament with Kevin Murphy were presented with yet another NUJ campaign. Jeremy Dear, then the NUJ national organiser for newspapers, introduced a reporter who had just been threatened with prosecution under the OSA. Martin Bright, home affairs correspondent of the *Observer*, had been in contact with a former MI5 officer turned whistleblower, David Shayler, and written a story on his allegation that MI6 had plotted with the international Islamic network Al Qaeda to murder Libya's Muammar Gaddafi. Shayler was a particular *bête noire* of government, and now the Attorney-General secured an order against Bright to disclose all the information he had, with a threat of prosecution if he did not. The NUJ found itself with another multiple secrecy case, for Shayler, who now made a precarious living as a journalist, had joined the union, and was already facing charges under the OSA. His case was a lost cause and he went to prison for six months, despite a union campaign in his defence.

Martin Bright, meanwhile, became the next NUJ hero to refuse to hand over material, and despite the antagonism of his editors and lawyers towards it was pleased to be associated with the union campaign. He spoke at the NUJ ADM in 2000:

> I will be handing nothing over. For this I realise I could face prison, although I find it hard to believe that [Home Secretary] Jack Straw would invite such a PR disaster. I wrote about alleged crimes by agents of the state, but instead of investigating a plot to kill a foreign leader, this government has chosen to attack the liberty of the press. No journalist can genuinely claim to represent the public interest if the police have access to everything they do.

During the ADM debate Dear gave the names of the MI6 agents alleged by Shayler to have been involved in the murder plot; the *Observer* had not dared identify them. 'They are David Watson and Richard Bartlitt,' Dear said. The NUJ was naming forbidden names again – but this time nothing happened. Bright's stance was borne out by a triumphant High

Martin Bright, Observer *reporter threatened with prosecution under the Official Secrets Act, (right) with NUJ General Secretary John Foster before the first hearing of his case at the Old Bailey. (Stefano Cagnoni)*

Court victory, in which Mr Justice Judge threw out the order against him with a ringing declaration on the freedom of the press in English law; no charges were laid.

Neither were they laid against a whistleblower from inside GCHQ – the first ever known. In 2002 Katharine Gun indirectly supplied Bright with the story that GCHQ had been bugging United Nations delegations in New York whose Security Council votes were going to decide on the invasion of Iraq. It was so deeply embarrassing for government that, despite the fact that no other papers had picked up the story, she was never charged. Although the 'public interest' defence that had kept Aitken and Ponting out of jail had been swept away by the 1989 Act there was still a possibility that Gun might be acquitted, but a stronger factor was probably the application from her lawyers for disclosure of the legal advice the Prime Minister had received on the lawfulness of the invasion. Whatever the reason, it did appear that the Crown lacked the confidence to proceed with the prosecution of whistleblowers whose cause might have public appeal.

During the Shayler and Bright cases another reporter faced the Official Secrets Act. Tony Geraghty, a veteran former military specialist with the *Sunday Times*, had written a book, *The Irish War*, which was on open sale. Ministry of Defence police ransacked his home and seized material, and

Geraghty was charged under the OSA along with a former military officer, Nigel Wylde. The cases never came to court.

With the secret state apparently in retreat again, the union coordinated an attempt to start a new movement, called ROSA – Reform the Official Secrets Act. A number of organisations joined up, including Liberty, whose director John Wadham was Shayler's solicitor, together with individuals including Bright, Geraghty and Wylde, plus investigative reporters and various 'spookwatchers' and campaigners. But support fell away after the terrorist attacks in the USA in September 2001, when with the cranking up of the 'war on terror' many people took fright. We were in a different century now.

The right to report

Press card wars

George Orwell's NUJ card is one of the union's treasures. That the great writer/journalist should have identified himself as a union member is a source of some inspiration. To journalists the NUJ press card is both a working tool and a badge of professional status. Getting it accepted by police and other authorities has been a perpetual concern of the union.

● ●

George Orwell

George Orwell (Eric Blair) (1903–50) was educated at Eton and served in the Indian Imperial Police. He became ashamed of his role in propping up the Empire, and took a series of menial jobs in Paris and London before turning to journalism under the pseudonym George Orwell. His first book, *Down and Out in Paris and London*, was published in 1933 and followed the next year by *Burmese Days*. He fought with the POUM militia against Franco's fascists during the Spanish Civil War, becoming deeply disillusioned with the communists, who considered POUM to be a Trotskyist front and murdered several of its supporters in Spain. The first result was his war memoir *Homage to Catalonia*, and his later novels *1984* and *Animal Farm* also

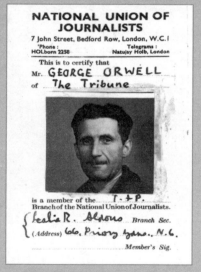

George Orwell's NUJ card. (NUJ Collection)

reflected this disillusion. Orwell joined the NUJ in December 1943 when he was recruited by Aneurin Bevan to be literary editor of the new left wing weekly *Tribune*, remaining a member until his death.

Former political editor Joe Haines wrote in the *Daily Mirror* in 1992 that the moment a young journalist received his or her NUJ card was the proudest of their working lives. Jeremy Paxman, presenter of the BBC's Newsnight, says: 'When I became a journalist, one of the first things I did was to join the NUJ. I couldn't believe I could get a union card without first demonstrating I was a proper journalist. I still can't believe I'm a proper journalist. But I've still got the union card.' The card establishes membership of a community that expects the privilege of cooperation and recognises that in return it is answerable for the carrier's conduct: whatever questionable activities journalists might sometimes get up to, the press card is a symbol of their professionalism. It informs the authorities that they should allow the bearer to carry on his or her business unhindered, and should respond favourably to any reasonable request for assistance. Its acceptance is a crucial but often overlooked aspect of press freedom. Acquiring a card is one of the main reasons given by journalists for joining the NUJ.

Orwell has not been the only world-renowned writer to carry one. H. G. Wells astounded American colleagues by flashing his card around at the Washington Press Club in 1922. According to the *Journalist*:

> Wells turned to the other British journalists present and said, 'Hey you fellows, bring out your cards', and every one of them did. The idea of respectable, not to say distinguished, English journalists being members of an avowed trade union excited extreme surprise, and there were many paragraphs in the American papers about the affair. It illustrates perhaps as well anything could the difference of temperament between the American and Englishmen in social and industrial affairs.

It wasn't really a press card then, nor even in Orwell's day. It was simply a union membership card on to which members glued their photos. It wasn't until 1960 that it even carried the word 'PRESS'. The card had always been taken for granted, but from the late 1960s that was no longer possible. There were big street protests over nuclear weapons and the Vietnam War, the IRA launched its 'mainland' bombing campaigns, and police were seeking more control of journalists working on the streets. Then, in 1972 the Metropolitan Police introduced a press card of its own; this was a laminated affair, sealed, with a photo of the carrier, and it launched two decades of 'press card wars' between the union and the police. The

Met card was widely taken up – three thousand were issued every two years – because applications were made not by the journalists but by their newsdesks, who circulated the application forms to reporters and made sure they completed them. The papers' photographers took the pictures, and that was that. Other police forces around Britain started to follow suit.

To the NUJ the system was anathema: to allow an agency of the state to control who could or could not work as a journalist clashed with a basic principle of independent journalism. Annual conferences in the 1970s called for a boycott of police cards, and the 1977 conference went so far as to instruct members not to hold them. Some members complied, but they could find themselves at a disadvantage on the streets because officers would not accept the NUJ card. Most members in London, at least, did not comply; it could have been more than their jobs were worth. To make it worse, the Met started refusing cards to some journalists – essentially, those working for the growing left-wing press.

One of these, freelance photographer Andrew Wiard, started a campaign in the London Freelance branch to get the union to introduce its own secure laminated card. There was resistance from the union leadership, who were almost as suspicious of the new generation of activists as were the police, but the 1979 ADM instructed the executive to introduce a proper press card – despite its objections that members wouldn't be able to record their subscription payments on it! Durham Paddock from Liverpool said it was 'diabolical' that London journalists were turning a blind eye to union policy and accepting police cards, while his own members were refusing those issued by the local force.

It took three years to get the decision carried out: at the 1981 ADM the LFB set up a laminating machine at the back of the hall to produce plastic cards for delegates on the spot. Wiard took Polaroid mugshots, branch secretary Tim Gopsill worked the machine. The conference took the point. Deputy General Secretary Jake Ecclestone saw the project through and the 'yellow lammy' went into circulation in 1982. Now the rival police and union cards were on a par.

The rivalry ended ten years later, with a union victory. In 1992 the Met threw in the towel. They had found it impossible to vet applicants, and police cards were turning up in the hands of couriers, taxi drivers and worse. In addition, some employers and agencies had started issuing their own cards, and officers on the ground were complaining that they didn't know which from among the proliferation of cards to recognise.

Conceding that the only people who could verify an applicant's bona fides were media bodies themselves, the director of public affairs at the Met, Mike Granatt, called together publishers, unions and agencies to set up a single national universally recognised and secure press card. These industry bodies would be called 'gatekeepers': they would issue the cards and be responsible for the conduct of their holders. As well as the NUJ, the broadcasting union BECTU representing camera and sound operators and other staff was included; they need press cards too.

The national paper employers, the Newspaper Publishers' Association, now threw the spanner in the works. At one of the meetings at New Scotland Yard the NPA attempted a coup: they brought along the managing editors of all the national papers to declare that they would run the scheme themselves, that the new card would be simply a replacement for the withdrawn Met card – and that there must be no involvement of the NUJ. They called the next meeting at the NPA's London headquarters. The unions were not invited.

Gopsill, now editor of the *Journalist* and the union's representative in the talks, got hold of BECTU's Deputy General Secretary Roy Lockett and the two of them gatecrashed the meeting. The managing editors sat along the side of the room, 'growling like Rottweilers', according to Gopsill, 'but they couldn't chuck us out because we had police protection'. Granatt, in the chair, went around the room asking all the other representatives whether they had any problem with NUJ participation. In an embarrassing scene – as they all said they did not – the NPA representatives got up and walked out of the meeting – in their own offices.

Afterwards, Gopsill and Ecclestone went to see Granatt: while the NUJ would withdraw its card if the scheme as initially proposed went ahead, it certainly would not if the NPA had control, they said, and the police would be back to square one. Granatt, a former union member as a local paper journalist in Kent, took the point. At the next full meeting he said it was NUJ involvement or nothing, and the NPA gave in.

The UK Press Card Scheme was launched in January 1993. Gopsill was its secretary for the first ten years, and NUJ involvement has been more than vindicated by the figures: among the sixteen industry gatekeepers, including the NPA and the Newspaper Society, the BBC, ITV and the Press Association, the union issues more than all the others put together: 13,547 out of 26,722 in 2006. In 2005 the gatekeepers' committee relaunched itself as the UK Press Card Authority, a limited company, and after years of cajoling

police forces for proper support for the scheme reached agreement with
the Association of Chief Police Officers for a publicity programme within
the forces drawing attention to the need for police to respect the card.

Number of press cards issued by the sixteen 'gatekeepers' in January 2006

BBC	1,820
BECTU (technicians' union)	715
British Association of Journalists	187
CPNA (photo agencies)	124
FPA (foreign correspondents)	1,842
Institute of Journalists	192
ITN radio (commercial radio)	260
ITV (commercial TV)	1,161
IVCA (corporate video)	126
NAPA (press agencies)	208
NPA (national papers)	1,981
NS (provincial papers)	3,125
NUJ	13,547
PPA (periodical publishers)	292
Reuters (national news agencies)	462
Sky TV	680
Total	26,722

As official security concerns mounted after September 2001 police
forces around the country, coordinated by the Cabinet Office in London,
began making preparation for the handling of such major emergencies
as a terrorist attack. One problem they faced was how to deal with the
hordes of journalists likely to descend on the scene, with the dread possibility of having to vet every one for security. Although the UK press
card is not 'secure' in the sense that its holders are not required to pass
counter-terrorism checks, it was agreed (with relief) that it would be
sufficient for identity purposes. And when the nightmare became real on
7 July 2005, as four bombs went off on London transport, the scheme
worked smoothly.

But government wanted greater security, with counter-terrorism
vetting that would require journalists to give personal information
including criminal records. Calls for a 'supercard' for access to Downing
Street had come from police a couple of times before, but solidarity among

the gatekeepers had seen them off without much trouble. The Press Card Authority is a rare example of cooperation in which unions, employers, agencies and associations work together: bickering is not tolerated, and the combination has so far succeeded in keeping the hand of the state out of determining which journalists can work.

So farewell then yellow lammy you were handy until you expired

This was the *Journalist*'s headline when the NUJ withdrew its own card in favour of the national UK card in 1992. But it was not in fact totally withdrawn: in the Republic of Ireland the authorities were perfectly happy with the NUJ press card, and it remains in use there. In Scotland, too, the union card was apparently no problem, and while the UK card is issued there, the Scottish employers are content for journalists to carry the NUJ-issued version and have

Campaigning photographer Andrew Wiard with his laminated yellow NUJ card. (Jeremy Nicholl)

not bothered to join the national scheme. It appears to be the English owners and editors alone who suffer from the union neurosis.

In 2006 the union secured a landmark agreement with the Met, which agreed to draw up guidelines confirming the right of photographers carrying the card to work unhindered. The negotiations resulted from persistent complaints from photographers in the rash of bomb alerts that followed the 7 July bombings, when panicking officers had restricted access. The guidelines were negotiated by the NUJ's national freelance organiser John Toner, who said: 'There were so many complaints last year by photographers who were denied reasonable access that we impressed upon the Met the need for clear instructions. They readily accepted that their previous efforts had not worked and that action was necessary.' It was a step forward in relations with the police, but Toner added, 'We do not expect that this will eradicate all problems overnight.'

The meat in the sandwich: photographers and the police

Official sanction for the press card is one thing; recognition by officers on the streets is quite another. Journalists have always been liable to arrest when things get tricky for police on the streets, and probably always will. Photographers, who have to be in the thick of things to do their job, find themselves bundled away, particularly when police are up to something they don't want the world to see.

Journalists and police have a complex relationship. Both need each other for their work, and the benefits are mutual. The police are the source of a huge amount of material in national and especially local media – more than the public probably realises. But the police like to retain the upper hand and journalists are quite often obstructed, harassed or even arrested while trying to work when police want them to stop.

Journalists have been soliciting formal recognition of the card and complaining about police obstruction of their work throughout the union's history; often at the same time. The Liverpool branch reported in July 1936 that they had met the Chief Constable of Lancashire, who had agreed to instruct his officers to recognise the card and give any help they could to the press. Two years later, in June 1938, the same branch was pressing the NEC to alert other branches to the 'excessive obstruction or interference with photographers by police officers', a hazard that was 'rapidly and alarmingly increasing'. But it was twenty years later, with the start of trouble on the streets of London, that police began to get heavy with photographers. In the 1958 Notting Hill riots in west London, the first serious urban strife in Britain since the Second World War, the Met began arresting journalists in numbers. The riots were caused by white racists attacking black immigrants, and demonstrations by and against the National Front (NF) became frequent scenes of violent disorder.

In 1974 Caudley George, a photographer with *West Indian World*, was arrested when he failed to produce a police card at an anti-NF march, and convicted, albeit with an absolute discharge. As he left the court, police taunted him and told him to get a Met card if he didn't want to be nicked again. Three months later, at another anti-NF march, George was grabbed again as he tried to protect a young black man seized by a man he thought might have been a fascist but turned out to be a plain-clothes police officer. Photographs showed him waving his NUJ card in the officers' faces. That day he was not arrested, but four other photographers were attacked. One of them, Ron McCormick, said there appeared to have been 'a deliberate attempt by the police to obstruct the press'. So alarmed were his colleagues that twenty-five of them got together at a union meeting and decided to picket the Home Office to call for an inquiry into the 'drastic deterioration of relations between journalists and the police'.

In 1977 London freelances Mike Abrahams and Homer Sykes were arrested while covering NF events and charged with obstruction, but the charges were dropped after union intervention. In 1980 north London freelance Peter Slepokura was arrested while snapping police breaking up an anti-NF picket. No evidence was offered in court when he too faced an obstruction charge.

It was during street fighting in Brixton, south London, that photographers came off worst; and one, David Hodge, was stabbed to death by looters. In the first outbreak of fighting in Brixton, in April 1981, photographers were targeted and beaten by police, who then tried to blame them for the rioting. Neil Martinson, who had photographed an arrest, was knocked to the ground and truncheoned on the head and in the testicles, and had his camera smashed and stamped on by police. With NUJ support he sued the Met and won compensation. A colleague, Larry Herman, broke a finger when a truncheon bashed him in the face as he was taking a picture. Assistant Commissioner of the Met, Wilford Gibson, made a statement: 'There were a number of people in organising positions … a lot of people, many of them white, with cameras' among the crowds. The notion of the youth of Brixton rallying to the call of middle-aged white journalists was baffling to most people, and when the Law Lord Leslie Scarman, appointed by government to investigate the disturbances, produced his groundbreaking report, blame was placed firmly on the police treatment of black people in the area.

Police attacks on photographers continued even after the introduction of the new UK card in the 1990s. Now their focus was mainly on the lively demonstrations of environmental campaigners and animal rights activists, which as well as photographers attracted another new breed: the video-journalists, people committed to providing alternative news footage to the generally hostile mainstream media coverage of such events. To police these people were no different from the demonstrators, and when they got in the way they were arrested, press card or no press card; one photographer who was given a warning – 'Next time you're nicked' – was told by an officer that he was 'always at the front' of the demo. 'Well, I wouldn't be much use at the back, would I?' he replied. Usually they were released without charge – after a few hours' delay that prevented them getting their images to that day's bulletins or the next day's papers. Cynics suggested this was the object of the police exercise.

Roddy Mansfield, a video-journalist from the Oxford-based Undercurrents news video collective, managed to get arrested a record seven times at various protests in 1993–5. Each time NUJ legal officer Sally Gilbert succeeded in preventing charges and in recovering his gear. One arrest took place at an animal rights protest over a farm near Oxford where cats were reared for vivisection. After weeks of problems at the farm the union negotiated an agreement with Thames Valley Police to send an official observer to keep an eye on the treatment of colleagues; the observer was NUJ executive member Jim Boumelha, who lives in Oxford. All passed peacefully; but

NUJ executive member Jim Boumelha (in armband) acts as a union observer at an animal rights demonstration near Oxford in 1999. (Mark Shenley)

Photographer Nick Cobbing is arrested in Oxford. (Andrew Testa)

the next week police banned the protest altogether. The activists marched through Oxford city instead, and Mansfield was arrested there, with stills photographer Nick Cobbing. The NUJ backed a case for wrongful arrest against Thames Valley Police, and the two won £18,000 in compensation.

The union's priorities were to secure members' release without charge, the dropping of charges if any were laid; and the return of any equipment that had been seized, undamaged, and with its film or other data intact. Almost invariably the union succeeded in its aims – though student photographer Maggie Lambert's case, over photographing the Twyford Down anti-motorway protest in 1993, had to go all the way to the Court of Criminal Appeal.

Cobbing, on the other hand, was one who did end up convicted. In May 1997 he was covering the occupation by environmentalists of the site for the second runway at Manchester airport, where the protesters were living in the trees. Cobbing climbed into an eighty-foot beech to photograph their eviction, cooperated with the bailiffs who were clearing the trees and came down when asked to, yet police took his cameras and film and held him for fourteen hours. By the time he was released, the papers had missed the pictures. He was charged and found guilty of obstructing the sheriff's officers and conditionally discharged, despite NUJ representation.

It was just more bad luck for Cobbing: fellow photographer Paul Smith, arrested and held for four hours on a different part of the site, faced the same charge but was acquitted. The distinction was that the airport site was split between two police areas. Cobbing was in Greater Manchester. Smith was in Cheshire, and when he came up before Crewe magistrates they threw out the charges. Sally Gilbert commented: 'It seems the authorities are anxious to stop these photographers getting their work out. By the time they come up in court the police somehow seem to be more prepared to accept the journalists' right to work on sensitive stories than they are at the time.'

The Brussels run

From time to time police set out to get hold of journalists' work, especially pictures, and the union always protects photographers being ordered to surrender their images (or reporters their notebooks) and advises them on how to prevent this happening. It fought one of its great test cases over this issue in 1988, when four photographers refused to obey a court order to surrender their pictures.

Journalists do have a measure of legal protection against the arbitrary seizure of their material by police, just as they have a measure of protection under the Contempt of Court Act when it comes to safeguarding sources. The Police and Criminal Evidence Act (PACE) of 1984 defines journalists' work as 'special category' material that requires the order of a crown court judge before it can be handed over, which gives a chance to argue against it. The NUJ always takes that chance, just as it does for reporters facing orders to identify their sources or surrender their notebooks.

The 1988 case was a tricky one, because the photographs that the Metropolitan Police were after when they applied to the Central Criminal Court (the Old Bailey) for a PACE order were of Met officers themselves attacking demonstrators at the mass pickets outside News International's Wapping newspaper factory in east London. Following numerous complaints of brutality, as officers both on horseback and on foot had waded into the crowds, Scotland Yard launched an investigation with a view to prosecuting the officers responsible. They approached newspapers and agencies, TV newsrooms and individual photographers in search of evidence.

The photographers had plenty of pictures but they didn't trust the Met – and they had reason, for when cases came to court four years later the Crown (rather too readily) accepted a defence that the delay in bringing the prosecutions made justice impossible, and the charges were thrown out. The photographers had followed the principle that the police or courts are welcome to any material that has been published or been offered for publication, but that is all. To hand over all their negatives (as were used then) was unthinkable.

If pictures are used by prosecutors and the photographers are subpoenaed to give evidence, they will identify the pictures as theirs and say where and when they took them, but that is all. They will answer no questions; police and prosecutors appreciate this and the NUJ is aware of no cases in which photographers have been put under pressure to go further.

In the Wapping case the journalists and broadcasters advanced various defences. Thames Television, for instance, said it had wiped all its tapes before the police came knocking. (To destroy the images once police have indicated they are going to apply for them is an offence under the PACE.) When Thames chief executive Richard Dunn gave evidence that the tapes had been wiped before the application, the judge looked at him and said, 'Well, Mr Dunn, I suppose we have got to believe you.'

The protection of unpublished images, and other material such as reporters' notes, is not just a union matter but is respected throughout the profession. TV companies had learned from earlier cases. The BBC had been badly caught out in 1984 after riots in the St Paul's district of Bristol. The police had applied for all the footage taken by news camera crews; but the court, as often happens, refused the general order and told them to reapply for images of specific incidents. The police asked the BBC to play them the tapes to help them pick what they wanted, which the BBC did – to the horror of the journalists, who protested mightily.

The Wapping case freelances – Jason Gold, Ilkay Mehmet, Andrew Moore and Andrew Wiard, the veteran press card campaigner – refused to comply with the Old Bailey orders. Their defence was ingenious and would prove successful: they could not hand over the pictures even if they wanted to, because they didn't own them. This was the first public outing of the NUJ's 'Brussels run': under this scheme, photographers gave their negatives to the NUJ, signing a letter to the effect that they were renouncing ownership and control of them for ever. The union gave them a receipt saying the same. A union official then took them to the HQ of the International Federation of Journalists in Brussels, where the exercise was repeated. The images were then outside the jurisdiction of the English courts.

Artist at work

London freelance photographer David Hoffman, held four times
by the Met police, got his revenge with £25,000 in compensation
– achieved after a remarkable piece of forensic work on his part. He
was arrested in May 1989 in Westminster while covering a demonstration by Muslims against the novelist
Salman Rushdie. The statement
of the arresting officer made false
accusations about his conduct – and
also got the time of the incident
wrong. The timing was significant,
and Hoffman devised an ingenious
method of proving his case.

*Photographer Dave Hoffman's self-
portrait in a police cell in 1987.*

Before his arrest Hoffman had
photographed the officer obstructing, and in one of these photos he
noticed the constable was wearing a
wristwatch, with the time just barely
visible. He took the transparency and
blew up the tiny section including
the watch hundreds of times, in the
manner of the Antonioni film *Blow-
Up*. Eventually he could make out
the time, and yes, the officer was

*Self-portrait of Dave Hoffman in a
police cell, 1989.*

lying. Horseferry Road magistrates
threw out the charge of obstruction
against him – because they couldn't
find an officer who was obstructed
– and Hoffman's startling photographic evidence secured his victory
in a union-backed civil claim for
compensation. The £25,000 offer
was made, as so often, just as the
case was to be heard.

*Self-portrait of Dave Hoffman being
arrested in 1993, taken with 20mm
lens at arm's length.*

Hoffman was arrested again for obstruction in 1993, at an anti-
whaling occupation of the Norwegian tourist office in London by
Greenpeace. He and another photographer, Mark Large, were held
for four hours – long enough to miss their deadlines. He managed to

▶

photograph his own arrest, by holding out his camera with a 24mm lens as he was led away. He added the image to a collection, which includes two photos he took of himself in the police cells by using the delayed shutter; for one of these he stood on his head.

At any rate, after the second arrest Hoffman brought another case, again with union support, and this time won £5,000.

The four photographers were summonsed for contempt and questioned at Preston Crown Court, where Judge Allott, who was on circuit, happened to be sitting. All four said they would not and could not ask for their pictures back. NUJ General Secretary Harry Conroy and joint President Barbara Gunnell also said they wouldn't give them back, if asked. IFJ General Secretary Aidan White flew from Brussels to take the stand and declare that he wouldn't give them back to the union. Judge Allott was not happy, nor were the police or the Crown lawyers, but there was nothing the judge could do save to quash the orders.

Since then, numerous photographers finding themselves in possession of images that may show individuals committing offences have followed the same route. To renounce ownership for ever, knowing that they can never get them back, is not a frivolous matter. Occasionally some have asked for material to be returned, to be rebuffed by the union. The film sits in a filing cabinet in Brussels, and from time to time producing an exhibition has been suggested, or a book, but nothing has materialised: it might be considered provocative.

The rationale behind the refusal to hand over is to protect not just the journalists, but the public too. On a practical and important level, if angry crowds get the idea that journalists are going to hand over pictures to the police they are likely to turn on them, and this has happened: Sky TV reporter Tim Arnold, an active NUJ member, was beaten by demonstrators at the Trafalgar Square anti-poll tax demonstration in 1990, and broadcast a heroic live report with blood streaming down his face.

Leaflets urging demonstrators to attack the press have been handed out at anarchist rallies in London: in 1994 the Class War group distributed leaflets proclaiming: 'The pigs and their friends in the media are always keen to try to get your mug on film. Don't think the media are on our side … they are our enemy. They should be driven out of the area.' Covering demonstrations that lead to fighting with the police is dangerous enough as it is, with journalists liable to attack by both sides; as Andrew Wiard put it, they are 'the meat in the sandwich'.

A free Irish state? – reporting the North

Censorship and the Troubles: whose side were we on?

Like all former colonies that achieve independence, the Irish Republic retained much of the law and political culture of Britain. The Irish government allowed a press that was independent of government control, but hedged it with harsh defamation laws and a rigid control of official information; it even plagiarised the Official Secrets Act. Having adopted these relatively mild restrictive measures, it then, like many ex-colonies, added some of its own. It established a public broadcasting system that was much more susceptible to government control than the British model; and compounded the pressure on journalists with direct censorship, the first in peacetime in the British Isles since the nineteenth century. Resisting it was a difficult and anguished duty for the union.

The ground for these measures was the hangover of the country's independence struggle: the conflict in Northern Ireland, in which the Irish Republican Army over many years waged a paramilitary campaign for Irish unity. Public attitudes in Ireland were ambivalent and divided, and the divisions among journalists constrained the NUJ's attempts to maintain free reporting of the North. For journalists had retained another British institution, the NUJ – and even confirmed their adherence to it when given the chance to break away in 1942.

Reports of the conflict broadcast on Radio Éireann – which became Radio Telefís Éireann in 1961 (TV came late to Ireland) – had always been from the government's standpoint, according to Ireland's premier media historian John Horgan.[3] They had even banned the phrase 'Irish Republican Army', and 'IRA', requiring journalists to speak mysteriously of 'an illegal organisation'. Then, the 1961 Broadcasting Act which set up RTE included a provision (Section 31) empowering the Minister for Posts and Telegraphs to prevent the broadcast of 'any particular matter, or matter of any particular class'. There was no protest, not even from the NUJ.

It was ten years before the power was used. In October 1971, just after RTE had broadcast comments by representatives of Sinn Fein, the

IRA's political wing, on a meeting between the Irish and British Prime Ministers, the Minister of Posts and Telegraphs Erskine Childers instructed RTE to 'refrain from broadcasting any matter ... that could be calculated to promote the aims and activities of any organisation which engages in, promotes, encourages or advocates the attaining of any particular objective by violent means'.

Now the NUJ did react. It asked for meetings with the Taoiseach (the Prime Minister, Jack Lynch) and with Childers, but was rebuffed. The 1972 ADM pledged support for members who took industrial action against the order, and in September that year there was a two-hour work stoppage in the RTE newsroom in Belfast. The journalists said in a statement that they had been 'journalistically compromised ... Our credibility with a considerable section of the Northern Population had been steadily eroded.'

No action was taken at RTE in Dublin; at a branch meeting a call for a one-day strike was not even put to the vote, because it was clear to the movers it would be lost. The union's full-time organiser in Ireland, Jim Eadie, revealed later that the Dublin members had also tried to dissuade their Belfast colleagues from taking their protest action.

The reason was that a sufficient proportion of RTE journalists supported the censorship, notably among the NUJ branch leadership, to make it difficult for those who, as Horgan writes, 'were opposed to the directive in principle [but] unwilling to oppose it publicly because of the fear that such opposition would expose them to the charge that they were IRA sympathisers or fellow travellers'. Most of those against the censorship were far from that. One of their arguments was that barring spokesmen from interview meant they could not be challenged over IRA atrocities, giving them effectively a free run; IRA statements could be reported, but the organisation could not be questioned about them.

The view of the collaborationists was vehemently expressed by political correspondent Joe Fahy in a letter to General Secretary Ken Morgan in January 1973. He declared that the union was being hijacked for a political campaign to challenge 'the right of a democratically elected government to govern in the national interest ... I will not support any direct challenge to the Government of Ireland on this issue.' He claimed the media were being 'abused in favour of illegal groups ... The men of violence have been portrayed on RTE as if they were the elected leaders of the Irish people.'

There were also NUJ members committed to the republican cause,
working for nationalist publications. One member, Seamus O'Toole, a
former editor of the *United Irishman* then freelancing for the magazine
Hibernia, was interned in the government's round-up in Northern Ireland
in 1971, but quickly freed after the NUJ appealed to Stormont. Some of
the most influential pro-censorship voices among RTE journalists were in
fact former members or supporters of the IRA who had taken the 'official'
route when the movement split in 1971. The 'provisionals' followed the
paramilitary path; the officials, doctrinally Marxist, opted for class politics
and formed the Sinn Fein Workers' Party in the republic, which won a few
seats in the Dáil – where it formally opposed Section 31. These people
were not pro-state right-wingers, but left-wingers against the provisional
IRA, whose militarism they saw as destructive of class politics.

On occasions when the union's Dublin Broadcasting branch – effectively an RTE closed shop – itself formally opposed the censorship, it did
so in terms of harsh criticism of the provisionals. In 1982, when Section
31 was declared unconstitutional by the Irish High Court, the branch in
its statement, while welcoming the court decision, felt obliged to castigate
the IRA's 'fundamentally anti-working class, anti-trade union, sectarian
and anti-democratic activities [which were] beyond the limit of human
decency'.

In 1973 the secretary of the NUJ Irish Council, Maurice Hickey,
wrote to Morgan: 'It is a dicey matter. I do not think "militant" action
is required and any "extremism" would cause a rift among our RTE
members.' Morgan agreed that the best way forward lay in an approach by
the national union to the RTE Authority (equivalent to the BBC board
of governors), but before that could happen there was a sudden crisis.
An RTE journalist, Kevin O'Kelly, interviewed two of the IRA's top
brass, though without naming them in his programme. The government
responded wildly, sacking the entire RTE Authority.

One of the interviewees – Sean MacStiofan, the Chief of Staff – was
charged with membership of the IRA. O'Kelly was called to give evidence,
refused to identify him, and was sentenced to three months' imprisonment
for contempt. 'What I did, any member in the same circumstances would
have done,' he said. The RTE branch was ready to take action to defend a
member and staged a forty-eight-hour strike in protest, supported by other
unions, and all broadcasting stopped – something that never happened
before or since at RTE, or at the BBC for that matter. There was a twenty-

RTE reporter Kevin O'Kelly, sentenced to three months' imprisonment for refusing to betray an IRA source in 1973. (NUJ Collection)

four-hour solidarity stoppage too on Dublin daily newspapers – a cross-media demonstration also unmatched in NUJ history. O'Kelly's sentence was reduced to a fine on appeal; he did not have to serve time.

Meanwhile, the replacement RTE Authority appointed by the government tightened the censorship by setting out guidelines on how it was to be applied, which their predecessors had always declined to do: any recordings of IRA voices were ruled out, and factual material could even be cut from reports.

In February 1973 a new coalition government came into power in Dublin (Fine Gael and Labour) and a new minister emerged, the urbane and erudite Conor Cruise O'Brien, colloquially known as the Cruiser – scholar, writer and diplomat, and for a time editor-in-chief of the *Observer* in London. He was also an NUJ member, and agreed to consult the union, inviting it to draft possible amendments to the 1961 Broadcasting Act. The union took up the invitation, but the RTE branch threw another spanner and demanded that the union pull out of the negotiations.

There was a further rebuff for O'Brien in angry scenes at the next year's NUJ ADM, held in Ireland, in Wexford. At a reception, the minister

suggested to Morgan that he might speak in the projected debate on
Section 31. When this was put to delegates it was brusquely rejected. For
once, all parties agreed. The executive member for Ireland, John Devine,
said: 'If the minister comes I won't listen to him. The directive [under
Section 31] has ensured continuous and ongoing censorship and resulted
in journalists being forced to read the minds of successive ministers.' It was
'crippling the whole range of current affairs broadcasting,' said RTE journalist Cian O hEigeartaigh. 'There is a gradual paralysis by red tape and a
refusal to take decisions, which can lead to the cancer of self-censorship.'
For good measure, the conference passed unanimously a motion calling
for the repeal of Section 31.

For years the Cruiser made an issue of this supposed censorship of
himself, but the truth is that he was never actually invited to take part
in the debate. He was as good as his word, though, and promoted a new
Broadcasting Act in 1975, which encompassed a much more detailed
directive, specifying the organisations to be banned, and required the
directive to be renewed annually by the Dail, allowing thereby a debate
each year. For another eighteen years it was dutifully renewed, but there
was never any serious debate; Dail members were even more compromised than the journalists.

Meanwhile, sporadic censorship continued. In June 1974 NUJ members
at RTE banned all court reporting for a month after a report of a trial was
cut. The subject of the censoring was Bridget Dugdale, a British woman
tried in Dublin for receiving paintings stolen by the IRA, and from the
dock she made a speech attacking British domination of Ireland. Although
she was not a member of any illegal organisation, an editor cut the speech
from the report. Then, in March 1980, the union protested publicly when
RTE bosses banned the reporting of a sensational arms trial. The journalists also took action a number of times over instances of censorship other
than Northern Ireland.

The NUJ maintained contact with O'Brien and now tried another
tactic: public debate. In February 1977 it staged the first of a number of
seminars and conferences with the aim of generating a political campaign
against censorship in Ireland. In March 1981 the Dublin Broadcasting
branch staged a gala dinner debate on censorship, featuring O'Brien and
an old adversary, Sean MacBride, a former IRA Chief of Staff and Irish
Foreign Minister. The Cruiser annoyed members by first announcing that
'Section 31 is here to stay … a democratic government has not just a

right but a duty' to stop terrorist organisations using the airwaves, and then suggesting that journalists could always find ways of getting round it. MacBride – who had also spoken at the NUJ ADM in Northern Ireland in 1980 – said it was 'indefensible to outlaw entire categories of people regardless of how innocuous their remarks might be'.

This event came two weeks after an equally remarkable conference organised by the NUJ in Birmingham. Reporting on Northern Ireland was just as fraught in the UK, where government and its appointees on the regulatory bodies frequently interfered with documentary programmes. Speakers in Birmingham included a Belfast lawyer named David Trimble, who said it was right to withhold information from people in the interest of security: 'It is all very well for you to say you want news, but there is an overriding public interest that has to be served.' Trimble would become leader of the Ulster Unionists and First Minister in the Ulster Assembly after the Good Friday Agreement in 1998.

Others taking part included BBC Panorama editor Roger Bolton and reporter Jeremy Paxman, who had been through the mill over the Carrick-more incident in 1979. Paxman said the BBC's system of upward referral of tricky stories 'creates severe inhibitions on the way we report Northern Ireland'. The most forceful contribution came from Mary Holland, a much admired reporter who had been sacked as Irish correspondent of the *Observer* – by editor-in-chief Conor Cruise O'Brien, indeed – because of her insistence on impartial reporting. She explained how censorship works through 'the pressures that are brought to bear on anyone who tries to report in a way that goes against the political consensus. For every programme that gets banned there are twenty that don't get made.'

Whatever might be happening within the broadcasting corpora-tions, the NUJ kept the issue of censorship on the public agenda in both countries. Eventually, in the 1990s, this political strategy was to have signif-icant success (just as it did for Sinn Fein). But for the journalists there would be more storms to weather first, each more turbulent than the last.

In 1981 IRA hunger striker Bobby Sands stood for election for the UK Parliament from his deathbed in the Maze Prison, and again the RTE bureau in Belfast was in the front line: they could not report the election fairly if they could not quote one of the candidates. They asked the Dublin branch to support a ban on all reporting from constituen-cies with IRA/Sinn Fein candidates, which at first the branch agreed to.

Sinn Fein President Gerry Adams issued a statement congratulating the
union – which probably didn't help – and the branch reversed its decision,
arguing that the action would have extended the censorship and prevented
the proper coverage of elections.

In Britain there was the *Real Lives* strike in broadcasting in August
1985, and then four years later the huge rumpus over Thames TV's *Death
on the Rock*. By chance, at the same time as the *Real Lives* action, RTE
banned an interview with Martin Galvin of Noraid, the group that raised
funds for the IRA in the USA. Now RTE journalists themselves staged a
one-day stoppage, in the form of a continuous mandatory meeting rather
than an all-out strike. One journalist said: 'It would never have happened
if we weren't shamed into it by [fellow members at] the BBC.' Heartened
by this action, when the Broadcasting Act directive came up for renewal in
January 1986 the union in Ireland called for a national twenty-four hour
strike. But once again the militancy evaporated and the event had to be
downgraded to a demonstration outside the Dail, which attracted a couple
of hundred people. But that day the RTE branch, which was capable of
action as long as no one else was telling it what to do, decided on a two-
hour strike which blacked out bulletins and current affairs programmes.

The scapegoat

The next crisis came in March 1988, when an RTE reporter was sacked.
British SAS troops had shot dead three unarmed IRA members in Gibraltar
– the subject of the controversial *Death on the Rock* programme in the
UK – and Jenny McGeever was covering the return of their bodies from
Dublin to Northern Ireland. Although she did not interview any banned
person, the voice of Martin McGuinness, the former IRA leader who
became a Sinn Fein MP in Westminster, was heard on the tape, briefing
journalists on how the Royal Ulster Constabulary were refusing to allow
the coffins across the border because they were draped with the Irish
tricolour. McGeever maintained she had warned editors that the tape
needed editing, but the decision was taken to dismiss her, all the same.

Jim Eadie, an ardent opponent of Section 31, wanted to fight the
sacking, but the branch did not. For one thing, McGeever was a freelance
on contract and was not a member of the Dublin Broadcasting branch,
which would take only RTE employees. She had begun her career as
a journalist on Radio Nova, one of a wave of stations set up as pirates

RTE freelance reporter Jenny McGeever, sacked for alleged breach of the Section 31 censorship law in Ireland. (Derek Speirs/Report)

because the government would not license commercial radio. At Radio Nova she had been Mother of the NUJ chapel and led a strike for union recognition. That was not good enough for Dublin Broadcasting, which refused to admit pirate journalists to membership; the union, unwilling to compel the RTE members, had allocated her to another Dublin branch.

The branch suggested she should go to a tribunal, even though RTE's own industrial correspondent pointed out at a heated branch meeting that as a freelance McGeever could not bring a case there. In fact she got fed up with the union and took her case to the High Court on her own, winning an eventual settlement. She wrote in the *Journalist* of the RTE editors being 'paranoid about any issue relating to the North'; one of them had said of her report that the 'Irish nation [was] standing still in shock'. Colleagues 'no longer regarded me as a worthwhile risk to be seen with. Friendship might be regarded as sympathy or identification ... How anyone could be left so isolated and afraid, when they feel so outraged by a measure affecting their ability to report objectively, is indicative of the level to which we have sunk.'

The union suggested that she be allowed to work out her contract, but this was rejected by managers. It seemed that a decision had been taken at a high level to make her a scapegoat. When RTE management summoned two of McGeever's editors to a disciplinary meeting, the

*Jim Eadie (standing) announces the NUJ-backed appeal to Strasbourg against Section 31 at
a Dublin press conference in 1989. From left: Seosamh O Cuaig of Radio na Gaeltachta,
lawyer Ann Neary, Jim Eadie, Deputy General Secretary Jake Ecclestone, Irish NEC
representative Kieran Fagan and writer/academic Kevin Boyle. (Derek Speirs/Report)*

journalists immediately threatened a forty-eight-hour strike if disciplinary action was taken. Jim Eadie, whose relations with the branch were by
now very strained, remarked that the members 'seemed to apply different
standards of protection to the three members'. The leader of the RTE
journalists, Charlie Bird – like Joe Fahy a political correspondent enjoying
good relations with senior politicians – attacked the union publicly: 'The
NUJ adopted a position on Section 31 which we oppose. This policy
affected only our branch, and we think it is ludicrous that other branches
are adopting a policy which [only] we have to implement.'

Nine months later Bird attacked the union again, resigning in protest at
a decision to take a legal challenge to Section 31 to the European Court of
Human Rights. He objected that the branch had not been informed of the
proposal in advance. A statement from the branch expressed 'grave concern
about the failure of the NEC to consult the union's membership in RTE'.
After Bird's departure the Broadcasting branch did subsequently endorse the
action, but the tension between branch and union was manifested when the
union sought signatories for the case (governments can be sued in Europe
only by individual citizens, not by corporate bodies such as trade unions).
No one in Dublin would put their name to it; eventually Seosamh O Cuaig

(Joseph O'Kwaig) came forward from RTE's Irish-language station Radio na Gaeltachta, out in Connemara in the far west of Ireland.

Just as the Irish had earlier copied British legislation, so in October 1988 UK Home Secretary Douglas Hurd announced a similar ban to Section 31, forbidding the BBC and commercial broadcasters to use the voices of representatives of listed paramilitary organisations in Northern Ireland, loyalist as well as republican. Broadcasting journalists planned a twenty-four-hour strike, but it was called off. Instead, the union in Britain swung into a lively campaign, under the title 'Time to Know', which organised a march and a rally to be held each year on 19 October, the anniversary of Hurd's announcement. In Northern Ireland itself there were protests in BBC and commercial broadcasting, just as there had been with RTE's Belfast journalists over Section 31. Despite the unionist dominance of Northern Ireland media, the NUJ's non-sectarian professionalism prevailed and the Dublin rifts were not duplicated.

At the first annual protest in London, in 1989, union leaders and MPs marched through the city centre to a rally, wearing gags. Labour Party deputy leader Roy Hattersley was given a rough ride when, as the main speaker, he launched into a fierce assault on Irish republicanism – his apparent price for taking part. Among the speakers were comedians, for in Britain, unlike Ireland, the ban was widely derided, especially over the practice known as 'goldfishing'. This was one of a number of techniques developed by the BBC for circumventing the ban: it involved actors voicing the words of Sinn Fein leaders while silent images were shown of them speaking those words. As lip-synching techniques were perfected, it became virtually impossible to tell that an actor was involved. Some in the union felt that censorship should be made manifest, not disguised – so better to use subtitles, as other stations did.

There were also embarrassing manifestations of overenthusiastic compliance to the ruling: some nervous producers dropped Irish songs from playlists and spiked interviews with people who were quite unconnected with the proscribed organisations. But the public ridicule did make the ban, again unlike in Ireland, a severe embarrassment to the government.

Meanwhile, a legal challenge to Douglas Hurd's broadcasting ban was going through the British courts, and when the House of Lords dismissed the NUJ's last appeal, in February 1991, that case followed the Irish one to Strasbourg. Again it was brought in the name of individuals, six NUJ members from different areas.[4] Both appeals failed. The European judges

used the 'national security' exception allowed by Article 10 of the European
Convention on Human Rights, which supposedly guarantees freedom of
expression, to find the restrictions 'necessary' and the complaints 'mani-
festly ill-founded'.

But by now political developments in both countries were bringing
the bans to the end of their useful lives. Negotiations between Sinn Fein
and the British and Irish governments were in progress and in 1993 the
Irish Minister for Communications, Michael D. Higgins, announced that
he intended to review the ban. The Fianna Fáil government of Albert
Reynolds wanted to use the cessation of censorship as a bargaining counter
in the talks, and it worked. The IRA declared its ceasefire, and Higgins
announced that he would not renew the directive in January 1994. And so
it went, as Horgan writes, 'without a dissenting voice in a parliament that
had declined to debate its pros and cons at any stage in the twenty-three
years since it had been introduced'. The chair of the NUJ Irish Council,
Christy Loftus, said: 'At last, journalists will be allowed to do their proper
job.' The UK ban was lifted in September 1994.

The union lets in some light

The NUJ didn't stop there. A spark from the anti-censorship campaign set
off a wider campaign for free speech and information in Ireland called 'Let
in the Light'. The brainchild of a group of journalists and civil liberties
activists, it was named after the pledge by Reynolds in a magazine interview
that he would 'let in the light on Irish society'. It brought together a wide
range of freedom of speech and information issues, from the broadcasting ban on Sinn Fein to the prohibition on abortion information, to the
country's culture of state secrecy, its artistic censorship ... and the defamation laws that were used effectively by Reynolds himself to silence his
critics.

As Paddy Smyth of the *Irish Times*, who was secretary of Let in the
Light, put it:

> The common thread was a stifling state paternalism based on the idea
> that we had to be protected from ourselves. For the NUJ, we had
> become convinced that we could end the ghettoisation of freedom of
> information issues, and the stigmatisation of campaigners, by creating
> a new public space where they could all be discussed together as part
> of a single problem.

The campaigners produced booklets on freedom of information and Section 31, briefings on censorship and the libel laws; they lobbied legislators and the UN Human Rights Committee, and in January 1993 held an electrifying two-day conference in Dublin, attended by twelve hundred people. From the US they flew in Carl Bernstein of Watergate fame and veteran columnist Anthony Lewis; from Britain there was Frances D'Souza of the anti-censorship organisation Article 19, and Jake Ecclestone, Deputy General Secretary of the NUJ. They were joined by former Taoiseach Garret FitzGerald, psychologist Anthony Clare and Aidan White of the International Federation of Journalists – and a surprise guest whose appearance, like a rabbit out of a box, raised the roof: the writer Salman Rushdie, on his first, highly secret, heavily protected visit to Ireland following the promulgation of the Iranian fatwa against him.

The campaign caught the spirit of the moment and articulated a popular demand for change in a remarkable way. Within a few years Section 31 was repealed, Ireland got a Freedom of Information Act that was a model of openness; arts censorship was relaxed and abortion information was legalised. An independent press council and ombudsman are being instituted in 2006, though reform of the defamation laws is still only a promise.

But there were also setbacks: Reynolds's Fianna Fail successors slashed the effectiveness of the FoIA with amendments that drastically raised the fees that could be charged and massively extended the scope of government confidentiality, while pushing for stricter privacy provisions against the press. In the North, following the IRA ceasefire, there was the Good Friday Agreement and the expectation of more tranquil times, but for journalists there was no respite – in fact things got worse.

More reporters were ordered to disclose their sources or their material, and more were threatened or attacked, culminating in the murder of Martin O'Hagan in 2001. But there was a more united resistance to censorship and to the pursuit of journalists by the state, particularly evident in the campaign against the attempted prosecution of Ed Moloney, the Northern Ireland editor of the *Sunday Tribune*, in 1999. Moloney is a widely respected journalist and author of an acclaimed book on the IRA, and his stand was as brave as any taken on the island. He faced a demand to hand over the notes of an interview he had conducted with a loyalist paramilitary charged with the murder of lawyer Pat Finucane. The man's identity was public knowledge. Yet Moloney refused to surrender his material on grounds of professional confidentiality; he prevailed, and the range and strength of

Ed Moloney, who successfully defied a High Court order to hand over notes of an interview with a loyalist paramilitary accused of murder. (Crispin Rodwell)

the support he enjoyed was without question a factor in the Belfast High Court's quashing the order against him. Moloney said: 'This is a victory for journalism ... the authorities in the UK and Ireland will have to think twice before they try to get orders for journalists' material.'

In 2002 a clutch of disclosure orders were issued by the Saville inquiry into the Bloody Sunday shootings in 1972, when thirteen people had been killed. Among those affected were two union members, Lena Ferguson and Alex Thomson of Channel 4 News, who on conditions of confidentiality had interviewed soldiers who had taken part in the shooting. Lord Saville ordered them to disclose the names of the soldiers. They could not and would not do that – and Alex Thomson declared publicly that he would willingly go to jail rather than comply with the order. Both were declared in contempt of the tribunal. They did offer to consult the soldiers if they could find them, and two of the five came forward of their own accord.

After two years, as the inquiry dragged on, Lord Saville bowed to their determination and agreed to drop the orders. Considering that the soldiers' anonymous testimony to Ferguson's and Thomson's programmes was partly responsible for the reopening of the Bloody Sunday investigation, and that it could never have been recorded had anonymity not been promised, there cannot have been many more telling examples of the importance to the public interest of the confidentiality principle.

NEW MEDIA:
THE FUTURE PRESENT

A small knot of people gathered in a corner of the hall at Blackpool's Winter Gardens during the NUJ's ADM in 1991. They were there because Andrew Bibby, a freelance from Calderdale, had come up with the idea of starting an email network for NUJ members. At that time very few people had heard of the internet and email was still a technological adventure, not the routine chore it was to become. Bibby's inspiration was the Poptel network, which had been commissioned to set up a city-based online network in Manchester modelled on initiatives in the USA. He was looking for volunteers to create an NUJ network, and found them: Mike Holderness from London Freelance, Martin Jenkinson from Sheffield and Gary Herman from Manchester, all computer-wise freelances. In 1992 they launched NUJnet, the first trade union bulletin board.

NUJnet never had more than 250 subscribers and its largely proprietary technology was soon overtaken by the internet, but it always punched above its weight. The NUJ hosted meetings of an inter-union working party known as TUDIC (Trade Union Digital Communications) on the use of websites by trade unions, and launched its own Digital Working Group which put the union at the forefront of European debates on internet copyright. At the 1995 ADM the group launched a site on the brand-new World Wide Web, jointly with the broadcasting union BECTU, whose President Tony Lennon was an enthusiastic participant. The URL was the hardly snappy http://www.gn.apc.org/media/. It was one of the first trade union websites, and the very first to offer members their own pages on it, to promote their work. It was administered by Holderness independently of the NUJ itself.

The pioneers were well ahead of the union itself, which went about the launch of an 'official' website in a bureaucratic and cumbersome way. 'When other people want to set up a website they set up a website,' BBC delegate Paul Mason, a technology enthusiast, said at the 2001 ADM. 'The NUJ sets up a committee.' It was not until 2002 that www.nuj.org.uk went on line. Lacking any dedicated staff, it was little more than a news site and is due for a relaunch – with Herman as a consultant – in 2007. A separate and more impressive site was launched for the NUJ training programme. Holderness's site, meanwhile, was switched to his branch, London Freelance, and has continued to expand into an impressive media resource. As for NUJnet, it was succeeded by a bunch of forums and mailing lists such as NUJphoto, NUJreps, NUJnewmedia, and CatHerds (for freelances). Journalists being what they are, one email network was never going to be enough.

The union struggled, too, to encompass internet journalists in its structure. Just as it took two decades for those working for the BBC to settle into the NUJ presence, so website journalists found themselves in an organisational limbo. The sites that employed the most journalists were spin-offs from major print and broadcasting outlets – to start with, national papers and the BBC – and the journalists belonged to the chapels and branches concerned. The union was organised along 'industrial' lines – newspapers, broadcasting, magazines and books, freelances, PR and so on – and many did not want a separate 'new media' sector because their interests lay with their 'old media' colleagues. But in the early years of the new century independent news sites covering business, travel and technology are fast growing; the journalists began to form chapels and a New Media Industrial Council was eventually set up in 2004. The great breakthrough came the next year with the first NUJ agreement at a dedicated website, and gratifyingly it was at the London bureau of aol. com – America OnLine, part of the world's biggest media conglomerate AoL Time Warner.

The union has been coming to terms with a period of technological change as drastic as any it had to weather during the previous century. Born in the 1900s of a developing popular press, and in the wake of the introduction of mechanised typesetting, fast nationwide transport and the rotary press, in the 1950s it expanded with the introduction of popular broadcasting, then was forced to rebuild itself in the 1980s with the introduction of computerised production. Currently it faces the retrenchment of the newspaper industry, the fragmentation of broadcasting into hundreds of channels and the spread of the internet on to thousands of sites, all in an unstable deregulated market. In 2006 the process of newspapers expanding their output online started to accelerate rapidly. National and local papers and broadcasters vied to augment their websites with audio and video content.

With these changes to journalists' work – as momentous as anything over the last hundred years – the need for a union is as strong as ever, to maintain both decent conditions and decent standards of work. It is important that our community remains independent, autonomous and democratic – not just for journalists, but for the whole of society. The centralisation of political institutions and the unaccountable power of big publishing companies have made the need for a trade union, controlled by its members, more vital than ever. This applies beyond journalism: with the accelerating concentration of control at the top of national and local government and the political parties, trade unions are the only truly democratic national institutions left in Britain. It is received wisdom that unions have had their day and lost their popular support – or as former NUJ Deputy General Secretary Jake Ecclestone once put it, 'the trade union movement is down to its last six million members'. That is still bigger by far than any other grouping in UK society.

Far from declining, the NUJ is growing. Membership, which dipped from nearly 33,000 in 1981 to below 22,000 in 1994, rose to 41,000 in 2006 (including 7,000 student members – an investment in the future). But this total is nonetheless a smaller proportion of the entire workforce of the media industry than it was in the 1980s. No one knows how many people there are whose work could be defined as journalism – official estimates put it at around 70,000 – but the NUJ is continually adapting so as to be able to speak and act on their behalf. It is a daunting challenge – but so it was in 1907.

AFTERWORD

by Jeremy Dear, NUJ General Secretary

There are few unions that can compare with the NUJ – fiercely democratic, defiantly independent and proudly speaking out both for members and for their professional rights.

The NUJ's history, like that of all unions, has its perceived golden ages and its darker days. But no one can doubt that over the past hundred years the union has made a real difference – standing up for press freedom, speaking out for equality and campaigning for better pay and conditions. It has not always been successful – but few would disagree with the notion that journalists and journalism would be in a much worse state today were it not for those who throughout the last century have fought tooth and nail in the name of the NUJ.

(Photo: Stefano Cagnoni)

When I joined as a student member in 1987 things looked bleak, not just for the NUJ but for trade unionism in general. Margaret Thatcher's government had introduced thirteen pieces of anti-trade union legislation, and media employers across the UK took advantage and unilaterally tore up collective agreements. Some managements believed the NUJ would wither on the vine. But the union proved stronger than that. Through difficult times dozens of unsung heroes kept the flame burning, often at great personal cost. They simply wouldn't allow *their* union to be eradicated.

Those who founded our union in the early years of the last century would look today with incredulity at the media – not just at the techno-logical change, unimagined and unimaginable a hundred years ago, but also at the unaccountable power of so many of today's media corporations. But I hope they would also look with some pride at the successive genera-tions who have built on their foundations.

The media industry has undergone radical change; the NUJ, while swimming with the technological tide, has stuck firmly by its founding principles – of justice, fairness and solidarity in the name of journalists and journalism. Those principles have served us well over the past century and they will serve us well in our future.

February 2007

APPENDIX I

THE CODE OF CONDUCT

The NUJ Code of Conduct was adopted in 1936. This was the original text:

Like other trade unions, formed for mutual protection and economic betterment, the National Union of Journalists desires and encourages its members to maintain good quality of workmanship and high standard of conduct.

Through years of courageous struggle for better wages and working conditions its pioneers and their successors have kept these aims in mind, and have made provision in Union rules not only for penalties on offenders, but for the guidance and financial support of members who may suffer loss of work for conforming to Union principles.

While punishment by fine, suspension or expulsion is provided for in case of 'conduct detrimental to the interests of the Union,' any member who is victimised (Rule 10, clause 3) for refusing to do work 'incompatible with the honour and the interest of the profession' may rely on adequate support from the Union funds.

A member of the Union has two claims on his loyalty – one by his Union and one by his employer. These need not clash so long as the employer complies with the agreed Union conditions and makes no demand for forms of service incompatible with the honour of the profession or with the principles of trade unionism.

I. A member should do nothing that would bring discredit on himself, his Union, his newspaper, or his profession. He should study the rules of his Union, and should not, by commission or omission, act against the interests of the Union.

2. Unless the employer consents to a variation, a member who wishes to terminate his employment must give notice, according to agreement or professional custom.

3. No member should seek promotion or seek to obtain the position of another journalist by unfair methods. A member should not, directly or indirectly, attempt to obtain for himself or anyone else any commission, regular or occasional, held by a freelance member of the Union.

4. It is unprofessional conduct to exploit the labour of another journalist by plagiarism, or by using his copy for linage purposes without permission.

5. Staff men who do linage work should be prepared to give up such work to conform with any pooling scheme approved by the NEC or any Union plan to provide a freelance member with means of earning a living.

6. A member holding a staff appointment shall serve first the paper that employs him. In his own time a member is free to engage in other creative work, but he should not undertake any extra work in his rest time or holidays if by so doing he is depriving an out-of-work member of a chance to obtain employment. Any misuse of rest days – won by the Union on the sound argument that periods of recuperation are needed after strenuous hours of labour – is damaging to trade union aims for a shorter working week.

7. While a spirit of willingness to help other members should be encouraged at all times, members are under a special obligation of honour to help an unemployed member to obtain work.

8. Every journalist should treat subordinates as considerately as he would desire to be treated by his superiors.

9. Freedom in the honest collection and publication of news facts, and the rights of fair comment and criticisms, are principles which every journalist should defend.

10. A journalist should fully realise his personal responsibility for everything he sends to his paper or agency. He should keep Union and professional secrets, and respect all necessary confidences regarding sources of information and private documents. He should not falsify information or documents, or distort or misrepresent facts.

11. In obtaining news or pictures, reporters and Press photographers should do nothing that will cause pain or humiliation to innocent, bereaved, or otherwise distressed persons. News, pictures, and documents should be acquired by honest methods only.

12. Every journalist should keep in mind the dangers in the laws of libel, contempt of court, and copyright. In reports of law court proceedings it is necessary to observe and practise the rule of fair play to all parties.

13. Whether for publication or suppression, the acceptance of a bribe by a journalist is one of the gravest professional offences.

The Code was drastically revised in 1976. Basically it was split into two: a Code of Professional Conduct covering the practice of journalism, and a Code of Working Practices covering relations between journalists themselves. In 2006 the union's Ethics Council embarked on a further revision of both codes, but this is how they stood in 2006.

Code of Professional Conduct

1. A journalist has a duty to maintain the highest professional and ethical standards.

2. A journalist shall at all times defend the principle of the freedom of the press and other media in relation to the collection of information and the expression of comment and criticism. He/she shall strive to eliminate distortion, news suppression and censorship.

3. A journalist shall strive to ensure that the information he/she disseminates is fair and accurate, avoid the expression of comment and conjecture as established fact and falsification by distortion, selection or misrepresentation.

4. A journalist shall rectify promptly any harmful inaccuracies, ensure that correction and apologies receive due prominence and afford the right of reply to persons criticised when the issue is of sufficient importance.

5. A journalist shall obtain information, photographs and illustrations only by straightforward means. The use of other means can be justified only by overriding considerations of the public interest. The journalist is entitled to exercise a personal conscientious objection to the use of such means.

6. A journalist shall do nothing which entails intrusion into anybody's private life, grief or distress, subject to justification by overriding considerations of the public interest.

7. A journalist shall protect confidential sources of information.

8. A journalist shall not accept bribes nor shall he/she allow other inducements to influence the performance of his/her professional duties.

9. A journalist shall not lend himself/herself to the distortion or suppression of the truth because of advertising or other considerations.

10. A journalist shall mention a person's age, sex, race, colour, creed, illegitimacy, disability, marital status, or sexual orientation only if this information is strictly relevant. A journalist shall neither originate nor process material which encourages discrimination, ridicule, prejudice or hatred on any of the above-mentioned grounds.

11. A journalist shall not interview or photograph children in connection with stories concerning their welfare without the permission of a parent or other adult responsible for their welfare.

12. No journalist shall knowingly cause or allow the publication or broadcast of a photograph that has been manipulated unless that photograph is clearly labelled as such. Manipulation does not include normal dodging, burning, colour balancing, spotting, contrast adjustment, cropping and obvious masking for legal or safety reasons.

13. A journalist shall not take private advantage of information gained in the course of his/her duties before the information is public knowledge.

14. A journalist shall not by way of statement, voice or appearance endorse by advertisement any commercial product or service save for the promotion of his/her own work or of the medium by which he/she is employed.

Code of Working Practices

1. A member shall study and obey the rules of the union and the code of conduct.

2. A member shall not act, by commission or omission, against the interests of the union or of the trade union movement.

3. A member who is terminating his/her employment shall give notice according to individual or collective agreement or custom and practice unless the employer consents to a variation.

4. A member shall not, by unfair methods, seek promotion to or obtain the position of another journalist.

5. A member shall not exploit the labour of another journalist by plagiarism or the unauthorised use of his/her work for any purpose.

6. A member who does linage work shall surrender part or whole of that work to conform with any pooling scheme approved by the NEC to provide a member with a livelihood.

7. A member who is a staff reporter shall not normally take photographs and a member who is a staff photographer shall not normally report. Freelance reporters shall not take photographs or freelance photographers report, if by so doing they deprive another freelance of income.

8. Members shall ensure, by support of union organisation and of their colleagues, that participation in union activity does not damage a member's employment, advancement or employment prospects.

9. A member shall not directly or indirectly attempt to obtain for himself/herself or anyone else any regular or occasional linage work, connection or commission which is rightfully undertaken by another member.

10. A member in staff employment shall first serve the organisation which employs him/her. In his/her own time, a member is free to engage in journalistic work, provided that in so doing he/she is neither depriving a freelance or unemployed member of work nor occupying a job which would normally be a full-time staff position; and provided that he/she has contacted the chapel in the office in which the work is to be done and established that he/she is not taking work which can be undertaken by a freelance or unemployed member.

11. A member in a position to commission freelance work shall always attempt to offer it first to a freelance or unemployed member of the union. No member with authority to commission work shall attempt to induce any freelance or casual to perform work for a lower rate of pay or under less favourable conditions than those laid down by any union agreement covering the work in question, or to allocate work to any non-member unless he/she can prove to his/her branch that no suitable member is available and willing to do the work in question. A member who commissions work shall do all in his or her power to ensure payments are made on time.

12. A member shall treat other journalists with consideration.

13. A member shall not accept employment on terms and conditions inferior to those provided for in collective agreements which apply to his/her place of work.

14. It shall be the duty of any member to inform his/her F/MoC of his/her terms and conditions of employment, on request.

15. Freelance members of the union employing salaried assistants shall do so in all respects in accordance with union agreements, the policies of the union and the recognised customs and practices of journalism.

THE UNION'S STRUCTURE – HOW IT WORKS

The NUJ is a democratic organisation. It employs nearly fifty staff to meet the needs of some 40,000 people, but all the main decisions on policy, spending, subscriptions and activity are taken by working journalists who give their time voluntarily to help their colleagues. It is open to any member to take part. Its structure has changed several times, but not by much. This is how it worked in 2006.

The top decision-making body is the **Annual Delegate Meeting (ADM)**, a gathering of representatives of all the Union's branches around the UK, Ireland and overseas. These delegates are elected by the branches.

Between ADMs, decisions lie in the hands of the **National Executive Council (NEC)**, a committee of (currently) 25 people elected annually to represent the NUJ's various sectors.

Both ADM and the NEC are chaired by the **President,** who is elected annually at the conference from among those elected to the executive. A **Vice-President** is also elected, who by custom but not rule succeeds to the Presidency after a year, and a **Treasurer**.

ADM can instruct the NEC, which itself can instruct the Union's officials, who are headed by the **General Secretary (GS)**.

The GS, currently Jeremy Dear, is elected every five years by a national ballot of all members. So are the Deputy General Secretary and the editor of the *Journalist*.

The GS is responsible for the day-to-day running of the Union, and directing the staff. But such important decisions as authorising industrial action must be taken by the NEC.

There is a range of national councils below the NEC, covering different sections and areas of activity. All again consist of voluntary members.

There is an **Industrial Council** for each of the NUJ's 'industrial' sectors – Newspapers and Agencies, Freelance, Magazine and Book, Broadcasting, New Media and Press and PR. There are also **executive councils**, covering all sectors, for Ireland and Scotland. The Irish Executive Council, which has a higher degree of autonomy, covers Northern Ireland as well as the Republic. There are also a **Wales Council** and a **Continental European Council**, although they have no executive powers.

Members of Industrial Councils are elected, every two years, by members in geographical areas within the sectors.

Two other councils are elected the same way: the **Ethics Council**, which covers professional and ethical matters, and the **Black Members' Council** (BMC) consist of members representing each industrial sector. Half the members of the BMC are elected at an annual conference of ethnic minority members.

Committees covering other areas of activity are elected at ADM: the **Equality Council**, the **Disabled Members Council**, the **Professional Training Council** and the *Journalist* **Editorial Advisory Board**.

ADM also elects members of the Management Committee of the union charity NUJ Extra, the **Appeals Tribunal**, which hears appeals by members disciplined under rule, and the conference's own **Standing Orders Committee**. And it elects the NUJ's delegates to the Trades Union Congress, the International Federation of Journalists and other bodies.

At local level, all offices in **branches** (covering local areas) and **chapels** (covering workplaces) are open to election by members.

It is a democratic structure from top to bottom, with hundreds of journalists volunteering for jobs that keep the NUJ going for the benefit of all.

NOTES

Chapter 1: The NUJ

1. Lord Northcliffe's role in the NUJ's first national wage agreement is covered in Chapter 2.

2. Steve Turner's period as General Secretary is covered in Chapter 4.

3. This was the dispute with Dimbleby Newspapers, covered in Chapter 2.

4. The Wapping dispute is covered in Chapter 4.

5. The 'chapel power' movement is covered in Chapter 2.

6. The NUJ Ethics Council is covered in Chapter 6.

7. The authors were unable to track down Tony Craig to interview him for the book.

8. The Pergamon dispute is covered in Chapter 3.

9. 'A Black Journalist's Experience of British Journalism', from *White Media and Black Britain*, ed. Charles Husband, 1975.

Chapter 2: Setting the rates

1. The IPC dispute is covered in Chapter 1.

2. The unrecorded nature of this meeting caused a problem for the inquiry into the supposed pensions scandal in 1985, because claims that the proposed changes had been ratified by the executive could not be confirmed. See Chapter 1.

Chapter 3: Starting over

1. NUJ chapel leaders who have been sacked or made compulsorily redundant for their union activities have included: Clifford Nixon, *York Herald*; John Bailey, *Sunderland Echo*; Peter Wrobel, IPC Magazines; Barbara Gunnell and Nigel Wilmott, *Independent*; Dave Toomer, *Bolton Evening News*; Rob Rooney, *Hull Daily Mail*; Dave Wilson, *Daily Mail*; Greg Challis, *Sheffield Star*; Trevor Davies, Irvine Hunter, Margaret Renn, Terry Pattinson and Tim Minogue, *Daily Mirror*; Eugenie Verney, Aberdeen Journals; Tony Harcup, *Harrogate Advertiser*; Mike Sherrington, Thomson Business Publications; Andy Courtney, *Ormskirk Advertiser*; Alan Mitchell, Haymarket Magazines; Chris Wheal, Morgan-Grampian Magazines; Tim Lezard, *Gloucester Citizen/ Western Daily Press*.

There have also been whole chapels that sacrificed their jobs in failed disputes, including at the *York Herald*, Latin American Newsletters, Aberdeen Journals, Pergamon Press, *Stockport Messenger*, Dimbleby Newspapers, *Nottingham Evening Post*, International Communications, *Essex Chronicle* and VNU magazines.

2.   There was a handful of provincial papers too that never lost union recognition, including the Liverpool Daily Post and Echo, *Manchester Evening News* and associated weeklies, *Rotherham Advertiser, Huddersfield Examiner, Oldham Advertiser* and *South London Press*.

3.   MORI asked 2,045 people (a large sample): 'Do you think that employees should or should not have a legal right to be represented by a trade union?' to which 89 per cent replied 'yes', 3 per cent 'no', 3 per cent 'it depends' and 6 per cent 'don't know'. Among intending voters there was a 93 per cent 'yes' from LibDems, 92 per cent from Labour and, amazingly, 86 per cent from Tory voters.

4.   Roy Greenslade, *Press Gang* (Pan, 2004), p. 341.

Chapter 4: Part of the movement

1.   Whitley councils, which had originated in the Civil Service in 1916, were an attempt to bring employers and employees together so as to avoid industrial disputes.

2.   And was extended, due to Richardson, by now General Secretary, omitting to include on the ballot forms details of where they should be returned: as Mansfield notes, 'The General Secretary's strong point never was detail and method.' (Mansfield, p. 307).

3.   The Wapping dispute is covered in section 3 of this chapter, 'Crisis: Wapping 1986'.

4.   Bundock, p. 328.

5.   The Accord with the NGA was entitled 'NUJ/NGA AGREEMENT: DIRECT INPUT IN PROVINCIAL NEWSPAPERS'. It had fourteen main heads, but the key points were:

● No new technology unless by joint agreement after negotiations involving both unions;

● No compulsory redundancy;

● NGA to retain all inputting of contributed copy and make make-up;

● NGA members transferred to editorial for retraining to join NUJ and by represented by NUJ;

● NGA transferees to continue to pay NGA subs;

● Arrangements for greater co-operation between editorial and production departments and setting up of 'joint chapels' in new technology houses;

● Joint standing committee at national level to supervise implementation of new technology agreements.

6.   The issue of personal contracts is covered in Chapter 3.

7.   Steve Turner declined to be interviewed by the authors.

Chapter 5: An international union

1. The authors are indebted for much of the material for this chapter to Professor John Horgan of Dublin City University; to Joseph Carroll, term paper on 'History and Structure of the Press', Dublin City University 1994; and to Gary Quinn, a postgraduate researcher at DCU.

2. 'Anti-Communism and Media Surveillance in Ireland 1948-50', by John Horgan, *Irish Communications Review,* 1998.

3. The origins of the NUJ Code of Conduct are covered in Chapter 6.

4. Two South African exiled journalists who became active in the NUJ became Union Presidents: Lionel Morrison in 1987-88, and Jim Corrigall in 2003-04.

Chapter 6: Whose press freedom?

1. The texts of the original Code of Conduct and the 2006 version are in Appendix A.

2. Editors knighted by Conservative governments of the 1980s were Sir Larry Lamb of the *Sun*, Sir David English of the *Daily Mail*, Sir Nicholas Lloyd of the *Daily Express* and Sir William Rees-Mogg of *The Times*.

3. Media Ethics and Press Regulation 2000.

4. The General Strike is covered in Chapter 4.

5. The UK Broadcasting Ban is covered in Chapter 7.

Chapter 7: Taking on the states

1. The union published a pamphlet, *Taking Liberties*, in 1978, covering issues around the secrecy trials and other threats to press freedom of the time. Edited by Ron Knowles, it included an article by a young barrister called Anthony Blair, who substituted for another lawyer known to the NUJ, Harriet Harman, who according to Knowles said she was too busy to write it. Harman became a minister in Blair's government after 1997.

2. NUJ members who were defendants in the Colonel B trial were Ron Knowles and Ken Ashton for the union; Dave Clark, Tim Gopsill, Phil Kelly, Russell Southwood and Nigel Thomas from *The Leveller*; and from *Peace News*, Albert Beale, Mike Holderness and Diana Shelley.

3. Material in this chapter is drawn from 'Journalists and Censorship: A Case History of the NUJ in Ireland and the Broadcasting Ban 1971-94', by John Horgan, *Journalism Studies*, 2002.

4. The six applicants in Brind and Others v. UK, the NUJ's case to the European Court of Human Rights against the Broadcasting Ban, were Don Brind and Fred Emery from the BBC; Vicky Leonard and Scarlett MccGwire from LBC, representing commercial radio journalists; Tom Nash, head of the union's minutes department, as a viewer; and freelance film-maker John Pilger.

BIBLIOGRAPHY

There is an enormous literature on British – and Irish – journalism over the last century. We have tried to indicate those works that have been particularly helpful to us, or which devote some space to the NUJ, its members or issues affecting it.

Ainley, Beulah, (1998): *Black Journalists, White Media*, Trentham Books, Stoke on Trent

Andrews, Linton, and **Taylor, H. A.**, (1970) *Lords and Labourers of the Press*, Southern Illinois University Press

Ayerst, David, (1971) Guardian: *Biography of a Newspaper*, Collins, London

Belsey, Andrew, and **Chadwick, Ruth**, (eds), (1992) *Ethical Issues in Journalism and the Media*, Routledge, London

Born, Georgina, (2005) *Uncertain Vision: Birt, Dyke and the Reinvention of the BBC*, Vintage, London

Bower, Tom, (1991) *Maxwell: The Outsider*, Mandarin, London

Briggs, Asa, (1961–95) *The History of Broadcasting in the United Kingdom* (5 vols), Oxford University Press, Oxford

Bundock, Clement J., (1957) *The National Union of Journalists: A Jubilee History, 1907–1957*, NUJ, Oxford

Cameron, Andrew, (2000) *Express Newspapers*, London House, London

Cohen, Phil, and **Gardner, Carl**, (1982) *It Ain't Half Racist, Mum: Fighting Racism in the Media*, Comedia, London

Chippindale, Peter, and **Horrie, Chris**, (1988?) *Disaster! The Rise and Fall of* News on Sunday, Sphere, London

Connelly, Mark, and **Welch, David**, (2005) *War and the Media: Reportage and Propaganda 1900–2003*, I. B. Tauris, London

Conroy, Harry, (1997) *Off the Record*, Argyll Publishing, Argyll

Crozier, Michael, (1988) *The Making of* The Independent, Gordon Fraser Gallery, London

Curran, James, and **Seaton, Jean**, (2003*) Power Without Responsibility: The Press, Broadcasting and New Media in Britain*, Routledge, London

Dickinson, Mark, (1984) *To Break a Union: The Messenger, the State and the NGA*, Booklist, Manchester

Donaldson, Roy, and **Sutherland, Kate**, (1990) *Strike! Pictorial Account of 12-month dispute at Aberdeen Journals*, NUJ Free Press Chapel, Aberdeen

Dyke, Greg, (2004) *Inside Story*, HarperCollins, London

Edwards, David, and **Cromwell, David**, (2006) *Guardians of Power: The Myth of the Liberal Media*, Pluto, London

Evans, Harold, (1983) *Good Times, Bad Times*, Weidenfeld and Nicolson, London

Garland, Nicholas, (1990) *Not Many Dead: Journal of a Year in Fleet Street*, Hutchinson, London

Greenslade, Roy, (1992) *Maxwell's Fall*, Simon & Schuster, London

Greenslade, Roy, (2003) *Press Gang: How Newspapers Make Profits from Propaganda*, Pan, London

Griffiths, Denis, (ed), (1992) *The Encyclopedia of the British Press*, Macmillan, London

Grigg, John, (1993) *History of* The Times *1966–81*, Times Books, London

Husband, Charles, (ed), (1975) *White Media and Black Britain*, Arrow, London

Hetherington, Alastair, (1989) *News in the Regions*, Macmillan, London

Knightley, Phillip, (1975; 2003) *The First Casualty: The War Correspondent as Hero, Propagandist and Mythmaker from the Crimea to Iraq*, André Deutsch, London

Koss, Stephen, (1981) *The Rise and Fall of the Political Press in Britain*, Hamish Hamilton, London

Lee, Alan J., (1976) *The Origin of the Popular Press*, Croom Helm, London

Lindley, Richard, (2005) *And Finally…? The News from ITN*, Politico's, London

Littleton, Suellen, (1992) *The Wapping Dispute*, Avebury, Aldershot

Lloyd, John, (2004) *What the Media are Doing to Our Politics*, Constable, London

Mansfield, F. J., (1943) *Gentlemen, The Press! Chronicles of a Crusade*, W. H. Allen, London

Marr, Andrew, (2004) *My Trade*, Macmillan, London

Melvin, Linda, (1986) *The End of The Street*, Methuen, London

Nevin, Donal, (ed), (1994) *Trade Union Century*, Mercury Press, Dublin

Northcliffe, Viscount, (1922) *Newspapers and their Millionaires*, Associated Newspapers, London

Reid, Alastair, (2004) *United We Stand: A History of Britain's Trade Unions*, Penguin/ Allen Lane, London

Robertson, Geoffrey, (1983) *People Against the Press*, Quartet, London

Scott, George, (1968) *Reporter Anonymous: The Story of the Press Association*, Hutchinson, London

Seymour-Ure, Colin, (1991) *The British Press and Broadcasting Since 1945*, Blackwell, Oxford

Shaffer, Gordon, (1996) *Baby in the Bathwater*, Book Guild, London

Snoddy, Raymond, (1992) *The Good, the Bad and the Unacceptable: The Hard News About the British Press*, Faber and Faber, London

Stewart, Graham, (2005) *The History of* The Times*: The Murdoch Years*, HarperCollins, London

Taylor, S. J., (1996) *The Great Outsiders: Northcliffe, Rothermere and the* Daily Mail, Weidenfeld and Nicolson, London

Tunstall, Jeremy, (1971) *Journalists at Work*, Constable, London

Tunstall, Jeremy, (1983) *The Media in Britain*, Constable, London

Waterhouse, Robert, (2004) *The Other Fleet Street*, First Edition, Manchester

Whale, John, (1977) *The Politics of the Media*, Fontana, London

Williams, Francis, (1957) *Dangerous Estate: The Anatomy of Newspapers*, Longman's, London

Wintour, Charles, (1972) *Pressures on the Press: An Editor Looks at Fleet Street*, André Deutsch, London

Wintour, Charles, (1989) *The Rise and Fall of Fleet Street*, Hutchinson, London

Woods, Oliver, and **Bishop, James**, (1983) *The Story of* The Times, Michael Joseph, London

INDEX

Page references in *italic* indicate illustrations